OATMEAL
and the
CATECHISM

McGill-Queen's Studies in Ethnic History
SERIES ONE: Donald Harman Akenson, Editor

McGill-Queen's Studies in Ethnic History
SERIES TWO: John Zucchi, Editor

Inside Ethnic Families
Three Generations of Portuguese-Canadians
Edite Noivo

A House of Words
Jewish Writing, Identity, and Memory
Norman Ravvin

Oatmeal and the Catechism
Scottish Gaelic Settlers in Quebec
Margaret Bennett

With Scarcely a Ripple
Anglo-Canadian Migration into the United States
and Western Canada, 1880–1920
Randy William Widdis

OATMEAL
and the
CATECHISM

Scottish Gaelic Settlers in Quebec

Margaret Bennett

JOHN DONALD PUBLISHERS LTD
EDINBURGH

McGILL-QUEEN'S UNIVERSITY PRESS
MONTREAL • KINGSTON • ITHACA

ISBN 0 85976 461 3

Published simultaneously in Canada
by McGill-Queen's University Press

ISBN 0 7735 1810 X

British Library Cataloguing in Publication Data.

A catalogue record for this book is available
from the British Library.

Canadian Cataloguing in Publication Data

Bennett, Margaret, 1946–
  Oatmeal and the Catechism: Scottish Gaelic Settlers in Quebec
Includes bibliographical references and index.
ISBN 0-7735-1810-X (McGill-Queen's University Press)
ISBN 0-85976-641-3 (John Donald Publishers)
  1. Scots–Quebec (Province)–Eastern Townships–History.
2. Scots–Quebec (Province)–Eastern Townships–Social life and
Customs. 3. Eastern Townships (Quebec)–History. 4. Eastern
Townships (Quebec)–Social life and customs. I. Title

FC2943.8.S3B45 1998   971.4'60049163   C98-900395-7
F1054.E13B45 1998

Typesetting and prepress origination by Brinnoven, Livingston.
Printed & bound in Great Britain by J.W. Arrowsmith Ltd, Bristol.

Contents

This book is dedicated
with love and gratitude
to Muriel, Ruth and Duncan

The author wishes to thank Will MacLean
for his generous permission to have
'Passage to America' on the front cover

Acknowledgements

At every stage of the preparation of this book I have accumulated a huge debt of gratitude. It will be clear from the Introduction the vital part played by Muriel Mayhew, Duncan McLeod and Ruth Nicolson—kinship, hospitality, and assistance of every kind. From the very first day I arrived in Quebec, there were (alphabetically) MacArthurs, MacDonalds, MacIvers, MacKenzies, MacRaes, Mayhews, McLeods, Mathesons, Morrisons, Murrays, Nicolsons, Shermans, Smiths and Youngs whose friendship, warmth, sincerity, encouragement and enthusiasm have sustained me over the years I have known them. Sadly, not all of them have lived long enough to see 'their book' in print, but I would like to record my heartfelt appreciation of each and every one of them, named and un-named.

The late Gordon MacLennan of the National Museum's Canadian Centre for Folk Culture Studies first suggested that I investigate the topic. I remain grateful to him and to Professor Herbert Halpert whose training, motivation and inspiration set me on the right track in the first place. As a teacher, mentor and friend, Herbert Halpert has influenced every project I have undertaken since 1969 when I first listened to his Folklore lectures as a post-graduate student at Memorial University of Newfoundland.

At the University of Edinburgh I greatly appreciated the advice and support from my two friends and colleagues who supervised my PhD study: the late Dr Alan Bruford and Dr John MacInnes. Good-humoured, critical, provocative, encouraging, amusing at every stage, they helped sustain my enthusiasm and I have no doubt whatsoever that the book is all the better for their careful reading and advice. On the technical side my thanks go to Neil MacQueen for advice, equipment, lab space and for ensuring that my tapes were copied and archived; to Tom McKean who helped with photography and advised me on word-processing; and to Ian MacKenzie for processing films and printing photographs.

The Universities of Harvard in Cambridge, Massachusetts, and Bishop's in Lennoxville, Quebec, were generous in their support when I wished to consult their libraries. In particular, I would like to thank Professor Emeritus Charles Dunn who arranged for me to work in the Widener Library and allowed me to use his personal office there. He generously gave me permission to use his own collection of Gaelic songs recorded in Quebec some twenty years before my first visit there. (Much of it will be incorporated in my second book, to follow.) At Bishop's University, librarian Anna Grant made me welcome by giving me the freedom to work in the Special Collections Room. She helped me locate books, maps, photographs and tapes, and allowed me to use copying facilities.

I am blessed with family and friends who inspire and encourage me. Right from the start, my 'companion in research' was my son, Martyn, whose five year-old curiosity led me down paths I would otherwise have missed; then, as twenty-four year-old, he returned to Quebec to bring his multi-instrumental contribution to the 1995 festival in Megantic that showed so many people, 'Scotch' and French alike, a perspective that would otherwise have been missed entirely. (see Conclusions). In Scotland, my mother, Péigi (Stewart) Bennett, with her endless ability to listen, not only discussed many of the details with me, but helped me transcribe and translate the Gaelic texts. And in Quebec, my father, George Bennett, visited me, shared his enthusiasm and helped with transport.

Friends whose hospitality was regularly appreciated are Percy and Jean Burnard, and Tom and Sylvia McKean who gave me havens of tranquillity in which to write. Finally, I reserve very special thanks for Marie Salton who not only proof-read several versions of text but also took a real interest in the topic. Her loyalty, cheerfulness, wit, and wonderful sense of humour, turned what can be a laborious task — correcting one's own mistakes — into a pleasure. My sincere thanks to each and every individual who made this book possible.

Margaret Bennett
Edinburgh

Introduction

When you're young, you're not so curious —
and when you grow old, it's too late to enquire.

[Ellen Legendre, Stornoway, Quebec, 1976]

In the Province of Quebec only two percent of the people claim to be of Scottish Gaelic extraction and out of that number a minute proportion have any ability to speak the language of their forbears. It would not, therefore, be unreasonable to question the value of studying the history and folk culture of a group representing such a small minority of the province's population. Statistics can be deceptive, however, for, in this instance, they do not deal with the fact that, at the time of their immigration, the group in question was concentrated in one small area of Quebec [Maps 2 and 3]. Furthermore, for over a century, the Canadian Linguistic Census ignored their language, counting them as 'English', since neither the census forms nor the enumerators were equipped to deal with languages outside the government guidelines.[1] As a result, it is now impossible to give accurate statistics of Gaelic-speaking settlers in the area, but, when faced with the 'folk-memory' of elderly inhabitants, the picture changes dramatically from the two percent portrayed by the Census. An article in *The Clansman News* of 1970, based on local interviews and entitled 'The Scottish Highlands of Quebec: Gaidhealatachd Chuibeic', states:

> At the time of the first Great War there were approximately two thousand five hundred Gaels in Marsboro [Marston] alone. We were talking with a man who was born in Milan, who told us that he did not know that there was any other language in the world but Gaelic until he was seven years old.[2]

In 1990, Christie MacKenzie (then aged 93), who was born and brought up in the village of Milan, Quebec, told me that she knew from family tradition the exact year the first French family arrived in their village: 'It was in 1879 when work on the railway began,' and her husband, John, born in Marsboro in 1892, added that 'in 1915 there were exactly four French-speaking families in Milan', and the rest of the population was Gaelic.

The existence of Quebec's Gaelic population was once relatively well known in Eastern Canada, for, when folklorist John L. Campbell visited Nova

Scotia in 1932, he was told of 'further Gaelic communities in Marsboro and Scotstown, Quebec' and he noted names of those he might contact. In the absence of official statistics on Gaelic-speakers in Canada, however, Campbell conducted two unofficial censuses of his own, the first in 1932 and the second in 1937. As a result of his research, he estimated the number of Gaelic-speakers in Eastern Canada in the 1930s must have been between 40,000 and 50,000.[3]

The *Census Reports* of Quebec's Eastern Townships that were issued by the Government in Ottawa for the years 1851–52, 1860–61 and 1871–91 would be altered considerably if the memories of Gaelic and French-speakers were to be taken into account. Instead of returning figures for the area that record the majority to be English-speakers, the statistics for language distribution in the following towns and villages could convincingly be reconstructed as follows:

Year(s)	Town/village	Gaelic	French	English
1851–91	Marsboro	c. 75%	c. 20%	c.5%
1851–91	Milan	c. 95%	c. 5%	c. 0%
1851–91	Scotstown	c. 50%	c.25%	c.25%
1851–91	Springhill	c. 50%	c.25%	c.25%
1851–91	Stornoway	c. 95%	c. 3%	c. 2%
1851–91	Red Mountain	c. 75%	c.20%	c.5%

In the light of this, the official two per-cent quoted for Gaels in the Province of Quebec is relatively meaningless. But, as the twentieth century draws to a close, the language that was once spoken by such a significant concentration of people is on the verge of extinction, as English is spoken by most of the second and third generation, French has rapidly overtaken the fourth generation and it is now well established as the language of the fifth. Many of the first settlers were monoglot Gaels whose children became bi-lingual in Gaelic and English; some learned 'enough French to get by' and a number became tri-lingual. A hundred and fifty years on, in 1997, there is only a handful of bi-lingual speakers of Gaelic and English, and I can name only one tri-lingual Gael — Jean MacIver — but cannot begin to count the number of descendants who are monoglot French speakers.

Since the official language of Quebec is French, it has become the adopted language of more than sixty 'ethnic minorities', whose history in the province spans thousands of years — the Cree Indians of the James Bay area, for example, can speak of five thousand years of trapping and fishing in Quebec, while 'boat people' from Vietnam and Ugandans from war-torn Africa can name the exact day they became Canadian citizens. All fit into what has become known as Canada's 'cultural mosaic', but, as the nation's history becomes increasingly complex, each province can only benefit from knowledge of the cultural groups which have shaped its past and contribute to its present; thus each piece in the mosaic merits special understanding.

Finnish folklorist Lauri Honko proposes that research into cultural identity promotes awareness of emerging national (or provincial) identity, thus changes and trends may be recognised as they take place.[4] Since Canada has such a range of cultural diversity, it may only be possible to understand the national or provincial picture by looking at it piece by piece. Thus, as American folklorist Lynwood Montell points out, 'Local history serves as a microcosm of a nation's history. Trends in attitudes, thoughts and economic concerns at the national level may be discerned and documented at the local level.'[5] And, as British anthropologist Anthony P. Cohen suggests, 'we should seek to learn about the whole by acquiring knowledge of its parts, rather than by ignoring them...*Local experience mediates national identity.*'[6]

In any multi-cultural society the 'parts' that contribute to the 'whole' may vary enormously in size and origin. Nevertheless, by looking at the historical background of one particular group, by examining the way of life and the values of the society from which they came, and by recording the traditional folk culture that has survived the emigration process (or has evolved from it), it should be possible to trace the influence of that group on a nation such as Canada. Furthermore, by explaining the significance of inherited patterns in the culture, some of the present day phenomena that emerged during acculturation can be better understood. Thus, in applying these principles, a grasp of the history and folk culture of Gaels from the Outer Hebrides who settled this comparatively small area of Canada will contribute to a better understanding of the Eastern Townships and of Quebec.

The area has already been the subject of several researchers and writers including (alphabetically) anthropologists, genealogists, geographers, historians, hobbyists, journalists, sociologists and travellers. All have contributed to a network of information, and, as will be seen presently, none can be ignored, though a few, relying mainly upon written or 'official' records, leave some disquietingly distorted impressions.[7] As Canadian historian, Leslie Harris pointed out in 1975 when he urged colleagues not to 'become overly committed' to manuscripts and documents as the only evidence acceptable to historical research : 'If we are to rely entirely on the written record, we may well be sadly disappointed. For [many of the topics we wish to research] there will almost certainly be no such record. *And yet, the evidence will exist.*'[8]

The evidence Professor Harris points towards is the oral tradition of the people 'whose story it is', and the research techniques called for are those of the folklorist, recording the spoken word as it has been handed down through generations. The global value, importance and urgency of preserving folklore was stressed in a document presented to the General Conference of UNESCO held in Paris in 1989.[9] Entitled 'The Unesco Recommendation for the Safeguarding of Traditional Culture and Folklore', it no doubt reached a wide audience, but, so far as international scholarship is concerned, Canadian folklorists had already been committed to the cause since before the turn of this century. Outstanding in his efforts to collect and preserve the folklore of Canada was Quebec's Marius Barbeau (b. 1884) who led the way for others (notably Helen Creighton, Edith Fowkes, Herbert Halpert and Luc Lacourcière). When Barbeau died in 1969, Canadians were reminded by the Press of the enormous contribution that the 'father of Canadian folklore' had made to the nation:

> During fifty years of research, much of it on long and arduous field trips, he produced a wealth of knowledge...he delved deeply into French-Canadian folklore and into the story of the Indian peoples, their legends and culture. He gave the National Museum a collection of 195 Eskimo songs, more than 3,000 Indian, close to 7,000 French-Canadian, and 1,500 old English songs.[10]

It was this same museum, later renamed the Museum of Civilisation, which first introduced me to the Gaelic settlement in Quebec, when, in 1975, after completion of four years postgraduate training in Folklore and a thesis researching the Scottish Gaelic traditions in Newfoundland, I was invited to become the folklorist in what was then labelled 'The Quebec-Hebridean Project'. In collaboration with social anthropologist Iain Prattis and cultural anthropologist Sharon Bohn Gmelch, my task for the six weeks' fieldwork project, funded by the Centre for Folk Culture Studies at the National Museum in Ottawa, was to 'record the Folkways and Religion of the Quebec-Hebrideans', to submit the products of the research and to produce a report for the Museum.[11]

I bought a map, drove to the Eastern Townships, reached the village of Milan, stopped at a country store named 'McLeod Bros', explained why I was there, asked the store-owner Duncan McLeod if he knew of any place to rent, and a few hours later moved into my new home and base for fieldwork. 'Aunt Annie's house', as it was known locally, had been the family home of Duncan's neighbour, Muriel Mayhew, who 'trusted [my] voice on the phone' and offered me the keys. Between the two of them, Duncan and Muriel were to have more influence on my decision to write this book than all of the academic references which have influenced my formal academic training. Furthermore, it was not so much my academic training that stirred their interest in my work — though both place a very high value on education; it was more the feeling that I was 'one of their own people' — a Scot, a Gael, and, most importantly, someone who knew their Island, as I had spent six of my teenage years there after my family moved from Skye to Lewis.

The prescribed period of fieldwork for the Quebec-Hebridean project quickly revealed that there was much more material than any folklorist could collect in so short a time. Consequently I decided to remain in Quebec for nearly a year, being entirely in accord with the sentiment of Scotland's best-known folklorist, Hamish Henderson: 'The collector-folklorist should never, in the heat of the chase, forget his humanist role.'[12] Realistically, the only way to get to know and understand the people and the place was to live among them.

In 1976 the community consisted of four distinct groups of people:

1. Descendants of the Lewis and Harris settlers who emigrated in the mid- to late-nineteenth century (all were contemporaries of my parents and grandparents, and none in my own age group; several Gaelic-speakers among them, but English had taken over most households).[13]

2. Descendants of the French settlers who came in the mid-to late-nineteenth century; (those I met were among the 'older generation' and all bi-lingual).

3. Recent French immigrant families from north of the area, in particular Comté Beauce and the Montreal area; (all ages, mostly monoglot speakers).

4. Recent Canadian and American immigrants, several from Montreal and other urban areas, and a number of American 'draft dodgers', all of whom had opted to become part of the 60s and 70s 'back-to-the-land' movement; (most aged between mid-twenties and forty, some with children; those who were English-speakers were rapidly learning French).[14]

To begin with, based on culture, education and age, my links were with the first and last group. Gradually I got to know the second group as 'les Poulins' ran the local post office; then, by staying on into the autumn and enrolling my five-year-old son in the school at Nantes, I was regarded as having a place within the remaining group. No doubt the process stood me in good stead for my first return visit in 1990, though, by that time, the groupings identified in 1976 no longer applied as the population had become so homogeneously French.

In the 1980s the area had the attention of other researchers, notably genealogist Bill Lawson who, in 1988, published *A Register of Emigrant Families from the Western Isles of Scotland to the Eastern Townships of Quebec, Canada*. While working from his home-based centre for genealogical research in the Isle of Harris, Lawson decided to undertake the compilation of the *Register* when he discovered that

almost every family in Lewis and Harris being researched had a branch in Canada...obviously records of the Island families would be incomplete without information on the destination of these emigrants...there was a place for a Register of all the Hebridean families who could be traced in the Eastern

Townships, with details, where possible, of which village they left from, and at what date.[15]

Whereas emigration records from the mid-nineteenth century give numbers without names, Lawson has identified some 800 families which he places into approximately 350 inter-related 'groups', including 118 from Uig Parish, 99 from Barvas Parish, 52 from Stornoway Parish, 18 from Lochs Parish, seven from Harris, and five from the Island of Grimsay off the south-east coast of North Uist. Having devised a system of references for the *Register*, Lawson also cross-referenced families related by marriage, though only the first generation of children born to emigrants is included, so it is not possible to reconstruct the genealogies of second, third, or fourth generations without access to further records. Fortunately this research has been taken up by a local person who has compiled an impressive computer database of subsequent generations which extends to approximately 8,000 families.[16]

The work of these genealogists is not only invaluable but also of enormous appeal to the thousands of Canadians and Americans whose hobby, if not passion, is Ancestral Research. In one sense, however, a list of names, dates, places, marriages and secondary migrations is only the beginning. The next stage must be to chart the places and tell the life-stories of the people in these lists, for, without language, culture, personality traits such as wit and humour, lists can record only faceless names. Before long they will be in danger of fading into oblivion, unless others add to the records of the genealogists. This was very much the motive of Johnnie 'Bard' MacLeod from Dell when he wrote thirteen 'letters' to his children and bound them in a manuscript entitled *Memoirs of Dell*. In a letter to Duncan McLeod he explained: 'If Dell is ever again inhabited, the future generations might know the type of people that had once lived there…it is too important to become obscure and forever lost.'

The research for this book is based on two phases of fieldwork: the first in 1976 and the second conducted in a series of annual visits between 1990 and 1995. As Lauri Honko points out in his article 'Studies on Tradition and Cultural Identity', 'What [folklorists] are studying is a process of ongoing identity negotiations…We may have to go back to the field and check whether our result still holds and what our one-time-spotlight analysis actually revealed in the…ongoing process.'[17] Yet it was not so much Honko's sound reasoning that prompted my return; it was, rather, the intense sense of urgency expressed by Duncan and Muriel during my reunion visit in 1990 when Duncan's book, *The Milan Story,* was being discussed. It had been the product of years of collecting files and boxes of magazine articles, newspaper clippings, locally printed songs, poems and sketches, and several shelves of books. 'But that's not the half of it…would you not take them and see if you could do something with them?' (I begin to feel slightly uneasy) 'But what about all those tapes you made in 1976? That Museum report doesn't cover it all…too bad, that's all we have of the old people talking…there's a lot more than that.' (I feel distinctly uncomfortable) Then, speaking to Muriel as though I were invisible, 'I suppose she'll wait till we're all dead and gone, and what use would that be to any of us? I've got enough to fill dozens of books…what's going to happen to it? When I'm gone they'll probably throw it all out.' And, as Johnnie 'Bard' MacLeod had reminded Duncan some twenty years earlier, so Duncan urged me: 'It is too important to become obscure and forever lost.'

Thus began my collection and documentation of the *folk culture* of the Hebridean settlers in the Eastern Townships of Quebec, relying heavily upon oral tradition, yet embracing many other disciplines — language, history, geography, literature, sociology, anthropology, religion, medicine, agriculture, botany, home economics. Eleventh hour though it be, I do not regard this folklore study as a salvage operation; it aims to be much more:

> The study of folklore is not the study of the past, though it necessarily includes it; rather it is as much the examination of the operations of tradition, from historical development of items, the stability and change they demonstrate, to matters of transmission — of items, of course, but especially of their meaning, of the values they purvey, and the varying degrees of artistic or operational competence which generate not only the items themselves but also their deep content and structure.[18]

'The values [these items] purvey' to Quebec's Gaelic settlers and their descendants are reflected not only in the strength of transmission from generation to generation, but also in the collective sense of urgency to have them documented 'while there are still a few of us left'. On that brief visit to the Eastern Townships in October 1990, I had been left without a shadow of a doubt that such an undertaking would be of enormous value to the people whose story it is. In the context of this book, the *items* will cover emigration history, community and domestic lifestyle, religious and social structure (including a few of the songs, poems, legends and folktales), customs and beliefs, material culture and foodways. Discussions of these major categories are supported throughout by the testimonies of many Townshippers, quoted verbatim, so that the 'voice' of the Gael will continue to be heard long after my tape-recordings have been archived.

Methodology and Key of Standardised Conventions

The 'folklore methodology' for this research project owes much to the inspiration and training of Professor Herbert Halpert of Memorial University of Newfoundland.[19] The 'tools of the trade' used were:

1. A cassette tape recorder with external microphone (Sony TC110B)

2. Several fieldwork notebooks in which to record notes on people and places visited; objects observed such as house and barn types, landscape

features; reminders of questions to ask and things that needed to be done; and notes on my observations of situations otherwise not recorded, such as informants' reactions of surprise, amusement or sadness.

3. A 35 mm camera

4. For the second 'phase', a portable word-processor (Macintosh Powerbook 140), replacing the fieldwork notebooks, cataloguing photos, and occasionally recording words spoken by informants when the tape-recorder was not suitable.

All the cassette tapes recorded were indexed, and most were fully transcribed. From the first collection both cassettes and transcriptions were deposited in the Centre for Folk Culture Studies at the Museum of Man at the National Museum in Ottawa. From the second collection, the cassettes were copied onto 7-inch reel-to-reel tapes and deposited in the School of Scottish Studies Archives at the University of Edinburgh. [See Appendix A]

Library research is based on books at The Special Collections Library at Bishop's University in Lennoxville, Quebec, the Widener Library at Harvard University in Cambridge, Massachusetts, the Main Library at the University of Edinburgh and the private collections of Duncan McLeod and Muriel Mayhew.

The actual words of informants are quoted as accurately as possible throughout, so that the voices of informants may be heard above that of the researcher. I am aware, however, that there are certain drawbacks to a printed text as a reflection of the spoken word. The problem is how to show physical or emotional aspects such as eye-contact (or lack of it), facial expressions, gestures, hesitations, emphasis, animation, laughter, anguish, and so on. Generally I have used square brackets and indicated the speaker's expression, for example [laughs]. Occasionally, for the sake of clarity, I have rearranged the sequence of a conversation, indicated where it occurs by [re-ordered]. And, while most of the voices 'heard on the page' were 'solo' when recorded, a few 'duets' are also included to reflect the dynamics between the speakers. This too is intimated wherever it occurs. I have established the following fairly simple method of transcription and have tried to follow it throughout.[20]

Quotations from books are indented, single spaced, and justified.

Quotations from tape recordings are indented left, ragged right.

Words that are emphasised in speech are in italics. e.g. 'Not *that* one.'

Words that are emphasised in a markedly loud voice are in bold italics. e.g. 'The next thing we heard was ***Bang!***'

Where the meaning of a quotation is unclear because contextual information has been supplied elsewhere in the conversation, I have added words within square brackets. e.g. 'And it [the harvest] had to be in by the end of September.'

Translations are in italics, usually square-bracketed.

Where I have asked a question to elicit further information, and have decided against reproducing the entire conversation, I have included the key words from my question within square brackets with broken underline. e.g. 'We went to the mill every fall [by horse and sleigh].'

An indication of contextual information required to clarify the tape transcription is based upon the system of bracketed and underlined text devised by Edward D. (Sandy) Ives. e.g.
I will attempt to explain all extraneous noises [clock strikes], account for all breaks [tape turned off while he goes for the photograph album], identify all photos, [looking at number 12], and add any information that will make the transcription more meaningful [As he said this, his wife looked in from the kitchen door behind his chair, and was shaking her head repeatedly, to show that she disagreed with her husband's remark.][21]

Words quoted from my fieldwork notebook are prefixed by an asterisk. e.g. ★'We used to go to Stornoway to the communions every June and October, and we'd stay overnight with relatives or friends.'

Words or phrases not understood in a tape transcription are indicated by square brackets and question-marks are used. e.g. 'And every time [— ?] went there, he'd come home with ?Oliver [?all of us? spoken while tapping his pipe, so words are difficult to make out.]'

'A modern folklore document permits the voice of the people to be heard exactly as it was uttered;' 'it represents a people's image of themselves, [and]…as a mirror of culture provides unique raw material for those eager to better understand themselves and others.'[22] And while this book is entirely about the Eastern Townshippers of Hebridean descent, it is written not only for them; it is equally for people in Lewis and Harris whose kinsfolk were separated from them and never returned, and for Quebecers and Québecois, whatever language they speak, whatever farm they farm, whatever woodlot they cut, whatever sugar bush they tap, that they may appreciate the events that led to its creation and the people who carved it out of a wilderness.

Notes

1. In Britain's 1991 Official Government Census, the forms delivered to every household offered a 'freedom of choice' to fill out an alternative form in any of Britain's *recognized languages* — they included Chinese, Hindi, and Urdu, but *not* Gaelic.

2. I am grateful to Duncan McLeod for this reference by an unnamed reporter. The figure is excessive for one village but applies to the township in which it is located. The local definition of Township is complex and will be discussed in Chapter 2.

3. He published his findings in *The Scotsman*, Jan. 30, 1933 and *Songs Remembered in Exile,* pp. 32–41.

4. Lauri Honko, 'Studies on Tradition and Cultural Identity: An Introduction' in *Tradition and Cultural Identity*, p. 10, my brackets.

5. Lynwood Montell, *From Memory to History*, p. 21.

6. A.P. Cohen, *Belonging,* p. 13, his emphasis.

7. The range includes Channell, (1896), Day (1863 and 1869), Doucette (ed., 1980), Lawson (1988), Little (1989 and 1991), Mackay (1892), McLeod (1977), Sherman (1971).

8. L. Harris, 'Without Strap Nor String', introductory address to the Canadian Aural/Oral History Association, St. John's, 1975; *Folklore and Oral History;* pp. 9–10.

9. Proceedings of the twenty-fifth General Conference of the United Nations Educational, Scientific and Cultural Organization, Paris, November 1989.

10. Quoted by Edith Fowke, op cit, p. 15.

11. Much of the thesis was edited and published in *The Last Stronghold*. The three reports were edited by Laurel Doucette for the Museum's Mercury Series Publication, *Cultural Retention and Demographic Change: Studies of the Hebridean Scots in the Eastern Townships of Quebec.*

12. Preface to Kenneth S. Goldstein's *A Guide for Field Workers in Folklore*, p. x.

13. As part of his fieldwork, Iain Prattis did a household survey over a thirty-mile radius which identified many more Gaelic-speakers than we ever met. Some had moved from the area, some were 'home on holiday', and even without the six months of snow it would have been impossible for one person to have recorded them all in the time available.

14. Alan Dundes discusses 'belonging' to one or more groups, and the factors which link members of a group. See 'Who Are the Folk?' in *Interpreting Folklore*, pp. 1–19.

15. Bill Lawson, *A Register of Emigrant Families from the Western Isles of Scotland to the Eastern Townships of Quebec, Canada,* p. 1. [Hereafter cited as *Register.*]

16. Since this is a work in progress the researcher would prefer no publicity.

17. Lauri Honko, *Tradition and Cultural Identity*, p. 9.

18. Gerald Thomas and John D. W. Widdowson, *Studies in Newfoundland Folklore: Community and Process,* p.xxii.

19. There are a number of standard guides to the field, notably, Kenneth S. Goldstein, *A Guide for Fieldworkers in Folklore,* and Edward D. Ives, *The Tape-Recorded Interview: A Manual for Field Workers in Folklore and Oral History.*

20. As a post-graduate student at Memorial University of Newfoundland (1969–75)I was most influenced by Herbert Halpert's training in fieldwork methods and analysis. I also note the ground-breaking work of Dell Hymes, especially 'Breakthrough into Performance' in *Folklore Performance and Communication.* I have considered (though not always agreed with) the proposed methods of Elizabeth C. Fine in *The Folklore Text: From Performance to Print.* Other major influences are Richard Bauman's work (especially in *Towards a New Perspective in Folklore*) and Dennis Tedlock's 'On the Translation of Style in Oral Narrative' in Bauman's book. See also J. Jeoffrey Patton, 'Writing Ourselves into our Texts: Dialogics in Folklore and Ethnography', unpublished M. Phil. thesis, The University of Sheffield, 1991.

21. This example is based on Ives's constructed example, op cit p. 92.

22. Lauri Honko, op cit, p. 5 and Alan Dundes, *Interpreting Folklore,* p. viii.

Number of Families

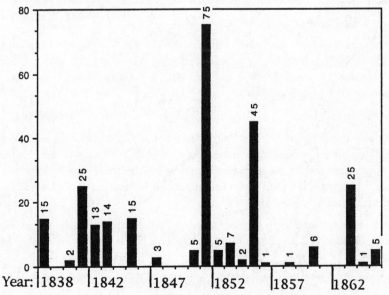

Table showing number of Hebridean immigrant families to the Eastern Townships, by year.

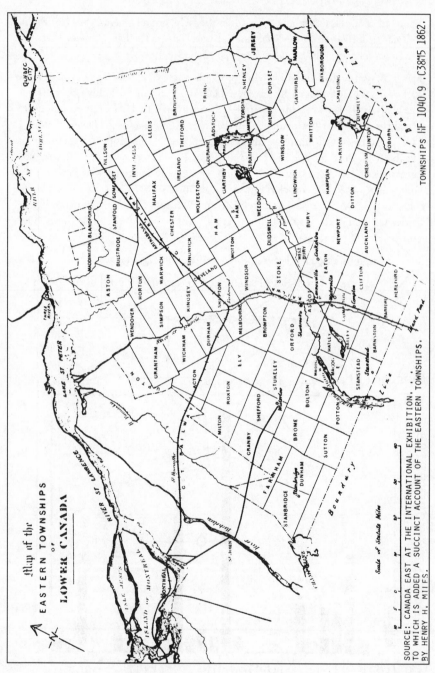

Map 1. *The Eastern Townships of Lower Canada, 1862.*

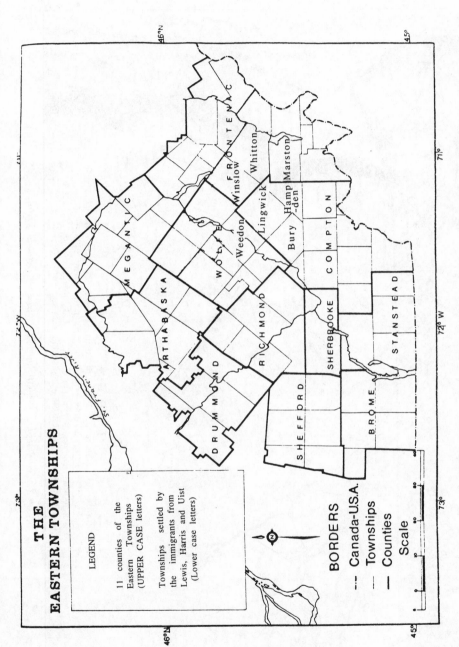

Map 2. The Eastern Townships, showing the counties and townships settled by the Gaelic immigrants.

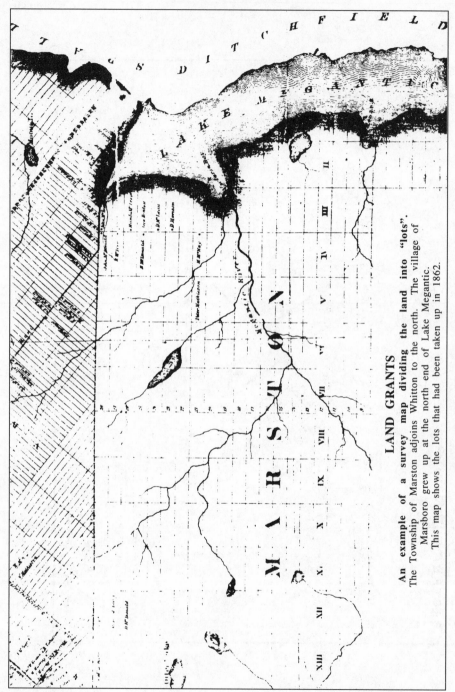

LAND GRANTS

An example of a survey map dividing the land into "lots". The Township of Marston adjoins Whitton to the north. The village of Marsboro grew up at the north end of Lake Megantic. This map shows the lots that had been taken up in 1862.

Map 3. An example of a land grant map, part of Marston and Whitton, 1862.

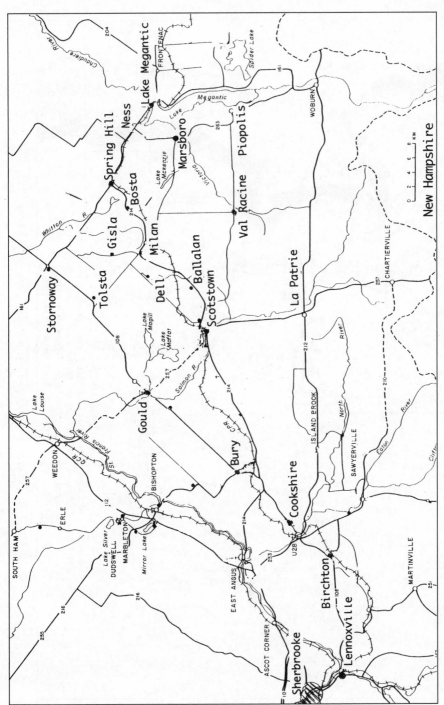

Map 4. Topographical map of the area settled by the Gaels, with names of towns and villages.

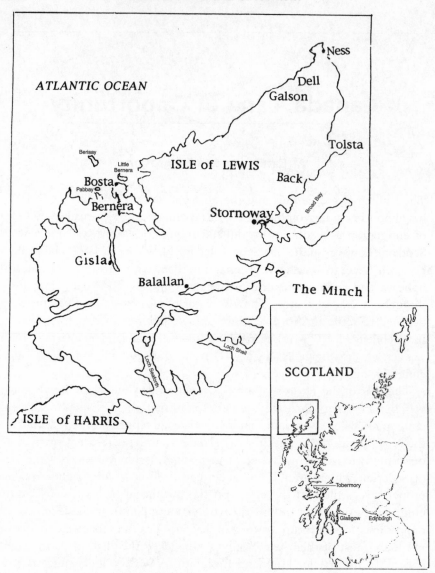

Map 5. Location Map.

1

Canada, Land of Opportunity

A Background to Emigration

The landing of the famous ship, the *Hector*, at Pictou, Nova Scotia, in 1773, has almost become symbolic of Highland emigration to Canada.[0] The idea of emigration as a solution to difficult living conditions was not new to Scotland, however, as the first Scots sailed for New York in 1732. The years in between were, to say the very least, unsettled, with turmoil and political upheaval and a complexity of issues which eventually led to mass emigration throughout the Highlands.[1] The vast majority of these early emigrants were destined to settle in North Carolina, but following the American War of Independence in 1776, immigration of Scottish Highlanders into the South was actively discouraged, and Canada became the destination of heavily laden emigrant ships.

The year of the *Hector's* sailing was significant to the Isle of Lewis, for it was in 1773 that the Island felt the effects of the first major wave of emigration, when over eight hundred people are reported to have set sail for the New World.[2] Many, in those days, *chose* to emigrate, as they saw it as an opportunity to rid themselves of the increasingly tyrannical effects of the Acts of Sederunt which, after 1746, sanctioned the landowner's rights over his property, regardless of the effect on the livelihood of his tenants. Some emigrants, especially among the young men, simply regarded it as an opportunity for adventure. In view of the harsh evictions that were to follow, no doubt most of them were soundly convinced they had made the right choice. In his article, 'Highland Emigration', W.C.A. Ross suggests that 'broadly speaking, in the eighteenth century people *go* from the Highlands, in the nineteenth, *they are sent.*'[3] As far as emigration to Quebec is concerned, this was the case for the majority of emigrants, as will be seen shortly.

By the turn of the nineteenth century there was steady traffic of emigrant ships between Scotland and Canada. The River Clyde saw most of the departures, with Glasgow and Greenock the most popular ports of embarkation, though three ships are recorded to have sailed from the town of Stornoway to Nova Scotia in 1803.[4] Many others followed the same route from a number of west coast ports, and for over thirty years people from the Outer Hebrides joined the passenger lists of emigrant ships, mostly to Cape

Breton. During this period, however, many departed without any choice in the matter, having fallen victim to the ever-increasing policy of eviction adopted by, or on behalf of, many of the landowners.[5]

From the mid–1700s to the early 1820s the kelp industry had been a very lucrative source of income to landowners, albeit at the expense of subjecting tenants to miserable, unhealthy conditions created by long hours of inhaling the noxious smoke from the burning, to say nothing of the effects of enduring perpetually cold and wet feet. Its rapid decline in the late 1820s, and eventual collapse in 1836, put pressure on island landowners to find alternative sources of income, and as a result, they began to clear land to make way for large, profitable sheep farms. Tenants were under perpetual threat of eviction, and lived a precarious existence. Not even faithful payment of rent could guarantee immunity against notoriously unscrupulous tacksmen, many of whom are reported to have employed cruel and aggressive measures to gain their own greedy ends.[6] Reports from that era contained in the Seaforth Muniments and other accounts, give a stark and savage picture of the situation that faced the poor tenants.[7] If the records of the evictions make gruelling reading (and they certainly do), then reality must have been unbearably hard.

Poverty and deprivation already characterised life when the year 1837 brought famine to add to the hardships. Again, emigration offered a solution, and the next year, 1838, sixteen families sailed for Quebec. Over seventy people formed this group of emigrants which began a Quebec-Hebrides link that was to endure for over a century and a half, and still remains to this day.[8] On the Hebridean side, the vast majority were from the Isle of Lewis, with a very small number from Harris and fewer still from North Uist; on the Quebec side they all settled in the area known as the Eastern Townships.

By far the most significant episode in the history of Hebridean emigration to Quebec is the Potato Famine of 1845-50. The disease and resulting failure of the potato crop in 1845, accompanied by impoverished grain and fishing harvests, heralded a five year struggle, the results of which affected the destiny of a considerable number of Lewis people. Once again, emigration to the New World became the solution — the *only* choice for those who wanted to survive. Commenting upon the effects of the famine throughout the Highlands, Michael Lynch states 'It was, by any measure, Clearance on a huge scale…carried through with a mixture of brutality and conspicuous philanthropy.'[9]

It is at this point that the story begins for most Eastern Townshippers of Outer Hebridean descent, although it goes without saying that the history of their ancestral home goes back much further than 1850, and is chequered by disasters that could arguably claim more lasting effects than the Potato Famine. Nevertheless, it is a fact of human nature that one is affected forever by trauma that directly hits the family, and the poverty and starvation of a great-grandparent is, for the Quebec-Gaels, the most memorable factor to have affected their fate.

Donald MacDonald's *Lewis: A History of the Island* deals with the pre-history, the Norse invasions, the shift to Scottish sovereignty with its accompanying complexities, and every stage of development to the present day. Among Eastern-Townshippers of Lewis descent, the book is looked upon as a handbook to the 'Old Country', as it is the best known of many books about the Outer Hebrides.[10] The author had a personal link with Quebec, and is warmly remembered by those who met him and corresponded with him. Christie MacKenzie who was born in 1898 and was a contemporary of his, remarked upon what she considered to be an outstanding contrast between the educational opportunities afforded to those who emigrated and those who remained in Lewis, citing Donald MacDonald's family as her example. She was proud that her kinsman should be so learned and eloquent,' agus sgrìobh e *History of Scotland'* [and he wrote the History of Scotland].[11] His *Lewis: A History of the Island,* has become the key reference book to keep in touch with the way of life in the twentieth century, and, as such, the real interest begins on page fifty, with the sixth chapter, 'The People'.[12]

Long forgotten are the trials, tribulations and even tortures of the early landlords, the MacLeods and the MacKenzies. These names have managed to shed any disgrace or outrage that could be attributed to them from the fourteenth to mid-eighteenth centuries. In modern times they are honourable names and proudly borne on both sides of the Atlantic.[13] A certain ambivalence creeps in, however, with the name of Sir James Matheson (though by comparison to his predecessors, the MacLeod and MacKenzie landlords, he was a paragon of virtue), for it was during his ownership that the Potato Famine occurred, the turning point in history, as far as Quebec is concerned. There is an occasional acknowledgement of the fact that he was reported to have helped some of the emigrants pay for the passage from Scotland to Quebec, but, beyond that, relatively little seems to be known about him in the Eastern Townships.

Because of his significance in the history and traditions of this area, it seems appropriate to offer the following brief summary of James Matheson's involvement with the Isle of Lewis.[14] Born and brought up in Sutherland, James Matheson entered the world of trade and commerce as a young man in London. He travelled to India and then to China as a tea and opium merchant where he amassed a considerable fortune. In 1842 Matheson returned to Scotland an extremely wealthy man, and in 1844 he bought the Isle of Lewis for the sum of £190,000 from the widow of the Earl of Seaforth, the last of the MacKenzie landlords.

It seems clear that Matheson aimed to raise the standard of living on the island, which, at that time, was very low. Aside from the lack of material goods, the population at that time was also struggling to emerge from the tension generated by the Disruption of the Church of Scotland.[15] Donald MacDonald suggests that Matheson 'could not have bought Lewis at a more unfortunate time'.[16] His plans for improvements (many, it must be noted, were ultimately for his own comfort rather than that of his tenants) were scarcely under way when the potato crop failed and the crofting population had little or no means of sustaining their families. The plight was common to the entire area of the Highlands and Islands, and, in order to alleviate the situation, the Highland Relief Board was established. For three years Matheson's factor avoided applying to the Board for aid, as he set up an intensive programme of road-making and land improving, which gave paid employment, and therefore a means of support, to the tenants. He set up schemes which offered credit on seed potatoes to be paid as a supplement of rent (after harvest) or in cash, or (the only option open during these years of failed crops) to be paid for in labour.

After three years under this scheme, the factor retired and was replaced by a much stricter individual, J. Munro MacKenzie, who changed the system of labour and relief. Lewis became included in the allocation of oatmeal by the Highland Relief Board, but the food did not by any means reach the population as 'direct aid'. Under the supervision of MacKenzie it was issued in exchange for labour, thus affording Matheson's estate further improvements paid for by the hunger of crofting families. Ironically, it was for his efforts during the years of the famine that a baronetcy was conferred upon James Matheson.

By 1851 funding for the Highland Relief Board had dried up and the Government was asked to step in to help avoid catastrophe by organizing emigration to the Colonies. With a policy for the settlement of Upper Canada already in place, the Canadian Government were developing a similar policy to extend to Lower Canada with its capital in Quebec City [Map 1]. In preparation for this new wave of immigrants, government pamphlets were printed and distributed in Europe to encourage emigration. For example, in 1835 A.C. Buchanan, the chief Government emigration agent in Quebec, issued a pamphlet that included the following information:

> There is nothing more important to emigrants, on arrival at Quebec, than correct information on the leading points connected with their future pursuits. Many have suffered much for want of caution, and by listening to opinions of interested, designing characters, who frequently offer their advice unsolicited…on all occasions when you stand in need of advice, apply only to the Government agents, who will give every information required, *gratis*.
>
> Emigrants are informed that they may remain on board ship 48 hours after arrival… *They should avoid drinking the water of the river St. Lawrence, which has a strong tendency to produce bowel complaints…*

Emigrants who wish to settle in Lower Canada or to obtain employment, are informed that many desirable situations are to be met with. Wild lands may be obtained by purchase from the Commissioners of Crown Lands in various townships in the province, and the British American Land Company are making extensive preparations for selling lands and farms in the Eastern Townships to emigrants.[17]

This area of Lower Canada referred to as 'The Eastern Townships' borders the America states of Vermont and New Hampshire.[18] Prominent among land speculators was The British American Land Company, founded in 1833–34 by a group of Montreal and London businessmen, and modelled after the Canada Company[19] which had promoted the settlement of Upper Canada. From the British Government the Company purchased

> nearly 1,000,000 acres in the counties of Shefford, Stanstead, and Sherbrooke…in the Eastern Townships of Lower Canada, [comprising] a tract of country, lying inland, on the south side of the St Lawrence, between 45° and 46½° north latitude, and 71° and 73° west longitude. This tract containing between five and six million acres, is divided into eight counties, and these are again sub-divided into about one hundred townships.[20]

There is an obvious difference between the size of the 'tract of country' purchased by the British American Land Co. and the acreage of the entire area. This is because much of the land was already settled and townships established in the late eighteenth century; descriptions of these early settlements, along with ink drawings of very impressive houses, farms, schools, churches, mills, factories etc. were published in Belden's *Illustrated Atlas of the Eastern Townships and South Western Quebec, 1881*, and give an invaluable picture of the range of conditions which existed in the Eastern Townships from the 1790s to the 1880s. The issue of land ownership appears to have been extremely complex, however, and it is quite clear from Belden's comments that land speculation was rife. His use of phrases such as 'fell into the hands of the B.A. Land Co.' indicate that not all parties were comfortable with the highly competitive and lucrative practices that were the order of the day.[21]

Depending on the location of the land, the British American Land Company set down terms for its disposal. Acting as emigration agents, their policy was to bring in British immigrants, and their prospectus highlighted advantages which were designed to appeal to would-be settlers:

> By agreement between His Majesty's Government and the Company, upwards of £50,000 of the purchase-money paid by the latter are to be expended by them in public works and improvements, such as high-roads, bridges, canals, school-houses, market-houses, churches, and parsonage-houses. This is an extremely important arrangement, and must prove highly beneficial to settlers…

The expenditure of the large sum above mentioned, will offer at the same time an opportunity of employment to honest and industrious labourers, immediately on arrival...[22]

With a modest down-payment and an instalment system to pay off the balance, it was an attractive proposition, provided emigrants had the capital for the down-payment. Naturally, the more fertile land west of the town of Sherbrooke was quickly taken up by those who could afford it, and prosperous farms were established mainly by English-speaking settlers. According to Belden, 'English, Irish and Scotch [sic] came,' and, since he states that they were all English-speaking, he confirms the tradition that some of the Scottish settlers were from the Lowlands.[23] All the Hebridean settlers were Gaelic-speakers, many of whom were monoglot as they had no need of the English language in Lewis or Harris. Although the term 'Scotch' has changed use in Britain (but not Canada), on both sides of the Atlantic it was commonly used to define people until the end of the nineteenth century. Over the years, however, any settler of Scottish background, Highland or Lowland, has always been referred to as 'Scotch', and since it is still the popular term used in the Eastern Townships and in many parts of Canada, Scotch will continue to be used in this book, where appropriate.[24]

Land speculation, by its very definition, is accompanied by certain risks, and by 1839 the British American Land Company was £72,000 in debt, having been unable to meet their own repayments for the St. Francis Tract in the Eastern Townships. Lengthy negotiations between the Company and the Government resulted in 1841 in an agreement that 500,000 acres should be given back to the Crown in order to cancel the outstanding debt. On the surface, this may seem harsh, but in fact the British American Land Company, who were to continue in their capacity as emigration agents, managed to keep the finest land, while the rougher, stony land reverted to the Crown.[25] That same year the Canadian Government passed the Land Act of 1841 which allowed free grants of fifty acres to be made to any British male subject. (Later, the land grant was increased to one hundred acres.) According to the the British Government *Papers Relative to Emigration to Canada*, in response to this scheme thirty-four families left Stornoway in 1841.[26]

Government publicity for emigration was efficiently in place when the Highland Relief Board could no longer provide food to save the Highlands and Islands from the devastating effects of the famine. Encouraged by the assurance that land grants from the Canadian Government would be freely available to emigrants, and no doubt affected by the Poor Law of 1844 which held the landlord responsible for the welfare of the poor, Sir James Matheson was strongly in favour of the government's renewed measures to organize emigration. In order to facilitate the move, he offered considerable assistance to his tenants: he would pay the ocean passage of destitute families to Upper or Lower Canada, Ontario or Quebec; he would forfeit arrears of rent; he would buy their remaining livestock at a fair price; and would supply clothing to those in need. Between 1851 and 1855, over 1,770 people are reported to have emigrated under Matheson's scheme, which, to the onlooker, may seem exceedingly benevolent.[27] The crofters were not, in fact, entirely free to choose their fate, as Matheson's factor, Munro MacKenzie, had a considerable say in the matter. T. M. Devine describes the situation in Lewis as producing 'the most remarkable instance of opposition' to Highland emigration. On the basis of MacKenzie's manuscript diary of 1851, Devine comments:

> Matheson's chamberlain, John Munro MacKenzie, surveyed the population in 1851 and selected c. 2,500 for emigration assistance. Only seventeen percent of the total agreed to accept. The fact, however, that over 2,200 were eventually 'emigrated' by the estate demonstrates how landlord strategy and coercion could sufficiently change attitudes even among those who were resolutely opposed to going.[28]

In order to 'change their attitudes', MacKenzie served eviction notices on those who were two years in arrears of rent and who were unwilling to emigrate. It was also intimated to these same individuals that they would be prohibited from cutting peat and need not expect any further assistance in the form of oatmeal or seed if they insisted on remaining in Lewis.[29] Needless to say, emigration became their 'choice'.

In his book *The Making of the Crofting Community*, James Hunter writes that Matheson's 'treatment of these emigrants was, by the standards of the time, decidedly generous — a model to other proprietors according to immigration officials in Quebec.'[30] Generosity, however, is only relevant to means. The sum involved in transporting almost eighteen hundred people across the Atlantic is recorded as £11,855, less than £7 per passenger.[31] During the previous five years, Matheson had already spent nearly three times that amount on meal and seed for the crofters (though we cannot ignore the fact that he received £33,000 worth of labour in return); he had also spent over £25,000 on roads and bridges (albeit leading to larger farms, shooting lodges and manses), and vast sums on other 'public' ventures. On a more personal level, his expenditure included £100,495 for the building of the castle, and £19,289 for shooting lodges at Morsgail and Uig.[32] Considering the facts and figures, the benevolent Sir James (a hard-headed businessman even in a famine) scarcely appears to have suffered significant financial hardship during these desperate years which took such a toll on his tenant crofters.

The plight of the emigrant, an all too familiar scene in European history, was their lot. They left behind their beloved homeland, family, friends and a life of poverty, and brought with them a few meagre possessions (usually the

contents of one wooden trunk) and a great deal of hope and faith. There are
no traditions of joy attached to the emigrants' farewell; nothing but the sorrow
of parting is echoed throughout their stories and songs.[33] Yet, from those who
survived the experience, emerge notes of optimism that could be heard
echoing among the Gaels wherever they settled:

> 'S a Chanada a nall d'àinig,
> Aite b'fhearr dhomh dùbailt.
>
> [Then I came over to Canada, A place twice as good for me.][34]

While it would have been impossible for the first emigrants to imagine
what was ahead of them — hardships that tested the utmost limits of
endurance, and ultimately a freedom of which they had only dreamed —
many of their descendants rationalize the trauma by concluding that most of
the emigrants set out believing it was for the best. For them, the struggle and
suppression of Hebridean crofting and landlordism was over; for those who
remained it was to continue until well into the twentieth century, and some
would affirm that it continues to this day.

From the Outer Hebrides to Quebec

> *Chì duine acrach fad uaithe.*
> *[A hungry person can see a good distance.]*

In their collective memories, most families have retained only brief references
to the actual emigration. There are, so far as I can ascertain, very few written
accounts, and those that do exist give only sparse details, such as a letter that
survives from a MacIver family who emigrated from Lewis in 1841. In her
book, *History of the Families of Sherman-MacIver*, Annie I. Sherman refers to
the letter which records that the Atlantic passage took seventy days.

Most Quebecers of Hebridean descent know approximately when their
forebears emigrated, as the following selection of excerpts shows.[35] They are
largely concerned with events that occurred after their forebears settled.
Typical of family recollections about this era were those of Christie
MacArthur who was born in Milan, Quebec, in 1888. Her father, Alexander
MacDonald, was one of the first settlers:

> My father was born in Scotland…on the Isle of Lewis…Well, my father, I think
> he was fifteen years [old] when he came to Canada…he was herding cattle,
> that's about all I heard. [laughs] Sheep or cattle, I don't know…[Did he ever say
> what made him leave?] I couldn't say, but they all came about that same time —
> but I think they were encouraged to leave…Well, they were kind of forced to
> leave…[36]

Although the 1850s are recalled by most families as the time of greatest emigration from Lewis to Quebec, some memories go back to the two previous decades. Duncan McLeod, whose grandfather built the first store in Milan in 1877, lived there all his life until he recently sold up and moved to Scotstown. A retired merchant, he is known throughout the district as a keen historian, a keeper of countless newspaper articles, features, clippings and books relevant to the history of the area. Based on his vast print collection and his own local knowlege, he published *The Milan Story* in 1977.[37] His family history in Quebec goes back to the early 1840s:

> Well, I had a great-grandfather, Alasdair, who came from — he came here from Ness but I believe he was a native of Back. And Murdo, another great-[grandfather], another MacLeod, not the same family, I don't think , he was a native of Back too. Angus MacDonald, my grandmother's father, was from Uig and his father, William, was known as the builder of roads, [he was called 'Uilleam a' rathaid'] and he built the road, and it's still visible. It runs from Miavaig ferry to the Uigan church. I have a picture of the road[38]...My grandfather, [Duncan L. McLeod, son of Alistair], was the youngest in the family, and he was born in Canada in 1848.[39]

When asked if he had 'any idea what made the people come out', Duncan replied:

> No, I don't. It was just to better their chance for their families. There were other people coming out and they decided [to do the same] — my great-grandfather Alasdair MacLeod] was a dominie...a teacher. Anyway he was known as a dominie. [He came in] 1841...There was Alistair, Malcolm, and Christina[40] in the family, and my [great- great-] grandfather, Murdo, came out with Alistair, and I believe Malcolm too, and he died that fall...And there's a Port Alistair on the coast of Lewis, up in the Ness area which is named after him.[41]

In 1990, at the age of ninety-three, Christie MacKenzie (née Murray) gave the following account in Gaelic, typical of many of her generation:

> Thàinig iad à *Scotland*...rugadh m'athair ann an Tolsta a Tuath...cha robh e ach ceithir là a dh'aois. Thàinig m'athair ann a' *eighteen fifty-two*, agus thàinig mo mhàthair ann an *eighteen fifty-six*..

> [*They came from Scotland...My father, he was born in North Tolsta [Isle of Lewis]...he was only four days old [when he left]. My father came over in 1852 and my mother in 1856.*][42]

Christie's husband, John, aged ninety-nine continued:

> My father and my uncle Allan came, it took them about three weeks until they landed in Quebec City. That's a hundred miles from here, and they drove from

there, I don't know if it was ox teams in those days or if it was horses. And they settled down in the woods, cleared a piece of land, built a home…They had to clear the land and cut down the woods and build a log cabin. Get the lumber sawed…1852, somewhere around there.

The considerably shorter time taken for the MacKenzies' voyage compared with the MacIvers in 1841 suggests that they were among the first to take advantage of steamships which were introduced in the 1850s. According to the National Museum of Navigation, the average passage from Liverpool to Quebec by sail was forty-two days, compared to twelve days by steamship.[43] Conditions were seldom 'average' and stormy weather often prolonged the time at sea.

The legendary 'babies were even born on the boat' story is confirmed by this account, recorded in 1991, from Alex MacIver, Christie and Johnny MacKenzie's son-in-law:

> My grandfather was born on the way across — my grandfather, in 1851. And there was three born here afterwards… *'Duine gun dùthaich',* they used to say — a man without a country.[44]

Duncan McLeod also recalled that his grandfather's youngest sister, Christie, 'was born on board ship on the St. Lawrence River, as the ship approached Quebec in 1841. It was said of her that she was born on neither land nor sea, but on the St. Lawrence River.'[45]

Muriel Mayhew (née MacDonald) of Milan who retains links with Lewis via her mother who emigrated fifty-six years later, also had family who emigrated in the mid-nineteenth century:

> My Canadian grandmother — that grandmother was three months old when they came over — Annie MacDonald, her people were from Bernera…[46] They came over in 1851…her mother was a MacLeod and her father was Neil MacDonald from Bernera — Breaclete, Bernera…The boat that they came over on, the 'Barlow', was three months — what did I say? Three months coming across, so she must have been six months [old] when she got here. She was only three months old when they left [Lewis].[47] The people were very sad at leaving, and they used to write poems, songs, I don't know where these songs are today or where they could be found, on leaving Lewis.[48]

The reluctance to leave is a theme that survives to this day, even when descendants acknowledge that the emigration of their forebears was eventually for the best. Muriel Mayhew re-told a story she had heard from her family which indicates that there was a keen awareness that emigration was a common fate in many parts of the Highlands and Islands where circumstances were even worse than they had been in Lewis:

I remember — this isn't Lewis, but my cousin Mina MacDonald, she was a MacLeod because my great-grandmother was a MacLeod, told me that the boats would come to take them — this is the time of the Highland Clearances, I suppose, and the people would be forced to go on and they'd be crying, and felt so bad, and this old man was put in the boat, and there was a man who ferried them onto the large boat. And at that time tobacco was at a premium and very few people even saw it. And this man had a pipe and he asked this man, this guard on the boat who made sure that none of them escaped, if he would light his pipe for him; well, he was on the windward side and he couldn't light his pipe. So that was a request not to be turned down by anyone, the only chance to puff at a pipe in those days. So he went to the other side of the boat, and when he went to the other side of the boat to light the pipe, this ferryman smuggled the old man off the boat and hid him at the bottom of the boat and took him off, and when the guard came back of course he didn't realize anybody was missing…And he didn't have to leave.

The fact that the old man outwitted the establishment is also a vital part of the story, as it reflects a 'native wit' and intelligence that people like to connect with their Scottish ancestors. It is not only in oral tradition that reports of Scottish characteristics survive. Many of the emigration agents stated that the hardiness of the Hebrideans was a desirable feature, fitting them for the hardships endured by steerage passengers on rough Atlantic crossings.[49]

The carrying of emigrants westwards was only one side of the shipping industry, as most of the ships were also involved in the timber trade.[50] As such, they were designed to suit both purposes, although after 1835 all ships had to comply with the 'American Passengers' Act'.[51] In many of them all the passengers went steerage, with accommodation set up on temporary decks that could be easily dismantled and removed when the passengers disembarked. The ships were then loaded with timber in Quebec and a profitable return journey made.[52] Some of the ship-owners are reported to have regarded a cargo of emigrants as suitable ballast for the outward journey of the timber trade.

Despite the 'improved' conditions brought about by the Act, there was no control over the hazards of the weather, or over the effects of disease once it managed to take hold in the crowded conditions below deck. The reality of the hardships suffered on board some of the emigrant ships was brought home to Catherine Parr Traill when, after a relatively luxurious voyage and a beautiful sail up the St. Lawrence, they landed in Quebec. She wrote home:

August 12. — We reached Gros Isle [sic] yesterday evening. It is a beautiful, rocky island, covered with groves of beech, birch, ash and fir-trees. There are several vessels lying at anchor close to the shore; one bears the melancholy symbol of disease, the yellow flag; she is a passenger-ship, and has the small-pox and measles among her crew. When any infectious complaint appears on board, the yellow flag is hoisted, and the invalids conveyed to the cholera-hospital or wooden building that has been erected…It is surrounded with palisadoes [sic] and a guard of soldiers.[53]

Although, in her excitement at landing, she becomes slightly irritated by the annoyance of quarantine, and the indignation of procedures such as fumigation of bedding, she writes later of the effects of disease, such as the distressing cases of cholera where in one family eleven people died, and in another, seventeen, leaving only a seven-year-old child to face life in the New World.[54] Surviving the Atlantic crossing may have been a great relief after a difficult voyage, but the threat of disease still remained even after quarantine and a journey on land to the final destination.[55] In 1968, former director of the National Maritime Museum in London, Basil Greenhill, wrote that 'the statistics speak for themselves…In 1847, the worst year, 17,500, 16 per cent of all who emigrated, died either on passage or on arrival.'[56]

So far as I can gather, there are no accounts from oral tradition about the returning timber ships — merely fading reports handed down from parents, grandparents and great-grandparents that the ocean crossing generally took six or eight weeks, the conditions on board ship were pretty spartan, often the sea was rough, the passengers seasick, and everyone was thankful to see land again.[57] Furthermore, I have not encountered any diaries of an actual voyage from Lewis or Harris;[58] in view of the circumstances in which they left, it is most likely that the very thought of writing an account of their misery was probably the furthest thing from the minds of the weary emigrants. There remains one piece of written evidence, in the form of a monument erected on the former quarantine island, Grosse Isle, situated in the St. Lawrence river, near Quebec City. It is a permanent reminder of the '5,294 persons who…found in America but a grave.'

In response to a letter which I wrote to the *Sherbrooke Record* in 1976 asking for information about emigration from the Outer Hebrides to Quebec, I received one reply from Cora McKillop Mimmaugh, the great-grand-daughter of an emigrant.[59] Although she was not from the Isle of Lewis or Harris, her familiy's experience was, nevertheless, typical of nineteenth century emigrants:

My ancestors, who came over in 1829, were not from the [Outer] Hebrides but from the Isle of Arran.

They were practically driven from the rented land by the Duke of Hamilton who owned the island. So they gladly accepted the offer of free land in Canada[60]…a land agent in Quebec met them and gave such a glowing account of this district that they were persuaded to come here. The ship they sailed in, the Caledonia, took 2 months to make the journey.[61] They suffered hardships a-plenty coming over, including sea sickness. They went to St. Nicholas (15 miles south of

Quebec City) by barge and then hired French Canadian teamsters to transport their belongings to the part of Megantic County they were destined for, 50 miles away.[62]

Severe hardships were suffered here the first winter as they had no idea of how cold a winter in Quebec could be, so were nearly frozen to death in their hastily built houses.

In fact they would have starved to death had it not been for the kindness of the U.E. [United Empire] Loyalists who had settled in Maple Grove a few years previous.

They all spoke Gaelic — some not even understanding English.

...I am a great grand-daughter of Mrs. John McKillop (widow) who came out with her family in 1829.

Emigration agents painted a fine picture of Canada and issued pamphlets intended to inform interested parties of the advantages of new country. To attract the Gaelic population, some of these were printed in Gaelic, such as *Ceann-Iuil an Fhir-Imrich do dh'America mu Thuath*, published in 1841.[63] Selected facts were generally enumerated, such as the description of the Eastern Townships as having an abundance of water in lakes, rivers and springs which would be good for both crops and water power; abundance of hardwood, which, after clearing, yielded fertile soil and an immediate cash return for the wood ashes; plenty of good grazing, and proximity to American markets. As the early histories of the Eastern Townships can confirm, it was perfectly true to state that churches, schools, colleges, mills and factories existed in that part of Canada, but selective truths gave intending settlers no idea of the vastness of the country. Immigrants had no concept of the fact that these amenities were as accessible to the land allocated to them as the University of Edinburgh might be to a person on St. Kilda. Economy with the facts was built into the techniques of emigration agents.

Nevertheless, the idea of land ownership must have seemed like Utopia to the impoverished tenant crofters of Lewis and Harris. Muriel Mayhew gave a general picture of the arrival of the earliest settlers:

They arrived in Quebec [City] and they came up the Francis River partly by boat, and then they came by horse and cart. There were people who transported them. Then they came to Lennoxville, and from Lennoxville they had to walk a good part of the way on a blazed trail.[64] There was one man left an axe, left his axe in Lennoxville, he was a carpenter, and his wife walked all the way back to Lennoxville from Gould to get it, [over forty miles, see Map 4]. And the only way they brought in provisions in the beginning was on blazed trails; carried flour on their back...From the British American Land Company they had been given over in Scotland various pictures which they believed and when they came here they were allotted sections of land by the British American Land Company, and they had to go to that land. And some of them had started for Ontario, but then they met other relatives or friends who were coming here, so rather than going on they came here. They settled first along the Scotch Road up in Bury, [then] eastwards from there, into Gould, and from Gould to Stornoway...[65]

There are many issues that appear to have caused confusion among the immigrants, especially since they were relying on competing agents to advise them. By way of encouragement, however, intending settlers were informed that there would be a house on each plot of land, ready for a family to move in. Naturally, expectations were based on information, and emigrants were filled with hope. The contrast between the propaganda and the reality of the situation is a frequent subject for anecdotes of emigrants and their descendants. Even for the more affluent, such as Catherine Parr Traill who emigrated in 1832 (in relative luxury) with her British Army Officer husband, the difference between what she read or was told and what she actually encountered was striking. In her book *'The Backwoods of Canada' being letters from the Wife of an Emigrant Officer, illustrative of the Domestic Economy of British America*, she recalls her conversation on the transatlantic crossing with an elderly gentleman 'who had been many years in the country.' He laughed when she said she'd heard and read of houses in Canada being built in a day: 'Yes, yes,' he replied, 'travellers find no difficulty in putting up a house in twelve or twenty-four hours, and so the log walls can be raised in that time or even less; but the house is not completed when the outer walls are up, as your husband will find to his cost.' Mrs Traill protested 'But all the works on emigration that I have read...give a fair and flattering picture of a settler's life...'

> 'Never mind books,' said my companion, 'use your own reason...Never tell me of what is said in books, written very frequently by tarry-at-home travellers. Give me the facts. One honest, candid emigrant's experience is worth all that has been written on the subject...'[66]

Published in 1836, the main aim of Catherine Parr Traill's book was to record the woman's point of view to the wives and daughters of emigrants (mostly from her own upper middle class background). It is highly unlikely that any poor victim of the potato famine ever saw a page of it, yet experiences she records and her impressions of the new land have much in common with that of all emigrants. As far as the promise of ready-made houses was concerned, the reality of the situation is still recalled with considerable indignation a century and a half later than Mrs Traill's record.

Eighty-one year old Russell MacIver whose 'great-grandfather came from a place called Loch Garvaig'[67] in Lewis, 'around 1850 or '52,' often heard his people talk of the family's first years:

> Well, I don't really know if they had to buy that land or not, because in some places there was supposed to be a small house built there for them, and it wasn't

much…Oh, they [the emigration agents] used to tell them a lot of stories, especially about the houses they have ready for them. When my mother came over she was one year old; that was around '75, I guess, 1875 or so. They were told 'what a nice house it was,' and there was no floor in it, and there was no glass in the windows, and you could pretty near walk out through the cracks — but it was a house! That passed [for a house], you know! [Just four walls and a roof?] Yeah. The companies that put them houses up of course they got paid so much for a house, but they were supposed to have been a lot better than that. I never saw that house, but I saw the first log house they made. And then after that they had a good house.[68]

Having struggled to eke out a living on a smallholding of three or four acres, a land grant of fifty or a hundred acres seemed like a vast area to be allocated to an immigrant family. Familiar only with the treeless Island of Lewis or the rocky Island of Harris, both with a predominance of peat, they anticipated making a living on soil that was rich and fertile surrounded by woods which were teeming with wildlife. Little did they realize that this fertile soil was covered with a forest so wild and dense that the branches of one tree tangled with the next, scarcely allowing light through its branches far less man or beast. Most of the people (apart from a few carpenters) had never used an axe, and their only knowledge of trees had been gained on their journey from Stornoway or Tarbert to their port of embarkation. Duncan McLeod of Milan commented that 'they were told all they had to do was tap a tree and they'd get sugar, the first ones that came over.'[69] Nobody explained what 'tap a tree' meant, nor that this wonderful sugar was only obtained after painstaking work — every forty gallons of sap collected from the trees yielded only one gallon of syrup, and only then could the process of making sugar begin. (See Chapter 5) Some of the emigration agencies had at least provided settlers with a large syrup kettle, which several of the emigrants presumed was to be used for dyeing wool, while others, having heard it was for syrup, must have been very puzzled during the trans-atlantic voyage.

The very first emigrants were quite unprepared for the extremes of the Quebec climate — the biting cold of -30 degree temperatures in winter (to say nothing of the wind-chill factor), and the searing heat or humidity in summer; and none could have imagined that much of the 'wildlife' they had been told about was in the form of plagues of mosquitoes and blackflies — torments completely unknown in Scotland.[70] There must have been many bitter disappointments in those early days, but once they had arrived in Quebec there was no going back. They had to face up to the hardships, accept the land that was allocated, and throw every effort they could into making it more habitable. 'There are very few countries where 'milk and honey flow' without considerable squeezing, scratching, and many heartaches.'[71]

Allocation of Land

There is no scarcity of topographical and survey maps and lists of land grants for the Province of Quebec, with the earliest significant to the study of the Eastern Townships dating to the second half of the eighteenth century.[72] Early topographical maps show additional details that may otherwise be forgotten, such as the Putnam and Gray *Map of the District of St Francis, Canada East* published by the Crown Land Department in 1863 (based on surveys from 1763 to the 1860s) which, along the road through Marston, states 'Road made by Americans in the year 1792'.[73] Aside from confirming the age of that road, the note also denies any claim that it might have been built by the Land Companies when they moved in.[74] The *List of lands granted by the Crown in the province of Quebec from 1763 to 3st December 1890*, printed by order of the Legislature of Quebec in 1891, records details from this considerable time span and can be readily consulted.

In 1842 The British American Land Company produced a map drawn from the actual survey by their Principal Land Surveyor, A. Wells. As land was purchased (or later granted by the Crown), the 'lots' were registered and the map grids were filled in accordingly, and updated as years went by. [Map 3] The actual process of land allocation, however, seems to have been one that was shrouded in mystery as far as the new immigrants were concerned. By today's standards the secrecy that seems to have been attached to the process is somewhat akin to that of the modern car salesman who is reputed to snap shut his price book the moment a customer looks interested. Not surprisingly, the oral traditions that survive concerning the procedure are those which were most meaningful to the Hebridean immigrants. Bill Young explained:

> I'll tell you how they made it [the land grants]. They formed up in a...line. First they drew lots — not for the land — they drew lots to see who'd take the place in this procession. And number one was the first, and number two was second, on down to the end of the line. And they started from a surveyor's point, outside one of the township lines, or something. They had those marked, I suppose — they were military maps. And the number one man would start, and he would take his axe and he'd mark a tree. And they'd sing, what was it, the Twenty-third Psalm in Gaelic. And they'd sing that over so many times, and they'd keep time walking through the woods. And when that ended, the number one man would make a mark on a tree, and that was his. That square that they'd...he'd walk the frontage and back, and two sides were the same as the distance they walked.
>
> And then the second man would take his place and he'd walk and they'd sing. And so it was got that way.[75]

It is unlikely that the actual measurement was made in this way, as survey maps show that 'lots' had already been surveyed and measured. More probably, the British American Land Company agents knew that these immigrants were

Gaelic-speaking Presbyterians who upheld their Calvinistic faith and looked upon the Bible as the very centre of their lives. Furthermore, they came from a tradition where every aspect of work could be accompanied by singing. Although they may have 'sung the survey' with a choice psalm (*Is e Dia féin a's buachaill dhomh*, 'The Lord's My Shepherd'), it did not mean, as they soon realized, that they were each receiving a choice piece of land. Who would dare question the land agent or the Provider of the 'pastures green' or 'quiet waters' when voices were raised in praise? Many a family must have felt quite deceived by the contrast between the picture that had originally been painted for them and the one that met their eyes in Quebec:

> Kenny Smith told us they used to sing the survey. Now, that didn't distract these agents from picking the best areas and taking it for themselves. Well, the poor settlers got what was left. And for digging a road through their settlements, grubbing it out, like, they were supposed to be paid in oatmeal and potatoes. Nobody ever told them potatoes didn't keep in the wintertime. So, there are instances of families living the entire winter on what little game they could get — and oatmeal. And others living for months on potatoes alone. And starvation did catch up to them, some of them.
>
> But that's the situation they faced. There was no help for it; they survived all winter…And, you see, they weren't accustomed to this country. They didn't even know how to handle an axe. And they were helped a lot by the French Canadian early settlers who put them wise to all these ways. And there's where they had the co-operation amongst the two of them! They had to co-operate to survive! And, eh, they certainly weren't equipped…but the fact that they stuck it out and…they burned the land in order to clear it — they didn't cut down the forest.

Quebec still has vast tracts of forest today, and though there are huge areas of second and third growth timbers, there are innumerable locations where the observer can stand and gaze at the density of the first growth, overawed at the daunting task that must have faced the first settlers who cleared the farmland.

For over a century and a half of Canadian history there has circulated a popularly held notion that Scottish Gaels who emigrated, either by choice or by enforced circumstances, settled in places that were very much like their homeland. Even in 1992, a third generation Scots-Canadian whose people all came from the Isle of Lewis remarked that 'of course Lewis is very much like Quebec.' She had never seen the land of her forebears, and, surprisingly, the fact that her mother had visited it several times had done nothing to dispell this long-held assumption. Nothing could be further from the truth: if one was set the task of finding two lands of the most extreme topographical and climatic contrasts, the Isles of Lewis and Harris (the Long Island) in the Outer Hebrides and the Eastern Townships of Quebec could scarcely fit better.[76]

The First Homesteaders

The insects have been a sad annoyance to us…
for these pests are numerous.
[Catherine Parr Traill, 1833]

Russell MacIver, whose family from Balallan, Lewis, settled in Victoria, eight miles from Scotstown, described their experience:

Well, when they started that was all trees — forest…I guess they'd have to tear it apart; I don't think they'd even have saws at that time, just axes…And all the best of timber was burnt, just burnt…And the stumps, they'd tear up around the stumps and put a few potatoes or a little grain around. Well, after a while the stumps would rot and then they could clear more land. They must have had an awful time.

Virtually every family who settled had a parallel experience to relate. A few miles away in Milan, the MacDonalds, grandparents of Christie MacArthur, were typical of new settlers clearing land:

They had to cut lumber down to make ashes; it was the *ashes* they were selling.[77] It was to Stornoway…[that] was the first place, and they had a store, where they had the necessities, and they used to bring that [the ashes] in there, and they would sell it. And I remember when I asked my mother what they were making she thought then they were making soda of those ashes.[78]

Russell referred to the product as 'lye' and confirmed it was 'potash — it used to go to Stornoway, I think, or Cookshire.' From these depots the wood ashes were transported to another location where they were made into potash by percolating water through them and evaporating the solution. (Most of the older generation made use of this knowledge on a much smaller scale, in the making of soap which will be described in Chapter 6.)

According to Catherine Parr Traill who watched, with trepidation, and then participated in the first clearing of timber from their land in Ontario in the early 1830s, there was a certain excitement and pleasure attached to the process. Helped by a team of oxen, the men piled up the timbers:

[And] a magnificent sight it was to see such a conflagration all round us. I was a little nervous at first on account of the nearness of some of the log-heaps to the house, but care is always taken to fire them with the wind blowing in a direction away from the building. Accidents have sometimes happened, but they are rarer occurrences than might be expected…Fiery columns, the bases of which are hidden by the dense smoke wreaths, are to be seen in every direction sending up showers of sparks that are whirled about like rockets and fire-wheels in the wind…The fire will sometimes continue unextinguished for days. After the burning is over, the brands are collected and drawn together again to be reburnt; and strange as it may appear to you, there is no work that is more interesting and exciting than that of tending the log-heaps, rousing up the dying flames, and supplying the fires with fresh fuel.[79]

In Traill's day, the ashes were not sold, but were 'scattered abroad'. The situation in the Eastern Townships probably reverted to this, as there was a drastic decline in the potash market in later years. The settlers then began to save the biggest lumber for railroad ties, which they sold in the 1870s and 80s while the railroad was under construction.

Christie MacArthur could remember a time during her youth when land-clearing was a major concern of second generation immigrants. By the time she was born in 1888, they had cleared several fields, but it was an on-going process which often lasted for decades. The entire family was expected to work at the various chores, and, although education was a high priority among the Scots, parents could scarcely afford to allow their children, especially the boys, to continue at school once they were physically strong enough to make a considerable contribution to the family work force: 'As soon as they were able to work they kept them at home — to plough, or harrow, or fix stones, or cut wood...do something.'

With the large timber removed from the land, the next task was to remove the huge roots and stumps that were left. Usually it was easier to get rid of the stumps after they had been left to rot for a few years and the land worked round about them. Whatever the settlers decided to do, the stumps and roots were stubborn objects to remove. Bill Young of Lennoxville described it this way:

> The first few years it didn't bother them. They planted around them...And then, they burned some, but the stump-puller, whether it came into this area or not in any great strength, I couldn't tell you. But parts of Ontario they made a stump-puller...

Some of the older men who had heard of 'stump-pullers' confirmed that they were not known to the Hebridean settlers in the Eastern Townships. As Russell MacIver commented:

> To get the stumps out? Oh, after they rotted enough, you know, I suppose they could hitch the oxen and pull some out...[stump-pullers back in those days?] No, I never heard they did...I'm sure they wouldn't have them then...At first, oxen and a dump cart. That was pretty fast getting around with one of them if you wanted to go somewhere! [Laughs]

Just as they had done on their treeless crofts in the Old Country, neighbours helped one another on countless occasions, and quickly learned to adapt to their new surroundings, trees and all. Bill Young summed up: 'Just brute strength, because they had bees, eh? They got together and pulled stumps, and raised barns, and they held *ceilidhs* afterwards.'

No matter what the work was — clearing land, pulling stumps, felling timber, burning brush, building cabins and barns, making syrup, spinning, quilting — if it could be done communally to lighten the load, then the homesteaders held 'bees'. This practice, common throughout Canada, was described by Catherine Parr Traill in the early 1830s as 'highly useful, and almost indispensable to new settlers in the remote townships.'[80] As far as the 'ceilidh afterwards' was concerned, that too seems to have been a universal feature, not necessarily under that name, as Traill's description of 'raising the walls of a house in one day' suggests..

> [Afterwards there was] plenty of Canadian nectar (whiskey), the honey that our *bees* are solaced with. Some huge joints of salt pork, a peck of potatoes, with rice pudding, and a loaf as big as an enormous Cheshire cheese, formed the feast that was to regale them during the raising.[81]

Neighbourliness was essential, and whether the stumps remained in the ground or not, each family had to plant their land as soon as possible in order to grow their food. In the first few years ploughing was, of course, impossible,[82] but they did cultivate the land using the implement familiar to them in Lewis, as Christie MacArthur described: 'They used to have a…an iron hoe, a *croman* — something like a hoe, but it wouldn't be so wide, just as wide as your hand.'[83]…And they used to plant potatoes there first.'

The earliest days were no doubt the most difficult for the new settlers who had to work enormously hard just to survive. The first year must have been their most difficult, as they were not only ill-equipped for the tasks of land clearing but they also had to adjust to a drastic change in climate. They discovered they would have to endure almost eight months of winter,[84] a spring so short that it seems to be over in a matter of days, and a summer that has weeks of unbearable heat and humidity, sapping every ounce of energy just when it is most needed to meet the greatest demands of work. At the same time there were the infestations of blackfly and mosquito to add to their misery. Bill Young told how they used to cope with this problem:

> Well, they made smudge fires. They made a fire outside at night that would put out a heavy smoke, or else they'd build it right in the cabin…They'd make a fire, and they'd just put green grass on top of it, or spruce boughs. Green, anything green creates a stench. And sit as close to that as you could.[85]

Only the clear, crisp air of autumn, with its brilliant maple reds mingled with glorious golds of the birch, afforded several weeks of living conditions which, by comparison, were comfortable. Families did the best they could to keep warm in their draughty shacks through the first winter. They eked out whatever supply of oatmeal or potatoes they had with whatever wildlife they could catch, some of them barely surviving. Bill Young continued:

> Contrary to the public idea, there was very little game in those days in the woods, because you take a section of woods that's all tree growth — there's no grazing for deer or animals of that type. So you're just not going to get anything! You might be lucky to get a few fish. Lake Megantic used to supply them with a certain amount of fish, but the woods didn't teem with game like they have it in these books. The woods around here didn't teem with anything except just blackflies and mosquitoes! It wasn't until the land started getting cleared and the meadows were opening up that the deer started coming in for grazing. You can't expect a deer to climb a tree and eat the leaves off it, can you? And these were hardships, and they raised their families, and they were cheated out of their land and they were cheated by the lumber dealers, and, you know — but they made it!

A first-hand account written by David Kennedy, who, as an infant, emigrated with his parents from Ayrshire to Ontario in 1829, tells of experiences which are very similar to those in the Eastern Townships. In his book, *Pioneer Days*, he recalls that even after they had been settled for a few years, their diet was still very limited:

> I can remember well seeing my mother putting potatoes into cold water to draw the frost out of them before being cooked, and then we had neither meat, milk nor butter to eat with them. The labour of clearing the first acres of unbroken land was all performed by the settlers when they subsisted entirely upon potatoes as a diet, baked and boiled time about, by way of change or variety, with sometimes a dish of greens made from cow cabbage or the tops of young turnips, were added in season. All this may seem strange when I tell you that the forests abounded with various kinds of game, and the creeks were full of speckled trout, yet it rarely happened that the settlers succeeded in capturing any deer. But the Indians that came up...in the fall of the year would kill deer by the dozen, and it was at such times that the settlers, if they had any money at all, could get a cheap supply of venison from the Indians. I can yet remember, although my father was a sportsman in the old country, yet he would never venture into the woods to shoot deer for fear of getting lost or of being attacked by the wolves or bears. So timid were the people that they would not venture outside of the house after dark, for in the evening the deer would come around the house in droves to get away from the wolves, which could be heard howling in every direction, and my father, who had a good rifle would quietly open a window sufficiently to get the point of his rifle out, and then shoot at a deer, and if it was wounded it would only run a short distance, when it would be caught and devoured by the wolves in a few minutes, so that nothing of it would be seen but the blood stained snow, so that my father's efforts to obtain a supply of venison were worse than useless, yet the deer were very plentiful.[86]

As soon as they had cleared part of the forest, however, the settlers found, to their relief, that the situation was much improved as far as wildlife was concerned. According to Mrs. Christie MacKenzie, born in 1897 and raised in Milan in the section locally known as 'the Yard', the profusion of wild life was such that the the first settler, a MacKay from Lewis, named the area accordingly:

> The fellow that moved in there first [was Angus Mackay — he started clearing the land] .. and it was just swarming with deer; he was right in the middle of the woods you know, and he used to call it the 'Deer Yard' — 'Yard *na Féidh*',[87] But then, of course, that name] is years gone afterwards...It was from his son that my father bought his lot, where Walter's house is there now. And by that time they had dropped the word 'deer', and it was just the 'Yard'. So that has followed it ever since[88]...It was pretty well cleaned off when my father was settled there...And there was very few people that had guns. A lot of the deer in them days had been killed with bows and arrows because they were so thick there, you know. It was nothing to go out and see one.

Mrs. MacKenzie herself had never seen anyone hunt with a bow and arrow, though she knew from family tradition that 'the first ones that were settled there did — Kenneth MacKay and Angus MacKay.' She did not know, however, if the Scots settlers had archery skills when they emigrated or if they learned them in Quebec. Russell MacIver remarked that 'when they first came over they couldn't afford guns, so they'd have bows and arrows.' [Sept. 16,1992.] A century and half later it is sometimes suggested that either the French-Canadians or the Indians taught the 'Scotch'[89] how to hunt with bows and arrows. While there may be some truth in this, strange as it may seem to expatriate Scots today, there is ample evidence to suggest that Scottish emigrants would have been skilled in archery before they left Scotland. As far as the Highlands and Islands are concerned, there are numerous accounts, both from oral tradition and in print. For example, in 1695, Martin Martin observed in the Isle of Lewis that 'the inhabitants are very dextrous in the exercises of swimming and archery,'[90] and in 1901 Dr R.C. MacLagan of Argyllshire published accounts of children learning the relevant skills and accompanying activities of archery in preparation for adulthood.[91]

Dealing with this kind of wildlife in the early days was a welcome task for the settlers who valued every good thing the land offered. Gradually they began to see the fruit of their labours; the first harvest gave encouragement as well as sustenance, and basic improvements made their homes more comfortable. Although life was not easy for them, they began to realize that the new country, despite its wildness and physical hardships, nonetheless offered a more hopeful way of life than the one they had left behind. Very quickly they saw improvements all around them. Together they carved out new farms, new communities, and life became much more comfortable. The physically demanding tasks of felling enormous first-growth timbers and then squaring logs with a broad-axe became the subject of 'settler stories' among a people who had never seen an axe, far less swung one with accuracy. They derived not only greater comfort from their efforts of house- and barn-raising, but also a sense of pride which has carried on through generations to the present day. Pictures of grandfather with his broad-axe are prized, and stories are told about timbers felled and squared by the finest craftsmanship.

In 1992, when I asked eighty-one year-old Russell MacIver if he could remember any of the older generation who were skilled with the broad-axe, or if he had ever seen a barn-raising bee, it all came back to him:

> I saw one — my Uncle Neil MacDonald. He put one up in Balallan here; I was pretty young. I saw them then, they had a bee to put the barn up. There was quite a few men there too…Gosh, I wouldn't know, but the whole neighbourhood, maybe twenty, thirty men…Oh, [the barn was] fairly big. They'd have the stable, and the hay-mow on top of the stable, and then the bay on the other side…Oh yes, [all the lumber was cut, and] everything was all ready and fitted and everything. Just put it up and into place. And the ones that made those fittings, they knew what they were doing! They was all ready to put the wooden pin in.

His friend, Duncan McLeod agreed that there were 'no nails then. We had a barn, the barn at Milan, just across the road from the store, was made that way.' Both men recalled that no matter whether the neighbours were Scotch or French, everybody lent a hand. Russell continued:

> I remember one year there was a French fellow, he used to live where MacIver lived first when he came over, and he came around one day and he asked my father 'You come tomorrow, help lift big barn?' [Laughs]. That was a big one, high — can you remember it? And they had a bridge going away up into it…Oh, [it was] about a mile further on…Oh yeah, everybody would help. My father was pretty good at that. It didn't matter how high, he'd walk on the ridges or anywhere, never bothered him. Of course there's a lot of people could do that.

The planning and cutting may have taken months, but when the big day came, there was no holding back. These men demonstrated a work efficiency level that would probably be the envy of every modern building site foreman:

> Well they'd put the frame up in one day. Then of course they'd have a lot of fitting after that — board it and put the stalls in, but it wouldn't take so many men or such hard lifts. [And] the roof, yeah, they'd have to lift that too, the same as the rest; have to have [?the top of?] it come to a peak. And they'd put like steps, like, going up to the, and some of them would cut their own clapboards; they'd be, oh, about three feet long, maybe that wide [8 inches], put

them on. Our cow-barn, that had the kind of roof that had clapboards. My father, no, my *grandfather* split them out of cedar. They didn't have a saw to do it there. They had chisels, hammers…Oh, they had a broad axe. And some were pretty good with that, just as smooth as that [and while he spoke, Russell drew his hand over the formica top of his kitchen table.]…Oh, they had pretty poor tools at first…they might have brought some [from the old country].

Although Russell and Duncan spoke as though it was almost natural for the men to know how to take part in a barn-raising, it is quite likely that the first settlers had to learn this kind of team work. In his autobiography, David Kennedy recalled how one man, a young, established farmer, taught a group of new settlers at the first barn-raising bee to be held among them. What he describes leaves no doubt as to the skill, strict discipline and co-operation of the men, to say nothing of the strength of the team.[92] Kennedy also recorded that they brought a few tools with them from Scotland, 'hammers and chisels, but not a saw.'[93]

How Are Things Back Home?

While most of the immigrants settled between 1851 and 1855, emigration from the Isles of Lewis, Harris and North Uist continued until after the First World War. According to emigration records, from the year 1856 there was a continuous trickle of new arrivals to the Townships, with a marked upswing of immigrants around 1863 and 1873. [Table 1][94]

During the closing decades of the nineteenth century, various departments of the Government of Canada produced further publications aiming to give confidence to those who had a mind to emigrate. These included a third edition of *The Eastern Townships: Information for Intending Settlers*, issued by the Department of Agriculture in 1881, and *The Settler's Guide, or the Homesteader's Handy Helper* by the Department of the Interior in 1896. A century later, however, I have come across no mention in oral tradition of such publications having influenced subsequent emigrants.

Fortunately those who had already settled in Quebec managed to adapt to the hardships of the harsh winter, and even to the summer's dreaded infestations. In the spirit of optimism and determination to succeed, they quickly adjusted to the initial shock of arriving in such a wild, wooded place with not a field or cottage in sight. Settled in their rapidly improving surroundings, they nevertheless longed to have some of their own family beside them, where they could see a realistic opportunity of land ownership for all who were willing to work. Some began to send letters of encouragement to relatives still struggling to make a living on a small croft. Despite the hardships of emigration, they lived in a land of hope and comparative plenty. Referring to the first of his family to settle in Quebec,

John MacKenzie remarked 'I never heard him saying that he wanted to go back — I know that.'[95]

After the emigration 'bulge' of the early 1850s, there was a steady flow throughout the remainder of the nineteenth century. There can be little doubt that most of those who came within twenty or thirty years of the first settlers did so at the bidding of kinsfolk who were convinced of the benefits of life in Quebec. Two such examples were cousins Roderick E. Morrison and Maryann Morrison, who, as children, came with their families from Geocrab in Harris. At the age of nearly a hundred and one, Maryann (who lived to be more than a hundred and seven) looked back over the century and recalled the circumstances surrounding the emigration of their families. Although I scarcely expected in 1976 to meet anyone who had first-hand experience of a nineteenth century emigration, I was privileged to record Maryann, whose memory went back almost another century to include that of her grandparents on Harris.

Born in Geocrab in 1875, Maryann recalled the way of life that was prevalent during her childhood. Like all the crofting families in those days, they lived in a small thatched cottage, a *taigh dubh,*[96] with the family housed in one end and the cattle in the other:

> Well, it wasn't a house made [with a slated roof, but with] straw on the top. And put down with tarpaulins on top [of the thatch] and ropes around that tarpaulin so it wouldn't move with the wind. They had little windows in them and they had...no stoves [like we had in Quebec, but], just the fire in the middle of the house; there's smoke going up and down and out and wherever it wants to go. No wonder my eyes is bad! But it didn't hurt then.
>
> Cows was over there and we were over here. As you come in, to go to see me, you'd go by like a little place — platform, you know, like a walk — that was going into the cattle and then going into our place. [There was a stone wall between the part where the people lived and where the animals were kept, and] you could go down there and milk them, and you could tie them and keep them in when you wanted to keep them.
>
> It was a good house, you know; there was no water coming through it or anything. And there was windows on it, and there was...we come in on that door and the cattle was going to their own place, and we weren't [uncomfortable]...We had two big beds with high posts; [box-beds] that's the beds we had.[97]

In his book, *Crofters and Habitants,* J.I. Little describes the blackhouses with 'no eaves or windows...' giving the impression of darkest stone-age dwellers,[98] and apparently missing the point that they were designed to cope with the weather, and the architectural principles involved are quite sound. While it is true that by today's standards material wealth was negligible and housing impoverished, Little seems to have no understanding of the actual conditions, or of the fact that, outwith the oppressive hardships of famine and landlordism, many Hebridean crofters still express a contentment with the way of life of their forebears. In vivid contrast to their deprivation of material goods, the occupants of these homes were in possession of a cultural richesse that made them among the wealthiest people in Europe — poetry, song, music, tales, legends were what they valued most highly, and the setting in which they nurtured these gifts was not, as Little suggests, one of perpetual discomfort.[99] In sharp contrast to Little's 'outside' view, American folklorist, Margaret Fay Shaw, who lived in a thatched house in South Uist from 1929 to 1935, quickly became accustomed to the peat smoke, and delighted in the songs and stories which she heard and recorded.[100] Commenting on the fire in the middle of the floor she noted that 'the pleasant thing about such a fire was that there was room to gather round it in the true sense.'[101]

Furnishings in the Morrisons' house in Harris consisted of basic necessities. Apart from the box-beds, one for Maryann's parents, and one for herself and her sister who was two years older (relative luxury compared to the shared facilities of large families), they had a table, a few chairs, a spinning wheel, and a loom. Maryann was not surprised to hear that this situation was widespread in all crofting communities in the Hebrides in her day, but was very surprised to learn that it continued to be so until well into this century.[102] As far as their small allocation of land was concerned, however, it was of the poorest kind — rocky, unproductive and difficult to the point that they could scarcely subsist: 'They were poor; they didn't get but a little plot, you know, to work on.[103] We had a cow and a calf, and all the potatoes we wanted, but that was all. No government money there! Not a thing.'

With no prospect of things improving, it became evident that they would do best by following Maryann's uncle and family who had already emigrated. Although she was too young to understand the set-up or the involvement of emigration agents, she recalled that

> It was a lady from Glasgow that sent the immigrants over; not us, but a lot
> of them. And when we were over here for — oh, quite a few years, she sent my
> husband — father — a letter telling him that he'd have to pay for his passage,
> you know, when he immigrated over to Canada.

For some time before their emigration, Maryann's family were involved with this 'lady from Glasgow' who was arranging for several families to emigrate to North America. Her elder sister was one of a number of local people who were employed by this woman in a small cottage industry:

> This lady was giving yarn to poor people — and [they were expected to] make
> it [into knitted goods] and send it back to her — that was all...I know my
> sister was knitting socks for this lady, you know, and the socks were going back
> to Glasgow, to be examined, you know, and my sister was paid for the socks she
> was making. I don't know what she was doing with the socks.

In her article, 'An Old Scottish Handicraft Industry', I. F. Grant discusses the nineteenth century demand for home-knitted socks — merchants gave out wool to women, usually widows, single women or those who were too old to work outdoors. Dr Grant notes that most of them could knit two and a half pairs a week, supplementing 'what little pittance' they had.[104] According to A.C. Cameron, the women in Skye received 6d. a pair for socks and 1s. 6d. for a pair of long stockings, and in the late 1860s it was recorded that the 'people of the Bays of Harris could not have made a living' without the women's knitting and tweed-making which were organised by two women, the Countess Dowager of Drumore, whose late husband owned Harris, and Mrs Captain Thomas.[105] Exactly what part this may have played in the Morrison family's emigration is not clear — perhaps the knitted goods were being sold to make funds to help cover the expenses of those who sailed across the Atlantic in this emigration scheme. It is also possible that the family were part of a scheme referred to by John Ramsay of Kildalton in his *Diary* of 1870 when, visiting the home of Captain Ramage on the shore of Lake Megantic, he recorded the fact that 'Captain R. had been in correspondence with Mrs Thomas regarding her scheme for sending out emigrants from Harris and Uist.'[106] Whatever the case, the two Morrison families set sail for Quebec in 1888 when Maryann was about twelve years of age. Their aim was to join her uncle and his family who had already set up a homestead some years earlier.

Although their voyage had taken place eighty-eight years before our conversation, Maryann's memory of sailing from Tarbert, Harris, to Glasgow, and from there to Quebec was very clear. This composite account in her own words tells of their voyage:

> We sailed from Tarbert on a little boat — a little steamer from Tarbert to Glasgow, and from Glasgow on a one called the *Siberia*. There was lots of immigrants coming over with us. In our family there was my mother, father, sister, and myself, and my grandfather, and my auntie, and she had three children. Her husband was dead, but she come with us. And my grandfather came with my father because his wife died when the children was young and he stayed with my father and mother. So he followed them over to Canada.
>
> [On the boat] my aunt, my sister slept on the upper, like two bunks. And my grandfather had to go to another section of the boat where there was old people like himself. But he would come down and see us every day, you know. You had freedom in the boat to go where you pleased, to see your people. The weather coming over — oh, we had one bad day on a Sunday, one bad day.

Though Maryann said little of the consequences of bad weather, it was clearly an unforgettable experience. In 1992, a hundred and four years after the Morrisons emigrated, Maryann's son, Angus, retold the story of his people:

Bha feadhainn aca, dh'fhàs iad tinn, bha iad cho fad air an eathar. Thug iad trì
no ceithear a sheachdduinean tighinn a nall...is nuair a *landadh* iad ann an
Cuibeac cha robh duine ann a Cuibeac a dh'aithnicheadh iad. Thàinig iad bho
[Bhaile] Cuibeac gu Megantic air an trèan, 's thàinig iad bhon an trèan ann a
Megantic 's bha daoine an sin a dh'aithnicheadh iad, 's chaidh iad a dh'fhuireach
comhla riutha...[Aonghas Moireastan]...Se...bràthair mo sheanar...Nuair a
thàinig iad a nall se *log cabin* anns a robh iad a' fuireach.

*[There were some of them became ill, they were so long in the vessel. They took three or
four weeks coming over...and when they were landed in Quebec there was nobody there
they knew. They came from the [town of] Quebec to Megantic on the train, and they
came off the train in Megantic, and there were people there they knew [meeting them],
and they went to stay with them...[Angus Morrison, he was my grandfather's brother...
When they came across it was a log cabin they were living in.]*

Although Angus's estimation of the duration of the voyage is closer to that
taken by his great-uncle, it probably matters little; as a young boy hearing
their story, he could well imagine how they must have felt with nobody in
this strange land to meet them. The group who came out in 1888, were,
according to Maryann, twelve days at sea. When the *Siberia* landed in Levis,
Quebec, Maryann and her family disembarked, and from there continued
their journey to Marsboro which was to be their home:

We got there on a train — to Megantic, not to Marsboro. There wasn't even a
car or anything then. We came from Levis, Quebec, to Lake Megantic...And
from there my uncle met us with a horse and a big cart, and we all jumped into
the cart and went to my uncle's house. He had a big family himself, but we had
just...my father had just two girls.

There was also her grandfather, who was well remembered as part of their
emigration story. Naturally, none of the present generation ever met him, but
they had family photographs to remind them [see Plate 3]. Angus's wife, Mary,
whose family are French, told of the circumstances that led to the old man's
emigration:

When they came here his wife had just died, and he wanted to come with
them. They said 'Wouldn't you rather stay here in Scotland and be buried near
your wife?' And he said 'No,' he said, 'I want to go with you.' [Angus's] mother's
father was over a hundred years old when he died.[107]

The Morrison homestead was in a part of Marsboro that was, and still is,
well off the beaten track. Angus and Mary took me there on a visit, and even
on a beautiful day in summer it was hard to imagine how the first settlers
ever found it. 'In the olden days this was the end of the road, there was three
families up here; we were in Cruvag, [Marsboro]' For Maryann it was to
become her home for more than half a century.

When the new immigrants arrived, the two families lived together until Maryann's father, Samuel, with the help of relatives and neighbours, built their first Quebec home, their own log cabin. It was situated on a neighbouring lot of land which Sam Morrison had obtained through a land grant. Although it was a sizeable piece of land, and they actually *owned* it, they faced the same arduous tasks of land-clearing as had the earlier Hebridean settlers. But for Maryann's mother, not the least hardship to bear was the homesickness she felt for Harris:

> It was a very poor place when we came, you know. Everybody was so poor, poor, poor. If we left Harris poor, it wasn't quite so bad here. But it was bad enough. But my father took up a farm, and one Sunday after we come over, he went out to the field and set up under a big tree, and my mother with him. And she was crying for her people all the time — nothing but her people, her people. And when my father set down, and her, under the tree — we were not with them; I don't know where we were, I and my sister was out somewhere — but they sit under a tree and my father look in his purse to see if he had money enough to take them back. The old lady that took us over, she wouldn't take us back. And…my goodness, that's a long time ago! Anyway my father took out his purse and see how much money he had, and if he had enough money to take them back, we were going back. But, no, he didn't have money enough, just enough for the passage. But now he said to my mother: 'When we get there…' — he had a boat, and a calf, and a cow when we left — well he sold that; and sheep; and lambs. 'But when I get to Harris again, we can't live there. We have no boat; we have no cattle; we have nothing to do.' So he decided to stay in Canada — which was better for them and for us. So that's the way I stayed in Canada, when…if my father had decided he had money enough to go over…he had just enough for the passage, but nothing when he'd get over there.

Although Maryann had no idea of how much the ocean passage had cost, she did know that they were expected to pay back the money which had been spent on them when 'the lady from Glasgow' brought them over. With what money Samuel Morrison had, however, he decided to make the best of their situation by improving their homestead in Marsboro and buying cows for the land he had obtained:

> Well, he bought cows with the land…but he didn't pay anything for the land. This old lady, after years — you know the one that sent us — she sent us a letter and tell my father it was time for him to pay for this passage, that he had to Canada. And one of [them] wrote back to the lady and told her: 'You should be ashamed to send any people to such a place as this. There's no place here for anybody, any better than in Harris.' We never heard any more about it. She never called after that, but she did mean that we'd pay it back…but we didn't. No, there wasn't no money; it wasn't like the way things are today. Everybody has a car, everybody has…

The fact that emigrants were unable to repay the cost of the ocean passage may not have come as a surprise to 'the lady from Glasgow', for, more than fifteen years earlier when Captain Ramage in Megantic discussed the scheme with John Ramsay of Kildalton, 'he saw no prospect of recovering any part' of the debt. He therefore asked Ramsay if he would 'see Mrs Thomas on [his] return to explain to her the improbability of realizing the cash.'[108]

Although still lacking in material wealth, the newcomers appreciated the closeness and support of family and friends. A consistent and recurring theme among the reminiscences of early settlers is the outstanding community spirit: the willingness to help each other, the ability to work together, and the efficiency of community efforts such as logging bees, barn-raisings, and house building. With the help of family and neighbours, the Morrisons' log cabin, featuring one large room on the ground level and three rooms upstairs in the loft, was soon built of stripped logs.[109] Even the children could help, as Maryann recalled:

> After the cabin is finished and you're going to live in it, they get moss in the woods, and they put it in the cracks, you know, all over. It was made very comfortable. We had a big, big stove, you know.

Maryann's family were happy to move into their new house, taking with them what few belongings they had brought over on the voyage from Harris:

> A wheel, a loom, and a [pair of wool] cards and…well that was all…only *cisteachan* — they called them 'chests' then. We had a lot of clothes coming over, [for bedding and for wearing, packed in the chests]. But we had plenty of blankets [that my mother wove in Harris] coming over which was very good for [the cold in Quebec] — heavy, rough — you'd have to sleep with one of them, without no sheets like we have now. Just the big blankets over you. We didn't mind that.[110]

All that was left to do when they moved in was to furnish their new abode: 'Well, when we went to our own house we didn't even have a chair to sit on. But there was nice neighbours around us and they come with a chair [for] us. But we managed very well after that.'

Content to have settled in Marsboro, the Morrison family formed part of the Hebridean community which, in those days, and for many years afterwards, was entirely Gaelic-speaking. She considered it fortunate to have sailed across the Atlantic with her cousin Roderick and his family, for eventually Maryann and Roderick married. Once again Maryann reflected on their childhood voyage, and with some pleasure recalled that 'we met on the boat.' For the children and adolescents it had been an adventure, though for some of them it must have been infinitely more traumatic, as they did not have the security of a loving family to surround them:

We had...do you know what's 'home children'? 'Home children' — some orphanage that has lots of children, and they gave them out for adoption, you know. We had a string in the boat we came on, between the immigrants and that gang. But they'd have to stay on their own line of the — they had a rope between, and they had to stay on that side, and we had to stay on the other side. So the immigrants and the 'home children' [were on the same crossing]...They were out for adoption here — lots of people was taking them from Homes. But we never had any of them.

The 'Home children' Maryann spoke of, or 'Home boys' as most of them were, came from orphanages in the British Isles and were part of a 'juvenile emigration' scheme that operated from c. 1870 to 1930, with a few agencies operating as late as the 1950s. As far as the Eastern Townships are concerned, the 'Home Boys' were mostly English, and were all destined to live on farms with Scottish families. They were 'spoken for', taken in, and were to become part of the family, working in exchange for their keep and (some say) a small allowance. The resettlement scheme offered them the opportunity of having a healthier and happier life among the Scots settlers who, to this day, speak warmly of the 'Home Boys' and the families who cared for them. In several instances boys were legally adopted, and though they may have changed their name from an English one to an unmistakeably Scottish one, local people always seem to refer to them as 'Home Boys', even well into old age.[111] From all accounts, no hardships they faced in Quebec offered any comparison to the poor and cruel conditions they left behind.

That, however, is only part of the story. The subject of juvenile emigration has attracted much attention over the years, with some of the issues involved coming under close scrutiny in recent years. For example, there are questions still being raised as to the moral standards applied by those involved in the network of organizations responsible for making the decisions. A number of studies have examined the records of British orphanages, and have exposed some staggering statistics.[112] During the sixty-year peak period, approximately 100,000 unaccompanied children, ages five to fourteen, were emigrated to Canada via the services of about fifty British agencies.[113] The network was highly organized and involved a number of orphanages all over Britain, with Dr Barnardo's Homes leading the way as the biggest juvenile emigration agency in the country.[114] In Scotland, well-known orphanages such as the Quarrier's Home at Bridge of Weir, near Glasgow, and the Aberlour Orphanage were involved. In her article, 'The Juvenile Immigrant: Halfway to Heaven or Hell on Earth', Marjory Harper confirms Maryann Morrison's observation of 1888:

The children were sent across the Atlantic in 'protected parties', which were usually allocated a separate section of the ship's steerage. On several occasions William

Quarrier accompanied his charges on the voyage and supervised their subsequent distribution...[115]

The personal experience of one of the Home-Boys who emigrated to the Eastern Townships around the same time as Maryann is told in the autobiography of John J. Mullowney, *America Gives a Chance*.[116] Born in Liverpool in 1878, his story may be typical: eight children in the family, father a drunkard, mother died, he and his siblings were put in an orphanage, treated well, educated with enthusiastic talks on lumbering, farming, and were given 'a rainbow tinted view of Canada and its climate.' A few months later the nine-year-old and his eleven-year-old brother were off on their adventure to the 'land flowing with milk and honey.'[117] The voyage was 'spent mostly below deck' but 'whenever weather permitted we enjoyed deck games.' On arrival they were sent to a Receiving Home, allocated foster parents, sent by train to Milan where he had to leave his brother ('I cried and cried'), and taken on by carter to 'widow MacDonald in Winslow'. She took one look at him and refused to have him; the carter, Murdo MacLeod, and his wife Mary at Spring Hill took him in. The family had two small children, and everyone spoke only Gaelic, which he mastered very quickly. At school, after proving himself 'in the usual manner' (a playground fight) he was more or less accepted. In contrast to all the 'studies' on the subject, John Mullowney's story is told with personal warmth and, perhaps surprisingly, not a single word of criticism. The impact is striking, and for the purposes of this study his observations of life with the 'Scotch' are invaluable.[118]

Though his initial circumstances were much more traumatic than those of the Morrisons, John Mullowney joined a household that had already been established — the MacLeods' two room cabin. As an adult, he looked back on his humble beginnings in Spring Hill as being the place where he got 'a chance in life' that he would never have had in Liverpool. In much the same way, the Morrison family looked upon Marsboro as giving them 'a chance'. Although they were well aware that the land they got was 'not exactly the best land' in the Townships, and in spite of his memories of land-clearing that seemed to go on forever — 'Oh boy, the big stones! I could take you around and show you stone piles that you wouldn't believe' — Angus Morrison is thoroughly convinced that emigration was the best decision his grandfather could ever have made.

Just before he retired in 1976, Angus and Mary Morrison took a holiday in Scotland and made the first return visit to Harris since their family set sail in 1888. Naturally they went to Geocrab, where they stood on the site of the Morrisons' ancestral home. In 1992, no sentimental, tear-filled eyes were reported by this fluent Gaelic-speaking Canadian; indeed his reaction was quite the reverse: 'Harris! Geocrab — have you ever seen it?...I'm telling you a sheep couldn't make a living there!'

NOTES

0. D. Campbell and R.A. MacLean, *Beyond the Atlantic Roar: A Study of the Nova Scotia Scots,* pp. 7–36; G. Patterson, *History of Pictou County,* see two passenger lists compiled from the memories of two emigrants on the 'Hector', pp. 450–456.

1. For extensive bibliographic notes and references see Appendix A.

2. The *Edinburgh Courant,* July, 1773 reports that 830 people left the Isle of Lewis.

3. W.C.A. Ross, 'Highland Emigration', *Scottish Geographical Magazine,* May 1934, p. 155. [My emphasis.]

4. For a concise, well-referenced summary of emigration to Nova Scotia, see Charles W. Dunn, *Highland Settler: A Portrait of the Scottish Gael in Nova Scotia,* pp. 11–23, [hereafter cited *Highland Settler.*] See also G. Donaldson, *The Scots Overseas,* pp. 57–80, which includes a discussion of ports of embarkation on the west coast of Scotland, especially the Clyde, and the Inner and Outer Hebrides.

5. James Hunter discusses the causes and effects of poverty, land shortage, landlordism and emigration; see *The Making of the Crofting Community,* pp. 15–88.

6. For individual examples of such tacksmen in Lewis, and a summary of their actions, see Donald MacDonald, *Lewis: A History of the Island,* pp. 159–164.

7. Hunter, op cit.

8. Bill Lawson, *Register,* p. iv.

9. M. Lynch, *Scotland: A New History,* p. 372.

10. So far as I can ascertain, this one book has served to remind descendants of the way of life they had already heard about from 'the old people' and it may even have influenced views about Lewis history held by people of the Eastern Townships. See also Alexander MacKenzie, *The History of the Highland Clearances,* J.M. Bumsted, *The People's Clearance: Highland Emigration to British North America 1770–1815,* and *The Scots in Canada.*; James Hunter, *Op Cit;* Dr Donald MacDonald of Gisla, *Tales and Traditions of the Lews;* D. MacKinlay, *The Island of Lewis and its Fishermen Crofters.* For earlier accounts, ,see Martin Martin and John Lane Buchanan.

11. From a conversation recorded in Sherbrooke, Nov. 13, 1990. Christie, whose family originated in Tolsta, Isle of Lewis, and her husband John, b. 1892, became acquainted with Donald MacDonald when he was researching his second book, *The Tolsta Townships,* published in 1984. He wrote several letters to their family.

12. Book 'owners' of Donald MacDonald's Lewis: A History of the Island are numerous, and most acknowledge 'dipping into it' from time to time. I have not, however, come across any who pay close attention to the section on early history as it has little bearing on the Lewis they know or the people they have met.

13. For a detailed genealogy of the MacLeods, see MacDonald of Gisla, *Tales and Traditions of the Lews,* (fold-out insert.)

14. See also D. MacDonald, *Lewis,* Dr D. MacDonald, *Tales and Traditions of the Lews,* and J. Hunter, *op cit.*

15. In 1843 a group of ministers left the Established Church to form the Free Church of Scotland. Inevitably many families and communities were divided over the issues that led to the Disruption, mainly on doctrinal grounds, though also on class lines, and thus an element of bitterness and unrest lingered for many years.

16. D. MacDonald, op.cit., p. 39.

17. Excerpted from Appendix B of C.P. Traill, *Backwoods*, pp. 273–274 (1989 edition). This appendix contains copies of her collection of papers and pamphlets relating to emigration, a copy of the American Passengers Act, and excerpts of the prospectus of the Canada Company and the British American Land Company. Pamphlets such as Buchanan's, above, give evidence of the nature of the useful (though limited and inadequate) advice that emigrants were given. During this time a large number of English settlers emigrated who were able to afford land under the terms offered. They are still acknowledged in the Eastern Townships as having gained the best farmland to be had . See Belden & Co, *Illustrated Atlas of the Eastern Townships and South Western Quebec, 1881.*

18. A detailed description of the Townships will be given in Chapter 2.

19. The business of Land Companies was to advertise Canada to prospective emigrants. The Canada Company, founded in 1824 by Scottish novelist, John Galt, had agents in Edinburgh, Glasgow and other towns in England and Ireland. It was incorporated by royal charter and Act of Parliament in 1826; the lands for sale bordered Lake Huron and Lake Ontario, with the largest tract of land being the township of Guelph. Extracts from the Company's prospectus are printed in Catherine Parr Traill, *The Backwoods of Canada, being letters from the Wife of an Emigrant Officer, illustrative of the Domestic Economy of British America,* Appendix B. [Hereafter cited C.P. Traill, *Backwoods.*]; O.D. Skelton gives a more complete history in *The Life and Times of Sir Alexander Galt.* (John Galt later became involved with the British American Land Company, as did his son, Alexander.)

20. Prospectus of the British American Land Company, in collected papers of Catherine Parr Traill, printed in *Backwoods*, Appendix B, 1989 edn., pp. 287–289.

21. Belden & Co, *Illustrated Atlas of the Eastern Townships and South Western Quebec, 1881,* pp. 12–14.

22. Prospectus, *op cit.*

23. Belden, *op. cit.* p. 13.

24. Writing in 1870, for example, John Ramsay of Kildalton, Islay, consistently refers to 'Scotchmen'; see Freda Ramsay, *John Ramsay of Kildalton: Being an*

Account of his Life in Islay and including the Diary of his trip to Canada in 1870 (hereafter referred to as *John Ramsay of Kildalton…Diary*), passim.

25. The complexities of the dealings of the British American Land Company are dealt with by O.D. Skelton, op cit, and Helen I. Cowan, *British Emigration to British North America*.

26. See British Government *Papers Relative to Emigration to Canada,* Vol. 31, 1843, p. 19.

27. MacDonald states 1,772 as the number, Hunter 1,771, T.M. Devine reports 2,200, and the number quoted by Helen I. Cowan in *British Emigration to British North America*, p. 213 is also at variance with these. Since the focus of this book is the oral traditions of the descendants of these emigrants, I have given an approximation. Genealogist Bill Lawson has researched the genealogy of a considerable number of emigrants from Lewis, and has compiled *A Register of Emigrant Families from the Western Isles of Scotland to the Eastern Townships of Quebec, Canada,* published by the Compton County Historical Museum Society, Eaton Corner, Quebec, 1988.

28. T.M. Devine, 'Landlordism and Highland Emigration' in *Scottish Emigration and Scottish Scoiety*, p. 96.

29. T.M. Devine, *The Great Highland Famine: Hunger, Emigration and the Scottish Highlands in the Nineteenth Century*, pp. 213–18.

30. Hunter, op. cit., p. 80.

31. The sum quoted is from Dr D. MacDonald, *Tales and Traditions of the Lews*, p. 277; the calculation is mine.

32. Drawing from various sources, Dr MacDonald lists the items of expenditure, allowing the facts and figures to speak for themselves; *op cit*, pp. 277–278. Only a few examples are cited here.

33. Though Quebec does not feature in her book, *The Emigrant Experience: Songs of the Highland Emigrants in North Amerca,* Margaret MacDonell includes several emigration songs that reflect the pain of parting, such as 'Imrich nan Eileineach' [The Emigration of the Islanders], pp. 106–113.

34. From a song-text printed in 1877 in *An Gàidheal*. Though composed by an Islayman, Hugh MacCorkindale who settled in Ontario in the 1860s, his positive attitude to Canada was characteristic of most Gaels who lived to enjoy the fruits of their labours.

35. Virtually all the elderly people, and many of the younger generation, know the year their people came to Canada. With ever-increasing interest in genealogy, and especially since the work of Bill Lawson (op cit), questions of genealogy arise in everyday conversation. In addition to Lawson's research, a local woman has compiled a database of approximately 8,000 names of Hebridean extraction. With current research on a scale such as this, it is not surprising that so many elderly people have a revival of interest in emigration.

36. I recorded Christie MacArthur in Megantic Hospital in 1976.

37. The book was privately printed in Sherbrooke but is now out of print. The author intends to update the manuscript and produce a revised edition.

38. Donald MacDonald states that roadmaking started in Lewis in 1791, and though the work involved was not generally popular, it was a means of earning extra cash. See *Lewis,* p. 53.

39. This paragraph does not coincide exactly with the tape as Duncan corrected it, July 1994.

40. Christina came out twenty-five years later, in 1866; she had been married to John MacKenzie [*Iain an Taillear*] in Lewis, then after she was widowed she emigrated with two of her children. Noted from Duncan, July 1994.

41. Recorded Sept. 27, 1991; transcription re-arranged here.

42. Recorded Nov. 13, 1990.

43. National Maritime Museum, *The Great Migration: Crossing the Atlantic Under Sail,* p. 8.

44. Sept. 24, 1991.

45. July 1994,

46. This part recorded Nov. 1990; the remainder in 1976

47. Part of the three months was taken up by the journey from their home in Lewis to the next village where they had to wait for the recovery of one of the intending emigrants who was ill. Then there was the journey to Liverpool, the main port from which the trans-Atlantic vessel sailed. (Duncan McLeod tells of a Lewis family, Grahams, who sailed from Belfast.)

48. A considerable number of songs of emigration and nostalgia for Lewis are still popular in Scotland today. Several songs composed in Quebec are in Duncan McLeod's collection of papers; see also, M. Bennett, 'Gaelic Song in Eastern Canada: Twentieth Century Reflections', in *Canadian Folklore canadien,* 1992, pp. 21–34.

49. C.W. Dunn, *Highland Settler,* pp.19–23.

50. There was an embargo on timber from the Baltic countries, thus Canada became all the more important.

51. Standards were set which required ship owners to provide for the comfort, safety and health of passengers. Specifications of minimum height between decks and bunks, minimum requirements of food and water and maximum numbers of passengers allowed on board were defined by the 'American Passengers' Act'. Ships were required to display an abstract for passengers to inspect; Appendix B, III, *Backwoods,* pp. 280–282 (1989 edn).

52. The Photo Archives of Canada has a photographic record of late nineteenth century ships loading timber (lumber) at Quebec. See also the National Maritime Museum publication, *The Great Migration: Crossing the Atlantic Under Sail,* p. 12.

53. Op cit, Letter II, p. 19.

54. Traill notes that nuns took the child in, as benevolent societies connected with the Roman Catholic and Protestant churches were set up to care for orphans. Op cit, p. 36.

55. Traill herself became violently ill several weeks later and describes the doctor's treatment of her: 'remedies applied were bleeding, a potion of opium, blue pills, and some salts…' Op cit p. 43.

56. *The Great Migration,* p. 7.

57. Vivid accounts of the emigrants' hardships, outbreaks of typhus, cholera, smallpox, dysentery and high rates of mortality on board ship are recorded by Charles W. Dunn in *Highland Settler,* pp. 11–23. For reports of quarantining, see *Backwoods,* pp. 19–43. For studies of ocean crossings, see Edwin C. Guillet, *The Great Migration: The Atlanic Crossing by Sailing Ships Since 1770.*

58. A notebook with a hand-written account was sent to the School of Scottish Studies and published in *Tocher 42.* (Though the ship was travelling to Australia the daily events on board ship were fairly similar.) See also *Towards Quebec: Two mid-19th Century Emigrants Journals,* edited by Ann Gifford. In *Scotland Farewell,* Donald MacKay refers to a young man from Loch Broom who kept a diary on board the 'Hector' in 1773; his notebook formed the basis for part of G. Patterson's *History of Pictou County.* (MacKay, pp. 93–94.) See also reference to Gaelic-speaking passengers in 'Account of a Voyage from Aberdeen to Quebec by William Shand, 1834' in *From Aberdeen to Ottawa,* Appendix 2, pp. 113–116.

59. This information is excerpted from the letter sent to me in December 1976 by Mrs Mimnaugh of Inverness, Quebec. Some of her information is based on *The Annals of Megantic,* compiled and published in 1902 by one of her relatives, Dugald McKenzie McKillop who left Quebec in 1883. He wrote a series of essays about his people's experience of emigration which were eventually compiled to produce *The Annals of Megantic.* Hereafter cited as *Annals,* the book has been reprinted in 1962, 1966, and 1981, largely through the efforts of Mrs Mimnaugh.

60. The Duke of Hamilton, who wanted to make a big sheep farm from the land occupied by his tenants, made an offer to each family, and to each son over 21, of 100 acres of land to *own* in Canada in exchange for vacating his rented land. Twelve families (86 people) left Arran at the Duke's expense in 1929. See *Annals,* p. 9.

61. The fare was £4. *Annals,* p. 9.

62. A team consisted of a single horse and cart hired to the emigrants at $5 a cartload of passengers. *Annals,* p. 9.

63. A review of *Ceann-Iuil an Fhir-Imrich do dh'America mu Thuath* [Guide for the Emigrant to North America] written by Rob MacDougall, appears in *Cuairtear nan Gleann,* Sept. 1841, p. 205. [There is also a copy of the pamphlet in the library of the University of Edinburgh.]

64. Blazed trails were tracks cut through the thick forest, along routes that were marked by 'blazes' cut into the barks of the trees.

65. Rec. 1976. Scotch Road was so-named because a number of Scottish settlers had obtained land in this section.

66. C.P. Traill, *Backwoods*, p. 57.

67. Russell pronounces the name as spelled here, then translates it as 'Sandy Lake.' He is referring to Loch Ganmhaig.

68. September 16, 1991.

69. Duncan McLeod accompanied me to record Russell, Sept. 16, 1991.

70. True, we have midges and clegs in the Old Country, but as a new immigrant to Canada in 1968 I will never forget my own first experience of mosquito or blackfly in the Newfoundland bush. There seemed to be merciless swarms of them, and they not only left angry weals when they bit, but the blackfly bites bled, and both itched 'like crazy' and kept me awake for nights on end. Worse was to watch my two year-old with streams of blood trickling down his neck because 'the flies are bad.' It is often suggested to newcomers that the reaction among the unaccustomed is often worse than for North Americans who have grown up with these insects and seem to have developed a certain immunity. I have not lived long enough to discover the time taken to develop such an immunity. See also Roberta Buchanan's note on the question of immunity in 'Country Ways and Fashions': Lydia Campbell's *Sketches of Labrador Life*–A Study in Folklore and Literature', pp. 305–306.

71. From the autobiography of John J. Mullowney, who settled in Milan, Quebec at the age of eight in the 1887; *America Gives a Chance*, p. 11.

72. All maps were consulted at the archives of the John Bassett Memorial Library at Bishop's University.

73. The names of the American surveyors are also noted.

74. As Duncan McLeod points out, it would scarcely have been a 'road' in those days, but more like a track.

75. All recordings of Bill Young were made in 1976; tape BEK:3

76. In his book *Songs Remembered in Exile*, p. 38, John Lorne Campbell notes this same phenomenon among Nova Scotians of Outer Hebridean descent.

77. In his book, *Crofters and habitants*, J.I. Little is mistaken in his statement, (p. 148) based on Parish Records, that there is 'no record of ashes sold for lye...'. Although *written* records may not store this fact, I have, nevertheless, tape-recorded a number of informants, including the Legendres, a French family in Stornoway, confirming that the ashes were sold for lye.

78. Christie was recorded in 1976; BEK 14:A.

79. C.P. Traill, *Backwoods*, p. 158–159 (1989 edn.).

80. Op cit, p. 121.

81. Op cit, p. 135.

82. In a letter home in Aug. 1833, Catherine Parr Traill said that the plough 'was seldom used before the third or fourth year.' Op cit. p. 158 (1989 edn.)

83. Donald MacDonald refers to a variety of hoes which were used after the introduction of the potato, including the *croman*, which 'had a short handle, with a long narrow blade like the sole of a lady's shoe and was mainly used for lifting potatoes.' *Lewis*, p. 72. Osgood H. MacKenzie describes women using the *croman*, op cit., pp. 150–151.

84. My own introduction to this was in 1976 when the first snow-fall was on October 10th. In a matter of days it was feet deep, and we did not see the ground again till the following May. At the beginning of June that same year I watched the last of the previous winter snow melt in low-lying hollows, then in a matter of days the temperature rocketed into the 80s. There is no part of the year that remotely resembles Scotland's 'snowdrops and daffodils' time.

85. In Newfoundland I recorded both Scots and French families tell of the same method of dealing with blackfly and mosquito, and adding to it that they would have to keep the smudge fire going all night just so they could sleep without waking up 'bitten to death'. [Folklore Archives of Memorial University of Newfoundland; for example, the Cormier tapes.]

86. David Kennedy's *Pioneer Days,* pp. 131-132.

87. According to John Shaw (Nov. 1994), the word 'yard' is used in Nova Scotia to describe a clearing in the forest that is stamped down by deer coming in to graze on new greenery during the snowy winter.

88. When I recorded Mrs MacKenzie in 1976 the area had gravel roads and there were no roadsigns to indicate back-roads such as the one leading to the 'Yard'. In the late 1980s the community council erected roadsigns in the entire area, and the site is now marked by its new sign, *Chemin de la Yard.*

89. As noted in the Introduction, the word 'Scotch' is common usage in the Eastern Townships, and also in other parts of North America. Since it is the term used locally, it will also be used throughout this thesis.

90. Martin Martin. *A Description of the Western Isles of Scotland circa 1695,* 1716 edn., p. 14. [Hereafter cited as *Description.*]

91. Robert Craig MacLagan, *Games and Diversions of Argyllshire,* pp. 44–45. My own uncles in Skye tell of making bows and arrows in their youth, up to the 1930s, and while they did not have to use them to hunt, as rifles were in use for small game, it was not beyond their scope to take aim at rabbits. As far as weaponry is concerned, bows and arrows were the normal weapons used by mercenaries in the Thirty Years' War. Even today, Edinburgh has an annual celebration of the ancient art, when the Royal Company of Archers display their archery skills each June in the Meadows.

92. David Kennedy, *Op cit,* pp. 102-104.

93. *Ibid,* p. 17. Carl Mayhew confirms this in his *History of Canterbury,* p. 25.

94. I have based this table on a count of all the families listed in Bill Lawson's *Register of Emigrant Families from the Western Isles of Scotland to the Eastern*

Townships of Quebec, Canada. There are several discrepancies between the year cited by Lawson and that given by my informants; for this reason, I suggest that the upswing was '*around* 1863 and 1873'.

95.   Recorded 1967; I also recorded John at the age of 99.

96.   In 1876 , Scottish archaeologist, Arthur Mitchell, sometimes referred to as 'the father of Scottish ethnology' delivered The Rhind Lectures on Archaeology, a series of six, which explored the topic 'Early Man'. All were based on his own fieldwork, mostly in Shetland and in the Outer Hebrides. His third lecture, 'The Black Houses and the Beehive Houses of the Hebrides' describes black houses in Lewis, the common abode of all the crofters, as Maryann confirmed. Mitchell visited black houses and described in detail what he saw. Published in 1880 as chapter 3 of his book, *The Past in the Present*, Mitchell's classic description of the blackhouse gives a sketch (woodcut) of the building, a floor plan (though it is, on first sight, slightly confusing, as it is not the same floor plan as the house above), and a detailed description of black houses with explanations of the functions of the features he observed. See pp. 48–54. Despite Mitchell's disturbingly condescending tone which characterized the entire book, and his tendency to judge the values of the people he observes by his own upper-middle-class Edinburgh standards, his work still stands as a model for ethnologists today. See also the description of a blackhouse in Harris in the 1850s by Osgood H. MacKenzie in *A Hundred Years in the Highlands*, pp. 85–86, and A. Fenton, *The Island Blackhouse* which features the Isle of Lewis.

97.   Recorded in Montreal in 1976; Tapes BEK 17 and BEK 18.

98.   Op cit, p, 16.

99.   It is essential for modern observers, especially academics, to set aside twentieth century values with glossy magazine appeal, and to consider the facts — ideally people who actually lived in a blackhouse should be consulted; there are also many tape-recordings in the Archives of the School of Scottish Studies. Alternatively, spend an afternoon in the blackhouse on the grounds of the Highland Folk Museum at Kingussie — I would like to thank the staff there for allowing all my students to discover that the warmth, cosiness and conviviality around the peat-fire was far beyond what they had imagined.

100. Margaret Fay Shaw published her invaluable collection *Folksongs and Folklore of South Uist* in 1955. She describes the differences between the *taigh dubh* and the later style with gable end chimneys. See p. 17.

101. Op cit, p. 4.

102. When I told Maryann that my own grandparents were born in Skye in 1881 and 1884 in such a house, she identified immediately with their generation. She was surprised, however, to hear that my mother, born in 1919, was also born in a thatched house, the only difference being that they had dispensed with the fire in the middle of the floor in favour of a chimney at the gable end. Maryann had imagined greater progress to have taken place in the Old Country. Most surprising to her was the fact that in the 1960s, during my teenage years,

there were still a few of these houses occupied in Skye, and on the Isle of Lewis almost the entire village of Gearanan consisted of thatched houses occupied by crofting families.

103. J.I. Little's description of Hebridean crofting with potatoes 'grown on lazybeds on the beaches' (sic) is very misleading. Apart from the fact that this is virtually impossible (the sea would wash them away at the first tide) the image he portrays shows no understanding whatsoever of lazybed cultivation. Donald MacDonald describes the 'inappropriately' named lazy-beds and the intensive labour involved; see *Lewis*, p. 68.

104. *Scottish Historical Review*, Vol. 18, pp. 277–289.

105. A.D. Cameron, *Go Listen to the Crofters*, p. 90.

106. *John Ramsay of Kildalton…Diary*, p. 88.

107. Mary was recorded with her husband on Aug. 8, 1992.

108. *Op cit*, p. 89.

109. Writing in the 1880s, Dugald McKenzie McKillop notes that the first log houses built by the Scots settlers (from Arran) in Megantic County were of round logs, approximately 18 x 18 feet, divided in two with bark partitions and, and the 'children were occupied in peeling bark.' *Annals*, p. 27. Buildings of stripped logs generally had saddle-notched corners, whereas the log houses built later were of square-logs cut by broad-axe, and had half-dovetailed corners. A few examples of the latter remain, such as the remains of the MacRae house in Gould. Interestingly, the previous method of construction, of stripped logs, was the choice of the most recent log-house builder, grand-daughter of the first MacRaes, Miriam MacRae Holland, whose house was built in the late 1970s. With stripped logs she employed the traditional saddle-notch corner technique, and carried out most of the work herself. For a general discussion on log building in North America, see H. Glassie, *Pattern in the Material Folk Culture of the Eastern United States*, pp. 48–124.

110. Blankets without sheets was common practice in the Highlands until well after the Second World War. As a child in the late 1950s I can recall my grandfather on Skye preferring to sleep under wool blankets. Since everyone else in the family had sheets, I asked him about it; he told me that sheets make you cold when you get into bed on winter nights. Considering the fact that the unheated bedrooms of a croft house were colder than the box-beds of the older thatched cottage, his reason for rejecting the modern trend made sound sense.

111. For example, in 1992, octogenarian Russell MacIver referred to one of his contemporaries in Scotstown as a 'Home Boy' as did Muriel Mayhew in Lennoxville, when referring to a local man who had made an important contribution to her neighbourhood. Similarly, in South Uist, boys who were adopted into crofting families were known as 'Homers'.

112. Some of these studies are cited shortly; see also the bibliography.

113. These figures are based on a sumary of the reports in *The Home Children:Their Personal Stories*, edited by Phyllis Harrison.

114. Believing it was 'for the best', Dr Barnardo developed his own programme and became the biggest emigration agency, sending 33 per cent of the entire number of child emigrants to Canada, between 1882 and his death in 1905.

115. Marjory Harper, 'The Juvenile Immigrant: Halfway to heaven or Hell on Earth' in *the Immigrant Experience*, pp. 165–183. A number of publications show photos, such as Gillian Wagner's major study on the subject, *Children of the Empire*, which also exposes some of the more shocking aspects of the 'trade'. See also A.G. Scholes, *Education for Empire Settlement: a Study of Juvenile Migration*, and H.L. Malchow, *Population Pressures: Emigration and Government in Late Nineteenth-Century Britain*, pp. 55–63.

116. I am grateful to Duncan McLeod for showing me this book, as it is not cited in the general studies on the subject.

117. The studies cited above state that the orphanages screened children for suitability. Any child suffering from signs of ill-health, malnutrition, feeble-mindedness, physical or mental defect of any kind, or any child judged to be dishonest or disturbed was not considered suitable for emigration. It was not unusual, therefore, for families to be divided.

118. As a young man, Mullowney moved 'across the line' to follow educational opportunities. He eventually became president of a medical college in the U.S.A.

2

Homesteading in the
Eastern Townships

The Townships

Today's visitor to the Eastern Townships is sometimes confused by the use of
the word township. Situated about a hundred and twenty miles south-east of
Montreal, the entire area comprises eleven counties. [Map 2] Only three of
these counties were settled by immigrants from the Outer Hebrides, namely,
Compton, Frontenac and Wolfe. A fourth county, Megantic, was, as already
mentioned, settled at an earlier stage by immigrants from the Isle of Arran.[1]
To add further confusion to defining the area under study, three of its main
landmarks, Lake Megantic (now usually referred to as Lac Mégantic), the
town of Megantic, and Mount Megantic, are all in Compté Frontenac, and
not, as one might expect, in the county of Megantic. The eleven counties,
which may be regarded as administrative blocks, are each sub-divided into
townships, which have administrative powers delegated at a local level. It is
to these townships that the first immigrants came,[2] and, out of what could
have more appropriately been labelled wildernesses, they gradually carved
small hamlets, villages, and towns. [See graph of settlement pattern, Fig. 1]

On the visitor from Scotland, the interminable stretches of thick forest
leave a lasting impression. Although there are reports and old illustrations of
virgin forests consisting of enormous coniferous trees, what remains today is
secondary or tertiary growth.[3] Spruce, fir, larch and pine grow so thickly in
some places that their branches seem to be knitted into one another, leaving
little space for light to reach the ground, far less a path for any human being
to walk through.[4] While almost all of the largest trees have been cut down
for timber many years ago, the rate of secondary growth is astonishingly rapid.
Many second growth forests consist of large areas of hardwoods such as birch,
maple, oak, ash, cherry and beech, as, needing more light, they were better
able to flourish once the tangle of soft-woods had been cut back. Fruit trees
and bushes also grow rapidly, often creating a pattern of raspberry and bramble
(blackberry) bushes straggling along the borders of roads and woods. Bill
Lawson, visiting from Harris, remarked that 'coming from an area where trees
can be grown only with the greatest difficulty [he] found it hard to adjust to
the idea of trees as large weeds.'[5] One is constantly reminded of the enormous
challenge that must have faced the first settlers.

Although very few species of wildlife were familiar to the first Hebridean immigrants, they soon learned to recognise a wide variety of animals and birds in the area — weasel, fox, wolf, muskrat, beaver, mink, lynx, wolverine, marten, otter, moose, red deer, black bear, caribou, raccoon, red squirrel, rabbit, hare and skunk are relatively common in the region, while species of birds include the blue-jay, chickadee, finch, hawk, robin, redwing-blackbird[6] and thrush.[7] The rivers have trout, salmon, and perch and swampy areas abound in frogs.[6] There is also a profusion of wild-flowers, some of which are recognisable to the Scottish observer, such as buttercups, daisies, bluebells, yarrow, goldenrod, thistle, vetch, to mention but a few. While this description is more of a sketch than a detailed painting, it depicts the kinds of features a visitor immediately notices, and is given not only to acquaint the reader with the landscape, but also to serve as a reminder of the observations that may have struck the new immigrants. Undoubtedly any of the settlers interested in fauna or flora would, in his or her own time, become acquainted with the species peculiar to the area, or perhaps, like Catherine Parr Traill, adopt the attitude of considering herself 'free to become their floral godmother and give them names of my own choosing' when she could not 'discover the Canadian or even the Indian names' of plants.[9]

Surrounded by what the emigration agencies referred to as 'wild lands', the *townships* that were largely settled by immigrants from the Outer Hebrides are Bury (established in 1803), Lingwick (established 1807), and Hampden (established 1867) in Compton County; Weedon (established 1822) in Wolfe County; and Winslow (established 1851), Whitton (established 1863–64), and Marston (established 1866) in Frontenac County. [Map 2.] As the newer townships were established, there was considerable secondary migration within the area, with records showing that most settlers in Weedon moved to Whitton, Winslow or Marston within two decades, thus eliminating one of the three counties, Wolfe, from the group.[10] Secondary migration sometimes depended on the relative success of the first settlers, some simply giving in to the fact that the land they were allocated was 'almost impossible', while others moved to be nearer the nucleus of the Gaelic community. By the turn of the century, a significantly high number of 'Scotch' farms were well established in the counties of Frontenac and Compton, with Gaelic as the prevalent (and in many cases *only*) language of the population.

The area under study may strike today's visitor as a complex network of small towns, villages and farms strung out along main roads, and interconnected by backroads of varying quality. The latter are usually referred to as 'gravel roads' for the wider, better ones, and 'dirt roads' for the less used, and at times impassable, routes. In the past ten years, town- and road-signs have been erected to help travellers locate directions, and, while they succeed in that, they are also misleading as far as other aspects of the area are concerned. For example, large signs, such as 'Bienvenu à Scotstown' and 'Stornoway Vous Acceuille' welcome visitors as they enter these towns, while new, neatly manufactured road-markers have been erected on back-roads that were once known only to the people who lived there. Signs, such as 'Ch. Dell' or 'Ch. Tolsta', meaning 'chemin' or 'road', may simply announce the name of a country road to the visitor, but to the people whose forebears cleared the land and helped to build the road, the new sign gives the message that they no longer belong. The signs are, however, in keeping with Quebec's unilingual legislation, which came into force in the 1980s. With French as the *only* official language of the province, it is perhaps understandable that the new generation of Québecois, many of whom are monoglot French-speakers, fail to understand that the towns and villages they now inhabit, and the farms they cultivate, have a colourful past that has helped to shape their present. And unless the story of that past is recorded, there will be many aspects of the present which will be difficult, if not impossible, to understand.

The issue of place names is an obvious example, as the older inhabitants, Scots and French alike, already know. Almost a century-and-a-half ago, the two groups shared the naming of places as the townships developed; with no difficulty one could relate to their origins simply by listening or looking at the map. Names such as La Patrie, Val Racine, and St. Romain stand out among the early French settlements, while Stornoway, Tolsta, Galson, Druim a' Bhac, Dell, Ballallan, and Gisla are some of the names that cannot fail to say 'Isle of Lewis' to the Scots.[11] Only the 'old French families', descendants of the first French settlers, such as the Legendres in Stornoway, understand the significance of the Scottish place-names and the local history that is so closely connected to them.

Just over twenty years ago, when the community councils of Spring Hill and Stornoway, by then entirely French, proposed a change in the names of their towns to French names, Spring Hill became 'Nantes', but the proposal in Stornoway was met by considerable opposition, led by the mayor, M. Legendre. He summarised the history of their town for those who had no idea that the Gaelic-speaking Scots were the first to settle the area, and persuaded the newcomers to pay attention. Not surprisingly, the incident is still recounted by many of the older people who report that the mayor insisted that 'as long as there is a Legendre in the town it will remain STORNOWAY out of respect for their good Scotch neighbours'.[12]

In recent years, the older French families, to their credit, have done their best to keep this part of their history alive by contributing details of the early settlers to the community's local history book, *Stornoway 1858–1983*, published in 1983 as one of the series, *Les Albums Souvenirs Québecois..*[13] Based on interviews with over fifty representatives of families who had been established in the area for several generations, and with occasional reference to Parish Records, the book records the fact that the area was opened to colonists in 1851 when twenty Scottish families arrived. Photographs showing land-clearing reflect the earliest beginnings of Stornoway, and are captioned by comments such as 'En 1853 arrivée de 73 autres écossais...' The editorial team are to be commended for their efforts in recording details of these early settlers, such as the fact that their cabins measured 10 ft x 12, & 6 ft high, their language was Gaelic, their religion Presbyterian, and their services of worship included the singing of Gaelic psalms.[14] A view of Scottishness is presented in a number of photographs, including one of a Murdo McLeod shown in full Highland dress, 'en uniforme de régiment écossais', and a family group in which the women are wearing tartan dresses.[15] The editors make reference to the Gaels' regard for customs, especially their adherence to the strict rules of the Sabbath, and remark upon the fact that they were given to composing poetry.[16]

There is no doubt that the French and the Scots of pioneer days held each other in great esteem, recognizing the joint efforts made to build their communities. As can be seen from anecdotes such as Russell MacIver's story of 'come tomorrow, help lift big barn', and the Legendres' reminiscences of their 'good Scotch neighbours', each group appreciated contributions made by the other. While they recognised their differences of ethnic origin and religion, their emphasis was on the common goals they shared. In the first decade of the twentieth century, André Siegfried wrote that the Scots in Quebec 'manifested a real goodwill towards the French and these latter were the first to recognize it.'[17]

Cultural enclaves created by the pattern of land grants was, as far as the settlers were concerned, an aspect of Canadian immigration that characterised the entire nation. They were aware, for example, that adjoining counties in the Eastern Townships had English and Irish settlers, while this part of the region happened to be granted to Scots and French. As neighbours, they shared common aims: they would work together, as families and communities, to tame this wild land, and in so doing would improve their own lot in life. As will be seen from further discussion, the increasing insecurity voiced by newcomers, which today embarrasses members of the older generation, was not characteristic of the early settlers. By way of contrast, descendants of the first French settlers, now in the minority, are proud to have shaped this area of the Townships alongside the Scotch.[18] This study was not undertaken, however, simply to record the past for a nostalgic minority, Scots or French; more importantly, it is aimed at today's population, many of whom are not descended from either group of first settlers, but have moved into an established area with little understanding of its past. It is hoped that the road-signs that now mark the towns and backroads, or the village streets in Milan, such as *Ruelle McLeod* or *Rue Nicolson* honouring Duncan McLeod's people, and Ruth and Dave Nicolson's family, may retain their significance, and not come to be regarded as meaningless labels that simply mark direction or place. It is just as important to remember that the new signs were erected by the present French inhabitants, who not only incorporated some of the old, established farm roads, such as Dell, Tolsta and Galson, but also created new street-names, chosen in the 1980s by the local community councils, which, by that time, did not have one Scotch voice to express an opinion. It is no coincidence that these road markers bear the names of McLeod, Nicolson, or MacDonald;[19] they are a deliberate choice made by former neighbours who have no wish to obliterate or forget the true meaning of neighbourliness. These same names are, today, also part of the identity of the older generation of French, descendants of *les habitants*, who appreciate their significance to the community in which they live.

House and Home

Just as the *taigh dubh* had been home to most of the emigrants, so the log cabin became home to the first settlers.[20] With hard work, perseverance, and the application of newly-learned insulation techniques, they very quickly attained an acceptable level of domestic warmth. Never again would the Hebridean immigrants endure the life-threatening misery of that first winter; on the contrary, they would enjoy an increasingly comfortable lifestyle, and even discover it possible to derive pleasure from the Quebec winter. They would also discover a range of practical solutions to the dreaded infestations of summer: muslin or fine wire mesh screens over the windows; a screen door hung in the cabin door-jamb; and perhaps a comfortable screen porch to surround one or two sides of the house to allow the inhabitants the luxury of sitting in the cool shade free from blackflies and mosquitos. Log houses continued to be built for many years, as most of the oldest residents, such as Russell MacIver, recall: 'Well I didn't see the first house, it was a log house, but my grandfather's house too was a log house, and that's where we lived — just stayed in the log house.'[21]

Warm, comfortable, and simply furnished, in Russell's young days all the houses were lit with kerosene-oil (paraffin) lamps, a few of which can still be seen hanging in kitchens or porches in case they are needed during a power-failure. Before lamps became common, the early settlers used candles, a relative luxury after the first winter relying on daylight, or a home-made crusie,[22] or simply the light from their open fire when night fell:

They soon became proficient in making tallow candles and these were followed by wax candles. Then came the first coal oil lamp in Lingwick, owned by the

Hanwrights. People came from near and far to see it. The light from the lamp cast a reflection on the ceiling which was a great curiosity to everyone.[23]

Lighting the lamp every evening is well-remembered, especially as it usually had associations of bedtime for children who longed to be allowed to stay up late enough to sit in its light. Christie MacKenzie recalls:

> Of course, we, as little ones, had to be in bed by daylight, because there was only a few lamps. There wasn't enough to go round [all the rooms]. Besides, a grown-up would have to carry the lamp for you — they wouldn't trust them to children.

Families were very close-knit in those days; as Kay Young[24] put it, 'There was always a grandparent — sometimes two or four grandparents in the one house.' The custom of extended families living in the one household was the tradition in Hebridean households (and continued to be so until after the Second World War). As such, it was quite common for newly-weds to begin their married life in the home of one set of parents. When Maryann and 'R.E.' (Roderick Ewen) Morrison were married in 1894, the couple were typical of their generation, as they spent their first few years of marriage in the home of the bride's parents: the same log house — warm, comfortable, and spacious enough — which, along with a barn, had been built soon after their arrival in Marsboro in 1888.[25] Situated in the adjacent settlement of Cruvag, it was also relatively close to R.E.'s family, and indeed to what must have seemed like a complete branch of the Morrison clan.

Cruvag was a tightly knit community, and every member contributed to its survival. The Morrisons, like all new settlers, not only attended to the everyday needs of home and farm, but continued the process of land-clearing, at the same time accumulating a healthy supply of timber for future building.

> Och, that's where four of my children was born, in a log cabin! But it got so small we had to move and get a place for ourselves…It was made very comfortable; we had a big, big stove, you know…Well, there was three rooms upstairs and one down. But, when we moved away from my father's house we had four boys — that was Danny, Sam, Peter, and Ewen. Four boys was born in my father's cabin. He had no boys at all, but the two little girls [Maryann and her sister, by then adults] so…they were in love with the boys. So, when we were leaving…we had four boys going, and my mother was crying and crying…she'd say to leave one of the children. My father said: 'Leave one of the children beside your mother for a week and then I'll take him home.' But he was attached to them and stayed with them, and stayed with them…He was brought up with them anyway, and we got along very well at my father's…Anyway we moved away and then we went to *another* log cabin that we went to live in. But [in later years] my husband built a big, big, good house…And we had lots of lumber on our farm, and it sold well, you know.

At her parents' pleading, they left their eldest son, Danny, who spent not just 'a week or so' but his entire childhood at the old homestead. Nevertheless, Maryann and R.E., who had nine more children, were content in the knowledge that they would be living close to their son even though he slept and ate at his grandparents' house.

As the Eastern Township communities developed, water-powered saw mills were erected on a number of rivers and their tributaries.[26] Inhabitants no longer had to depend upon the broad-axe to hew every log for construction,[27] or on pit-saws to manufacture planks for flooring. Instead, they could have large quantities of wood, sawn evenly into planks with minimal effort. While a number of small saw-mills operated in the area, the town of Stornoway became known for its larger-scale mills built on a tributary of the St. Francis River, and owned and operated by the Legendre family. Although Parish Records of the area apparently do not record any contribution made by the Scottish settlers to milling — J.I. Little states that the 'Lewis Scots did not produce a single successful miller'[28] — the Legendres record that their saw-mill, built in 1853, was constructed by Donald [S.] McLeod, a well-known mill-wright in his day: Les frères Legendre font construire le premier moulin à scie par Donald McLeod qui construisit plusieurs moulins dans la région.[29] *[The Legendre brothers had the first saw-mill built by Donald McLeod who constructed several mills in the region.]*

As a result of the appearance of this and other saw-mills, fashions in house building changed; no longer did the log house dominate the landscape, but new timber-framed houses began to appear. In a transitional stage, log houses were vertically planked with wide boards, primarily to keep up with changing styles, but also to add further insulation.[30] And, as fashions evolved and clapboard siding became the desired mode, building techniques were re-adapted and carpenters began to use timber studs to construct the main frame, over which was vertical planking, tar-paper vapour barrier, and finally, horizontal clapboarding. The size of house built by the Scottish settlers also became much larger than the small cabins which were necessarily economical in the early years. Timber was plentiful, and, at the cost of a winter's work, family and community effort could produce an impressive quantity, ready to be milled to whatever specifications were required by the builder.

By today's standards, the wood used was impressively thick, and the width of the planks indicates that the trees used were of a size that is now rarely seen. While the construction of walls usually had planking of a uniform width, about nine inches, floor planks were not required to be a standard measurement. In older houses it is not in the least unusual to find floorboards up to 18 inches wide. The carpentry employed in building these houses was of a standard that constantly elicits comparative comments from many of today's old-timers who remark upon joints like 'you never see nowadays';

dove-tails and notches like 'today's builders wouldn't know where to begin'. The reality of these comments was vividly brought home to me during fieldwork, as the following comments from my field notebook illustrate:[31]

July 27, 1992:
c. 2 km south of Marsboro visited a ruin of one of the old two-storey houses. Log construction, hand-squared and notched, meticulous carpentry. At some later stage, it had been vertically planked, some of the planks as wide as 16 inches, circular sawn,[32] then on top of that again was 5' clapboards — possibly 3 stages of 'outward appearance'. Took photos of all the joints visible; very long timbers — and such craftsmanship! Nails were squared (some rectangular) iron, hand-forged, some c. 6ins long. Roof metal finish (tin?); cedar shingles on upper surfaces of walls also. The foundations were of quarried granite, large blocks c. 4 ft long, (possibly from Scotstown quarries?) and part was built like a stone wall with cement. In one corner of the house was a rowan tree, in full leaf and green berry, now towering above the remains, a stark reminder of the lives that planted it, and a strong reminder of the ruined croft houses at home with their living rowans. The cleared fields above and beyond the house were still used as pasture for cattle. The land was luscious and the farm was bounded by stone walls (from field clearing, some of them huge) on one side, and on the far side by a stone dyke with cedar rail fence on top — an interesting combination of Old and New World styles. On the hill above the house was a grove of apple trees like an abandoned orchard; more fields stretched to the crest of the hill and beyond. One location between two fields was the site of abandoned farm implements, such as the remains of harrows, and harvest machinery (binder), rims of cart wheels and an old tractor seat. Also the remains of a cart, just the wheels and an axle, sat at the edge. The view from the top of the hill over Mount Megantic and other layers of hills is spectacular. Must find out who owned the land, who cleared it, etc.[33]

Aug. 11:
Angus Morrison in Marsboro said it belonged to MacDonalds; it only fell down this spring. The farm next to it is owned by Foleys, a French family with an Irish name. The reflection of the hard work to carve out such a splendid farm was strong; the expanse and 'generosity' of the land allocation is such a contrast to the pitifully meagre land the emigrants left in Lewis and Harris; yet the silence over the land, no human habitation on it, but only cattle in the adjoining [French] farm is almost eerie.

In keeping with the appearance of many of the very oldest homesteads, several of which now stand in ruins, can be seen the vigorous rowan tree, not many yards from the house. So far, I have not come across anyone with a story about who planted the rowan, or where they got the seed, or the sapling.[34] Nor have I heard any acknowledgement that they kept away witches or evil spirits[35] though there is probably little doubt that the first settlers planted them, according to tradition, for just these purposes. In recent years, inspired by a visit to Lewis where she saw rowan trees growing outside the homes of relatives, Muriel Mayhew made the connection to familiar images of her native Quebec, and asked me to look out for saplings in the Milan area so that she could transplant one into her garden in a suburb of Lennoxville. Although there was already a profusion of trees, bushes and flowers growing, Muriel explained that the addition of a rowan would be more meaningful to her than any of the existing trees, as it would serve as a reminder to her of both Milan and Lewis.[36]

Whatever the skills in carpentry may have been when the Hebridean settlers arrived, there is no doubt that these skills were developed to a very high standard in Quebec.[37] Christie MacKenzie clearly remembers the family home in Yard na Féidh where she grew up. It was a well constructed two-storey timber-frame house, painted over with linseed oil 'that was a sort of a preventative for the weather, like, so that the rain wouldn't be soaking through the lumber.' The bedrooms were upstairs (except for one), and the main living quarters on the ground floor:

> I can remember — I could point out everything to you, [as] if it was there. Oh, it was very humble. There was a cupboard in one corner [of the kitchen], the table was in the centre, and the stove was away back, like. And it was a dry sink you know; there was a sink there where you put your pans and your pail of water, and all that, but the water had to be spilled outside, away from the house, like, somewhere…And if it wasn't handy to go out with your pan, you had a pail in the shed [adjoining the kitchen at the back], like, that you filled, and when it was full they took the pail out and emptied it…
>
> There was a little dining room — it wasn't much. But usually when we had company they ate in the dining room. It was a smaller table in there…
> And there was a bedroom downstairs. My father and mother always slept there, and whoever was a baby at the time. The cradle was in there…it was sort of long and on rockers, where it would sway back and forth. It wasn't one of those cradles that stood still. The last in our family was twins. So the cradle that I remember best was a long one — there was a baby at each end of the cradle. [And the baby would be in the cradle] until they'd be big enough to be creeping around — *walking* around.[38]

The house was modestly, but comfortably, furnished. 'Well, there'd be chairs, of course, and — usually there was a bench on both sides of the table. There was so many of us, you know. There wasn't always chairs enough to go around…' Christie did not know where her parents bought some of their furniture, but she did recall that her 'father made the benches' and cradle.[39]

Christie's childhood dates back to the years when Maryann and R.E. Morrison were setting up their new home. By that time, as Maryann recalled, furniture was almost 'all bought, and very cheap.' That is, cheap by today's standards; it was produced by a small factory that had been set up in Scotstown by an enterprising company. Though prices have increased considerably since the days when lumber was so plentiful and inexpensive, the furniture factory is still in operation today. Wooden kitchen chairs in a variety of styles, most with spool backs and legs, still feature in many homes in the area.[40]

First impressions of some of the older Hebridean homes in Quebec give an instant reflection of many aspects of the lifestyle of previous generations. 'Aunt Annie's house' in Milan (Marston township), where I first lived when I went to Quebec in 1976, had remained unoccupied for several years, apart from occasional summer visits by her daughter and son-in-law, Muriel and Herbert Mayhew. It was, therefore, 'just as she left it', and, from my point of view, an ideal place to live. An old-style house, two-storied, and 'smallish' by local standards (as had been their family of three), visitors approached by the front door which faced the main road through Milan. An open porch ran along the complete length of the front, so that visitors were immediately shaded from the elements as soon as they stood under the sloping roof. Only after living in the house did I discover the advantages of the porch: in summer, the cool of the evening breeze allowed respite from the day's sun which steadily heated up the house, and in winter when driving snow created drifts at every corner, one could arrive at the door and find a moment of protection before entering the house. The front of the porch was formed by a low wall (c. three feet high) which was punctuated every six feet by square timbered pillars supporting the edge of the roof. Grey painted tongue-and-groove planking formed the floor, which seemed springy and hollow, being set on widely spaced joists keeping it clear of the damp ground. There was ample room on the porch for a few chairs, a bench and a rocking chair, and some neighbouring porches even had a swing. The eaves were finished off by ornately cut trim which I began to recognise as characteristic of the work of the old-style carpenters: in varying designs, eaves, lintels, windows, door frames, and porches of the older buildings were usually finished in meticulously carved decoration then painted in a contrasting colour which, against the main colour of the house, showed up like lace on a garment.

One of the greatest improvements to the old-style houses was undoubtedly the introduction of a supply of running water, with all the accompanying advantages to house and home. Some families were fortunate enough to have their homes located near a spring, while others had to sink a well for household water supply. Ruth Nicolson recalled that several individuals in the area were able to use a hazel divining-rod, such as Donald M. Campbell, nicknamed 'Malavy' (pronounced with the emphasis on the middle syllable).[41] In his manuscript recollections, *Memoirs of Dell*, written in 1971, John Austin MacLeod, locally known as 'Johnnie Bard', recalled that 'anyone who anticipated the sinking of a well would usually need his assistance…and it was even used to locate a gold ring that had been lost in the vegetable garden while his niece was thinning carrots.'[42]

While all the houses had kitchens, none of the first houses had a bathroom. The addition of what was then considered a luxury to the older houses — the now-essential bathroom — was very much a parallel to the modifications made to older croft houses in the Hebrides. The main difference between the two sets of improvements is that Quebec began considerably earlier than the Outer Hebrides. In Duncan McLeod's family, for example, his grandfather had modern plumbing and running water in the kitchen and bathroom before the end of the nineteenth century. By the 1930s nearly all the houses in the villages and towns were improved, though in outlying areas, such as Cruvag, people still relied upon their wells and springs until the 1940s.[43] Homes in Lewis and Harris, however, were still catching up in the 1960s and into the 70s.[44] Although carrying water from a nearby well or spring was commonplace in both locations, the difficulties of keeping the source free from ice, and then carrying the water through deep snow would no doubt be an added incentive to make improvements as soon as possible.

The interior of Aunt Annie's house consisted of two main rooms downstairs, the sitting room and a large kitchen, both heated by stoves, with cast iron 'registers' directly above. A common feature of the older houses, these ingenious devices are set into the pine ceilings and through the floor above, thus allowing heat to circulate in the upstairs rooms.[45] A vent that is operated from the floor above controls the amount of heat admitted to the bedrooms. A simple wooden staircase ascended from the small hallway opposite the front door, and led to the upstairs landing and two bedrooms and a bathroom which had been converted from what had once been a third, smaller, bedroom. The landing was big enough to accommodate a 'spare bed' and a dresser. All the rooms were decorated in the style which had been prevalent between the World Wars. The sitting room at the front of the house was shaded by the porch, and was seldom used as it was almost always bypassed to get to the kitchen. As the 'best room', it was carpeted and was heated by a free standing, cylindrical stove which was fired by logs. There was a couch, two armchairs, an occasional table, a bookcase, an oak pedestal desk incorporating bookshelves at each end, and a few lamps. Most of these items were store-bought, and while not particularly characteristic of the area, and only 'old-fashioned' in the sense that many were from the forties, fifties and sixties, the acquisition of new furnishings, particularly for the best room, is in keeping with prevailing practices. As I. F. Grant wrote, when describing the furnishings and plenishings of homes in the Highlands and Islands of Scotland:

> It would be out of keeping with the people's attitude of mind to cling to the archaic and the folksy. Like their forebears they adopt the current styles. One often sees in modern Highland houses the mass-produced three-piece suites so widely sold all over Britain and if there is more comfort and not room for quite so many, the row of Highland folk sitting on the sofa is by blood and attitude of mind the same as the men and women who once sat on the old *seise*.[46]

Access to the large, square kitchen was via the sitting room. Dominating the room was the cast-iron and white enamelled range, with its stove-pipe set into the brick chimney on the back wall. Summer or winter, it had to be lit each day, as it was the only cooking stove in the kitchen. It was also the main source of heat in winter, and, as in every house in the neighbourhood, the wood-shed kept a good supply of logs cut, dried and stacked well in advance of winter. Furnishings consisted of a kitchen table and six chairs, a wooden rocking chair, an electric fridge (1950s vintage), and day-bed which was laden with cushions and a very heavy, home-made tweed patch-work quilt, and a cuibhrig, (hand-woven coverlet), both folded up when not in use. The day-bed was (and still is) a feature of many of the older houses; rather like the bench or 'settle', the *seise*, in Hebridean homes, it was (and is) often used for seating, especially when visitors increase household numbers.

The kitchen had a back door which opened into the location known as the 'summer kitchen', a spacious, airy room, part of which was designated as the wood-shed. A common feature of the early French homes also — Mary Morrison remarked that 'it kept the house cooler to sleep at night' — its construction was similar to the front porch, only the walls full-length and had a series of windows which in summer were screened and in winter glazed. On the hottest of days it seemed cool, and afforded an escape from the heat of the stove which could be quite oppressive. After the coming of electricity, Aunt Annie had added a small electric cooking ring which allowed her to cook a modest meal without having to light the stove at all. This was the exception, however, as the wood-stove was the preferred method of cooking.

The bedrooms had cast-iron and brass bedsteads, with a little dresser in each, and a wash-stand with facilities in one room. The beds all had hand-made patchwork quilts, old style, as opposed to 'craft quilts' that have, to some extent, taken over in modern times. The rest of the bedding consisted of white cotton or linen, some of which was trimmed with hand-embroidery or crochet, with a plentiful supply of woollen blankets, several hand-woven in Quebec or Lewis. The floors were covered in 'canvas' (linoleum) and had colourful, home-made rugs (hooked and braided) beside the beds and dressers, [see Chapter 7]. Examples of all of these items surrounded me during my fieldwork visits in 1992 and 1993 when, again, I lived in Milan, this time in the home of Ruth Nicolson, who also cooked on her wood-stove every day of summer.

Aunt Annie's immediate neighbour, Mary 'Allan' MacLeod, had a larger, slightly newer house, yet it had many of the same features, especially those I am about to describe. (So also did the other 'Scotch' homes in Milan, Scotstown, Marsboro, Gould, and Lennoxville which I visited.) Whether we sat in the kitchen or in the best room, the surroundings told their own story: walls are usually decorated with a number of pictures, mostly portraits of grandparents and great-grandparents, well-dressed and well-groomed, in studio pose. A few in oval-shaped frames look solemnly at you wherever you move in the room. Fifty-year-old photos of communion services show throngs of faithful Presbyterians, entire villages of people clad in black, now immortalized in a group pose outside the church. Most of the pictures are reminders of the past. Still in the present, however, are bookshelves or tables with a few well-used Bibles visible; you could be in a cousin's home in Lewis, as far as that goes. Closer inspection of the row of black spines will reveal an extended range of gold-leaf titles: *Biobull* [Gaelic Bible], *Tiomnadh Nuadh* [Gaelic New Testament], *Holy Bible, New Testament,* and *Sainte Bible* [Holy Bible in French], and hidden among them the slim volume of the *Shorter Catechism.* Familiar biblical texts hang on walls, giving their message to all who enter the house. As far as the Québecois-Hebrideans are concerned, access to the scriptures and to the catechism is fundamental to their way of life. Just as the lives of their forebears were upheld by a strong faith, so also the tradition continued in Quebec to be central to every aspect of home and community, no matter what fate befell. Maryann Morrison, who tasted life in both the Old and New Worlds, reflected on what had sustained her kinsfolk through generations: 'They lived on oatmeal and catechism.'[47]

Regarded as 'quite ordinary', and generally taken for granted, a blend of Old and New World *symbols* co-exist in every homestead. So integral to the identity of the Hebridean settlers are these images of 'home' that nobody commented upon them of their own accord, except for two 'incomers', both Eastern Townshippers who had married into the 'Scotch' area. One was Duncan McLeod's wife, Kay, who remarked to me in conversation that 'you wouldn't really need to speak to a soul if you wanted to know if they were Scotch or French around here. Just walk up the path and into their houses, and you'll see for yourself — the rowan tree, the bookshelves, the pictures, the photographs…it's all there.'[48]

Notes

1.	The Isle of Arran, off the west coast of Scotland, was Gaelic-speaking. In her report to the National Museum of Man, Ottawa, social anthropologist Sharon Gmelch erroneously locates the place of origin as the Aran Islands which are part of Ireland. See L. Doucette (ed), *Cultural Retention and Demographic Change in the Eastern Townships of Quebec.*

2.	In his *Register* Bill Lawson refers to township destination of emigrants.

3.	According to homesteaders 'across the line', where the terrain was similarly wooded, there are reports from oral tradition that the first branch of the pine and fir was a hundred feet from the ground. From S.M. Morse, New Hampshire, b. 1893.

4.   This growth pattern is common in Canada, thus the emigrants who settled in Nova Scotia, Prince Edward Island, New Brunswick, Ontario, and Newfoundland must all have experienced similar periods of readjustment, to say nothing of the task of land-clearing that was common to all.

5.   B. Lawson, *Register*, p. v.

6.   The redwing-blackbird, *agelaius phoeniceus*, is described under the heading of 'Meadowlarks, Blackbirds and Orioles' in Roger T. Peterson, *A Field Guide to the Birds*; see p. 211 and plate 53.

7.   Several local histories refer to the fauna of the area. Catherine Matilda Day mentions several (though not all) of the above in her book, *Pioneers of the Eastern Townships*.

8.   C.P.Traill wrote a letter home telling about the profusion of frogs and remarked upon the noise they made; *Backwoods*, p. 146. As a newcomer to Quebec in 1976, I have clear recollections of my first summer in Milan: apart from the heat, humidity and biting insects, there seemed to be a perpetual noise of frogs, day and night. Coming from a country where the sound of birdsong wakens me each morning, I thought it strange to waken to the croaking of frogs. It struck me that there is comparatively little birdsong, despite the fact that the nearest tree is never more than a few feet away. There are no frogs in Lewis or Harris, but a wide variety of seabirds can be seen and heard all over the islands.

9.   *Backwoods*, p. 136. See also Catherine Parr Traill's later books, *Canadian Wild Flowers*, (1868) and *Studies of Plant Life in Canada,* (1885).

10. See Bill Lawson, Register. Throughout the book, secondary moves that took place relatively soon after emigration are noted.

11. On August 13, 1992 I drove along a number of back-roads with Duncan McLeod and recorded him talking about landmarks such as farmsteads, schools, churches, graveyards, mills, gold-mines, and place names that were not on the most recent Ordnance Survey map. He pointed out and named 94 sites, all of which were of significance to the Gaelic settlers, that are not on the O.S. map. Unfortunately the scope of this book does not allow further elaboration on the subject. The recording is, however, the only one that Duncan knows to be in existence telling of the place-names of the district. Hopefully it can be published at a later date.

12. Tape-recorded from the Legendre family in 1976. The story of the Stornoway Town Council's attempt to change the name to a French one is now frequently told to demonstate the strong loyalty that existed between the Scotch and the French.

13. I am grateful to Duncan McLeod for lending me his copy of *Stornoway 1858-1983*. The editorial team was led by Guy Lalumière, and the book was printed in Sherbrooke to mark the celebration of the town's 125th anniversary. It is an invaluable source of information about the town and its people, as it presents profiles of a number of families, with photos and significant dates.

14. There is a photo of Stornoway's Gaelic church on p. 12, and a close-up of an open psalter on p. 8. (Details recorded in *Stornoway* do not agree with J.I. Little's caption below the Gaelic church photograph in *Crofters and Habitants;* he incorrectly refers to hymns (sic) sung without organ accompaniment — there were, of course, no hymns in the early churches as they followed the customs established in the Free Church.)

15. Op cit p. 36.

16. Included is a translation into French of an example of a Gaelic poem by the Rev. Malcolm N. MacDonald.

17. André Siegfried, *Le Canada, les Deux Races*, p. 73, (translated by Henry B.M. Best in his article "The Auld Alliance' in New France'), in *The Scottish Tradition in Canada*, p. 15.

18. Recordings which were made in 1976 of Mlle Ellen Legendre and her brother Alphonse, confirm this attitude, and will be included later in the text. Their family were among the first French settlers in Stornoway, and, typical of their generation, are fully aware of the interaction between the two groups.

19. These three examples are all in Milan. When I lived there in 1976 there were several families in the village of those names, but no streets were named, either officially or unofficially. Duncan McLeod and Ruth Nicholson, the only two left in the 1990s, told me that a few years ago the local community council were asked by the Township's central administrative body to name all streets and roads. As a result, they had to choose new names for roads hitherto unnamed. Duncan and Ruth were not at the meeting when the names were proposed, but were pleased that 'there still enough of the older Milan folk to keep the others right.' [Milan, Aug. 1991]

20. There are many similarities between styles in Quebec and the New England States. Henry Glassie discusses log cabin styles, construction methods and design in *Pattern in the Material Folk Culture of the Eastern United States*, pp. 48-166. See also Robert C. Bucher, 'The Continental Log House' in *Pennsylvania Folklife* (1962), pp. 14 -19; Henry C. Mercer, 'The Origins of Log Houses in the United States' in *A Collection of Papers Read Before the Bucks County Historical Society*, (1926), pp. 568 - 583 republished in *Old-time New England*.

21. The prevalent style was squared-timber logs with half dove-tail construction. For a comparative style, see Glassie, op cit, p. 156, Fig. 45B.

22. In *The History of Canterbury County, Quebec*, p. 30, Carl Mayhew notes that the early pioneers used a 'dish of grease in which was placed a floating type of wick... This was called a crusie.'

23. Annie Isabel Sherman, *History: The Families of Sherman-MacIver with Stories of People and Places on the Eastern Townships*, p. 31.

24. Originally from Milan, Kay (née Catherine MacLeod) has lived in Lennoxville since her marriage to Bill Young after the Second World War.

25. Marsboro is in the township of Marston.

26. J.I. Little's map of saw-mills, Op.Cit. p. 161.serves as a useful guide to the Stornoway area, though it does not include mills that were erected in other locations. Duncan McLeod pointed out the sites of several mills that operated along the Big Woods Road, between Milan and Marsboro, when he was a young man. Recorded Aug. 13, 1992.

27. A photograph of a broad-axe 'utilisé par les Ecossais', [used by the Scots] can be seen in *Stornoway,* p. 12.

28. *Crofters and Habitants*, p. 165. Several relatives of John MacKenzie, Christie's husband, were mill-wrights and millers (see Chapter 4). Also, several of Duncan McLeod's family operated mills — Norman H. McLeod operated a water-powered saw mill near the Marsboro Mills cemetery, and his grandfather, Duncan L. McLeod, ran one in Milan; their employees were Gaels.

29. Alphonse 'P'it' Legendre, in *Stornoway*, p. 165. See also photographs of the site, and of subsequent mills, pp. 31-32.

30. There is one example of such a house in Milan. Formerly the home of Duncan MacLeod's grand-uncle, Roderick [*Ruaraidh* or Rory] MacDonald, it is now owned by Wayne Mouland. Today, it would be impossible to tell from its outward appearance that the modern clapboarding covers a log house over a hundred years old. Those who know it still refer to it as 'the Rory house'.

31. I have retained the style of my notebook as it gives my own impressions at the time.

32. There were clear marks of a circular saw running over the grain of the wood.

33. Photographs are in the Photographic Archive of the School of Scottish Studies.

34. There are many examples of letters written by immigrants asking relatives to send seeds of a favourite plant. For example, one letter home requests an elderly parent to make a paste of flour and water, like a glue, and then stick the seeds to a paper, in order to send them (original letter in a student project at the School of Scottish Studies). Also, Catherine Parr Traill wrote to ask her mother to send in next parcel the seeds of flowers and the stones of plums, damsons, pips of apples, along with plants of her favourite flowers, primroses and violets. See *Backwoods,* pp. 149-150, 1836 edn.

35. By comparison, my uncle on Skye, remarked upon the rowans when I asked him about those growing on his croft in 1991: 'Oh, the old people planted them to keep away the witches.' And although he laughed as he said it, there is, nevertheless, no apparent conflict of belief to a family of faithful church-goers.

36. There are many Scottish references to rowans; see, for example, John Ramsay, *Scotland and Scotsmen in the Eighteenth Century*, vol. 2, p. 454.

37. I. F. Grant discusses the skills of carpenters in *Highland Folkways*, pp. 244-246. As expected in fishing communities, there were many highly skilled coopers working with wood, while in wooded areas of the Highlands techniques of use of pit-saws had taken over from the adze in the eighteenth century. Grant recalls that even 'in the treeless Island of Uist' she was surprised to find an

enormous pit-saw, and points out that these islands found a certain amount of wreckage from ships which was utilized by local builders.

38. This arrangement of parents and infant children in a downstairs bedroom is exactly as it was in many Hebridean croft houses from the 1920s onwards. My mother and her brother, Peigi and Murdo Stewart, were born in a *taigh dubh* in Skye in 1919 and 1916; the family moved into a newly built croft house (now regarded as 'traditional style') in 1921. Murdo remarked that 'Granny and Seanair always slept in the downstairs small room, the *clòsaid*,' which is also where the cradle was when there was a baby in the family. Cradles were a common feature of Highland homes. See I. F. Grant, *Highland Folkways,* p. 176 and M. Bennett *Scottish Customs from the Cradle to the Grave,* p. 72, photo after p. 171.

39. The bench, or *seise,* was a common feature of the blackhouses. See I. F. Grant, op cit, pp. 170-172, sketch p. 171.

40. Further information about the Scotstown furniture factory is recorded in a discussion between Russell MacIver and Duncan McLeod, taped Sept. 16, 1992.

41. Fieldwork notes, Aug. 11, 1993.

42. *Memoirs of Dell,* p. 50. I am grateful to Duncan McLeod for lending me a copy of the manuscript.

43. Mary and Angus Morrison said they drew water from the well until they left in 1942. Some of Mary's French relatives had a windmill which pumped water into the house and allowed them the convenience of tap water before it was generally available. She said that not all houses with a water supply had a toilet installed at the same time; that came later. (July 1994).

44. By co-incidence, it was the installation of 'water schemes' in a network of rural villages on the Isle of Lewis that precipitated my family's move from Skye to Lewis in 1958. My father, George Bennett, was the civil engineer who surveyed the area, and until 1964 he was responsible for a series of projects involving the installation of water mains supplies. The projects were said to be 'no engineer's picnic' as the accessibility of some of the outlying settlements (through peatbogs especially) proved enormously challenging. In the Ness area, for example, the only means of bringing in equipment and supplies was by helicopter, which, in those days, was quite revolutionary. To locate the source of water, however, he used 'one of the oldest methods known to civilization, a water diviner cut from a forked hazel stick.' (Tape recordings and photographs in the Archives of the School of Scottish Studies.)

45. 'Registers' are still relatively common, and can be readily purchased at hardware stores and antique shops. This is the type of heating in Ruth Nicholson's house, and in summer she not only keeps the vents shut but sometimes places a heavy mat over them to exclude heat from the wood-stove. In Scotland I have seen them in the floors of older churches, with warm air rising from a boiler below.

46. I. F. Grant, op cit, pp. 177-178. Furniture, household supplies and clothing were available to all parts of Canada and the United States via mail order catalogues such as Simpsons and Eatons.

47. In his article, 'Pottery and Food Preparation, Storage and Transport in the Scottish Hebrides' Hugh Cheape remarks that '...since the Reformation in the 16th century, Scots have proverbially been reared on the hardy diet of porridge and the Shorter Catechism.' *Food in Change,* p. 117.

48. Paraphrased from field notebook, 1976. Kay died in Oct. 1980. The second individual was former school-teacher, Myrtle Murray, whom I recorded at the age of 94 in 1992.

3

Making a Living

The Year's Work

Having managed to carve fields out of forest, the homesteaders faced the annual task of removing stones. Of every size imaginable, they seemed to be everywhere; it was as if each year grew a new crop. As a result, learning to work on the land began in early childhood: as soon as a small child was able to pick up stones and deposit them on a selected site, then the fields had gained another labourer. Those who were born on the new farms grew up accepting it as a part of the season's work. 'Oh, yes, well, we had no choice,' remarked Angus Morrison who, like everyone of his generation, 'did his share.'

> Oh boy, the big stones! I could take you around and show you stone piles that you wouldn't believe...And mind you, they started in with ox [sic]. They didn't have horses at all — ox! You know what they are! You may as well have an elephant as one...You may as well have an old cat as [them], you know how slow they are, ox. [But in my day], we had three horses.

Angus's wife, Mary, put in a good word for oxen, however, affirming that the French settlers also farmed and logged with them.[1] 'My brothers worked with ox; well, they weren't very fast,' but some people improved the situation by harnessing an ox with a horse. 'Well they used to fix the trace...' so that the two animals would work as a more efficient team. Unless a rock was of such an enormous size as to defy removal, the men tackled it: 'They'd go with a team of horses; like there's the stone...and they'd put the chain around and turned the stone around like that — you'd just haul them out. Big stones too.'

Rocks weighing well over a ton were tackled in this way.[2] No matter whose land it was on, several men would be required to help, and judging by a photograph which was taken on one of the French farms near Stornoway in 1932, there were several ingenious approaches to rock moving: in this case, a huge wooden contraption, like a pyramid-shaped cage, had a pulley at the apex, by means of which a monstrous boulder, tied around by a chains, was winched aboard, secured within the frame of the cage, then wheeled across to the edge of the field to be dumped.[3]

Smaller rocks (of several hundredweight) were towed away on a home-made 'stone-boat',[4] and deposited at the side of the field. Despite the fact that they were living in an area with such a profusion of wood that there was never any need for stone construction, a great many of them were used in the making of dry-stane dykes, a tradition learned in their native Islands of Lewis and Harris. Russell MacIver described what they were like:

> They had some fairly good ones made into a stone wall in the old days — [the men would] take them onto what they called a stone-boat. They'd drag, you know, and roll them on there and roll them off. [laughs] And boy, the stones! Those stone walls are on some of them farms yet…They'd build them on this side, on that side, and then throw them [rocks & rubble] into the middle…Some years ago there was a millionaire lived here, over here, had a lake, and along the road there, they built a stone wall. Oh, it was just perfect, you know. He hired men the year round, making that stone wall. Old men that couldn't do very much, and he hired them just to make that stone wall! There's some of that left yet, 'course it's falling down some.

In fact there was no practical reason to have a laboriously built stone wall in this part of Quebec which abounds with timber. The most common method of constructing a boundary fence, and by far the quickest, is cedar railing, common throughout much of Canada and the United States.[5] As far as Russell MacIver or men of his generation are concerned, it is difficult for them to imagine why anyone but a millionaire, with enough cash to pay for labour that had no logical purpose, would go to the trouble of erecting a long, perfectly built stone wall. As a result, such a wall is seen as having some kind of aesthetic value.[6] It became clear to Duncan McLeod, however, after his first visit to the Old Country, why the previous generations did not seem to question the choice of construction method, nor did they lack the skill involved. For Duncan, the sight of rural Scotland's ubiquitous networks of dry-stane dykes dispelled what had, till then, been something of a mystery. Clearly, the early settlers who built stone walls were highly skilled, as was characteristic of Highland crofters and farmworkers. They simply did so as a matter of course, just as their forebears had done for generations.

To Russell, however, it was not entirely surprising that when a road construction crew appeared many years later and needed massive quantities of road-fill, they welcomed the sight of ready-made material. They seemed completely unable, however, to discriminate between 'stone piles' and the carefully constructed stone walls. 'When they put the road through they used pretty near all them stones.'[7]

When the homesteaders had removed the biggest stones that horses and men could tackle, there still remained a few giants, literally the size of houses. These were simply left in the fields, like odd-shaped monoliths. Finally, within the past twenty years, most of them were removed and deposited in random piles forming massive boundaries between some of the farms, as Russell MacIver explained: 'Them *big* stones, not too many years ago they used the bulldozers on them.'[8] It had taken more than a century and a half to create today's landscape, and, as Angus Morrison added, 'I tell you, they worked hard.'

Having spent much of his life farming in Victoria near Scotstown, Russell MacIver was well into adulthood before he realized that poor, stony ground was *not* characteristic of the entire Eastern Townships, even although it was all the Scotch settlers knew. A mere fifty miles west was a different story, one that affirmed there was indeed 'beautiful land to be had'. This was the element of truth that had been broadcast in the 1830s, 40s, and 50s by the land companies which had been so eager to entice Hebridean emigrants to settle. Russell still recalls his surprise at this discovery:

> In near Lennoxville, my brother-in-law had a farm in there, and I helped him plough one time; that's before they had the tractor — he had horses — and we were ploughing. I couldn't even find a little stone like a hazelnut to throw at the horse! My God! That looked funny! And at home, I'd be breaking plough points and tipping over, and spending weeks hauling stones into the stone walls.

But plough they did, and every spring would plant their crops in preparation for the following autumn and winter. Despite the drawbacks of the early days, their hard work was rewarded by increased productivity. As Bill Young's generation recalls, virtually every family who had persevered with their land gained a high level of self-sufficiency:

> Everyone had their own garden. I'm speaking of — like in the village. Like farming, everybody went right in for it. It wasn't specialized like it is today, but it was diversified. They raised what they needed...Sheep supplied the wool for their blankets, and stockings, and mittens. And their cattle and pigs supplied their meat for the winter.[9] And their hens, the eggs. And they planted the brown buckwheat, which you don't get any more today, which made lovely pancakes. And they had scones, which were the old stand-by; and they were barley, and they were buckwheat, and there were potato ones; and, you name it, they had them, eh? And Mrs. Mayhew, and the wife, and a few other women in the town are about the only ones left that can make those things today. And whenever they have a Scotch supper, everybody goes to it, because that's where you get solid food![10]

Since spring came late by comparison to that in the Outer Hebrides, settlers had to adapt to the ground remaining frozen until late May or early June when ploughing could begin. The main crops were much as they had been at home: oats, barley, rye, hay, potatoes, turnips, with the addition of wheat, buckwheat, and 'sometimes a little corn', known elsewhere as Indian corn or maize. It is well known in the Eastern Townships that oats, barley, and, to a lesser extent, rye, were staples in the Old Country, and that Lewis and Harris 'would be too cold and wet' to grow wheat or corn. Curiously, however, most people do not seem to realize that buckwheat is virtually unknown among their kinsfolk overseas. So popular had it become by the turn of the century,[11] that it was assumed without question that buckwheat was part of the old-style Lewis and Harris diet. No Highland or Island crofter I have ever asked has come across it, except those who have visited modern, urban 'health food shops' who have seen it on labels on a shelf.

In *The Book of the Farm,* intended as a text-book guide for nineteenth century British farmers to consult while training their farm-workers, Henry Stephens acknowledges that buckwheat has been grown in the British Isles:

> This plant is comparatively little grown, being easily susceptible of injury from frost if the seed is sown earlier than the middle of May. The crop is sometimes cut green and used for soiling. The grain is used chiefly for feeding game or poultry.
> In Ireland the term 'buckwheat' is sometimes locally applied to some of the varieties of common wheat, with which the true buckwheat has no connection.[12]

Despite his meticulous attention to the details of growing and harvesting all of the above-mentioned crops, Stephens does not, however, give any further information.

In a study based on readings of early herbals, botanical works, and folklore documentation, Geoffrey Grigson suggests that the name *buckwheat* is derived from the German *Buchweize,* meaning 'beech wheat' since the small, dark, triangular, sharp-edged seeds resemble beechmast.[13] It was introduced into Europe from Asia in the sixteenth century, and until the nineteenth century

> buckwheat was widely cultivated in Great Britain, giving a poor man's flour as well as food for cattle and hens...Early colonists took Buckwheat to North America, a good crop for the poor soils of New England.[14] America has not abandoned it as we have, and in the drug-store or the cafeteria no breakfast is more delicious than a golden pile of Buckwheat cakes soaked with maple syrup.[15]

In Quebec, however, the 'golden pile' is still very much a feature of the kitchen table, and does not appear to have reached the cafeteria menu yet. *The Canadian Encyclopedia* confirms that buckwheat, <u>Fagopyrum esculentum</u>, is grown in Canada 'mainly for human consumption (e.g., flour for pancake mixes, bread and ethnic dishes, breakfast cereal) and is also used for livestock and poultry feed...and as a source of buckwheat honey'.[16]

Among the Eastern Townshippers of Hebridean descent, buckwheat is just as important a part of the diet as barley and oatmeal. Although I have not come across anyone who is aware of when this became the case, perhaps it is not entirely surprising, since it was already established among British immigrants as a staple crop at least as early as the 18th century. This is confirmed by emigrant letters, such as one by Elizabeth Russell, who in 1792 wrote home to England: 'We live in a log house...and have a nice little Farm about us. We eat our own Mutton and Pork and Poultry. Last year we grew our own Buck wheat and Indian corn...'[17]

My own first introduction to buckwheat was in 1976 when it was served to me as buckwheat pancakes. Having never seen the growing plant, nor what I assumed to be 'the grain that produced the flour that made the pancakes', I can well understand the confusion of the Irish[18] or any other individual. Buckwheat, not being a *grain*-producing crop, bears no resemblance whatsoever to its part-namesake. As can be seen from the photograph, it has broad leaves, produces small white, or pinkish, flowers, which, after they fade produce little triangular seed pods which turn brown when ripe. In the autumn the crop is harvested and threshed, just like the grain crops. (Chapter 6 will deal with food preparation.)

Vegetables grown were, for the most part, the same as the kinds they grew in the old country — at least an acre of potatoes, half an acre of turnips, and smaller plots with carrots, beetroot, cabbages, and onions. Several varieties of beans grow well in Quebec, as do peas, and are easily dried, although relatively few Scotch farmers seemed to grow them on a large scale, and dried beans were usually listed among items obtained from the store.[19]

Planting time was always very busy, with work for everybody in the family. Just as it was with the island crofts, at potato planting time even the smallest pair of hands could be put to work.[20] John MacKenzie of Scotstown said that some families, though not his own, used to plant their potatoes after the new moon had appeared, because they feared a crop failure if they planted when the moon was on the decrease.[21] In view of the fact that the potato famine of 1846 — 51 had been the ruin of so many crofting families, little wonder that their descendants were prepared to observe whatever law of nature was prescribed to prevent another disaster. Nevertheless, John himself used to plant 'just when the ground was ready.'

The warm summer weather comes suddenly in Quebec, and is accompanied by a rapid acceleration in growth. During this period, hoeing, weeding and thinning were daily demands. I have yet to encounter anybody who lists thinning turnips among his or her favourite activities for a summer's day; a necessity without immediate rewards is what it seems like. Perhaps Scottish crofters and farmers can yet take encouragement from the practice in Quebec, where a favourite dish of early summer is boiled turnip or beetroot greens, utilizing the fresh, young plants which, in Scotland, are usually discarded during the thinning process. Since there was always more than one family could possibly eat while they were fresh, a large quantity were bottled for the winter. Today, among the few farmers who remain, it is more common for these greens to be frozen.[22]

One of the benefits of land-clearing was the noticeable increase of wild fruits such as raspberries, blueberries, choke-cherries, crab apples and high bush cranberries. Regarded as one of nature's miracles that the birds should be instrumental in dispersing the seeds, the appearance of wild berries and fruit was a welcome gift to hard-working families. Having realized that certain fruits grow well in that area of Quebec, many farmers planted apple orchards of several varieties in a field near their homes. Christie MacKenzie remembers when some of the orchards were created in Milan: 'We planted some [apple trees]; we got some from a fellow that was selling them. And some grew wild later on...' To this day, the harvest of apples that appears on these domestic orchards is profuse, even where farms have been abandoned and trees left untended, they suggest that America's folk-hero, 'Johnny Appleseed', has done his rounds among the Gaels in Quebec.[23]

Although planting time always seemed exceptionally busy, the busiest time of all arrived in late summer and autumn, with food and fodder crops requiring to be harvested before the onset of cold weather. Frosts could suddenly appear in September, and snow as early as October, and because of the severity and duration of the Quebec winter, a great quantity of food had to be stored for both animals and humans. Fortunately, during haying time they could be almost assured of good weather, and seldom, if ever, did they have to endure the prolonged adverse weather that too often characterises a Hebridean summer, flattening the hay and corn, and bringing despair to crofters. Yet again, everyone who was on the farm was called upon to do his or her share.

Not everyone in the family could be home for haying, however, as it was one of the few seasonal occupations that could bring in extra cash to a family, provided one or two could be spared from their own farm-labour. Visiting the area in 1870, John Ramsay of Kildalton noted that

> The young men from this district often go to various parts of the United States during the seasons of the year when they can best be spared from their own farms, and they then get employment at high wages, and, after working for some time, return again to their home with the money they have earned. [Mr Ross in Lingwick] expressed a doubt how far such a system was prudent, as he felt that their labour on their own land was as necessary and likely to yield a greater profit than any wages they could possibly earn.[24]

Paid seasonal labour was, however, a common and necessary feature of many communities of new settlers, as the Ayrshireman (mentioned in Chapter 1), David Kennedy, recorded in his memoirs of homesteading in Ontario in the 1830s and 40s:[25]

> We always found some of our neighbours very anxious to secure our assistance and in that way we earned over forty dollars in a few weeks. This proved to be of great help to us in the way of purchasing a supply of provisions and groceries and other needful things, such as wheat for seed, besides a quantity of miscellaneous articles...'[26]

There are no memories of neighbouring farmers who employed men on these terms, as all the neighbours, Scotch and French alike, were in the same economic situation. For the Eastern Townshippers of this area, paid work meant 'going across the line' to Vermont or New Hampshire. The opportunity was regarded as a mixed blessing: on the one hand it could be the means of paying off debts that had accumulated over the winter, or loans on farm equipment and seed that had been necessary for progress, or even survival; on the other hand, it meant extra hardships for those left behind, to say nothing of the encounters of those who went. Only the oldest people in the community remember young men going. Age was not a barrier to going haying, however, as Russell MacIver and Duncan McLeod recalled one afternoon in 1992. (In order to project as much of the atmosphere as possible, the transcription is given in full):

Russell: Another thing they used to do from around here, when it was haying time in Vermont, they'd walk from here up to Vermont to do the hay, and it was all that crooked sticks, you know. They didn't have mowing machines then. [laughs]

MB: No. A scythe?

Russell: A scythe, and by gee, there were some o' them were good. I used to do some of that too. My father was pretty good at it — he was strong. And one time there was a bunch of men went up to Vermont, my great-uncle, Neil Beaton — he wasn't very big, he wasn't very old either. And he [the Vermont farmer] went to hire out fellows to cut and scythe too, he had quite a bunch o men. And [looking at Neil] he said 'I won't pay you a man's wage.'
   'That's all right,' said Uncle Neil, 'then I'll do a boy's work!'
   'Oh,' he went on, 'why don't you keep up with the rest?'
   He says 'You pay me what you pay them and I'll keep up.'
   Well, the fellow thought he'd try it — he paid him. The others couldn't keep up to him then! [laughs] You met him, Duncan — it's just because he was small.

MB: And witty!

Russell: They used to have to walk up there [to Vermont] and walk back.

Duncan: They had to live by their wits.

Russell: But there was some o' them'd go up by team [of horses and wagon]. My father had a cousin went up one time by bicycle, then came back. And places where there was clay, they'd get stuck and have to carry the bicycles. **Huh!** But there were some of these fellows they weren't very honest, from around here, although they were Scotch people they'd go up there in teams, they'd steal chickens, they'd steal stuff [just to keep from starving on their journey]. [laughs] Well, that was something to eat, and they figured it wasn't stealing.

MB: Where would they stay when they went up on those farms?

Russell: There was a couple o' them stopped at a farm and asked if they'd give them some dinner. 'Oh, we haven't any dinner cooked,' [they said].
And one fellow, pretty sarcastic, he said 'Too bad we didn't telephone ahead that we were coming!' They didn't have any telephones anyway! [laughs]

Duncan: Well, the time that Dave Nicolson's grandfather went [to the Vermont harvesting] and died there, they were in the haying, that'd be July probably. And his wife didn't hear about his death until they walked back in September or October.

Russell: My, I heard them talking about that in the [Scotstown] Hotel there lately. It was one hot day, oh, it was awful hot — terrible! And they took out this ice cold water and he drank so much it just killed him.

MB: That was Dave Nicolson's grandfather?[27]

Russell: 'Course they couldn't do nothing, they just buried him.

MB: He must have been up in years when he went haying, then?

Duncan Oh no, I suppose he'd be 30 or 40. That's a long time ago.

MB: Yes, and really, they were going for extra money, income, weren't they?

Duncan The only ways they had then of earning cash.

MB: Yes, to go haying... Would they take their own scythe?

Duncan: [louder, to Russell] Would they have their own scythes or would the farmers — ?

Russell: Oh I think they'd get them up there. That'd be an awful thing to carry when you're walking, or on a bicycle. [laughs] If you went in a buggy you might take them, wrap them up in something.

Duncan: I think they walked, though. I don't think they had any buggies.]

Russell: Most of them walked.

MB: Did they ever say what kind of treatment they got? OK, they earned some money, but where they stayed, or how they were fed when they were there?

Russell: Oh, I don't know, they used to — oh, I think most of them would feed them pretty good. But going up there, or coming back, walking, they were always sure of a good meal if it was a Scotch family. They were never turned down by the Scotch although they're supposed to be so tight. Whatever, [among other strangers on the road] a lot of them'd turn them down. But they said the Scotch were kind; they had nothing for themselves but they could still give you some dinner.

MB: D'you think they would sleep in barns or stuff like that?

Duncan: Oh yes, anywhere at all.[28]

Meanwhile, at home, the work of the farm still had to be done, as every farmer has to prepare for long winters demanding more than six months of indoor feeding — an enormous load of hay, even for only a few cows and a horse. The men and youths who remained usually handled the horses and machinery, while everyone else busied themselves with fork, rake, or simply a pair of hands. Maryann Morrison probably did as wide a range of tasks as any woman of her day:

> Well, I would be in the load. I used to rake the grass [hay], make bundles of it, you know. And — this was before the boys got old enough, you know, to go in the load of hay [i.e. on the cart], or in the oats, or barley, or whatever we have. So, I used to be in the load of hay, or oats, or barley — whatever was to be cut. But when the boys got old enough to do that, I never went. But I worked very hard on the farm. He was on the ground, pitching loads of hay over...over to me stamping on it, up and down. And [we had] a pair of horses, and I could drive the horses.

On a summer day in 1992, Maryann's son, Angus, the fourth of her thirteen children, stood on the land that his parents had farmed and, at the age of eighty-two, he pointed out what had once been a hayfield. Reflecting on his younger days he remarked: 'My mother was in the load and my father pitching hay up on the cart the day before my brother Peter was born — now that's work!' While acknowledging the fact that they all worked extremely hard, he remembered with pleasure the cohesion of family and community during their years at Cruvag. Reminded that it was relentlessly hot, sweaty work bringing in the harvest, Angus laughingly recalled how he and one of his brothers invented a shower, which, having no bathroom in the house at that time, they all enjoyed at the end of the day's work. Angus's shower must be one of the earliest instances of the use of solar power, if not in Canada, then certainly in the Eastern Townships. Their invention was housed in a small log cabin, built by them for the purpose. On the roof the boys installed a tank which they had salvaged from an old car. (They were later to replace it with 'something bigger'.) To the tank they fitted a hose leading into the cabin, and on the end of the hose a shower-head with a faucet (tap) that they had purchased in a store. Every morning they would make sure to fill the tank with icy water from the nearby stream, and then they relied upon the heat of the sun to warm it, as indeed it did. At the end of the day they looked forward to a refreshing shower, with preliminary cautions of 'don't use all the water' to the one who got in first.[29]

The Morrisons' ice-cold brook, flowing down through the farm, below thick, shady trees was also an important food preserver in summer. By lowering a wooden food-box containing meat, or an earthenware crock containing butter or cream into the cold water, they could keep these foods fresh and cool through the hottest summer day. [30] 'Just feel how cold that is, even today!' The fact that the community lacked electricity and indoor plumbing throughout all of Angus's childhood and much of his adulthood was only inconvenient upon reflection.

The demands of farm work are for every day of the year where there is livestock involved. Though the situation varied from farm to farm, Russell MacIver's family were typical: 'Oh, we had sheep, cows, horses, hens...Well the most we ever milked was seven, but we had a few young stock.' In his day he shared in all the chores connected with the care of animals, but in Maryann's time, milking, along with many other tasks, both inside and outside the house, were considered 'women's work'. The division of labour may have kept the women constantly busy, but, as far as Maryann was concerned, there were many pleasures that could be enjoyed in the course of a season.

Aside from the work horses, the Morrisons also kept a finer horse which gave Maryann the sort of independence her mother and grandmother in Harris could never have had:

> I had one for myself to drive. When I'd go to the Ladies' Aid, I'd take two or three women with me. I had quite a big wagon. It wasn't a small one — you could have three in the same seat...I had a very good horse.

Although the family did not think that there was anything unusual about it at the time, Angus reflected on his mother's skill with her horse and wagon, and realized that she was a very capable woman:

> Tha cuimhne agam. Bha each brèagh, cha robh e glé mhór, bha e *special* dha na boireannaich, bha e *quiet,* agus bhiodh mo mhàthair, reidheadh i dh'àite sam bith leis. 'S nuair chuimhnicheas mise air na laithchean sin — O bha *wagon* — ceithear cuidhlichean air. 'S a's a' gheamhraidh bhiodh, oh rud ris an canadh sinn *cutter* . Yeah. [Coltach ri *sleigh*?]...Se. *Sleigh* a bh'ann. Ach, 's e rùm do dhithis a bha sa' *chutter*, ach bha *sleigh* eile againn 's bha dà shuidheachan innte. Rinn sinne bith-beò ag obair a's a choille.

> *I remember. It was a beautiful horse [called 'Pat'], it wasn't very big, it was a special horse for the women; it was quiet, and my mother could go whatever place she wanted with it. When I think on those days! Oh, it was a wagon [she had] with four wheels on it. In the winter it would have been, oh, a thing we called a cutter. Yeah. [Like a sleigh?] Yes, it was a sleigh.* [31] *But there's room for two on the cutter, but on another sleigh we had there was seats in it. We made our living in the woods.*

Comparatively few people kept sheep; cattle were, and are, preferred by most farmers, possibly because the earliest settlers discovered, fairly soon after their arrival, that they thrive better on newly cleared land than sheep do. They are also much better able to cope with the winter's snow, and the threat of preying animals.[32] Even in recent years, the few people who kept sheep complained bitterly about the number killed by wolves. The MacArthur farm in Milan was probably the last Scotch farm to have kept sheep, as Christie's son, Donald, a bachelor in his sixties, finally got rid of them all in 1990.

Animal Husbandry

Aside from keeping cattle for dairy products and beef, horses for farm labour and transport, and sheep mainly for wool, most farms raised a few pigs for domestic consumption. From childhood, every member of the family took a share of the work involved in the care of animals. The men and youths generally undertook the heavier work, while the children and adolescents were assigned suitable tasks such as helping to feed the cattle. The women, meanwhile, did most of the milking and dairy work which, until well into the twentieth century, was considered 'women's work'.[33]

Although farmers generally bred their own cattle, horses, sheep and hens, only a few bred pigs. Angus Morrison recalled walking with his brothers from Cruvag to a farm in Marsboro, about four miles away, to buy piglets, and returning home with the wriggling animals under their arms. The majority of families, like the Morrisons, bought their piglets to fatten for the winter.[34] 'We didn't raise our pigs but the other farmers did — you'd buy a pig for two dollars, maybe three dollars.'[35] At the end of autumn the pigs, having been well fed all through the summer, weighed about 200 pounds and were ready to be slaughtered 'after the first fall of snow.'[36] According to Christie MacKenzie, some families adhered to the old belief that pigs should only be slaughtered when the moon was on the increase, otherwise the meat would shrink when it was cooked.[37] It was also thought that the weather could be forecast by studying the spleen of the pig, as recorded in the following verse by Johnnie 'Bard' MacLeod :

> Among these people were weather prophets untold,
> Who forecasted the weather of winters of old.
> Tho' some of them swore by Dr. Chase's almanac,
> Yet, others, the spleen of the pig, butchered out back.[38]

In his *Memoirs of Dell*, Johnnie 'Bard' explains how the forecast was made: if the pig's spleen was long and fat, there would be a hard winter ahead; if it was short and thin, they could expect a mild winter.[39] He also adds that nothing was wasted, not even the pig's bladder which was either made into a money bag or a tobacco pouch, or, by means of a straw, it was blown up into 'a balloon for the kids'.[40]

During a house-visit at Ruth Nicolson's in Milan in August 1992, the subject of winter preparations arose, and, while the men took a back seat, it was discussed by the three women in the company — Ruth, her sister, Bernice (Laurila, née MacDonald) and Christie MacArthur's daughter, Isabell (Mrs Ross Beattie). All had clear memories of the importance of these preparations, and of the fact that most families had at least one pig to slaughter. Generally, when an animal was butchered at the onset of winter it would keep for a long time simply hung up in a shed or other out-building, for, once the temperature dropped below zero at the end of October, it was likely to remain so until well into the new year. Isobel, whose parents' farm is still in operation on 'MacArthur Corner', spoke as I wrote, remarking:

> *I think the spring time was the hardest time to prepare meals. In the fall my father always butchered four pigs and as soon as the weather was cold enough he'd store it in an out-building. And in the winter we'd eat *four pigs*. There were a lot of hired men around to feed too. And we always had potatoes and turnips to see us through, though the carrots would be long gone by Christmas. And then when spring would come and the weather would be warm and we had meat left over we would try burying it in the snow banks to try to keep it fresh. And although it was cold it wouldn't have the frost in it. And then after that, [when the weather got milder], it was put in the brine to keep it.[41]

Preserving food was of prime importance and although there were several methods in use, it was universally accepted that it would be much better to share meat than to let it spoil.

Donald MacLennan, from Scotstown remembered a story his father used to tell, and, though in old age, Donald was still amused by it, he was in no doubt that it had a didactic message. Although he originally heard the story in Gaelic, Donald's own family had been using English as the language of his home for many years, and thus he re-told the story (in 1976) as he knew it best:

> In some community over in Scotland, in Lewis there, when they used to kill their pig and they had no refrigeration — and so they'd have fresh meat, they cut…the family'd kill a pig this week, and they'd cut it up and divide the pieces amongst the whole community. And the next week somebody else'd do the same, and they'd have fresh meat all year round.[42] But this year there was a disease, or an epidemic that killed off all the pigs but two. And there was a fellow there, he was very, very tight, and didn't like to share with the others; and he went to the other fellow that had the live pig, and he told him: 'You know,' he said, 'it's not going to be fair for us — we've got the only two pigs, and when we kill them and divide them up amongst the people we're not going to have enough for ourselves.'
>
> 'Ah, well,' the fellow says, 'keep it then.'
>
> 'Oh,' he says, 'we can't do that. They'll think we're awful stingy. Well,' he says, 'I don't know what to do. What would you do?'
>
> 'Oh,' he says, 'I thought of an idea. You kill your pig, and hang him up, and announce you're going to cut him up in the morning, and,' he says, 'some time during the night hide him, and you can have the meat to yourselves.'

Well, he thought that was a good idea. But this other fellow, he went and he told all the neighbours what he was going to do. And after he had gone to bed, he went, and all the neighbours went and they took the pig, cut him up, and handed him around.

And anyway, early the next morning the fellow got up and he was going to go and hide the pig, and he went and his pig was gone! Now he was in an awful stew, and he ran over to this fellow that had advised him to cut it. 'You know,' he said, 'somebody stole my pig, during the night.'

'Oh,' he said, 'that's a good story.' He said, 'You keep telling that and people are going to believe you.'

'Oh, yeah!' he said, 'but they did! They did!'

'You just keep on telling it just like that,' he said, 'people'll believe every word you say!'

My father always used to use that expression when he'd catch us telling a lie, or when he thought we were. He'd say in Gaelic: '*Cum sin a mach, agus creididh daoine.*' [Tell it like that, and people will believe [you].]

No doubt the daily committment to caring for animals was enlivened by the telling of stories, and, as far as this was concerned, there appears to have been very little difference between the routine work of Highland crofting and that of Quebec farming. Naturally, there were the necessary adaptations to a harsher climate and the proportionately larger tracts of land.

Farmlife in Quebec offered a wider range of animal husbandry than the settlers had experienced in Scotland. Furthermore, it brought the image of the settlers into focus with the story-book Canadian stereotype, projected for more than two centuries as that of the fur-trapper. Usually he himself is clad in fur, is pictured in the snow, far from civilization, and preferably near to native peoples. School-book accounts tell of how he makes a modest living selling his furs at the end of the winter. A lesser known side of the fur trade was part of community life among the Scots in the Eastern Townships, as several individuals ran their farms especially for the fur trade.[43] As a boy and as a young man, Duncan McLeod was well acquainted with the 'fox men' as they were known, for he and his boyhood companions used to enjoy their own small part in feeding locally bred silver foxes:

Well, the Mathesons, they had the big one…1920, that's when Jimmy [Matheson] first got his breeding stock…But when he started his business here in town…people complained. So then he bought this farm about half a mile out the road…Well, he kept say 250 or 300 females, and he had so many males to service them, and then first of all in the spring there would be more, probably 750 to 800, up to a thousand[44]…Then there was Walter MacDonald up in the woods, just above Lois there, he had the second largest. And then there was some who kept just one or two or three.[45]

Well [the furs] were sold out of Montreal fur market, New York, and possibly in the London fur market…Oh, right after the Second World War, oh, 1947, 48 [the bottom dropped out of the market]...Yeah, once in a while I see an article on the silver fox fur...

Well, [to feed them] when we'd catch rabbits we'd bring them to [Jimmy], and he'd give us anywhere from 15 cents to 25 cents...Yeah, we'd trap them with snares...And eh, well, he used to buy meat from the meat packers, the red meat that wasn't fit for humans, I s'ppose. Then there was the 'fox-feed', that's what they called it. It was, eh, I don't know what was into it, but little pellets. But then I used to hear them say that in 1946 or 47 it cost them $45 to feed a fox, and that's all they got for the furs. So that's when they went out of business.

Russell MacIver also recalled snaring rabbits, and very much regarded it as part of the way of life for adolescent boys. He was reminded of a misadventure which, more than sixty years later, amused not only Russell but one of the other 'boys' involved:

We used to set snares for rabbits, and we'd sell the rabbits to the fox men, [usually to Matheson's Silver Fox farm in Milan, about five miles away]. And sometimes an owl would come along and he'd eat half of a rabbit, and we'd set a trap and he'd get caught. And we had two big horned owls at home one day, and Alex Campbell from Dell, he thought he'd like to have them. So he asked if he could have them, and we said 'Yeah, you can have them'. So he took them home and he put them in the hen house, and they killed all the hens! [Laughs!] Last time I saw Alex it was a few years ago, when Danny died...He asked if there was any deals going on with the owls yet! That was about sixty years ago [since the owl incident].[46]

Besides fox farms, Duncan recalled that there were also mink farms, although they operated on a much smaller scale:

[Jimmie Matheson also] had a mink farm, yeah. There was only two of them in Milan that had a mink farm, Jimmy Matheson and the fellow next door to him, Johnny Dan [MacLeod]...I don't remember too much about [how they were kept, but] oh yes, you'd have to have their own quarters [pens].

In addition to commercial ventures, there was generally an opportunity for independent trappers to make a few dollars to supplement the family income. Russell MacIver's family were all keen sportsmen, and as adolescents they not only snared rabbits but also learned to trap small animals:

One winter my father had a box-trap set for weasels[47] — Oh, the fur was worth something — and the weasels'd go in and of course something'd come down on 'em. One day, going to Milan, Murdo [Matheson] was ahead with a team [of horses] and we were behind with the other team. When he came down and he looked in and he yelled *'Tha sguireal agad!'* [laughs 'You have a squirrel.'] So, they let the squirrel go...I used to catch a few of them — a dollar, and a dollar and a half. That was big money you know, for a young fella!

[laughs]…There was a fellow from Sherbrooke used to come around, a fellow Gilman, and then there was another Gilman in Megantic. And they used to make money themselves too. They'd buy hides…Oh they'd call here.

The image of the Canadian hunter, though stereotypical, nevertheless reflects an aspect of life, which, from an early age, became part of the Eastern Townships identity. As may be gathered from the accounts from Duncan and Russell, young boys grew up with an aptitude for hunting. Starting with small game, they quickly progressed to the largest and most exciting possible, learning from their elders how to use guns as easily as they had learned how to snare and trap. One of the main differences between shooting and snaring, however, is the accuracy that is required for marksmanship, whereas snaring and trapping depend more on knowing where to locate the wire-loop snares and the various kinds of traps. In the context of an afternoon visit, Russell MacIver and Duncan McLeod looked back over the years when hunting was not only a way of life, it was also one of the most interesting topics of the *taigh-céilidh*. Sitting around Russell's kitchen table on a summer's afternoon in 1992 may not have been a traditional setting for such a céilidh, especially considering the fact that both men had been well acquainted with customary *céilidhean* of the past. Times had changed, however, and it had been many a year since either of them passed a long winter's evening listening to stories and songs and sharing such anecdotes. Although I asked a few questions, it was not, by any means, an interview situation; it was simply a spontaneous and lively exchange of anecdotes. During the two-hour visit, the two men returned to the topic of hunting no fewer than three times, and I had the impression that if we could have returned on subsequent days or evenings, there would have been no shortage of stories to sustain the interest of an enthusiast.

Duncan: I used to hear that old Rory's father, or Rory himself, with the Indian, Archie Annis,[48] they'd hunt the moose on the snow-shoes all the way between Milan and the mountain. And the moose would play out, floundering around in the snow, and they'd kill it then.

Russell: My grandfather and Wild Alec they used to do that, they'd run the moose down in the deep snow — just cut their throat.

MB: They'd be on snow-shoes themselves?

Russell Oh, yeah.

MB: Who made the snow-shoes?[49]

Russell: Themselves. Some of them were real good at it.

MB: Where did they learn that?

Russell: Oh, just learned it, I guess.

MB: Did they get the idea from the Indians, or the French, or — ?

Duncan: There was Indians in the country in the early days; not many of them, but some; they might have learned it from them.

Russell: I had an uncle, and my gosh he was good with a knife. He used to fix up deer heads; did you ever see any of them?…Well he'd skin the neck and the head, take all the bones out and then make wood that looked like a deer's head, and oh! He was good! D'you want to see one of them heads?

MB: Yes!

Russell: Wait till you see it! Well, c'mon we'll see it.…[MB stops tape to go into adjoining room to see the deer heads. Very impressive. Russell also shows a number of photos; we all return to kitchen to resume conversation]…That deer had an old mark on his foot and he had a scar over his shoulder, and he had a new one on one leg too, and my Uncle Dan MacDonald claimed that he shot it that day or the day before; well, he could have because it had that wound on the leg. But my father could hit them where they should be hit! [Laughs] He was a good shot, and it made no difference if they were on the gallop or standing still. He had what they call an autoloading Remington and it had a peep-sight here [at the top of the barrel] and sight here [in the middle] and a sight down at the end. And he looked through, and he could see it was lined up, it took in the three sights, he didn't have to aim, he could see that — *Bang!* Usually he'd come home and he'd have a whole bunch of partridge tied to his waist — belt — and cut the heads off.

MB: You had plenty to eat then, with him hunting like that?

Duncan: Oh his father was an excellent hunter.

Russell:…Yeah. I remember one time, I didn't see it done, but my Uncle Johnny was fixing up some deer and he used to soak the [skin] — well he made moccasins and everything. To fix up the snowshoes he'd put them in brine, he'd have another pail of brine there, and my grandfather took it out and gave it to the hens. It killed every one of them! [laughs]

MB: Oh, dear me! I hope you ate them!

Russell: Oh, *they* did — I may not have been born then, but — Another time, we used to set snares for rabbits, [Russell tells the anecdote quoted above.]…

MB: You caught the owls alive?

Russell: Yeah. They got trapped .

MB: Oh my, the birds and hens seem to come off rather badly in those stories.

Russell: But salt or brine will kill a hen awful quick, just the least little bit.

The conversation turned to a discussion about the MacIvers' farm. Having lived on it and worked on it for many years, Russell could remember every field and crop, and greatly regretted the decline in farming over the years. He looked back on the days when farming and hunting were their way of life, and recalled the enthusiasm with which his father used to pursue his sport. It is easy to imagine why Russell's father gained his reputation as a skilled hunter:

Russell: We had a hayfield there at that time and then nobody lived there, and we cut hay for quite a few years but then we quit. My father called the farm 'Sportsman's Rest'; and he was quite a sportsman. Oh, yeah. Every fall, the same as Duncan's father they'd go out to Woburn and hunt. There was one fall my father killed around a hundred and thirty deer. You could kill two in anybody's name and then ship them, [i.e. send them by post or by rail to that person]. And he'd go to the Post Office with a list and he'd give it to the post-master. And those that'd come in he'd save them for me; get him to check back, you know, any name at all. There had been a fire went through in the spring, and then by fall oh, there was a lot o green stuff, you know, and the deer just came pouring in. And you could see them up against that black stuff with the green. He said one day he was just standing there and he killed five. Never moved out of his tracks, and before he got home that night he had two more.[50] He had seven, [then he'd] make up some names [for the requirements of the licences]. And then he'd come home with a big sleigh full of deer; he came to Milan and Norman Doak and Norman McLeod, Duncan's father —

Duncan: And George D.A. [MacDonald] and his brother Walter.

Russell: Yeah.

Duncan: I can remember as a kid, eh, on the railway, at the railway station there'd be, oh, two or three, five or six, seven or eight deer ready to be loaded on the first train that came through going to Montreal.

MB: Yes —

Duncan: There was no restrictions on killing deer the way there is today. (MB: Yes.) Well, there might have been restrictions, eh, like he said that you had to have a name to ship them out. But you had to have somebody to buy them from you.[51]

Russell: Johnny Doak, he used to put his father's name on [the shipping tag], and his father never shot a gun in his life! [laughs] But Johnny shot a lot.

MB Yes.

Duncan: He was Ruth's uncle, brother of her father.

Russell: Yes, my father'd come home with a pung sleigh[52] full of them. We couldn't eat em all, he'd give em away, you know. Eat them.

MB: And sell the hides?

Russell: Yeah. And my Uncle John, he'd make up a lot of [stuffed] heads. In that house we had at the farm we had a shed, we had a good shed, and all this way [pointing down the length of the adjacent wall] all deer heads, down that way, and back this way, and that way [indicating the four walls of the room].

MB: All four sides.

Russell: And there were some of them in the velvet yet. Do you know what that is?

MB: Yes.

Russell: And boy, there was some good ones.

MB: I guess it would be OK to have a bit of deer meat now, still. Do you ever get any, any more?

Russell: No, I haven't hunted for a long time.

MB: You used to go hunting yourself too?

Russell: Yeah. I killed a few of them. I never got one of the real big ones. I got some of the ones that —

Duncan: Well, the big ones were all killed by your father and his friends!

Russell: I guess so.

Duncan: By the time you came along there were just small ones left! [laughter]

Russell: Oh, I've seen some big ones, yeah. I never could get them.

Whether or not Russell 'could get them' may never be known, as the men who hunted with him are mostly all gone. In all probability his account of his own skill as a hunter was more in keeping with his reputation for modesty and understatement as well as his wry sense of humour. During our afternoon visit Russell gave the impression that even in his old age hunting and trapping were, in his mind, still a way of life, though perhaps not as necessary to his psychological well-being as it had been for one of his uncles, known locally as *Alec Fiadhaich*, or 'Wild Alec':

Russell: I saw my father, he used [the mechanical seeder] one time when Wild Alec had cleared a spot, and he went West, and my father went up and used the Cyclone Seeder. That was over next to that Mrs MacArthur's farm. My great uncle Alec, they called him 'Wild Alec'.

MB: Why did they call him Wild Alec?

Russell: Oh he was a hunter and a trapper. He used to claim he could put the *buisneach* on somebody! Did you ever hear about the *buisneach*?[53]

MB: I did, yes.[54]

Russell: Laughs] Like, put the *buisneach* on a fellow's cows and they wouldn't give any cream. I never put much stock in that, but you used to hear a lot of stories.

MB: Were people a little wary of that?

Russell: Oh, I don't know.

MB: Did anyone ever put the *buisneach* on someone making butter?[55]

Russell: Oh I've heard doing that, so it wouldn't churn. But those stories, you know, whether there's any truth —

MB: Who knows?

Russell: And that poor old fellow, I think he was about eighty-seven, or eighty-five, one fall, after he was losing his eyesight, and he took a bunch of traps out in a storm to the Black Lake out near Spring Hill [towards Bosta]. The Rosses tried to stop him, but no, he wouldn't stop. He didn't come back, 'n they went looking for him and found him dead in the woods, frozen stiff.

MB: Eight-seven is pretty old to be going trapping.

Russell: Yea, and especially when he was going blind.

MB: Maybe that's the way he wanted to go?

Russell: Oh I suppose, that's just what he'd like. First thing they found was his bag of traps, then they found his hat. And where they found him, he had a hatchet and he had been chipping at a tree, just like he was a little kid, and he was there. [to Duncan:] Were you there then?

Duncan: I was pretty young. But my father took me with the Star car out to Bosta, top of, Bosta Hill. I thought it was Bosta Hill, brought him out of the woods. He put him in the back of the cart, and I rode there with him on the way home. I was only eleven, I guess; 1927.[56]

Russell: Yeah. I remember that fall, we went to his funeral in a pung sleigh, and the next day we went in a cart over to the town line, to Alex Murray's [funeral], you know.

The image of the hunter has always been close to the hearts of the old-timers. It is not, however, in keeping with the modern American image of 'huntin' season', when lines of pick-up trucks topped with gun-racks appear along the backroads in New England and Quebec. To old-timers like Russell MacIver, it was as much a part of family tradition as hunting the *guga* had been for their forebears in Lewis. The Quebecers knew the woods and surrounding territory as well as Nessmen knew the seas around the Butt of Lewis; they knew when to go out, and when to recognize approaching 'white-outs', just as their people had learned to forecast Atlantic gales.[57] Furthermore, a good supply of wild meat ensured a winter of plenty, and if the men enjoyed the sport and the yarns in the *taigh-céilidh*, then all the better. The Old and New World hunters experienced one major difference apart from the size of their quarry: in the New World they enjoyed the kind of freedom to hunt the deer that was afforded only to the landowners of the Scottish Highlands or wealthy European sportsmen.[58] Not even today could it be considered a birthright of disenfranchised crofters who, lacking the considerable wealth required to be able to pay for the privilege of hunting, can only dream of the liberty Russell's people enjoy, or risk severe public prosecution if they transgress the boundaries of their class.

Lumbering

Cutting wood and moving stones was all part of the settlers' farming routine, for without these activities they could neither improve their land or maintain an acceptable degree of self-sufficiency. The ambition of most families, however, was to attain a better standard of living, and this required a steadier income than the summer haying could bring in. As a result, many of the men either operated a small wood-cutting business on their own land or opted for seasonal work in a lumber camp.

The Morrison homestead at Cruvag, Marsboro, for example, had extensive stands of timber, and after they had cut what they needed for house and barn building, they began to work at cutting trees, both for themselves and for other businesses. As a young man, Angus worked in the woods for several years before he and his wife, Mary, moved to Montreal. In 1992, they looked back over the years the family were involved in lumbering before they sold the family farm in 1943. Angus began:

> Anns a' choille? *Well*, bha mise 's mo bhràthair — bha dà bhràthair agam — bhiodh iad a' gearradh na *logaichean*. Bha each agamsa, 's bha each aig mo bhràthair, 's bhiodh sinn a' tarruing na *logaichean*. Bhiodh sinn a' cuir ann am pìl iad. Bha siud mu Shamhainn. 'S an geamhradh nuair a thigeadh an sneachd, bhiodh sinn 'gan tarruing le *sleighichean*. Bhiodh sinn 'gan tarruing ochd mìle 's naoi mìle —

> *[In the woods? Well, my brother and I were — I had two brothers — they would be cutting logs. I had a horse, and my brother had a horse, and we would be hauling logs. We would put them in a pile [cut to measured lengths, and stacked neatly in the woods]. That was around Hallowmas. And in the winter when the snow came, we would be hauling them with a sleigh. We'd be hauling them eight or nine miles —]*

Angus and his brothers took over from their father, R.E., who had already begun to raise their modest standard of living by selling timber to a big company in Megantic which made both paper and boards. As Mary joined in the conversation, Angus reverted to their common language, English, and continued. (Mary's words are included here in italics here):

> Yes, yes, yes — to a company in Megantic. And my father was jobbing for years, jobbing for a company in Megantic, a big lumber company, they had lumber limits all over Marsboro. And my father jobbed for this company for years. We were the first family in Marsboro to buy a car — and a radio. My father bought the car, and my brother bought the radio. *It had a big horn like coming out of it, and* — Earphones.

Canada's timber trade was fed by lumber operators of all sizes, not only in Quebec, but right across the country. Men could get a job in the woods so long as they were willing to work hard and live in spartan conditions. Lumber camps were established in many remote locations, and when word got around that men were needed, either for cutting or for the 'drive', there was no shortage of labour. For a people who claim to have scarcely seen an axe,[59] far less made a living with one, the Hebridean settlers took their places beside the more experienced French-Canadians, and joined crews all over the Eastern Townships, 'down across the line', and into Maine. According to other accounts of Maine lumbercamps, they were manned largely by Canadians from Quebec and the Maritimes.[60] According to Donald Morrison who grew up in Red Mountain and spent most of his adult life in Scotstown, 'at that time, if you were a man, you weren't supposed to be *considered* a man until you'd done either a stint in the woods, on the drive, or you'd worked a couple of years in the quarries in Vermont.'[61]

Training for this 'stint' began early. Even today, young boys scarcely old enough to go to school are taught to swing an axe, and within a very short time, the routine of how to stand, how to hold the axe, how to aim, and how to use it safely all become second nature.[62] Although many young men in the Eastern Townships still work in the woods for a living, 'times have changed' (partly due to mechanization, and partly due to choices in further education) since the days recalled by men of Russell MacIver's generation:

> Yeah, there was a lot at one time. They'd go in the logging camps in the Fall and there was no way they'd get out till the spring. There was a lot o them. My father used to go in and he was head [chief] 'chopper' there. He'd notch a tree, and [the loggers] they'd just come along and look at the notch, and then they'd cut it down, because they wouldn't have to find out where it'd go [i.e. in which direction it would fall]. He had it all figured out where it wouldn't get lodged. There was a French fellow one time, he came home and [we] asked him if he had a good job in the woods. 'Oh yes! I chop head first in the tree all winter!' [laughs]

At this point Russell touches on an aspect of lumbercamp humour that pervades every discussion on the topic. No matter who tells the story, no matter where the lumbercamp happened to be — Quebec or Maine — no matter if the men were felling trees or on the drive, sooner or later an amusing anecdote at the expense of the French-Canadian is told.[63] Like the one told by Russell, the humour is usually based on *double entendre*, either due to a mispronunciation of a word, or an incomplete grasp of English grammar. (Interestingly, Russell did not seem to notice the *double entendre* within his own part of the story — his father was the 'head-chopper'[64]?) It would be too easy to leap to the conclusion that this type of humour is a manifestation of some kind of ethnic put-down, like the Polack, Newfie, Kerry or Teuchter joke, depending upon where it is told. We must also consider the fact that these same people, the Eastern Township 'Gaelickers', (as school-teacher Myrtle Murray called them) told similar jokes about their own people. The scenario is familiar in Scotland, where favourite subjects for these 'jokes' are often elderly Gaelic-speakers unaccustomed to speaking English, who make naive and amusing mistakes; there is an element of warm affection in many of them, just as there is in the re-telling of the amusing linguistic irregularities of small children. While most of these types of jokes can also serve to remind us how illogical English grammar is, seldom do the tellers acknowledge that they notice these idiosyncrasies.[65] Of even less concern to the tellers of lumbercamp jokes is *why* people tell them; lumbercamps aside, why do people tell Auschwitz, Abervan, Space Shuttle or Chernobyl jokes?[66] It is no more because they are pleased that such dreadful disasters happened than because the 'Gaelickers' are pleased that many of the French-Canadians cannot speak fluent English. To a large extent they enjoy the fact that they speak it with such colourful and memorable idiosyncrasies. And like the above categories of 'black humour', the lumbercamp jokes help alleviate some of the tensions generated by the dangerous, arduous work and the inhospitable living conditions.[67] There was, in short, little else to joke about, or to remember with pleasure about the lumbercamp way of life.

Johnnie A. MacLeod from Dell recalled his winters of working in a lumbercamp in the late 1920s. As far as the woodsmen were concerned, he said that logging was a fairly miserable job, whereas there was 'real prestige' attached to the river drive. When Johnnie, a Gaelic-speaker, joined the camp crew, he found that he was the only fluent English-speaker among a crew of eighty-five Frenchmen, all brought in for the woods operation. Regardless of the dominant language in the lumber camp, he was to discover over the years that the routine was fairly standard.[68] They all slept in the one bunkhouse, years later memorable for the bed-bugs, lice, body odour, and stifling atmosphere. 'Day' began when they all had to get up at 3.30 a.m. and go outdoors to eat breakfast of beans, bread, and tea. Then began the work of preparing for the drive by putting pulpwood into the river. At 9 a.m. they stopped for the next meal of the day — beans again. Work resumed immediately, tree after tree after tree, till they stopped for lunch at 2.30 p.m. —

same as breakfast.[69] Back to work then, till nightfall, and the fourth meal of the day, a welcome plate of boiled beef and potatoes, which was eaten at the camp, again outdoors. Back in the bunkhouse, and in spite of their fatigue, the men enjoyed their own entertainment of songs, stories, jokes and the occasional fiddle tune and step-dance. It was their only respite from a hard, unsafe, stressful and often lonely way of making a living. Despite the warmth from the bunkhouse stove, they often went to bed wet, and always with their clothes on.

Decades later, Johnnie Bard still exchanged lumbercamp stories with friends, such as the ones that he wrote in his unpublished manuscript, *Memoirs of Dell*: 'Joe Leblanc tol'' about 'my fadder was two years a policeman an' a haf', and another man used to like to speak about his horse, saying things like 'You tro' de hors' over de fence som' hay'.[70] It was only stories like these that made life more bearable.

Nevertheless, the stereotypical image of the Canadian lumberman reflects none of this discomfort to the world in general. He is still seen as the epitome of the outdoorsman — strong, tough, healthy and happy. Young men were, and are, still attracted to the life, ever hoping for adventure and wealth as they set out for camp. For some families, however, one man's winter in the lumberwoods brought no financial rewards, but instead cost them dearly. Inevitably, tragedy struck, and many a young man was 'cut down in his prime', as the songs tell it. Incidents and individual are remembered long after their generation has passed away. Russell and Duncan continue:

Russell: And that used to be a long winter too.

MB: Oh I bet. When would they go in — October or November?

Russell: Oh, at the first cold weather.[71]

MB: And they wouldn't get out till when? [pause] April or May?

Russell: Yeah. And then some of them'd stay for the drive on the water [when the ice broke]. There's a first cousin of my grandfather MacIver, Donald MacIver, same name, he came over from Loch Garvaig, and he just came over in time to go on the drive in spring. And he went up to Connecticut. He didn't know anything at all about handling and stuff, you know, and he got drowned. He's buried in the MacIver cemetery. He was thirty years old. He was a nice fellow, strong and healthy. But there's quite a knack in handling them logs in the water.

MB: I bet.

Russell: There's some fellas could walk on them, and drive them, and ride them down the river. 'Course there's a lot of them got drowned too.

MB: Yes, they had dangerous work.

Russell: Yeah.

MB: Were there many accidents felling them? — cutting them?

Russell: Oh sometimes. Cutting the trees? Yeah, there was a Tormod Matheson…he got killed by a tree.

Duncan: I think it's marked on the gravestone that he was killed by a falling tree.

Russell: And I think there was, there's maybe a Beaton in the MacIver cemetry there got killed by a tree, a young fella. He was out with MacKenzie in Marsboro. Oh there's quite a few.

MB: A hard life.

Russell: Yeah.

Duncan: That was, eh, a lot of people went down across the line into Maine to work in the woods. There was more men went down there than there was here, I think.

Russell: Oh yes.

Duncan: And then down what they call the Connecticut River, eh, down through New Hampshire. The Connecticut Valley Lumber Company was quite a big outfit there.

Alex MacIver recalled the attraction of the river drive in 1935. Although he did not work in any of logging camps doing the 'miserable job' of getting the trees to the river, he joined the next stage of the work: *'When I was nineteen I used to hire on for the log drives. And some of the drivers were younger than that. You'd pack your lunch and work for ten cents an hour for ten hours a day.'[72] After he married Jean MacKenzie, daughter of Christie and John, they both moved to Maine where Alex became pumpman for the railway steam engines at Holeb. 'Once you were in there, that was you — you couldn't get out till next spring,' Jean added. Both Gaelic-speakers, when I recorded them in 1992 they were among the very few who were still completely fluent and using Gaelic on a daily basis. In both jobs, Alex found himself as much in the company of Gaelic-speakers as he had been at home in Quebec. 'Oh, yes, everything was in Gaelic.' He joked about 'one fellow who used to pretend he did not speak Gaelic,' projecting the notion that superior beings spoke English. 'He tried to let on that he couldn't remember it!' Jean, added 'I'm sure he must have heard it all his life at home, the same we did.'

Alex regarded Gaelic songs and stories as central to life in the lumbercamp bunkhouse as they had been in the *taigh cèilidh*, where, as children, they had gathered with their parents and grandparents. Whether at camp or at home, the songs, poems, rhymes, riddles, proverbs, jokes, stories and witty remarks of the *taigh cèilidh* (see Chapter 5) were dear to the heart of every Gael, who, for generations, regarded them as vital to the perpetuation of language and culture.[73]

The days of the river drives are over, however, and though there are extensive woods operations of felling and hauling in the Eastern Townships and beyond, huge machinery does the work of teams of men, and the television has taken over from the singers and storytellers. Today, the yarns of the old-timers are relegated to summer afternoons on the front porch, the kitchen or occasionally the Hotel. As Russell remarked, he is often reminded by the media, and by the huge, heavily-laden trucks that drive through the Townships, that lumbering was essential to the economy of most families, and was not just the monopoly of a few well-heeled contractors as it is today: 'I saw them on television this summer. I think it was the Gatineau River; they made the last log drive there…down at Trois Rivières…'

Railroad Work

Aside from seasonal work on the drive, there was a steady, local market for railroad 'ties' [sleepers], especially in the village of Milan which is said to be the highest village east of the Rockies on the Canadian Pacific Railway line. No visitor can fail to notice the line that cuts through the top of the village, as every train that goes through blows a long, loud whistle that stops every conversation for its duration. I have tape recordings that are suddenly interrupted by 'There she blows!' or 'Count the coaches! Count the waggons!' Even in the middle of her baking, Ruth Nicolson would stop, go to her window to watch, and smile with pleasure as the train whizzed through. 'My, that always makes me lonesome,' she remarked on a summer's day in 1993, reflecting on the fact that everybody in Milan looked on the railway as important to the village. To Ruth, her 'lonesome' feeling reflected a nostalgia for the ever-busy way of life she knew as a younger woman, and also the many times she had stood with her children and grandchildren counting over a mile of boxcars in the heyday of the railway.

Myrtle Murray's first impresion of Milan Station gives a striking impression of the vitality of the community in the 1920s, and of the importance of the railway to the entire village :

> The first time I got off the mail train, the night before our school was to start, here was this sea of faces, mostly men, but some girls, at the CPR station at Milan. And I thought 'Good Heavens! What are they doing here?'…The younger and freer ones, but men too, came to meet the mail train. They all arranged themselves on the platform, and as you came out [of the train] you looked over the sea of faces. If I had my life to live again, I'd teach school among the Scotch![74]

Myrtle was to discover that meeting the train was a regular pastime, and had been so since the railway first went through Milan. According to Duncan McLeod whose family moved into the area in the late 1870s while discussions on the railway route were going on: 'When the survey crew was going through they had three possible routes and the one where it is now is the central one…the most feasible is where they are at the present time.' And for Duncan's grandfather, Duncan Lewis McLeod, already established in a 'toting business' [transporting merchandise] near Tolsta, in the township of Winslow, the coming of the railway was the main factor in his decision to move to Milan. There he set up a new business, operating under the name of D.L. McLeod, which has been well-known throughout the area for over a century.

> Well, the store was started in 1877 by my grandfather. He had been in business over in the Winslow area, and when he heard that the Trans-Continental Railway was being extended from the Sherbrooke area east to Lake Megantic, and when he knew that they were going to come through some area in the Milan area, he and another man went over there and staked out a claim to some land. He built a store and he built a home for his family, and also it was used for a number of years as a hotel public rooms in Milan, that's when there was nothing but the railway going through there.

Christie MacKenzie's family, already in the area, recorded the fact that 'it was in 1879 the railroad came through Milan,' and although her father did not work on the actual construction, the whole township was affected by it. For many families the choice of route offered an opportunity to earn extra cash while living at home. Men who did not work on the line were generally employed in the woods, felling timber to be hauled to the sawmill, or in the mill sawing logs into eight-foot long railway 'ties'. Russel MacIver continues:

> And they used to make a little money too. When the CPR was going through here they'd cut ties for the CPR. Oh they didn't make much money but they got a little bit. And near Sherbrooke, and they're still up there — once in a while you can see the top of a tree that had been squared and left the top [lying on the ground after they'd cut a number of 8-foot sections], maybe that much, you know, when they used to level so many feet and then cut it off.

There was extra work for carpenters, as the village expanded to include two hotels, McLeod's, which was a temperance hotel, and a second one which was not. Farmers who sold cattle would ship them from Milan Station, just across from McLeod's store, and often had to spend the night in the village. Duncan continued 'Well, when we built the building that's there now I guess anybody going through *had* to stay overnight if they missed the train service.'

Memories of a community that once buzzed with activity contrast sharply with the present day village where trains no longer stop, but whizz through several times a day. Muriel Mayhew, whose home was a short distance from the station, remarked on the fact that the village was busy enough to support two hotels: 'That was because the drovers were coming through with the cattle, from one place going to another — they had to stay overnight, at a hotel.'

To the children of the village, there was never any shortage of excitement. Duncan reflected on times spent as a boy when he and his friends would go 'just across the track from where I lived' to the railway platform:

> I remember when we were kids I used to, like on Friday afternoons, when people'd drive their sheep and their calves and cows and we'd go and help them — especially the sheep! You know Christie Belle MacArthur?...she was the first woman I ever saw with rubber boots on!

For years after the line was established, tree-felling continued to be vital to the economy, as Milan became one of the main shipping stations for the area. D.L. McLeod expanded his business and became agent for the export of timber. To this day, local men 'who could swing an axe with the best of them' are recalled with admiration. Duncan continues:

> With the broad axe, eh, I know my grandfather used to buy birch, squared birch, and that used to be shipped overseas to Europe. And they squared it because they could get one or two more logs in than if they left them in the round. And some of the fellows there, Christie MacKenzie's father, *Iain Beag Donn,* he was one of the best, and he was the smallest man in the town there.

Lumbering was a way of life, with mills of all sizes springing up all over the Eastern Townships. The hours were long, and the men would look forward to the end of the week, when they could enjoy the freedom from the camp and time to socialize. Muriel's father George MacDonald, who grew up in Stornoway, was Duncan's source of the following story:

> He used to tell me about when he was a young man he worked in a sawmill at Reedsville which was a town about half way between Stornoway and Spring Hill. It was named after a Mr Reed who owned the sawmill and he was doing a bit of lumbering in that area. He used to tell me he worked ten hours a day, six days a week, but on Saturdays they got off an hour early and they'd walk to Stornoway which would be six miles, I suppose, and they had their pay — I don't remember he ever told me how much they earned in those days, but — A lot of fellows were drinkers; they'd head right for the hotel, and they'd buy a tumbler full of whisky for ten cents, and you could buy the whole bottle for a dollar. But they probably didn't have more than two or three dollars a week pay, so there weren't too many [men] that bought the bottle, but a lot of them were going by the glass.

No-one denies that there were several family heart-aches caused by the Saturday night sprees, and while little is mentioned of the women waiting and wondering, much is made of the fact that it was 'a man's world' and, rough as it might be, 'a stint in the woods, on the drive, or a couple of years in the quarries in Vermont' were all part of that world.

Quarrying

To work in a quarry, it was not actually necessary to 'cross the line' into Vermont, as there were quarries in the Eastern Townships. No doubt the idea of going to the States, where wages were higher, appealed to many of the young men, some of whom married and settled there. It was dangerous work, no matter where it went on, and despite safety precautions, fatalities happened. The one that is best remembered is that of a young man from Scotstown, Peter MacRae, who was killed in the Scotstown quarry. His death is generally recalled in the context of discussions on second sight, and accounts of it can still be heard at informal storytelling sessions, such as evolve during a visit, or cèilidh. Sitting by Ruth's kitchen stove in 1991, Duncan McLeod spoke of 'an old fellow by the name of AD Morrison' who was reputed to have had second sight:

> The day that [Peter MacRae] was killed, he walked into the post office on his way to work, and the AD [sic] was in there talking to the postmaster, Jack Scott, and he saw a halo around Peter's head. And after Peter stepped outside he told Jack that there was going to be a death, a tragedy of some sort...I don't know what his job classification was, but he worked in a quarry, and he was down in the lower depths of the quarry when a stone, a loose stone, hit him on the head and killed him.

Duncan's story is very similar to one told fifteen years earlier by Bill Young of Lennoxville, who mentioned no names when he reported a stange encounter that turned out to be a forerunner of an accidental death:

> There was a fellow walking home one night from Scotstown out to Lingwick road where he lived. Now, I think he was sober; he never had a record of being inebriated. And right on the road, just outside the town limit, he stopped — he heard a train coming, and, you know, the railroad runs on the other side of the river, and he thought, 'Oh, it's a train.' But he looked down, and he couldn't see the track. Suddenly this train went right by in front of him, right on the road! What that meant or not, nobody knows, but it was only a month later than that, his brother was killed in a quarry, eh. That happened right up the quarry road. This train came out of the quarry, and he swore to it. He swore to it.

Where possible, the granite was split by hammering in various wedges along joints which occur naturally in the rock. In order to extract or fracture enormous sections of granite, gunpowder was used. Apart from the blasting operations for which the workers needed to learn specialized skills, many of the men who worked in the quarries had learned the techniques of splitting rocks during their land-clearing operations.[75] Rock drills, wedges and 'feathers', which were the tools of the trade, can still be seen in antique shops or at local auctions. To the men who actually used them, however, they represented heavy labour, sweat and toil. Johnnie 'Bard' MacLeod recalls how they used these same implements to break up enormous boulders on their farm:

> We would drill holes in it and split it. We borrowed drills, feathers, wedges and hammers. When the drills got dull we would take them by horse and buggy to Milan, to James MacKenzie, the blacksmith to have them sharpened. Papa would sit on the rock and turn the drill after each wollop. We used two hammers, [my brother] Donald and myself striking alternately[76]

Quarrying in is no longer in operation in Scotstown, though the towns of St. Sebastien and Lac Drolet still have huge operations that have adopted more modern, and hopefully safer, methods of work.

Milling

The year's crops would scarcely be harvested when autumn, with its blaze of red maples, would appear. With daylight beginning later each day, and the air becoming clearer and crisper, time was of the essence in preparing for the winter that might set in as early as the beginning of October. Farmers would usually arrange to have their grain crops threshed by one of the threshing-machines that did the rounds of farms in the district. On threshing day, all hands were required to help, and, as Ferne Murray recalled, during her childhood in Marsboro, it was not only those on the field who were busy, but 'the women would also have spent days cooking and baking. Sometimes they had to feed as many as eighteen or twenty helpers on threshing day.[77] At the end of the day, the family would be all set for their annual visit to the meal-mill, or 'grist-mill' as it was called locally.

For nearly a century and a half the name 'Legendre' has been synonymous with milling in the Eastern Townships. As already mentioned in Chapter 2, the Legendre brothers had their first saw-mill built in 1853 by a Lewisman, Donald S. McLeod, who was, in those days, well-known for his skill as a mill-wright. According to Ellen Legendre (born 1897), daughter of the first Legendre, a retired nurse whom I interviewed in 1976, the first grist-mill was built in 1862. The site was fairly close to the family home, by the Legendre River, the source of power for all their mills, and although the first grist-mill burned down in 1883, it was rebuilt on the same site.[78]

This was not the only grist-mill in Stornoway, however, as Russell MacIver recalleds that 'there was another one just as you got into Stornoway on this side — Layfield, he owned that for a long time.' The second mill was built by

Layfield & Palister in 1857, at a time when there was enough business to keep two mills going in the Stornoway area. The Legendre family were eventually to gain monopoly of the milling business, however, as the Layfield & Palister mill, which first changed hands in 1914, was bought by Alphonse Legendre in 1929.[79]

Alphonse's daughter, Ellen, described her recollections of the days when their grist-mill was in great demand. They produced several kinds of flour according to what customers requested: barley, buckwheat, wholewheat, and occasionally rye. She remarked that the wholewheat flour of modern times, formerly known as 'graham flour', does not compare with that of earlier days which was milled with more of the germ and bran left in the flour than in more recent commercial products. Of the two most common flours, barley and buckwheat, the French people preferred to have buckwheat while the Scots liked both.[80] Ellen's brother Alphonse, locally called 'Pit' [written thus, and pronounced like 'Pete'], who had spent many years working in the grist-mill, recalled some aspects of its operation.

They kept several different kinds of grinding-stones, each set for its own special purpose: one set for barley, one for buckwheat, one for wheat, one for oats, and another for cattle and pig feed, which was usually milled from oats. The stones themselves were made of very hard granite, which Pit thought might have come from Vermont, rather than from local quarries — 'it might have been shipped by train to Quebec.' The method of making mill-stones was apparently well-known in Lewis before the first emigrants set sail, as Lewis historian Donald MacDonald noted that, not only were the skills exported with some of the men, but a mill-stone was sent from Lewis to Megantic.[81] To this day, the nickname *A' Muillear*, as in the family of Johnnie MacKenzie, *Seonaidh A' Muillear*, still testifies to the trade of his forefathers.[82]

On closer examination of these massive mill-stones, it can be seen that a series of grooves have been cut into them, giving the illusion that the actual mill-stone is composed of wedges..[83] The grooves are, however, cut into a solid piece of stone in order to give 'bite' to the grinding surface as the stone turns . A great deal of care had to be taken in using the mill-stones, as failure to adjust them properly for the amount of grain being used meant unnecessary wear on the grinding surfaces. Most of the business was in producing flour, though occasionally they were asked to make buckwheat groats.[84] As Pit said, 'All they had to do for that is to not to put the two stones too close together, so it wouldn't crush the grain [more than was required for the groats].'

Through experience, the Legendres perfected their methods of production.[85] Barley flour could be ground coarse, medium, or fine, according to the request of the individual customer, but buckwheat flour was always the same. Pit said that 'there should be no black specks in it,' for their presence indicated that the miller had the stones too close, or 'too sharp — if the stone is too sharp, it will cut the buckwheat, and that's what will make those little black spots. If it goes through the screens it will be in the flour.'

This was to prove to be a very significant statement which would explain a frequent comment about 'little black specks' [Chapter 6 will take this up again] It also showed that the Legendres had perfected the method of milling which pleased the taste of their Scotch customers. When the grist-mill closed down — 'Il cessa de servir en 1945 quand les cultivateurs cessèrent de semer des grains' — the Legendre mill was greatly missed.[86] Fifty years on, it is still regarded as a loss to the surrounding communities, where the taste for good buckwheat flour has not lessened in the least, for, try as they may, the devotees of the old-style milling cannot seem to find any buckwheat that compares to the Legendre milling.[87] People send for miles around, each time hoping that a new source will measure up to their expectations, but so far the Legendres have no rivals.[88] Local people have come to refer to the product they buy today, ('it's full of little black specks'), as 'French buckwheat'. While it is certainly true to say that it is grown and milled in Quebec, that was not a term familiar to Ellen Legendre in 1976. As far as her family was concerned, the milling process was the same for Scotch and French Canadians customers alike. In 1992, when trying to locate a supply of the 'old-style' buckwheat flour, Ruth Nicolson commented that the type of buckwheat plant, or species, greatly affected the final product: 'The one is the *silver-hull* — that's the French buckwheat and the texture isn't the same; it's more of a floury type, the silver-hull. And the other is the *beech-nut*…but I may not be able to get any now.'

Until the end of the Second World War, people travelled to the Stornoway mill from villages as far away as Milan, Dell, Scotstown, Gould, Victoria, as well as from Marsboro, only five miles away. Christie MacKenzie from Milan remembered when a trip to the mill was part of the family's annual preparation for winter, as it was for most families. Here, her husband, John, who grew up in Marsboro, supplemented her description by adding a few comments (shown here in italics):

> Well, we used to raise our own barley flour, and our own buckwheat flour — take it to the mill. We had to drive all the way from Milan to Stornoway when I was growing up. And we'd have a barrel of the barley flour, and maybe a barrel of the buckwheat flour. Oh boy, that'd be a sled full of bags, and then the flour was gotten into some bags, and the outside of the grain. — *[The middlings and the shorts were]* — was kept for the cattle — *[coarser, would be for feed]*.[89] Oh, it was very nice, and fine — white. We always used to get it very nice. I seen some of it since I, we've been here in Scotstown that you'd buy, that would have the black specks in. We used to call it the 'French buckwheat'. It wasn't as nicely done as they used to do it. And the barley flour the same — lovely.

In Victoria, near Scotstown, Russell MacIver had similar memories. From a Gaelic-speaking family though unable to speak Gaelic himself, he shared the admiration of most of the community that the Stornoway millers were totally tri-lingual: 'And those old Legendres, they could talk Gaelic just as good as anybody else. And the second generation and the third generation they could talk a little.'

From all accounts, the Legendres had a very good relationship with the Gaels, as there are many warm-hearted memories of going to their mill. As Isobel Stewart of Dell put it: 'Oh, they were lovely people.' Isobel's neighbour, Johnnie 'Bard' MacLeod, also shared the community's esteem for the Legendres, but one childhood memory convinced him that there was more to cultural understanding than language alone. He recalled that even though the family had to rise very early for the annual fifteen mile trip to the mill, so that they would be there by nine o'clock, 'the boys loved it.' One year, however, they reached Stornoway only to find everyone dressed in their Sunday best. Unknown to them, it was All Saints' Day, a Catholic holiday, and no work could be done, so they had to go all the way back home to Dell and return the next day.[90]

Payment for milling grains in those days was, like many business transactions of the time, on an exchange system. For every load milled, an agreed percentage was left with the Legendres, who in turn had a market outside the area. As a child, this way of doing business was always a great mystery to Ellen, who later found it amusing that she took so long to realize just how the system worked: 'I always wondered why keep a mill going if they didn't pay! But they'd measure so much for each bag...we'd keep that for ourselves.' This system of payment was by no means unique to the Legendres, as it has been common in Scotland for many centuries. Peter Ellis of the National Trust for Scotland mill in Angus explains:

> A mill has stood on the site of the Barry Mill since at least 1539...it used to be said that all roads lead to the mill...Historically, at a mill, no money would have changed hands but payment in kind, and the miller would have extracted his toll, or 'multure' which normally amounted to 1/6th by volume of the grain...Once the miller has extracted his 'multure', the remaining grain would have been milled into the meal required by the customer.[91]

Though the Legendre mills had closed many years before I interviewed Ellen in 1976, she still recalled with pleasure the autumn days when they operated at full capacity:

> I can remember when there were teams and teams at the grist mill there, and there were also teams that would come to the carding mill at the same time, but they weren't able to go back home the same day — they'd sleep here. And the good Scotch people had barley scones. And father would invite them to the house, and they'd be with us, and they'd give us the barley scones, and we'd enjoy those. I remember that very well.

Twenty years later, Duncan McLeod recalled 'the old people' talking of when they would have to wait to have their grain milled. It became a social occasion, a day out, and more than that for some people, as there would be so many teams of horses lined up, that many of them would not get home till the next day.

Carding Mills

As well as operating timber and grist mills, the Legendre family had a carding mill, also water-powered, which served Stornoway and the surrounding communities in much the same way as the other mills. According to Ellen, the carding mill was built in 1862. A brief history is given in *Stornoway 1858/ 1983*, which states:

> Les premiers moulins à carde et à foulon furent construits en même temps que le premier moulin à farine à même la maison des frères Legendre peu après leur arrivée en 1853. Après l'incendie, ils seront reconstruits en 1883 et cesseront de fonctionner vers 1950.[92]
>
> [*The first carding and fulling mills were built at the same time as the first grist mill beside the home of the Legendre brothers a little after their arrival in 1853. After the fire, they would be rebuilt in 1883 and would cease operation around 1950.*]

When I first visited the Legendres it had been only about twenty-five years since this mill beside their family home ceased to operate. Once in great demand, the carding mill is also remembered by all the older generation who had dealings with it. Also by the Legendre River, the mill still has a large water wheel that once powered the two carding machines inside. The equipment for the mill came from the United States, and, according to Pit Legendre, in its day was the biggest and best equipment available.[93] The carding machines consisted of a number of drums, about three feet wide, which rotated against one another when the machine was set in motion. The drums were clothed with small, curved metal teeth, similar to those on the hand cards, but set in leather instead of wood, so that they could be easily replaced when worn out by simply winding on new cladding. There were two exceptions among these drums: the first drum of the series, situated at the back, had large metal spikes, about an inch and a half long, and it was called the picker. The final drum of the series, situated at the front where the carded wool came out, was clothed in velvet, and was called the 'doffer'. The picker did the work of teasing the wool as it entered the machine to be carded, and it could be removed from the machine at this stage if anyone wished to have the wool for a quilt batting rather than for spinning.[94] The majority of it, however, went through the entire process, and when it came off the doffer, which was always kept sprinkled with water to make sure it was smooth, the rolls were long and fluffy, and ready for the next stage in the process, which was spinning. (see Chapter 8)

Wood-Carving and Snowshoe-Making

The oft-quoted phrase 'A woman's work is never done' tends to create an impression of men whose hands become idle the moment dusk falls and they can no longer work out of doors. Meanwhile, the women continue to attend to all the domestic chores that are indeed never-ending, and when they finally do sit down, it is not without knitting, sewing or darning needles, or the likes, in hand. No doubt there were, and are, domestic scenes that fit the stereotype, but equally, there is plenty of evidence that many of the men had hands that were far from idle. In every kitchen can be seen examples of work that would fit Russell MacIver's expression, 'my gosh he was good with a knife.' Such impressive skill was probably quite characteristic of the earliest Hebridean emigrants, since a similar observation was made by Martin Martin as far back as 1695: 'Some of the Natives are very dextrous in engraving Trees, Birds, Deer, Dogs, etc., upon Bone, and Horn, or Wood, without any other Tool than a sharp-pointed Knife.'[95]

Aside from the highly-skilled carpenters in the Eastern Townships who are remembered for their meticulous work in the home and on the farm, most of the men would 'turn a hand' to maintenance work and small woodwork projects.[96] In Aunt Annie's kitchen, for example, one only needed to pull out the cutlery drawer to see this: there was a variety of wooden utensils, such as hand-carved spoons and spatulas of different shapes and sizes, each with its own use.[97] There was one little gadget which was neither spoon nor spatula, which Muriel informed me was her mother's syrup-stirrer. It was only six inches long, handcarved, and shaped like a little spade, complete with a 'hole-in-the middle' handle. Next door, in Mary MacLeod's kitchen, was another unique range of well-used utensils, including a doughnut-lifter that had been made for her by a neighbour. It was about fifteen inches long, fashioned rather like a fencing sword, but entirely of wood, and perfect for the job: when held by the handle, its shaft was long enough to keep the cook's hand a safe distance from the extreme heat, and the pointed end could single out a cooked doughnut to lift it out of the hot fat, while the guard at the top of the shaft prevented it from rolling onto the handle and burning the hand that held it. Not only ingenious, but also decorative, the handle of the doughnut-lifter was carved from a single piece of wood, and had a two-link chain that was used for hanging it up after use. It was this feature that attracted me to enquiring further, as it seemed to display skill and care that were well beyond the basic requirements of a functional kitchen utensil.

The ability to carve chain-links out of a solid block of wood requires geometrical precision, concentration and skill that would test any craftsman.[98] Referring to the examples of wood-carving I had seen, I asked Russell MacIver 'Was there much of that?' Enthusiastically he replied:

> Oh, yes! that's about all I ever saw! There was two [very skilled wood-carvers] anyway. There was one [example] hanging in Duncan's store for a long time, and it was a cousin of mine that made that — Murdo Matheson. By gee, that was fine work and all. [How did they do it?] Oh, jack knife. Took a long piece of wood and you had chain lengths [that were carved out of this one piece, without join or break]. And [just for an interesting variation], you had one place and you had a little 'house' [?cage] like, with a ball loose in that, on a swivel. He [Murdo Matheson] was good with a knife. Boy![99]

Duncan McLeod was able to tell Russell what happened to the wooden chain that had so often been admired in the family store, and recalled a second example of Murdo Matheson's work which he later showed to me:

> That one, the long one — it's Bernice [Laurila, née MacDonald] who has that, Ruth's sister up in Nipigon, Ontario. He [Murdo] took a six foot length of white birch, and when he'd finished the chain, the chain measured seven feet two inches...The chain that he gave my father measured about three feet. He was going right along when he hit a knot in the wood and it broke off there, so he gave it to my father.

'He was a woodsman and he was a cook,' Russell continued, 'and a little while like that, he'd work. One winter my father had a box-trap set for weasels...' and without pausing to draw breath, Russell went on to tell the anecdote that is already quoted above. Such was his style, that for every discussion on a serious or practical subject, Russell would have an amusing story to tell. There would be no hint to the listener that Russell was about to light up the conversation with one of his stories, as his facial expression would remain serious until well into the story. With only a faint suggestion that his eyes were beginning to smile, he would complete his story and laugh.

Continuing his conversation about the weasel and the fact that 'a fellow Gilman...used to...buy hides...' (quoted above), I asked Russell if he ever cured any of those hides himself.[100] The flow of the conversation reflects how seamlessly Russell is able to weave in his amusing anecdotes:

> Russell: No, I never did.

> MB: And was it deer-hide that they used to put in the snow-shoes?

> Russell: Yeah.

> MB: Did they just use it green [uncured]?

Russell: It was pretty strong stuff, that deer-hide, and they'd slice it into laces. Oh, I've seen my uncle make it.

MB: Did he have a special wood for the frame? [repeated]

Russell: Oh, I don't know. I think it was hardwood anyway. I suppose it may be maple or birch.

Duncan: And beech — beech would bend, you know.

MB: And then just thread them up with strips of hide.

Bill Young had told me that the Gaels originally learned snow-shoe-making techniques from the French-Canadians. When he was growing up 'they would soak the cow-hide first, then do the lattice work with the wet strips, and when it dried the tension would be suitably tight.' At the MacIver family homestead in Victoria, 'Sportsman's Rest', Russell recalled tha there was never any shortage of deerskin to use:

> I had a great uncle, John MacIver, he married a, I think she was part Indian — of course she had no Gaelic — and there was a bunch of 'em making snow shoes, and they were talking away there, and *bròan sneachda* — you've heard the name *brògan sneachda*?

MB: Brò — ? No? [not sure if heard correctly]

Russell: No? Well that's snow-shoe in Gaelic.

MB: *Brògan sneachda!* Oh yes, yes!

Russell: And they were talking away there — '*Brògan sneachda, brògan sneachda* — ' Well she woke up [having dozed off in her chair], she says 'Who broke his neck?' [laughs][101]

Despite the fact that Russell claimed not to speak Gaelic — 'Well…my mother made up her mind that we'd speak English when we went to school so we didn't learn Gaelic. Well, that was a mistake; a bad one too — ' Russell had enough Gaelic to allow him to enjoy such jokes which rely upon word play between the two languages.

Having seen most of the twentieth century, Russell and his contemporaries witnessed enormous changes. Gone are the days of gruelling, hard work, of mending and making do, of communal labour that involved neighbours regardless of the language they spoke. Everyone completely understood the importance of co-operation within their community. Over the years the standard of living has increased far beyond the original hopes of the first settlers. Perhaps it is not quite as high as that of their wealthier neighbours 'across the line'; nevertheless the standard of living far surpasses the crofter-fisherman level that those who have travelled to the 'Old Country' have seen when visiting their ancestral island. As far as the old-timers are concerned, however, money had little to do with it, for, as Russell pointed out, he receives more in government pension in the 1990s than he ever did when he worked for his living and earned a wage. Scarcely a conversation about the 'old days' goes by without someone expressing regret at the passing of an era, when 'making a living' was synonymous with community cohesion and vitality.

Notes

1. There is a photo of an ox used by the Legendre brothers for hauling wood to their saw-mill. See *Stornoway 1858-1983*, p. 15.

2. There seems to be no discrimination between a *rock* and a *stone*. Both can be little or enormous.

3. *Stornoway.* p. 32.

4. In his book, *The Past in the Present*, Arthur Mitchell describes Hebridean people using carts without wheels for the removal of stones from fields. Initially Mitchell thought it a peculiar practice, but he quickly saw that it was the only way of coping with the terrain on which they were working; see p. 97. Also, I.F. Grant writes about 'slypes' which were used to drag stones from fields; *Highland Folkways*, p. 204, and though the name is not known in Quebec, her description and the sketch of a 'slype' are closest to what Russell MacIver described. See Fig. 65, p. 283.

5. Fences and their importance to the landscape in Canada and America have been widely researched. See Harry Symons, *Fences*; George E. Harney, *Barns, Outbuildings and Fences*; T.S. Buie, 'Rail Fences' in *American Forests*, (Oct., 1964), pp. 44 - 46; Douglas Leechman, 'Good Fences Make Good Neighbours' in *Canadian Geographical Journal*, (Oct., 1966), pp. 467 - 496; Eugene C. Mather and John F. Hart. 'Fences and Farms', in *The Geographical Review*, (April 1954), pp. 201 - 223; and Vera V. Via, 'The Old Rail Fence', in *Virginia Cavalcade*, (Summer, 1962), pp. 33-40. On the same subject, Catherine Parr Traill writes these 'zig-zag fences of split timber…are very offensive to my eye,' and she laments the fact that everything is done by 'the most practical method, with little regard for beauty.' See *Backwoods*, p. 56.

6. Stone walls are relatively common in New England, probably for similar historical reasons rather than for practical ones. In the Bluegrass area of Kentucky, a wealthy farmer, of English background, had his slaves build a stone wall reminiscent of the style he knew in England, with upright, diagonal capping stones; see H. Glassie, *Pattern in the Material Folk Culture of the Eastern United States*, pp. 99-100.

7. In Newfoundland, 1972, I was shown a picture postcard of a wall built around the turn of the century which was later demolished by road-makers.

8. The most remarkable examples of these are to be found between Stornoway and Nantes (formerly Spring Hill); the farms are all owned by French farmers today.

9. The omission of mutton is deliberate, as will be seen in the next chapter.

10. In 'Diet and Social Movements in American Society: The Last Two Decades' (*Food in Change*, pp. 26-33). Mahadev L. Apte and Judit Katona-Apte discuss the increasing awareness of 'ethnic foods' and the general change in 'food behaviour'.

11. Several of the early Canadian settlers, including C.P. Traill and David Kennedy, refer to growing buckwheat.

12. Henry Stephens, *The Book of the Farm Detailing the Labours of the Farmer, Farm-Steward, Ploughman, Shepherd, Hedger, Farm-Labourer, Field-Worker, and Cattle-Man*, p. 255.

13. Geoffrey Grigson, *The Englishman's Flora*, pp. 251-252. Despite his title, Grigson includes references to works from Scotland, Ireland and Wales.

14. This region borders with Quebec and shares many similarities in climate, landscape, and soil type.

15. G. Grigson, op cit, p. 252. The *Oxford English Dictionary* gives 1548 as the date of its appearance, and states that the 'seed in Europe is used as food for horses, cattle, and poultry; in North America its meal is made into buckwheat cakes.' [O.E.D.] As far as Canada is concerned, however, buckwheat cakes, made with yeast, do not fit the description of food made in Quebec. See also Marjorie Tallman, 'Buckwheat cakes', *Dictionary of American Folklore*, p. 41.

16. *The Canadian Encyclopedia*, vol. I, p. 235. Manitoba produces 85 per cent, and Quebec 15 per cent of Canada's crop, which, in 1981 was estimated to be 53,000 tons, valued at $20.5 million. About two-thirds of it is exported.

17. From the Elizabeth Russell Papers, Toronto Public Library, edited by Innis, p. 6.

18. See Stephens, op cit, above reference.

19. In September, 1976 I took part in a day's threshing at Paul and Julia Doerflers's farm, where beans were one of the crops put through the threshing machine. A variety of kidney beans, they had been left to dry on their 'bushes' and the entire plant was pulled up and threshed.

20. Within my own family on Skye, there were at least ten cousins, some of them small children, who would be expected to help with the planting. We were each given our instructions for the day, and, following the adults, made our contribution to the planting. Families who had fewer members relied on the help of neighbours.

21. Comparative beliefs, see Richard M. Dorson, *Buying the Wind*, pp. 118-124.

22. In *The Book of the Farm*, Henry Stephens describes turnip cultivation methods in great detail, (pp. 149-158) but makes no mention of eating the young plants.

He recommends that the thinnings should be left on the field and used as 'green manure'. Also, A. Fenton deals with turnip husbandry in *Country Life in Scotland,* but again, no mention is made of eating greens. See pp. 142-145. So far I have not come across any information about the existance of this practice in Scotland.

23.   There are many examples of these orchards, such as the one on the abandoned farm in Marsboro, mentioned above.

24.   *John Ramsay of Kildalton...Diary,* p. 91.

25.   Catherine Parr Traill also wrote in one of her letters home that many of the men were 'obliged to hire out to work for the first year or two to earn sufficient for the maintenance of [their families]' and they also needed ready cash to cover settler's expenses. See *Backwoods,* p. 101.

26.   David Kennedy, *Pioneer Days,* pp. 53-54.

27.   The late Dave Nicolson was Ruth's husband.

28.   The French farmers also went haying to make extra cash for their families. Mary Morrison's grandfather used to tell of similar experiences in his youth, though Mary was of the opinion that most of them stayed on the Quebec side of the border, and generally worked for an English farmer 'who had the good land over near Cookshire.' They would walk from Marsboro, and spend the much of the summer working. '*In the late 1800s when he got married he had just returned from Cookshire and he said he was well off because he had $17 for the summer's work. And he bought his wedding suits, the shoes, and the rings, and he had money enough left over for what they needed to start housekeeping.' [Conversation, July 1994]

29.   Fieldwork notebook, August 12, 1992.

30.   A. Fenton writes about the 'Butter Wells' which served the same function in Scotland. Op cit, p. 157.

31.   The 'cutter' was fairly high compared to other sleighs, and had a set of steel ribs between the body of the sleigh and the runners, keeping it well off the ground as it travelled. The other sleigh was a 'pung' which had two steel runners attached directly to the body, thus it travelled much closer to the ground than the cutter.

32.   In the late 1980s two farms in Scotstown and Gould introduced Highland cattle to the area. The choice was initially based purely on preference for the Scottish Highland breed, but since their introduction they have proved to be 'as hardy as it says in the books'. They can survive the bitter Quebec winters with only the shelter of the trees to protect them. Miriam MacRae Holland showed me the wintering for her cattle, fairly close to her house, in a thick belt of trees. Field notebook, Aug. 1993.

33.   This pattern is the same in the Highlands and Islands. My grandfather, b. 1881, never milked a cow in his life, though his sons, b. 1915 and 1921, did all dairy work.

34. This was also common in other areas, for example, in Megantic County, among the settlers from Arran, Dugald M. McKillop's mother related that when she was about sixteen (c. 1830) she and her sister were sent to carry home one little piglet each. *Annals,* p. 73.

35. Recorded Aug. 8, 1992.

36. Methods of slaughtering are discussed by Bruce Walker in 'The Flesher's Trade in Eighteenth and Nineteenth-Century Scotland: An Exploratory Investigation into Slaughtering Techniques, Tools, and Buildings' in *Food in Change,* pp. 127–137; see also Lamont Pugh, 'Hog-Killing Day', in *Virginia Cavalcade,* (Winter, 1957), pp. 41 - 46.

37. This belief is prevalent throughout Scotland, Canada and America. See Opie and Tatem, *A Dictionary of Superstitions,*. pp. 262-263; M. Bennett. *The Last Stronghold,* p. 86; Richard M. Dorson, op cit, p. 128

38. Verse 4 of 7 eight-lined verses of an unpublished poem by Johnnie 'Bard' MacLeod. I am grateful to Duncan McLeod for a copy of the text. Dr Chase's Almanac is as much of a household name in North America as Whitaker's Almanac is in Britain. It has been published for many years and is still very popular among country people and farmers.

39. Op cit, p. 81.

40. As a child in Skye in the late 1950s, I saw my grandfather, John Stewart, blow up a sheep's bladder after he had butchered a sheep. He tied the opening in a tight knot, and said that in his youth boys would dry the blown-up bladder to use as a football.

41. Field notebook, Aug. 12, 1992. Methods of preparation are discussed in Chapter 5.

42. The story implies a belief that all the crofters in Lewis kept pigs, whereas very few actually did; they were more commonly kept by the tacksman.

43. The fur trade was flourishing in Canada in the 1920s. For example, the silver fox industry in Charlottetown, P.E.I. was described as a 'generator of instant wealth...' See Gillis, Heather M. and J. Estelle Reddin. 'Tapioca Pudding — Food's Interconnections', in *Canadian Folklore canadien,* p. 47.

44. In his book, *The Milan Story,* Duncan had estimated this number to be 2000, but his brother, Roderick, said that 750 would be more accurate. (Duncan is ammeding the text for a second edition.)

45. Harvey MacRae in Gould had a small farm of around twenty foxes. Fieldwork notebook, from his daughter, Miriam MacRae Holland, August 1992.

46. Alex Campbell from Dell became a minister and moved out to Seattle. In many of the old barns can be seen a variety of metal 'leg-hold' traps (gin-traps) of different sizes, many of which are now banned by law. For a more detailed account of snaring and trapping, see P.A.L. Smith, *Boyhood Memories of Fauquier,* pp. 130-132.

47. This is a simply made, rectangular wooden box with a trigger device inside that releases a sliding door, which, when set, is suspended over the opening. Common in many part of Canada and America. See H. Glassie, op cit, p. 169, Fig. 49.

48. Muriel Mayhew's husband, Herbert, also knew Archie Annis, a full-blooded Indian, who lived in a cabin in the woods near Canterbury. According to Carl Mayhew (brother of Herbert), *History of Canterbury, Quebec*, p. 60, Archie Annis was 'supposed to be a Chief of the St. Francis Indians…and [when] game was plentiful…he used to come to the Canterbury Section to hunt.' Although he was a hunter and trapper for most of his life, he was also very well educated, and a graduate from Dartmouth College in New Hampshire. In C.M. Day's book, *History of the Eastern Townships*, pp. 137-8, there is a much earlier account (1869) of the St. Francis Indians, where one man is referred to as 'Capt. St. Francis, Chief of that tribe of Indians.' Mrs Day also reports hearing about a battle involving the tribe on October 5, 1759 where they sustained great losses at the hands of the white man.

49. Mrs Simcoe described the troops practising walking on the Plains in snow shoes, March, 1792. 'the Racket is made of Deer or Elk skins, the frame is of light wood an inch thick, 2 feet long, 14 inches broad.' *Mrs Simcoe's Diary*, p. 55.

50. Christie MacKenzie also commented about the profusion of deer that surrounded her family home at *Yard na Féidh* after they first cleared the land. See also, David Kennedy, *Pioneer Days*, pp. 131-132.

51. By comparison to Scottish game laws, restrictions are minimal. All adults can, for an affordable fee (between $5 and $10), apply for a licence to hunt bear, deer, moose, etc., with 'rifle, flintlock, or bow and arrow.' The restrictions are more on the season and use of weapon, rather than the cost, with fines levied for hunting 'out of season', or with the wrong weapon; for example, bow and arrow season for deer precedes rifle season because the noise of the rifles would scare too many of them and thus spoil the bow and arrow season if the order were reversed. Flintlocks are still used by a few enthusiasts during what is commonly called 'black powder season'.

52. The runners of the pung were sometimes of wood, rather than steel. Across the border in New Hampshire, the same term is used for a vehicle that slides on small skis rather than full-length runners, a system not unknown in Scotland, such as in non-mechanized woods operations. (Demonstration of log-hauling by an Argyllshire team, Royal Highland Show, Edinburgh, 1994).

53. Dwelly gives *buitseachd*, meaning 'witchcraft, sorcery, enchantment'.

54. It was not my intention to divert Russell from his story, which, from the previous statement I erroneously surmised was about to lead to another familiar topic among the old-timers, that of belief in the supernatural. Russell himself was able to weave in the little diversion while keeping his mind on the story. Both are retained here to give a more realistic impression of the dynamics of the conversation.

55. I recorded an account from Donald MacLennan in 1976 (BEK: 5A).

56. 'Star' was a trade-name for a type of automobile made by the Durant Auto Company. It had an enclosed front cab (similar to Hackney cabs) and the roof at the back could be removed, like a modern pick-up truck. Duncan's father had removed the back for this trip, and on the return journey Duncan had to sit in the back with the dead man. Bosta was named after the Lewis placename, near Bernera, Uig.

57. The *guga*, solan geese, nest on the cliff face of Suilisgeir, forty miles off the coast. The Nessmen have to haul their boat up a sixty foot cliff for safety, and usually stay on the island for three weeks. Photos from the 1960 hunt can be seen in Donald MacDonald's book, *Lewis,* Plate numbers 39–43, with notes p. 128.

58. Provincial game laws have changed from the days when Russell's father hunted; nevertheless, compared to the Scottish situation, hunting licences are easily obtainable.

59. This is also claimed in Cape Breton, despite the fact that there are Gaelic stories in oral tradition mentioning axes. For example, I recorded the nursery tale, 'Murachan is Marachan', in Newfoundland which mentions *tuagh,* an axe; see *The Last Stronghold,* pp. 130-136. David Kennedy also notes that the early settlers had tools, including 'hammers and chisels, but not a saw.' *Pioneer Days*, p. 17.

60. Edward D. Ives's book, *Larry Gorman, The Man Who Made the Songs,* tells of the life and songs of a Prince Edward Islander who was famous for the satires he composed in lumber camps in Maine. Ives's second book, *Joe Scott, the Woodsman Songmaker,* is about a New Brunswicker who worked as a lumberjack. Two very different characters and life stories, both books describe life in the lumber camps in Maine.

61. The late Donald Morrison worked as a customs official; he was a very keen local historian with a lively interest in every aspect of Gaelic tradition in the Eastern Townships. He was recorded in October, 1976.

62. In 1976, a neighbour, without any prior consultation, taught my five-year-old son to swing an axe so that he would be able to chop logs for the fire 'like all the other men'. The lessons were very successful, though the following year in Scotland, the sight of a very small six year-old swinging an axe caused considerable alarm.

63. See also Richard M. Dorson, 'Canadiens' in *Bloodstoppers and Bearwalkers*, pp. 69-102.

64. 'Head chopper' was the official title of a woodsman who was good enough to take on the job, such as 'Big Neil', Russell's father. [Duncan McLeod, July, 1994.]

65. The subject of why we laugh at jokes has been discussed at length by behavioural psychologists whose methods of observations are useful to folklorists. Of particular relevance to this context is Mihály Hoppál's discussion on 'folk humour' in Transylvania at a village gathering. Hoppál examines the social setting of certain types of humour and identifies the 'comic feature' using

concepts of modern linguistics. See M. Hoppál, 'Genre and Context in Narrative Event: Approach to Verbal Semiotics' in *Genre, Structure and Reproduction in Oral Literature*, eds. Lauri Honko and Vilmos Voigt, pp. 107-128.

66. Two articles in *Western Folklore* Vol. XLV, No. 4 discuss the subject and give a large number of examples: Willie Smyth in 'Challenger Jokes and the Humour of Disaster' 243-260; Elizabeth Radin Simons, 'The NASA Joke Cycle: The Astronauts and the Teacher', pp. 261-277.

67. A number of recent studies deal with this issue; see, Robert Cochran, 'WHAT COURAGE!' Romanian 'Our Leader' Jokes', *JAF*, Vol. 102, No. 405, pp. 259-274 and Mary Beth Stein, 'The Politics of Humour: The Berlin Wall in Jokes and Graffiti' in *Western Folklore*, vol. XLVIII, pp. 85-108.

68. *Memoirs of Dell,* pp. 191-193.

69. Descriptions of lumbercamps invariably include the mention of beans as the staple food. As with the brose-fed bothymen of the North-east of Scotland, the repetitive daily routine is described in many songs of the lumbercamps. For comparative examples, see song texts and Hamish Henderson's notes to the Scottish Tradition record, *Bothy Ballads: Music from the North East,* 1971, reissued on CD with booklet by Greentrax, Edinburgh, 1993.

70. Op cit, p. 193.

71. In 1976, my only personal experience of all the seasons, the first snow fell on October 10; we never saw the ground again that year, as the snow got deeper and deeper as the weeks went by.

72. Fieldwork notebook, Sherbrooke, August 5, 1992. Alex, who was suffering from ill-health, died two years later.

73. See also Chapter 3, *The Last Stronghold,* pp. 55–81.

74. From the Eastern Townships Collection, Bishop's University; recorded Aug. 18, 1982 by I. Loutit and G. Hutley.

75. For most of this century, Lewismen have operated a fairly large quarry at Marybank, outside Stornoway. In the 1950s and 60s the foreman of the quarry was an Aberdeenshire man who had gained his expertise in the huge granite quarry at Rubislaw. Though I have found no descriptions of quarrying methods from Lewis dating to the nineteenth century, in his book published in 1858, *Buchan,* the Rev. John B. Pratt describes the use of 'plugs and feathers' in a granite quarry near Peterhead. He notes that when blocks are too large even to be removed by cranes, such as those 'above twenty feet square and eight feet thick,' they are 'cut by iron wedges, and *plug and feather,* a little gunpowder being used where no joints can be found.' Op cit, p. 124 and Appendix CC, pp. 376-377, P. For a modern description of methods and techniques, see the *Blasters' Handbook,* produced by Canadian Industries Limited. (Thanks to my father for making his copy available to me.)

76. *Memoirs of Dell.* p. 23.

77. Noted in conversation, Lennoxville, July 1994. Johnnie 'Bard' also recalls the threshing machine coming to their family farm in Dell; op cit, p.145. See also

George Ewart Evans, chapter 13, 'Threshing', in *Spoken History*. Although set in Ireland, the tape-recorded reminiscences of threshing day (pp. 196-203) are similar to those on Scottish farms.

78. Rivier Legendre is a tributary of the St. Francis River.

79. *Stornoway 1858-83,* pp 30-31. For a map of mill sites in the area, see J.I. Little, *Op cit,* p. 161. Though not all the mills that once operated are included, it nevertheless affirms the importance of milling in former days.

80. According to J.I. Little, in 1852 Scots in the Eastern Townships grew three times more buckwheat than the French. *Op cit,* table 5.5, p. 139.

81. Donald MacDonald, *The Tolsta Townships*, p.148, and *Lewis: A History of the Island,* p. 78.

82.   John MacKenzie's grandfather had been a miller in Gress, Isle of Lewis, before he emigrated. J.I. Little states that the Lewis Scots did not produce 'a single successful miller'. *Crofters and Habitants,* p. 168.

83. In his book, *Mills and Millwrighting*, which deals mostly with English examples, John Vince refers to one type of millstone as the 'French stone' which 'was made up from several sections of stone, cemented together and bound with an iron band.' Op cit, p. 17-19, with photograph on p. 18.

84. Hulled buckwheat.

85. The technology involved in building and operating mills was of concern to all frontier communities in North America. See Janice Tyrwhitt, *The Mill*, Marion Nicholl Rawson, *Little Old Mills*, and Ivan C. Crowell, 'Little Old Mills of New Brunswick', in *Collections of the New Brunswick Historical Society*, No. 19 (1966), pp. 79 - 87.

86. *Stornoway,* p. 31. 'It stopped working in 1945 when the farmers stopped sowing grains.' [Translation]

87. In a more detailed discussion on the millwrighting, Stanley Freese observes that dressing and balancing mill stones is a 'fine art on which much of the efficiency depends...the work should be so finished that the 'nip' or closeness of the stones will only permit a piece of brown paper being placed between them and the centre, and a piece of tissue paper at the periphery.' *Windmills and Millwrighting*, p. 49.

88. I have brought buckwheat from different sources (as far away as North Carolina) to Milan, each time precipitating a discussion on the subject of milling. My Fieldwork Notebook records, e.g., that 'Ruth is still looking for the real old kind of buckwheat; 'July 29, 1993.

89. The 'middlings' referred to partly ground grain, and 'shorts' to the husks or bran, the outside part of the grain. Both were suitable for cattle-feed. S. Freese refers to 'middlings' as 'an intermediate product from the flour dresser.' Op cit, p. 161.

90. Op cit, p. 146.

91. Peter Ellis, 'The Modern Miller's Tale', *Heritage Scotland,*, 1983, Vol. 10, No. 2, p. 11.

92. *Stornoway 1858-1983*, pp. 30-31, based on interviews with the present generation of Legendres. [I do not know why the future tense is used here.] On my tape-recording, Ellen Legendre said that the mill was built in 1897 after their first carding mill was destroyed by a fire.

93. I did not see the machines described here, but I was taken to a similar carding mill in the Codroy Valley, Newfoundland; description and photographs in *The Last Stronghold*, pp. 148-149.

94. 'Batting' is the filling or padding used in quilt-making.

95. Martin Martin, op cit, p. 200. (Quoted from the facsimile of the second edition, 1716.)

96. For a general reference work on the subject, see W. L. Goodman, *The History of Woodworking Tools*. More relevant to pioneer settlers and their skill is Erwin O. Christensen's *Early American Wood Carving*.

97. I. F. Grant discusses hand-carved wooden utensils such as ladles and spoons in *Highland Folkways*, pp. 192-92. She refers to the care taken to make these utensils, and, having noticed a heart carved on some of the older items, suggests that some may have been betrothal gifts. The examples she gives confirms that wood-carving was practised throughout the Highlands in the nineteenth century. See also Mary Earle Gould, *Early American Wooden Ware and Other Kitchen Utensils*.

98. Simon J. Bronner discusses the hobby of chain-carving among workers in the furniture industry in Indiana; see 'Folk Objects' in *Folk Groups and Folklore Genres: An Introduction*, ed. E. Oring, pp. 210–14.

99. According to Johnnie 'Bard' MacLeod of Dell, his brother, Roddy, was another man who was good with a jack knife as he even carved a violin out of a hollow, dry block of spruce. (He adds that he bought catgut strings from store in Scotstown, made the bow using horse hairs from their own two horses, but admits that the 'final sound was pretty bad!') *Memoirs of Dell*, p. 28.

100. Eighty-two year old Ontarian, Jesse Saunders was tape-recorded in 1976 telling how he learned to make snowshoes as a boy. 'There's a secret to rawhide,' he said, as he gave the details of the tradition. See *For What Time I Am in the World*, pp. 131-133.

101. Scots settlers in Canada frequently recount stories about first encounters with new concepts or words which are new to them. David Kennedy tells an anecdote about an old Scots setter who, on seeing prints of snow-shoes in the snow for the first time exclaims 'D'ye ken what kind o beast it is?' D. Kennedy, *Pioneer Days,* pp.63-64.

4

In Sickness and in Health

From the day they arrived in Quebec, the immediate concern of new settlers was not just making a living but simply staying alive. If they managed to survive the freezing temperatures of winter and spells of unbearable humidity and heat in summer, how would they deal with illness and disease? The Gaels had a 'common sense' attitude to health, and were attuned to diagnosing illness based on everyday observation. They also benefited from generations of traditional knowledge while, at the same time, remaining open to new ideas.[1]

Nowadays, even the very oldest residents of the Eastern Townships have lived their entire lives during a time when formal medical assistance was available. Before the turn of the century, there was a doctor at Stornoway and one at Scotstown, thirty miles away, and people in outlying settlements such as Marsboro and Milan could be reached by horse and sleigh or buggy, as Christie MacKenzie recalled:

> We never felt that we were without a doctor; he'd always come when he was sent for, day or night. He'd hop a freight train, or he'd take a sleigh if it was winter, and horse, and come — or some buggy in summertime. Even before cars, they'd always come.

While professional medical advice was sought for major problems, a wide range of conditions was treated at home with familiar cures, preventatives, tonics, charms, and essential midwifery skills. Muriel Mayhew gave a very typical account of one local practitioner:

> *My aunt Helen was born in 1890 and she told me that when she was a child she remembered her mother — my grandmother — who was a widow, going around to help people who had someone sick in their homes, and she would go out and gather herbs and she used to boil these herbs and make medicine — for pneumonia, colds, arthritis, and so on — and Uncle Willis was very good like that with people who were sick; he used to gather herbs for people. There was one herb he gathered that was good for your stomach, you'd chew it — I've chewed it, and I think it was good. Anyway, when anyone was having a baby they would call my grandmother, even in the middle of the night. And when Bernard Matheson was born, his mother was at her parents' home in Stornoway. And my grandmother who lived in Stornoway then, half way up the hill below the Roman

106

Catholic church, she was called in the middle of the night to go. And she got up and Helen remembered the big snow drift she had to walk through. And she was put to bed when she got to this house and she had to sleep with the aunt — that was Tina MacAskill, who later became a nurse herself. And my grandmother would stay a couple of days and when she left to go home she would get paid with a sack of potatoes or vegetables.[2] She often went out like that to help people who were sick.

Until after the Second World War, childbirth was generally taken care of by local women who had earned their reputation as midwives. They managed to cope with almost all births, except occasional cases that were particularly difficult. Even then, very few women had the help of a doctor, and most of the older women dismissed the very idea of it with comments such as: 'I had thirteen of a family and didn't see no doctor!'

At the age of a hundred, Maryann Morrison recalled that her father's sister, who came over from Harris to Quebec with them on the same boat was 'very good to the ones that she'd go to, you know. And everybody was after her...' Though she lived till she was over 107, Maryann could not recall anyone of her own generation whose case was urgent enough to have required a doctor:

> Well, I never heard of anybody like that; I heard of one woman that had a hard time; she had twins. And she told them to go out and bring the axe in and kill me. She was in pain, you know...But she got over it...the baby came some way or another, you know. But no, that was the only one I heard of that had a tough time with the babies.

From the next generation, Christie MacKenzie remembered two of the midwives in Milan:

> Dave Nicolson's grandmother — she was an awfully good one [and] Mrs Campbell, she was [too]...But really, for people that didn't have a doctor or a nurse handy, it was remarkable how they got along. And most houses had a houseful of kids.
>
> My mother had fifteen children, and only on one did the midwife have to send for the doctor. It was the one ahead of me...the eleventh one. She was coming feet first, and she couldn't get her turned around. So they had to wait until the doctor got there. But her last, the fourteenth and fifteenth, were twins. She was forty-four years old and the midwife took her through.

Unlike today's mothers who are encouraged to resume normal activities as soon as possible after the birth of a baby, mothers in those days were expected to stay in bed for at least a week, and sometimes two.[3] If possible, the midwife would stay at the house to look after the mother and baby and help with the running of the household. Alternatively, there was always a grandmother, who would most likely be helping the midwife in any case, or a female relative, who looked after the family and the housekeeping during the confinement. Older children were generally relied upon to give extra help with the chores, and though 'he would if he had to,' the father of the new baby seldom took part, as most of the tasks were regarded as 'women's work'. Christie MacKenzie remarked, 'There was a lot of that.'

> Of course, on the farm, like we were, the farmer didn't have time. He was busy from morning until dark at night. I know that my father did very little around us as children.

All the babies were breast-fed, usually for a year, though exceptionally as long as three years, unless there was some physical reason to prevent the mother from nursing. When she wanted to wean her baby, the mother would have her breasts bound for a day or two to relieve discomfort and suppress lactation. A roller towel, of the sort that hung behind every kitchen door, was most often used as it has the ideal dimensions.[4]

If a new mother suffered abmormal discomfort or pain from swollen breasts or cracked nipples, she was treated with a homemade ointment, as recalled by Katherine M. MacKenzie in her letter: 'Kenneth (Doak) MacDonald Scotstown's mother made a wonderful healing ointment; she was my husband's aunt. He could give you the recipe as Ivy used it to heal my breasts when our oldest boy was born.'[5]

Though Kenny died before I could record him, his wife, Ivy, recalled the recipe, which, for more than a century, had been an old standby for family and community.

> That was from Kenny's mother…She was Mary Campbell before she married…She was [from Milan and lived] on a farm up the hill that goes up to Dell…It should have been *lamb,* lamb tallow, but no-one had lambs around, so we used deer, and it's very much the same, and rosin. And you melted rosin… you could buy it in those days. People used it for, you know, violin bows, and so on — that rosin, see. And we we crushed it and melted it and mixed it into quite a thick, oh, kind of a sticky paste. [When I made it, I would make] say, a couple of cupfuls of melted stuff — I never measured it, And that was just because Kenny's mother made it and she told me how to make it, so I don't know if I had the right proportions, but it worked anyway. [You'd use] a whole lot more fat than rosin, you know, [and a little block of rosin, about maybe an inch or so. And to store it,] well, I used to use little cold-cream jars, and things; I used to save all those little jars and things, you know, and use it for that. And it was just wonderful for healing — just wonderful for healing. [I'd keep a jar in the house] — always, always, *always.* [Aug. 11, 1992; re-ordered]

Ivy went on to tell a family anecdote about her husband who was badly burned as a child and was treated by his mother with the ointment:

But when Kenny was a little boy, he was playing in the woods, and you know, people in those days used to burn trees to clear land, and this ash that was left was just like velvet — soft, soft, just like velvet. And when he was about ten years old he jumped into a pile of these ashes, and he went right up to his knee in one, and there was still coals in the bottom of that. And he burnt his whole leg until it was just, eh, cooked. And his brother took him on his back and took him to his grandfather's across — oh, it was nearer to the grandfather's than it was to their own home. There was an old man there and he poured kerosene oil on this poor leg, and the poor boy nearly fainted, you know. So somehow they got him home, and the first thing his mother did was to eh, pat all this stuff as best she could, and then she just smeared that whole leg with this ointment and it healed…It was so healing, and why, I don't know.

Knowing *why* something works is not essential to using it, as 'tested and tried' remedies go back through centuries of tradition. The efficacy of 'deer's grease' had been common knowledge in Gaelic Scotland for generations, as I.F. Grant discovered when researching her book, *Highland Folkways*.[6] There is also an old Gaelic proverb that suggest that animal fat was generally valued in traditional medicine: *'Saill na bà a mach's a steach mur leighis sin an Gàidheal chan eil an leigheas ann.'* [A cow's fat cures the Highlander of inward or outward disease].[7]

Apart from Kenny Doak's ointment, there were other ways of treating cuts and abrasions, depending on the seriousness of the wound. Patent medicines were available through peddlers, 'such as the Raleigh man', who travelled the area and sold 'every kind of product'. Isobel Beattie recalled that she 'used to love to see the Raleigh man coming'.[8]

She remembered that he sold Red Liniment labelled 'for internal and external use' which was said to be very good for cuts: 'My father used to put it on the horses if they had a cut, or on the cows if they had a sore teat; it was good for everything.' Ruth also remembered the Raleigh man although her family 'used balsam of myrrh — even for the foxes, if they lost a tail, it'd cure it! It would cure the infection anyhow!'

The Raleigh man also sold a substance called Electric Oil which was recommended for cuts and abrasions.[9] While it was said to have been effective for fairly bad cuts, Christie MacKenzie pointed out that the cut would have to have stopped bleeding first. If not, 'you would have it stitched. Of course, if you had [to have it stitched], you had to try and wind it so that the blood wouldn't be flowing, and get to the doctor with it.' Most families 'always had a bottle of it in the house,' although they were still inclined to rely upon older methods or a combination of both old and new.

Sometimes Electric Oil was combined with butter, as in the treatment of small hacks or cuts on the feet, a frequent affliction of summertime when all the children were barefoot:

And we used to walk barefoot, you know. And you remember the cracks, or perhaps you don't — Well, when we'd bathe our feet before going to bed, my mother would give us a woollen string and run it through the butter. Put butter onto our toes, and oil — it would relieve that. I think the salt in the butter was really good.

The use of butter for medicinal purposes dates back much longer than Hebridean emigration to Quebec, as Martin Martin refers to 'an ointment made of Camomile and fresh butter, or of Brandy with fresh butter' in his *Description of the Western Islands of Scotland, circa 1695.*[10] Woollen threads, pieces of yarn or silk also played a significant part in a range of traditional medical practices.[11]

Not all wounds were treated by a doctor, however, as most people had neither the money nor the transport to seek medical help. Isobel Stewart of Dell vividly remembered one very bad cut she got as a girl:

It was caused by me on my bare feet, jumping. I was a real tom-boy; I loved to climb! I was up in a tree, and I jumped down in this tall grass and there was a broken bottle there. And it cut down the whole [?ankle] — almost like an X. Oh, oh! Was that sore! So I went running into the house, bleeding like the dickens. And my mother said 'What in the world happened to you?' And I told her. She just opened the stove; she got a piece of white cloth, and she opened the stove, and she took a handful of ashes out of it. And she slammed that right on to that cut! *O Thighearna!* [Oh, Lord!] I thought I was going to die!

   It wasn't the heat, or anything, it was just the lye in the ashes that burnt me. Oh! Was that sore! And that's all she put on it. Every day she'd take that bandage off and wash that cut, and put more fresh ashes on it — and that healed...That's what healed that cut. I never saw a doctor or anything.[12]

Flour was another readily available substance that was commonly used to treat bad cuts, or even accidental amputations. Bessie Smith recounted one particular incident that stuck in her mind above all others:

I remember one time, one of my brothers was working in the woods...He was working on a saw — he had one of them — and he fell on his hand. And it was in the woods when they were working there, and my father tore his shirt, you know, so as to get him home — he was bleeding to death. And of course the nearest doctor would be in Scotstown, near on seventeen miles. And do you know what my mother did? I'll never forget about it. You know in them days we used to get the flour in barrels. And she just went with her hand and took the flour out — white flour — until the doctor came. So he wouldn't bleed to death she was putting flour on it to stop it, you know. Of course the blood was oozing out.

By the time the doctor arrived, a thick, coagulated mass, consisting of a mixture of flour and blood, had formed over the cut and the bleeding was minimal. Bessie then watched the doctor dress her brother's wound. He took some, though not all, of the sticky covering off the cut and bandaged it up. In time, the arm healed perfectly and was as good as it had always been.

Fortunately, not all Bessie's encounters with cuts were as traumatic as that one. Over the years she herself treated many minor cuts, generally using either gum from a spruce tree, or a spider's web, applied over the cut, because 'that seals things up.'[13]

Dramatic as some of these treatments may seem, the most dramatic of all was that used by the local bloodstopper, the late A.D. Morrison from Scotstown. He was well known throughout the district for his gift, and though many people talked about it, no-one could explain his power and no-one seemed to doubt it.

I first heard about 'A.D.', as he was commonly called, from Bill Young:

There was an old gentleman around Scotstown when I was a child. — now I'm — [laughs] — I've been exposed to enough modern way of thinking that I don't put a great deal of faith in a lot of these things, but I do definitely know that he could stop bleeding. No doubt about that! I've seen him do it, and you can't deny your own eyesight, eh? And there were numerous cases where — you see, doctors weren't available those days and, if there were, they would [have to consider] the distance they'd travel [which] was mostly by horse. And [instead] they'd always call on this old fellow if there was any serious accident, and he definitely could [stop blood]. There's no doubt about it! Well, I don't know [how he did it] — he just came into the house, or say [to the person who came to him] 'Well, go home. The bleeding's stopped.' And it's true — absolutely true.

Now, there was a case where there was a young girl came into the Sherbrooke Hospital here, years ago, in the wintertime, and of course the roads were blocked up — there was no travel those days — and she had her tonsils or something removed and she haemorrhaged, and you couldn't stop the bleeding. But of course, medical care wasn't as fancy as it is today. And they called, by telephone, to Scotstown, and had him come on the phone. And they swear by it, and don't see any reason why they shouldn't, because I've *seen* him stop bleeding in Scotstown…His name was A.D. Morrison…and this old gentleman could definitely stop bleeding.[14]

In 1909, Alexander Carmichael collected a *rann* from a Ross-shire woman of a hundred-and-three who had heard a man in Strathspey recite it in her childhood. In his notes to *Carmina Gadelica* he says that 'belief in this power is now obsolete in the Isles but is still common in Caithness and Sutherland and the mainland of Ross- and Inverness-shires. He cites 'but a few' of many accounts he heard of healers who had power to 'stop the escape of blood from man or beast without any sort of manipulation, without personal contact, and even at a distance.[15] Carmichael's *rann* from Ross-shire can be estimated to pre-date 1820, some thirty years before A.D.'s people emigrated to Quebec. As with other emigrant traditions which survive in the New World long after they become extinct in the Old, faith in the power of the blood-stopper appears to have lasted over a century and a half longer among descendants of Lewis emigrants than Carmichael's report suggests.[16]

Even in the closing decade of the twentieth century, faith in the blood-stopper seems to be a perfectly normal part of the local belief system. As retired nurse, ninety year-old Ivy MacDonald, remarked:

> Isn't it strange how there's people who could stop blood?…Well, Lennox Murray's sister used to have awful nosebleeds. And they lived on a farm in the Yard then, and a cousin of my mother's was a nurse, and her mother called Margaret one day, and she said 'Mavis is having such a nosebleed,' she said, 'I don't know what in the world to do for her.' Margaret told her what to do, she said 'I've *done* all that.'
>
> Margaret said 'Would you mind if I call 'Cracky Morrison' (they called him).' And Edith said 'No, anything at all.'
>
> So in about an hour or so, Margaret called Edith back, and she said 'How is Mavis?'
>
> 'Oh,' she said, 'her nosebleeds have stopped.' And she told her when it had stopped, and it took her a little while to get hold of this man. And it stopped when she spoke to this man. Now, if you tell me why or how! Well this was *over the phone;* you see, he didn't even communicate with the girl's mother, or with the girl herself. [Some time later] he asked the nurse, Christie MacLeod, one day if she was afraid of lightning, and she said 'no.'
>
> 'Oh well then,' he said, 'I can't pass on my gift to you.'…She was telling me that, and wondered what he would have done, or what he would have, you know…goodness knows…It was just that bleeding, that was the only thing he did, just stopped bleeding. Strange thing.[17]

Unusual gifts of healing, often attributed to supernatural power, have been reported in the Old Country for centuries — there were bone-setters, for example, who were relied upon as essential to the well-being of many communities.[18] It is not something unique to Gaels, however, as there are accounts from all over the world. In Quebec, Marius Barbeau, often referred to as the father of Canadian folklore, recorded the craft of a French-Canadian bone-setter in the 1940s.[19] He was approximately contemporary with another bone-setter in Milan who is still remembered by the Gaelic community. His reputation extended throughout the townships, and, from several accounts, it seems that he was more often called upon to re-set joints that had been dislocated than bones that had been broken.

Loooking back over eighty years to her childhood in Milan, Ivy MacDonald gave this account of the bone-setter:

He was a Smith, and he lived, you know where you go up the hill and go to Dell, you know a road straight through, they call it the Town Line, and he lived in there somewhere. And he could set bones and he could do wonderful things. My father would have a knee-cap that went out [of joint] and it would get so painful that his eyes would get bloodshot, and he'd have a fever he was in such pain. And the doctor could never do anything about it. And my mother would hitch up a horse, maybe in the middle of the winter, and go in there with him, and he'd do something about that, and it would snap back into place. And the first time he did it, he told Papa now to stay in bed for two weeks. Well, Papa didn't stay in bed for two weeks, so I suppose the tendons or ligaments were stretched so that sometimes for very little they would go out. Oh, I've seen his lips just purple from the pain. Just in agony. So he [Smith] could set bones, though this wasn't a bone, I guess, 'cos there wasn't any bone that could go out of place. Well it would be the patella, like the patella, the knee cap, sits on tendons there, and it would slip off. [And if somebody broke an arm or a leg] he was wonderful, I guess…Isn't it strange how there's people who could stop blood, and so on?

Isobel Stewart also recalled seeing him in action when, as a child, she visited in the Smith home:

I remember when we were kids, one night, someone who used to work in the lumber camps came in and sat in a chair. And we were standing there with our eyes popping out of our heads and he went over and he grabbed that guy's arm here [elbow] and here [shoulder] and there was a quick snap and we thought he was killing the man. But he got up — and he'd set the arm. He was in the lumber camps and he was lifting the logs or something and he pulled his shoulder out, and [Smith] set it in no time flat. Apparently he had done this to several people — it was just in him.

The power of the seventh son is widely acknowledged in the field of traditional medicine, and though neither Smith nor Morrison were known to have been seventh sons, there were other gifted healers who were. Mrs K. MacKenzie, formerly of Whitton, wrote this account in her letter:

My father was a seventh son so had the healing power over King's Evil, and as a small child was made to wash his hands in water and apply [the water] to the cervical sore. One application by the healer and two by the patient if they couldn't stay at Grandpa's house. He had many people call on him while we lived in Quebec, but being a humble person he never mentioned his doctoring after moving to Ontario. I met people in later life who swore they were healed.

'King's Evil' or scrofula, is an unpleasant, painful condition which appears as an outcrop of boils on the neck. Being a specific ailment, it was not treated with poultices like ordinary boils; instead, the sufferer would have to visit someone who was born with a special gift of healing as Muriel Mayhew recalled:

Oh, a seventh son of a seventh son of a seventh son. There was this lady, a
MacIver, who had what they called *tighneas a righ,*, king's evil, on her neck, and
her parents got the seventh son whose name was Alex Campbell — he lived in
Dell — to come. And I don't know what he did, but he put his hand on her
neck and washed it or something and it was supposed to cure it.

The Eastern Townships' cure for King's Evil seems very similar to the
nineteenth century one reported by Alexander Carmichael, who gave two
accounts of a man in Sutherland who was well known for his power. In
preparation for washing his hands, he would draw pure cold water from the
well 'before breaking fast or silence…and he never sent any person away
unhealed or unhappy.'[20]

The most common 'magical cures' of all are, of course, those for warts.
Widespread as these cures are, however, they are no better understood than
any other supernatural power. An informal survey of any group of people
usually turns up a range of seemingly illogical, unconnected, bizarre methods
— try rubbing a piece of fat on the wart then burying it, or putting a chalk
mark behind the stove, or rubbing it with a special stone — people
everywhere will swear by these 'firm cures'. A typical response from anyone
who is asked about wart cures is to laugh and sound sceptical, then tell about
other people's odd ideas. Isobel Stewart confirmed the pattern:

> Oh gosh! They used to take a penny, some of them used to give you a penny for
> every wart [laughs] — and in a few days they were supposed to be gone!…and
> they'd give buttons too, you know. But I never heard of any disappearing [laughs]
> but [my son] Mike said that two of his disappeared after he'd sold them.

I assured Isobel that I would hesitate to buy anybody's wart, for, having
been told the same cure by a seven-year-old in Newfoundland, I was then
asked if I would buy the wart on his thumb. Satisfied that I had 'collected
another cure', I entered the bargain with mock-seriousness, and gave him
the nickel he asked for. About three weeks later he triumphantly showed me
the perfect thumb, announcing that it had worked, but my pleasure at his
long-awaited cure was somewhat tarnished by the fact that, in the meantime,
a wart appeared on my own thumb.[21]

Before the turn of the century, Alexander Carmichael recorded wart cures
from Gaelic Scotland which were just as impossible to explain: going to a
graveyard to 'dip the wart in water lying on a gravestone' was recommended;
alternatively, you could 'rub the wart against the clothes of one who has
committed fornication.'[22]

In a discussion on 'odd [or magical] cures', Christie and John MacKenzie
laughed together as they recalled hearing of someone in Milan who was told
to 'spit under a stone' to get rid of pain. Christie remarked: 'I suppose if some
people heard of these things, they'd think, 'Oh my, they weren't very bright.'
More than likely, however, they were just as bright as the group of newly

qualified, very sceptical doctors at the Western Infirmary in Glasgow who 'invented' a wart machine and, under lab conditions, conducted a controlled experiment with a group of school children. They discovered that the success rate of their 'magical machine' was much higher than that of a patent medication and it was also better than leaving the warts without any treatment.[23] One of the doctors, Dr David Clow, concluded that, as with more formal medical practices, the significant feature of traditional medicine is: You don't have to *understand* how something works to use it; and if it works for one person and not for another, then he or she will try something else that does work.

For common ailments, there were standard practices used in nearly every household. Remedies for colds, coughs and sore throats were numerous and diverse, as most families would swear by their own methods of finding relief. Adults, especially the women, usually had to carry out daily chores while suffering any of these afflictions. Occasionally, however, as the result of a severe infection, the victim was confined to bed, and precautions taken lest the condition worsen or develop into pneumonia.

In Maryann Morrison's household at Cruvag, the family cold remedy was usually taken as a nightcap: 'I never got anything for a cold but just ginger and hot milk, and maybe put a lump of butter in it or something like that.' She added that 'if you had a sore throat as well, then you would add honey,' which was bought at the store.

In 1992, while walking with me over the deserted farm the Morrisons once owned, Maryann's daughter-in-law, Mary, picked a bunch of yarrow as we went along. Every summer for as long as she could remember, Mary had gathered it 'for medicine — *'You make an infusion of it if you have a cold in the winter and you breathe in the vapour. An old neighbour of ours said she wouldn't last the winter without it.'[24]

In Christie MacArthur's home in Milan, a hot lemon drink was given to anyone who had a cold. If lung congestion developed, then the chest was smeared with goose grease and covered with flannel or woollen material.[25] Her daughter Isobel recalled a slight modification in the next generation of the household: *'Do you remember those cloths we had to wear around our throats — if you had a sore throat? The Raleigh man, a peddlar, used to sell them; they had camphor in them and of course you'd smell it. It would clear your tubes.'

Goose grease was also a standard treatment for congestion in Christie MacKenzie's home. If the patient also suffered from a sore throat, then the neck area was rubbed and wrapped around in a manner that seems universally known: 'When you'd have a *very* sore throat, I've known of taking your stocking off and winding it around your neck...It went on warm, off your foot.'

Spending as much time as possible out of doors 'in the good fresh air' when they were young, Isobel Stewart recalled that most of them generally enjoyed good health. When she, or her brothers or sisters did catch a cold, however, their mother would melt lard and rub it on their chests before bedtime. They also used to squeeze the blisters of gum on fir trees and eat the rosin, as they believed it would relieve colds. Occasionally, when the cold was very bad, they were confined to bed and subjected to a more elaborate treatment:

> Well, they used linseed a lot for poultices. When a person had a very, very bad cold, they'd put poultices like this on you…They boiled the linseed — I don't know, I've seen my mother do it, but I don't know just whether she did anything besides boiling it or not, and then cooling it off and putting it on the cloth and then, when that would come off, she'd have a piece of flannel to put over it, to keep the cold — boy!

Though twenty years younger than Isobel, Ruth's sister, Bernice, had lived with their grandmother after their mother died, and therefore had experienced the medical practices of an earlier generation:

> *Grandmother made poultices of linseed boiled up into a real thick sort of porridge, and then put into an old piece of folded cotton, thick enough not to burn [your skin through the cloth]. And she applied that to the chest for a bad cold — I had pneumonia so she was very careful. It kept the heat.

Living up the road on their father's farm, the treatment Ruth recalled was slightly more modern and depended upon the Raleigh man rather than the general store which sold linseed: *'And did you ever have the red cough syrup? Oh my, that was dangerously hot, but you put hot water and a bit of sugar in it.'

Before the Raleigh man cornered the market, and, it may be noted, sold commercial variants of old, established local remedies, people made their own cough mixture. As Katherine M. MacKenzie recalled, the ingredients were readily available to the old folk, as cherry bark was the main component in the mixture.[26] To this day, that is still the main ingredient listed on the labels of many commercial products.

Christie MacKenzie had several different recipes for cough mixtures she used to make: 'Some made with molasses and onion, boiled together. And some with onion, and honey and onion. Some with honey and lemon together.' And if one of the family suffered from more severe respiratory ailments, he or she was kept in bed.

Bronchitis, pleurisy and pneumonia were generally treated with a type of poultice, or 'plaster' as it was called. The principle behind this procedure is that the local application of heat will relieve the pain caused by inflammation of the lungs, and also loosen the congestion. The 'plaster', therefore, acts as an expectorant. Mustard was the main ingredient, and was always mixed with flour to prevent skin irritation. Isobel Stewart described how they did it, and gave a cautionary reminder to apply a barrier cream to protect the skin while the plaster was working:

> You mix it with flour, about two parts mustard and one part flour. Mix it like a paste, almost like a pancake, and put it on cloth, you know. And put it on [the person] for about ten or twenty minutes, take it off, leave it for a few minutes. And [remember, first of all] put oil or cold cream or something like that on so it wouldn't blister…And we used to put one on the front and one on the back of a person that *really* had pneumonia, a good dose of it.

When young children suffer colds and respiratory complaints, earache is a very common symptom of inflammation, and it is this painful condition, rather than the common cold, which causes most distress. Keeping the patient warm was standard, and, in some households, a couple of drops of warm Electric Oil were put into the aching ear. Isobel Stewart, who had this done to her as a child, used the same treatment on her son. Although she said that 'Mike claimed it was very effective,' Isobel doubted that she would continue the practice, as she had since read that modern medical opinion discouraged 'the introduction of foreign substances into the ears.' There is no doubt, however, that the effectiveness of any of the traditional remedies for easing pain was due to the application of heat, regardless of whether it was in the form of a warm blanket, drops of heated oil for earache, or, the method used for toothache by their Lewis forebears, a 'green turf…heated as hot as can be endured' applied to the side of the head.[27]

The same principle was at work in the Quebec-Hebridean treatment of toothache, though, according to Christie MacKenzie's description, one might wonder if the cure was not as dreaded as the affliction. 'Oh, carbolic acid. Imagine that! I still remember the way it used to burn your throat…Oh, you'd put it on a little absorbent cotton and put it on the cavity. Oh boy! It used to stop the toothache, but boy, it would burn your tongue too! Yeah.' For anyone unwilling to try such a drastic cure, there was an alternative method: pour whisky into the mouth and keep it around the tooth to dull the pain. (Swallowing the medicine also seems to have helped, though eventually the victim may have needed treatment from the dentist in Lennoxville.)

Apart from gum-boils associated with severe toothache, one seldom hears, nowadays, of boils afflicting other parts of the body. In Quebec, as in Scotland and elsewhere, they were once very common, because few household had a sufficient supply of hot water for regular bathing. As a result, people were much more susceptible to boils and other inflammation. For example, when a splinter, thorn or any tiny particle that could carry infection, pierced the skin, it often resulted in the eruption of inflammation, festering or a boil.

Sometimes, for no apparent reason, an outcrop of boils appeared on an individual, more often in boys, at times the result of abrasions sustained during some rough and tumble. The standard home treatment was the application of a poultice to draw out the pus or poison. Isobel Stewart recalled two methods which were used effectively by her family, both consisting of ingredients readily available in or near every home.

The first one was made from a common plant, and though Isobel could not recall the name of it, her description suggests a variety of plantain or docken:

> Now there's a weed and I can't tell you the name of it — it's a very common weed that's in everybody's yard. The seed that comes up, it looks like a bird seed; the leaves are kind of shiny.
>
>   But you can take those leaves — it's good for poison of any kind — and wet it, and put it on, and you can feel it drawing after a while. Oh, and does that pull! And you take it off, and if you have lots of them, put more on, but you got to keep it damp all the time — just keep sticking it in water and keeping it damp. And that can really draw.

The second poultice was made from two ingredients found in any Quebec kitchen:

> Molasses and soap — the brown soap we used to get…I mean if you lived [here] and they used to buy the Sunlight soap and the Home Comfort. [And for this one you'd use] Comfort soap — it was in brown bars. And scrape a little of that off, put it in a saucer and mix it with molasses. Put that on, and that draws too.

Other recipes for poultices consisted of butter and salt mixed together, or bread soaked with boiling water and placed in a rag was also applied. Maryann Morrison commented, however, that if one of her family got a boil, they would just let it take its own course, as it would fester and break by itself. As with most ailments, nature eventually does take its own course, though most people prefer to do whatever they can to help relieve accompanying misery.

The old saying that 'an ounce of prevention is better than a pound of cure' fits well with all systems of traditional medicine. As in my own childhood in Skye, children were given a variety of tonics and preventatives, especially during and after the winter, when everyone is thought to be more suseptible to colds and flus. Fruit that had been bottled or dried in the autumn was highly valued for its vitamin content, as there was very little available during the long snowy season.

The most memorable tonic of all was the end of winter mixture of sulphur and molasses. Isobel Stewart described the procedure which, in their household, was an annual ritual at the onset of spring:

Molasses and sulphur! We'd all line up there and everybody'd have a spoonful of it…We'd take it once, then you'd miss four or five days…You'd have to take it three times, and miss two or three days between. Oh, that was *mi-chàilear* [distasteful], but we took it!

Although it was said that such a tonic 'cleaned out the blood', nobody seemed to know exactly what this meant.[28]

Fear of disease was very real, especially as there was always someone in the community, old or young, who had succumed to the most dreaded affliction of all — tuberculosis.[29] Once as rife in the Eastern Townships as it was in the Highlands and Islands of Scotland, 'TB' affected most families. Home-nursing was common, and those who suffered from it were given a daily tonic said to be beneficial to the patient. A discussion with Isobel Stewart drew close parallels between the tonic she knew and the one my own grandmother made: egg beaten with milk and brandy, though in Skye the shells were included, prepared a few days in advance by soaking them in the brandy, which softened them enough to allow them to be beaten in with the other ingredients.[30] Isobel's account was typical of many families:

A lot of our family died of TB. Now, they had to drink raw eggs till they were coming out their ears, that was supposed to have been a cure for it. There wasn't anything else for it, except I've known people to mix brandy in…Buy it at the Liquor Commission. And sugar, I guess, to add some, though some didn't bother with it…Just beat them up [with milk] like an egg-nog. But the shells, I've never heard of…Oh yes, there was an awful lot of our family died with it…Oh my, it was awful! Terrible!

Bessie Smith also described a home tonic which was given to anyone who suffered from TB: it was simply the liquid resin, or 'gum', extracted from the little blisters on the bark of fir trees. This was collected in a bottle, and every day the patient was given a spoonful of it mixed with a little sugar. According to Bessie, it was a most unpalatable medicine.[31]

Coming from the almost treeless islands of Lewis or Harris, the use of sap or resin from the trees must have been learned in Quebec. Its value was certainly known among the Micmac Indians, for, according to William Epps Cormack who journeyed across Newfoundland with an Indian guide in 1822, they used it for healing ulcers.[32] Isobel Stewart had a similar cure for an ailment that still defies modern medical science: 'The gum from the tree they say is good for people with cold sores — even people with asthma, they say…They just burst the bubbles, eat it, just eat it as it was, yes.'

Discussions of topics such as the above were once a regular part of the activities of the *taigh céilidh*. In the general course of conversation, one of these subjects would come up, say, warts or cold-sores. The entire company would then offer opinions, tell of experiences, and discuss the merits and demerits of each remedy. Thus, even when an illness or ailment was not present, the traditional medical knowledge was passed down from one generation to the next, in the same way as local history, weatherlore, placename lore, stories and songs. These discussions were all woven into the fabric of life. Judging by the fact that all the information recorded here is from elderly people, most of whom said that they could recall 'only a fraction of what the old people used to do before they had doctors,' it would be safe to assume that the Eastern Township Gaels were the custodians of a wealth of medical knowledge. Many of these traditions originated in the Isles of Lewis and Harris and have survived for generations, while others, equally as old, were assimilated in the New World. The gradual amalgamation of the wisdom of the Gaels, French and the native Indian population greatly enriches Quebec's folk culture.

Today, like most of the western world, Eastern Townshippers have come to rely upon formal medical knowledge, now much more readily accessible than in former times. Even so, there is still a strong interest in the wisdom of their forebears, and several of the traditional remedies are retained, while others are adapted to accommodate modern ideas — for example, common colds and coughs are still treated with hot lemon and honey with the addition of aspirin or another analgesic. Nevertheless, there are still a few conditions which, having failed to be healed by modern methods, are treated with the old-fashioned remedies. Information about them turns up when least expected: for example, in July 1995, not long after her eighty-first birthday, Ruth and I were about to set out from her house when she remark that she couldn't put her lipstick on because of a 'darned ol' cold sore — but never mind, it should be gone in a day or so' because she had tried Angus Willis's cure. Her former neighbour from Milan, Angus MacDonald, was Muriel's cousin, 'Uncle Willis's son' , who, as Muriel said, was 'very good with people who were sick.' *'Take the axe and burn a piece of newspaper on top of it. Then apply the ash that it leaves to the coldsore — it's an old cure. Angus died last year [1994] but Constance [his long-time partner who is French], reminded me to try it.'

What seems remarkable about this procedure is the fact that it *has* to be done *on top of the axe,* even in a household such as Ruth's where the cast iron kitchen stove is still the focus of all domestic life. Since she has the ideal, safe surface on which to burn a piece of newspaper, I asked Ruth 'why the axe?' to which she replied, 'Gosh, I don't know.' As with many traditional remedies that have been tried over the years, that's just the way it is.

Though Ruth and I left our discussion at that, it is quite conceivable that, consciously or not, the axe features as part of the cure because our forebears had a belief that an axe has special power in healing — it could 'cut pain', [33] or it could be placed between the patient and the outside world to keep the fairies away. [34] The newspaper is a feature of modern life, but a very similar burning-to-ash routine was followed in parts of Scotland where a piece of linen was burned to produce the ash was used in the treatment of the navel of a new infant.[35]

There is no 'closed medical system', with tradition giving way to formal medical school training. Instead, these systems may work hand in hand, or they may operate like a network, with freedom to go back and forth between them. There is also a third option which links tradition and formal medical training — that is, the array of patent medicines sold by peddlers like the 'Raleigh man', or, for that matter, today's modern pharmacy. Both succeed by borrowing the tested and tried treatments from tradition (like a piece of flannel), adding a new element from modern science (say, camphor oil) and, most important of all, packaging and marketing the goods with more enthusiasm and conviction than both the other methods put together.

Today, with a much wider access to print than there once was, there is a noticeable increase of interest in preventative medicine. The ageing population have more time to read and to absorb new ideas, some of which arrive unsolicited in the mail. As a result, these ideas also get woven into the discussions, usually introduced with a reference to the source. While mental and emotional health are valued as much as physical health, there also is the belief that, while each one can do his or her best to prolong general health, only God can sustain it.

Notes

1. Traditional medical practices have been recorded by countless writers, starting with Martin Martin, *Description…circa 1695*.

2. Payment to midwives was generally in kind, although if a patient was too poor to offer any reward it would make no difference to the attendance of the midwife. Among the French, the practice was similar. Roger Paradis points out that when the role of the midwife changed from being the sole attendant at a birth to that of Doctor's assistant, the midwives were hardly ever rewarded; the doctors simply departed without offering to pay his assistant, and the patients, often poor and hardly able to pay the doctor's bills, generally assumed that the doctor would be paying the midwife who gave of her services before, during and after the delivery. See 'Henriette, la Capuche: The Portrait of a Frontier Midwife', p. 125.

3. The same practice was also standard in Scotland. M. Bennett, *Scottish Customs from the Cradle to the Grave*, pp. 42 — 44.

4. I saw this done in 1976 when, after the death of an infant, a young mother needed relief from the pressure of her swollen breasts.

5. All information from Katherine M. MacKenzie is contained in personal correspondence to the author, 1976.

6. *Highland Folkways*, p. 314.

7. From Assynt, Sutherland, collected by Babi NicLeòid, in *Gaelic Proverbs,* p. 15.

8. Raleigh products are still sold widely throughout North America and 'Raleigh men' still travel the backroads of the Southern Appalachians.

9. Consisting of camphor and oil of thyme, 'Electric Oil' is still produced by Northrop Laboratories of Toronto and marketed commercially as 'Dr. Thomas's Electric Oil'.

10. Op cit, p. 177; see also use of melted butter, p. 179.

11. In older Scottish tradition, the use of thread or wool usually had a supernatural association, e.g. red thread worn to avert the evil eye; see J. G. Campbell, *Witchcraft and Second Sight in the Highlands and Islands of Scotland,* p. 61.

12. Vance Randolph notes that ashes were applied to cuts in the Ozarks because they 'make the cut heal without blood poisoning'. *Ozark Magic and Folklore,* pp. 124–25.

13. I have recorded several Gaelic-speaking people in the Codroy Valley, Newfoundland, who described the same treatments for cuts, including the emergency flour barrel method for the accidental amputation of a finger. Spruce gum, which is sometimes called rosin or turpentine, is extracted from the small bladders that form on the trunk. *The Last Stronghold,* p. 58.

14. In the late 1940s French-Canadian folklorist Luc Lacourcière recorded a blood-stopper in Montreal who also operated over the telephone. 'Médicine Populaire et Magic' in *Medicine et Réligion Populaires: Folk Medicine and Religion,* (ed. Pierre Crêpeau), p. 146.

15. Op cit, 1992 edition, p. 653 ff.

16. In the 1920s, Vance Randolph recorded detailed accounts of blood-stoppers in McDonald County, Missouri, who relied upon a Biblical text from Ezekiel, Ch. 16 . Op cit, p. 122 — 24.

17. See also Richard M. Dorson *Bloodstoppers and Bearwalkers,* pp. 150 — 65.

18. I.F. Grant gives an account of bone-setters in the Highlands, see *Highland Folkways,* p. 314.

19. Marius Barbeau, 'Boily le ramancheur', *Liaison,* 1948, 145-153.

20. Op cit, pp. 651 — 2. There are also reports of 'silvering the water', or placing a silver coin, sometimes one with the king's head on it, in the water before beginning the treatment.

21. Codroy Valley, Newfoundland, 1975. This method is widely known in Canada.

22. *Carmina Gadelica,* 1992 ed., p. 401.

23. The 'machine' was a broken X-ray machine, unplugged and re-labelled for the experiment. Dr D. Clow, recorded by M. Bennett, SA1985/130.

24. Fieldwork notebook, Aug. 1992; *Culpepper's Complete Herbal,* London, 1653, states that 'a decoction of yarrow is excellent for colds in the head, influenza, etc.' Op cit, p. 310 (1992 edn.) See also, R. Paradis, 'Henriette, la Capuche: The Portrait of a Frontier Midwife', *Canadian Folklore Canadien,* Vol. 3, No. 2, p. 122.

25. Also among the Gaels in Newfoundland, op cit, p. 58.

26. Cherry bark was also used in Newfoundland, op cit, p. 58.

27. Martin Martin, op cit, p. 181.

28. In Skye, my mother mixed sulphur and treacle, as her mother did. We were also told 'it cleaned the blood', though, unlike Isobel, we quite liked the taste of it. The custom is very old and widespread — it is even mentioned by Charles Dickens in *Oliver Twist*. The main difference in Quebec is that spring arrives three months later than in the Old Country.

29. An old Scottish medical belief that a decoction of nettles and mugw0rt taken every spring would prevent 'consumption' (tuberculosis) is recorded in Robert Chambers, *Popular Rhymes of Scotland*.

30. Although two of her daughters died from TB, she still gave her grandchildren a similar tonic. I recall a dash of nutmeg or cinnamon, but not the shells or brandy given to my mother's generation.

31. Turpentine (distilled pine resin) was once widely used for human and veterinary medicine in many parts of rural America. While working in the Southern Appalachians c. 1912, John C. Campbell noted that 'turpentine taken externally and internally, alone or in a combination with varous other ingredients, is a favourite household remedy.' *The Southern Highlander and His Homeland*, p. 205.

32. W.E. Cormack, *Narrative of a Journey across Newfoundland,* and *The Last Stronghold,* p. 139.

33. See also Wayland D. Hand's references to belief that an axe will cut pain: 'Popular Beliefs and Superstitions from North Carolina', *The Frank C. Brown Collection of North Carolina Folklore*, p. 10 and p. 191. In the context of international folk narrative Stith Thompson cites 'the magic axe' having similar properties, Motif D1206.

34. Any 'piece of cold iron', such as a knife, a razor or an axe would serve the purpose of keeping away the fairies. M. Bennett, *Scottish Customs,* pp. 11–22.

35. M. Bennett, op cit, pp. 36–37.

5

Faith of our Fathers

The Presbyterian Church

According to Bill Young, the most memorable qualities that characterised the early Hebridean settlers were 'pride, poverty, and the Presbyterian religion. Those were the keynotes!' Without exception, the first settlers were Presbyterian, and, though no other term is used today, according to descriptions of the church services held during the first two generations, they were closer to the format of the 'Free Church' in Scotland. The term may well have been used by the first settlers, as John Ramsay of Kildalton records in his *Diary* of 1870 that he 'stopped at Lingwick…to call for the Free Church minister who is a resident there.'[1] As Maryann Morrison pointed out, the church she went to in Marsboro was just the same as the one her family had left in Harris — the building was unadorned; the Minster stood in a high pulpit, below which was a 'box' for the precentors and elders; the services were solemn and always long — 'sometimes too long'; the fundamental truths of the Bible were taught; selected chapters and verses were memorised along with the whole of the Shorter Catechism; and only metrical psalms were sung, led by a precentor practised in the old style of 'lining out'.

Maryann explained that there was no organ or instrumental music, because 'There was no music in Jesus's funeral, or birth, or anything. They went by that, you know.'[2] Instead, every district had a few men whose strong, clear voices would lead the psalm singing, and for many years her own husband, R.E., was a precentor in the Marsboro Church:

> [There were] two men in the pulpit, and one would read his psalm, and the next one beside him would read the next. Two men in the *little* pulpit [usually called the precentors' box], and the minister sat above you. That's the way we were. But [my husband] was a good singer…very, very good. And he was an elder for years, and then we moved from that place and moved to another — to Lake Megantic, you hear about lately. And then they made him an elder in that congregation when he went there. Just the two elders…they would have a [psalm] each, you know: 'You sing this one, and I'll sing that one.' And they went like that, two or three verses in the psalms. And it was lovely — the roof would fall off the house![3]

In 1992, at the age of eight-seven, Ivy MacDonald, Ruth's aunt-by-marriage, spoke for the next generation on whom the church services also made a deep impression:

In the old days they had two [precentors]. It was usually one who did it, but then if he played out [laughs] there was another one to take over, you know. Oh, I remember years ago, as a little girl going to a church — have you been up to the cemetery where Ruth's people are buried? Well, it was before you get to that; there was a church there, a great, big Presbyterian Church, and there was a cyclone and the roof blew off so they never rebuilt it; they built the one up in Milan and then one up at the MacArthur Corner. Now what was I going to say about that?…Oh yes! Going to that church, one day my brother had croup and he couldn't go to church, and we lived out near the St. Leon road then, and Papa had two horses and they were snappy horses, good. And Mama couldn't come to church without bringing my brother too, so Papa and I went to church. And he said, 'Now you go in.' He had to put the horses away — it was a cold, cold day. And oh! There was this *huge* big church full, *full* of people. There was a big stove with pipes going, looked to me like miles of pipes, you know, to a chimney to warm the church. And I remember standing there feeling about that high, [she indicates two feet] you know. And I suppose when I closed the door, half of them turned around to look at me, you know, and I remember walking up, when Papa came in, walking to our seat and feeling so small with all those people there, you know. You can't believe all the people that used to be here! And when they'd sing, just the walls and the roof would just *reverberate*.[4]

The history of the Presbyterian Church in the Eastern Townships would fill its own book; indeed, the Special Collections at Bishop's University in Lennoxville have a large section of papers, files, photos and memorabilia which Muriel Mayhew, who is very much involved in the project, showed me. This chapter, however, can present the subject only from the viewpoint of the people whose lives it affected, and not from any theological standpoint.[5] Old photographs of church events and ministers seem to appear in everybody's album or in framed pictures on walls or dressers. And attached to every one of them are stories of the church, the minister, or both. Childhood memories always include the 'long services that lasted for hours' and the stern preachers whose fiery sermons left indelible impressions on young minds. Then there were the amusing anecdotes which allowed the over-serious Presbyterian to laugh at himself, at the same time satirising the stereotypical features of his church. One of the local favourites was told by Kenny MacLeod of Scotstown:

There was a minister who was preaching for a call. And of course, he wanted to make a great impression so that they would think he was quite a man. So, when he got up into the pulpit, he said: 'I tell you what I'm going to do today,' he said, 'I'm going to preach,' he says, 'on the prophets. And,' he said, 'that'll be my text today — the prophets.'

So he started in on Isaiah, and then he came to Jeremiah, and then he came to Ezekiel, and then he came to Daniel. The hour had gone by; and the hour and a half had gone by. 'Now,' he said, 'we'll start on the minor prophets. Now,' he said, 'for instance, where are we going to put Habakuk?'

This old fellow jumped up, he said: 'Put him in my seat! I've been here too long now!'[6]

Nevertheless, there was enormous public respect for the minister, who was generally regarded as the most important person in the parish. As the only one with any formal theological training, he was never directly questioned about the content of his sermons, though there might be plenty of discussion outwith his hearing. Reflecting on the sermons she used to hear in her youth, Muriel Mayhew was struck by the fact that 'it was mostly Old Testament theology. And they were learned men — good theologians, typical of the Presbyterian Church in those days. And all trained in Scotland.' And as in any walk of life, there was a wide range of personalities, some more memorable than others, some best forgotten, and some so well-loved that, on death, they were eulogised in song. Hand-written copies would circulate among congregations, to be 'sung to the tune of' some well-known Gaelic song. This example is one of twenty-six verses composed by Ian Morrison of Dell for the Rev. Roderick MacLean, minister of St. Luke's Church in Hampden, who died in 1908 at the early age of fifty-three:

Tha Hampden bochd an diugh fo ghruaim
'S an teachdair àluinn air thoirt uath
'S bhith 'g chàradh anns an uaigh,
Thug sgeula chruaidh r'a h-aithris dhuinn.

Fonn:

Far och, is och, is mo leòn;
Tha fear mo rùin an diugh fo'n fhòid!
Tha fear mo rùin an diugh fo'n fhòid!
'S chan éirich ceòl no aighear leam.

Poor Hampden is desolate today,
The gentle, bright teacher is taken from them
It is he who will be laid in the grave
Who brought the firm truth to us in his oration.

Chorus:

Woe is me, woe is my affliction;
My beloved one is today beneath the clay!
My beloved one is today beneath the clay!
No music or mirth will rise from me.[7]

The last Gaelic-speaking minister to preach in Milan was the Rev. Donald Gillies, originally from St. Kilda, who, after spending a few years in Cape Breton, moved to Quebec to take up a vacancy as student minister in Marsboro in 1930. He spent 1931 in Milan, and though he was 'called' to

Cape Breton after graduation, he kept lifelong ties with friends he had made, returning year after year as guest preacher at communions or special services. The last of these was the Gaelic service in Milan in July 1976, when I had the privilege of recording him preach. Judging from the welcome he received, and the obvious pleasure of having him 'in their midst', had the bards lived as long as the Rev. Mr. Gillies, no doubt one of them would have composed a song for him when, well into his nineties, he died in 1993.

Donald Gillies thoughtfully gave the insider's perspective of the ministry, and it is interesting to note that, above all the formal theological training he received at college in Scotland and in Canada, he valued the learning he received from the people who surrounded him in everyday life:

> I learned more of theology from the people I associated with here…the age
> before me, you know. There was [a very strong faith among them]. And it
> dominated the Kirk in my own home before I left, in St. Kilda, more than
> theology that I learned in the college. The foundation I got! I learned some [at
> college. But the more your learn], the more you feel…how ignorant you are.
> Nevertheless, as far as the 'real McCoy' of theology, as we may put it, you get it
> in the home and from the environment of the area that you're living in — that
> you and I were brought up in. We had to go to church twice a Sunday and
> once on Wednesday…You couldn't get an excuse to stay away from church; it
> was an unpardonable sin to stay away. That was how strict it was.

No matter how far home was from the church, it went without saying, 'you never missed a Sunday'. Bill Young recalled the 'twenties of his childhood and the 'thirties of his youth till he joined the army at the start of the war:

> [In my grandparents' house] they got up early on Sunday morning and they got
> ready for church…in the morning and the services were in Gaelic, and I *had* to
> go. Now, I was reaching the point where I could understand a bit of it, and I
> had to sit through this whole thing. And then, they'd go home, and I had to go
> to Sunday School. And then I'd go home, and we'd all have dinner, and there'd
> be relations or somebody dropped in. They'd be all sitting quietly around on
> the verandah, or something, if the weather was good. And then, somebody
> would be elected to say a prayer, and we'd all have to go into the house, and
> we'd all have to get down — kneel down while prayers were said. And then in
> the evening, back we'd go to church. Now, you had to have something like an
> earthquake or the end of the world for to stay home from that! You *had* to go
> — there was no way [you would be excused].
> We had eh, perhaps, as far as from here down to the corner there, to walk in
> the winter. A lot of people would come in from outlying districts and,
> especially in the morning service, they'd come in sleighs in the winter, and put
> their horses in sheds, and come in, and oh, a [?storm?] never stopped them. And
> Kate's folks never missed a Sunday.

Still strong and active at the age of eighty, in 1992 Maryann's son, Angus, cheerfully contemplated the possibility that all the exercise they got walking back and forth to church may even have contributed to the longevity in the family:

> 'S bhiodh sinn trì mìle a' coiseachd — a dhol dhan eaglais. Anns a' mhadainn bhiodh sinn a' dol gu *Sunday School* mu dheich uairean, 's nuair a thigeadh sinn as a' *Sunday School* dheidheadh sinn dhan a' choinneamh Ghàidhlig. [Thòisicheadh e] mu aon uair deug, 's bhiodh e as déidh meadhon-latha. Bha na ministearan a' cumail na seirbheis glé fhada, uair a thìde is uair gu leth. Choisicheadh sinn dhachaidh a rithist, dà mhìle eile. Anns an fheasgar, choisicheadh sinn dhan eaglais a rithist — chun na *h-Evening service* mu sheachd uairean. Bha sin da mhìle dheug anns a latha a' coiseachd dhan eaglais…Bha sinn a' coimhead glé mhath le deise bhrèagha 's brògan, ach bhiodh sinn a' dol dha'n sgoil air ar casan rùisgte — cha robh brògan againn…Dìreach ach Làtha na Sàbaid!

> [*We would walk three miles to church. In the morning, we would go to Sunday School around ten o'clock, and when we would come out of Sunday School we would go to the Gaelic meeting. [It began] around eleven o'clock, and it would be out at mid-day. The ministers used to have very long services, an hour or an hour and a half long. We walked home again, two more miles. In the evening, we walked to the church again for the Evening service around seven o'clock. That was twelve miles a day walking to church… We were looking very good with beautiful suits and shoes, but we would be going to school on our bare feet — we didn't have shoes [on us then]…Only on Sundays!*[8]]

At home as well as in Sunday School children were taught obedience to the Ten Commandments, and though both mother and father had important roles in the teaching, as far as the traditional structure of the church went, there was no opportunity for women to voice an open opinion. The church, as well as society, was male-dominated, and if this situation ever came into question, then Paul's advice to the churches was enough to settle the issue: 'Let the women be silent'. Christie MacKenzie noted that, while it was true that the women could never express an opinion at congregational meetings, they could still have an indirect influence through their husbands. Bill Young also noticed that while the women adhered to this custom in church, they liked to air their opinions at home:

> Well, you know, the women in those days, they never very often, in public, questioned a man's positions; but they did in private! [laughs] Well, I've heard them. But you know, Kate's father and mother came home, and she'd sometimes mention something about the service. And your father would growl, and he wouldn't say too much, but perhaps he'd go, 'Tch — ' or something.

That may have been one technique of concluding the discussion, but there were also homes where women were remembered as controlling the entire household when it came to putting their religion into practice. When Johnnie

'Bard' MacLeod looked back on his early days in Dell, he acknowledged that the church had a powerful influence over the community, but within the MacLeod household he was convinced that his own mother 'seemed to be possessed with religion':

> She seemed to feel that God would hold it against her if she would miss a prayer meeting anywhere within the confines of the church parish. These meetings were always held on a Thursday at two o'clock in the afternoon. Consequently, whatever Papa might be doing with the team of horses would usually have to be postponed at noon on that day so that Mama could have one horse to go to the prayer meeting with.

He remembered too that the first time she saw a bicycle she said she'd seen 'the devil going by on wheels.' Within their home she let it be known that 'playing cards was sinful — she'd never have them in the house'. Like many of her generation, she regarded dances as taboo, and as for the use of tobacco, 'poor Papa could never enjoy a relaxed smoke in her presence.' It was not until she discovered that Billy Graham, the American evangelist, broadcast on a Sunday that she relaxed her views about playing the radio.[9]

Just as the traditions of the church were connected to every aspect of daily life, so they also blended with ancient beliefs dating back to a pre-Christian era. Not that any would acknowledge it, but, as in Gaelic Scotland, the rowan tree, for example, with its ancient connections to supernatural powers, would be more likely to be found beside the ruined homestead of one of the first settlers, all faithful Presbyterians, than planted next to the modern home of a non-believer.

Despite the frequent references to the austerity of fundamental Presbyterianism, almost everyone acknowledged that the church played a very positive part in uniting the community. There was a certain security in knowing and observing the limitations set by the church, even if at times one felt restricted by them. The Bible had a central place in every kitchen, and 'Sunday best' clothes were regularly in use. Ivy MacDonald looked back over the years and, comparing today's relaxed attitude to the days of her youth, she exclaimed, 'Oh, my goodness! In the old days, indeed in *my* day, we'd never *think* of going to church without a hat, never!'

Gabhail an Leabhair: Family Worship

No matter what day of the week it was, it began and ended with family worship, a familiar feature of Highland Presbyterian homes since the Reformation. Each household followed a set pattern of *gabhail an Leabhair*, [lit. 'taking the Book'], usually by the kitchen stove, as was the case in Christie MacKenzie's home in Milan:

My father and mother always had family worship, but he couldn't read the Gaelic. But oh boy, his father could read the Gaelic [Bible] and sing; he was a precentor in the church for years and years — Murdo MacKenzie, *Murchadh [— ?]* we used to call him. — Well, they opened with a *beannachd* [blessing], the *adhrachail* [devotional] and they'd read the chapter, and those as could read the Gaelic would sing a psalm too. And then they closed with prayer; everybody got on their knees, [just around the kitchen], yeah, and no matter how busy they were, this was done right after breakfast, before they'd go out to work. And then, in the evening again, after supper, before going to bed…Well, there may be one or two that [still] do in Scotstown, but not very many.

In the opinion of the Rev. Donald Gillies, the strength of the Presbyterian Church had its deepest roots in the Highland tradition of family worship. He pointed out that, generation after generation, when people faithfully adhered to the custom of their forebears the village churches were filled to capacity, and furthermore, people 'knew their Bible':

The church started at home. If you haven't got a church started at home, you're not going to have a church outside…The home is the church, now, you see. And eh, you know, the parents, they saw that [the children] went to Sunday School…To begin with, that generation was entirely a different generation [to the present one]. They had the Bible — that's all that they were concerned about. A concordance wasn't in their minds [i.e. needed]as well as that — they had a full knowledge of the Scripture…when you met a fellow man that was dedicated and devoted to the church, and lived according to the doctrines of the church…[in response to] certain questions even in the Bible and — he didn't need the concordance; he would tell you exactly where it was! There was family worship at home.

Bill Young, who was brought up in Scotstown, recalled childhood memories of the same custom: 'And every night before bed-time there was a reading from the Bible, and…I remember as a child having to turn around and kneel on the hard floor while I was saying prayers, and it went on and on till my knees were sore.' Isobel Stewart continues:

Oh, yes, yes, everywhere! Everywhere! They'd read the Bible and they'd sing a hymn[10]. And everybody'd get down and kneel. We took it for granted that was *it* — that was what we were supposed to do. But today they never do that. [But some of the old people still do it, read their Bible in Gaelic.] Oh, yes, like Annie [MacDonald, Dell], she won't let Angus go to the barn till he reads the Bible — he's the one that reads the Bible [in that home].

Naturally, an ability to read Gaelic was a factor in deciding who would lead the family worship, but usually the one regarded as head of the household did so automatically. Maryann Morrison explained how the tradition was faithfully followed from one generation to the next. When she was a child, her father, led the family in worship; then when she and her husband were first married, Maryann's father was still regarded as head of the household as the young couple lived with her parents:

> But when we moved [into our own cabin my husband] started to do it, and I told him ' Now, you'll have to take my father's place,' I said. And he did, he did. He'd read the Bible and pray...When they [the children] grew up, ready to read, he would take one [verse] and they would read the Bible verse about...So like that they got a good [grounding].

And, as her son Angus recalled, though Maryann had a more silent role than her husband, she could also take over the reading when appropriate:

> Bha i fhéin a leughadh a' Bhìobuill gach maduinn 's gach oidhche...bha, 's gheibheadh i sinn a h-uile duine againn air ar glùinean...leughadh m'athair 's bhiodh e a' deanadh an ùrnuigh, ach mara biodh m'athair ann [bhiodh] mo mhàthair a leughadh a' Bhìobuill. 'S bhiodh i cheart cho math air. 'S e eildear a bha na m'athair.

> [She herself was reading the Bible every morning and every night...yes, and she would have every single one of us on our knees...my father would read and he'd say a prayer, but if my father wasn't there, my mother would read the Bible. And she was pretty good at it. My father was an elder.]

As the years went by, R.E.'s health began to fail, so gradually Maryann began to assume more of the duties of family worship:

> When his — her father couldn\'t read or say a prayer, I used to read the Bible at the bed. And he'd say: 'You read the Bible, and I'll say a prayer.' So we did that, you know. And before he died, he told me: 'I can't get to pray like I used to be, but I'm going to — you read the Bible, and I'll take this psalm for a prayer today.' Just a short psalm he took for a prayer :

Mo shuile togam suas a chum	'Se Dia t'fhear-coimhid; se do sgàil
nam beann, o'n tig mo neart.	air do làimh dheis gu buan.
O'n Dia rinn talamh agus nèamh,	A' ghrian cha bhuail i thu san là,
tha m'fhurtachd uile teachd.	no ghealach fòs san oidhch'.
Cha leig do d' chois air choir air bith	Ni Dia do choimhead o gach olc;
gu'n sleamhnuich i gu bràth;	ni t'anam dhìon a chaoidh.
Tàmh-neul cha tig sin air an neach	Do dhol a mach, 's do theachd a steach,
s fear coimhid ort a ghnàth.	coimhididh Dia a ghnàth;
Feuch, air fear-coimhid Israeil,	O'n aimsir so a nis a t'ann,
codal cha'n aom no suain:	's o sin a mach gu bràth.[11]

After R.E. died, Maryann moved to Montreal with Eva, and it was only natural that she should lead family worship in her daughter's home. For nearly

thirty years in the city nothing changed her ways, no matter who came or
went — she would read and pray aloud in Gaelic every morning when she
got up, and again before going to bed. And, as I discovered, those who visited
with her were included in the daily devotions. Maryann lived to be a hundred
and seven and when I recorded her in 1976 at the age of a hundred, she
regetted she no longer sang, as she felt her voice could not do justice to the
psalms of her youth, or to the hymns that became popular in later life. With
no more housework to take up her time, she spent many hours silently reading
her Gaelic Bible — 'Well, this is what I understand better than English.' She
also enjoyed reading sacred poetry: 'Did you ever read Padruig Grannd's book?
[My mother] used to be repeating those…I have a book here…Well, it's very
good. And if you like to read it, I'll give it to you. Lots of good reading in it,
lots.' Maryann was typical of her generation: over a lifetime of studying the
Bible, she had committed to memory large sections of it and also many of
the metrical psalms. Her fluency and clarity were not just a reflection of her
competence in reading the Gaelic Bible, but more an indication of her
thorough knowledge of the Book that was at the very centre of the lives of
her people.

Bookshelves had an important place in the home, (see Chapter 2) and, from
the ones I looked at in Milan and Scotstown, there was a good number that
reflected the strong faith of those who lived there. I was able to tell Maryann
that I had already made my acquaintance with Padruig Grannd's *Dain
Spioradail* (Peter Grant's Spiritual Verses, a book of hymns) on 'Aunt' Annie's
bookshelf in Milan. It sat beside *Pilgrim's Progress,* several works by the familiar
religious writers such as the Rev. Andrew Murray, and Gaelic collections of
religious verse such as *Laoidhean agus Dain Spioradail* by Murchadh MacLeoid
and *Dana: A Chomhnadh Crabhaidh* by Seumas Mac-Ghriogair. My first sight
of Aunt Annie's shelves of religious books immediately reminded me of
neighbours' houses in Lewis and of my own grandparents' home in Skye,
where, every Sunday, as children we were encouraged to 'read quietly' on the
Day of Rest. And so it was in Quebec, until, in her old age, Maryann's weeks
had seven 'days of rest' which she spent contentedly surrounded by her
beloved books. Perhaps she sensed an awe at her attainment of such peace, as
she quickly pointed out that she had not always been so content to observe
even *one* Day of Rest. As young girl, she and her sister positively resented the
restrictions imposed upon them by the strict code of the church. And, from
all accounts, Maryann may have spoken on behalf of generations of children.[12]

Sabbath Observance and Unforgettable Saturdays

Thoir an aire Latha na Sabaid, a naomhachadh, mar a dh'aithin an Tighearna do
Dhia dhiut, sea laithean saothraichidh tu agus ni thu t'obair uile…

['Remember the Sabbath Day to keep it holy. Six days shalt thou labour and do all thy work but the Seventh is the Sabbath of the Lord thy God. In it thou shalt not do any work...'[13]]

The words of the Fourth Commandment were imprinted on every mind even before children learned to read, and the implications of 'keeping the Sabbath holy' punctuated every week of life. Though the phrase 'Sabbath Observance' is known far and wide, it is often associated with the Presbyterian Islands of Lewis, Harris and Skye, when visitors discover just how literally it is observed.[14] They may not realise, however, the extent of the preparation that takes place the day before. But in Lewis, Harris, Skye, or Quebec, there is a general consensus of opinion that 'by the time Sunday came around you were ready for a rest.'[15]

> Saturday! Of course we had the well-house out back, you know, and we had the rope, with the bucket on the rope. We had to bring in the water; we had to bring in the wood. And if we had a [home-made toy] cart — we didn't have many toys, of course — we had to put our toys away...Everything had to be put away on Saturday — you had to bring in all your wood.

Isobel Stewart's experience in Dell was fairly typical of most families, and, having regularly taken part in the weekly household routine, Bill Young could remember as if it was yesterday:

> There was filling wood-boxes, splitting the kindling, piling the wood...That had to be all done the day before; even the meals had to be prepared the day before. You might put the kettle on, or something like that, but the rest was ready. Cooking was put aside — [you'd hear] 'This pie is for Sunday; this cake is for Sunday; this cold meat's for Sunday.' Sunday there was nothing to be done!

The oft-quoted Fourth Commandment made it perfectly clear what could, or could not, be done on Sunday: , 'except for the works of necessity and mercy'. Isobel continued, 'The only thing, they'd milk the cows, or something that really *had* to be done, but no stable was cleaned, or anything like that.' Writing in the 1880s, however, Dugald McKenzie McKillop noted that his people from Arran soon discovered they had to change their custom of bringing in the water on Saturday night for Sunday because by morning it was completely frozen and useless. No doubt with the advent of efficient stoves and bigger kitchens the custom was re-instated, as Katherine M. MacKenzie, formerly of Whitton, indicated in a letter to me in 1976: 'All work had to be finished by 12 midnight Saturday, drinking water for the next day, food and fuel all prepared.' Looking at the positive side, some 'children' remembered they rather liked not having to make beds on Sunday, and the sight of Sunday supper dishes on Monday morning made the prospect of school more attractive.[16]

There were times, however, when it was difficult to understand a faith that would keep people from harvesting crops during a week when the only fine day turned out to be a Sunday. As a new bride, Angus Morrison's wife, Mary, could clearly recall the adjustment she had to make when she moved from the French Catholic home of her parents to the Presbyterian stronghold of her in-laws in Cruvag. Her mother-in-law, Maryann, had a certain sympathy with Mary, as she told her how a stern uncle once rapped her sharply across the knuckles for picking a few raspberries by the roadside to eat on the way home from church. Mary found it difficult to reconcile this kind of behaviour with the Christian faith; furthermore, the story related in the four gospels is well known: 'Jesus went on the Sabbath day though the corn; and His disciples were an hungered, and began to pluck the ears of corn, and to eat...' His response to the Pharisees is also well known; nonetheless, there is no mention of being able to eat raspberries. [17]

Kenny MacLeod of Scotstown, also strictly brought up to observe the Sabbath, found that his generation began to adopt more relaxed attitudes as they left home. Kenny could nevertheless joke about the old ways, characteristically attributing the strictest observances to a village other than his own: 'Well, they tell a story about the Scotch, and how strict they were. Take out in Marsboro — Saturday they used to tie up the rooster till Monday morning!'

No doubt in Marsboro they told different stories, though even those from personal experience could be slightly exaggerated in the mind of a child, as Maryann Morrison demonstrated:

> And my grandmother, we hate[d] my grandmother keeping us in on Sunday. We couldn't go out and play with the other children. And she would keep us there — read the Bible, read the psalms, read the Catechism on Sunday. But you can go out any other day to play — but [at the time] we hate[d] my grand-mother for that! Oh, they were all religious people, my mother's side.

Even if they had been allowed to go out to play, Maryann would have found very few 'other children' to play with in the neighbourhood, for they too would have been under the same strict rules. And things were no different 'over in Dell' as Isobel Stewart remembered:

> Of course in the wintertime we weren't allowed to [sledge or play in the snow]. And to whistle! That was one of the biggest curses! To whistle on Sunday — now, isn't that strange? Oh, no, everything had to be very quiet on Sunday. Gosh! Nothing like today — *ugh!* [Isobel's expression of disgust is directed at the way things are today, though she was not considered to be particularly religious.]

Whenever the subject comes up, similar sentiments are re-echoed time and time again. Bill Young showed another aspect of Sabbath Observance as he spoke of his memories as a youngster in the 1920s and 30s and even into post-war years:

> Sunday was a dead day at out house. A dead day. You dressed up; you had your breakfast, and sat quietly around the house all day. You done nothing else. You didn't even whistle…And my grandfather had a big, gold watch-chain. Well, it might have been dipped [i.e. plated], I don't know! But it was a big, heavy thing. And he'd take that off, and he'd put his shoelace on it when he went to church, because you're not supposed to show any vanity, eh. Remember that? No vanity. The women ought to wear a dress with collars and long sleeves. I can remember the first young girl who went to church in short sleeves…and the church pretty near all got up and sat on the other side of the aisle!
>
> Not too long ago, right in the church in Scotstown, Murray got up one night and preached against it. He would never allow anyone in there in that [— ?] Immodesty, vanity!

Only religious books were allowed to be read on Sunday, though in some homes, this rule applied to every day of the week. Bill Young's grandmother was an enthusiastic reader of spiritual books, which seemed reason enough for her to decide on behalf of the entire family:

> Well, it had to be religious, something religious. Oh, heavenly days! I remember the first Western story she ever caught me with in the house! Well, I got rid of that fast — or she did! It wasn't on Sunday either! Whooosh! That was clear trash.

Apart from attendance at church morning and evening, the day was usually spent with family, relatives or friends sharing dinner and a quiet afternoon together. Inevitably there was an opportunity to go over the morning's sermon and elaborate on some of the points raised in the sermon. Sometimes there were lengthy discussions on points of theology, depending on who happened to be there. When the Rev. Donald Gillies first came to Milan as a student, he sat in on many such sessions and became very much aware of the fact that many individuals were so well-versed in the Bible that they could quote chapter and verse at great length without the aid of any reference to print:

> You could mostly find them talking about what had occurred in the service, or what the service was all about, or you would find…two or three of the elderly individuals talking there about…oh, scripture. This, is what you would find here. I know — for a fact.

The Revd Mr Gillies may not have realized, however, the extent to which the congregation respected the statements and opinions of the clergy, for, as long as the minister was 'in their midst', no real controversy would break out. When Kay Young exclaimed: 'In our grandfather's time, you didn't question the minister!' her husband, Bill, emphatically agreed:

Oh, you didn't question him — he was omnipotent, eh. The minister was the man, and, if he called at your house, you were honoured. Highly honoured. There's a story of an old fellow who went to church and he didn't agree with the minister on something. And it never stopped him from going to church, but he wouldn't go in the church. He'd sit outside in the entrance and listen to the sermon, but he wouldn't go in the church because there was something the preacher had said or done outside the church that he didn't agree with. But he didn't hold that against the religion at all. No, the preacher was accepted, regardless, because of the religion he taught — not on account of the man — and he'd had to have Gaelic — he had to have it!

Na h-òrduighean

Twice a year, usually in June and September (or October), the Presbyterian Church celebrated the Sacrament of the Lord's Supper, or *Na h- òrduighean,* as this five-day event was called. Lasting from Thursday to Monday inclusive, this series of church services was looked forward to immensely by everyone in the community, as Duncan McLeod explained:

> The communions, oh, it was a chance for people to get together. They came from a 25 mile radius…What they used to do back then when there was a sizeable community, while the Gaelic service was on in the church they would have the English service in the grove beside the church.[18]

Not only were these biannual events the highlights of the church year, they were also important social occasions, as people from outlying districts could visit friends and relatives they saw only very rarely — at weddings, funerals, or *na h-òrduighean*. People would drive in by horse and buggy from many miles around, and every family within easy reach of the church could expect to have a houseful from Thursday to Monday. Myrtle Murray, who became the school-teacher in Milan in the 1920s, remembers the impression communion season made upon her as a new-comer to the area:

> A different custom in their religious world was the *òrduighean,* spring and fall…I never heard of them or never saw them till I went to Milan…Some people would travel to each *òrduighean,* and they would go to the homes and stay with friends or relatives. I remember my husband [Jack Murray from Milan, whom Myrtle married a few years afterwards] saying when the *òrduighean* was on in Milan, you never planned to sleep in your own bed, you slept wherever there was room. Probably twelve or thirteen people would come from Marsboro, or Middle District. The Milan people would go to these other places, Marsboro, Megantic, Middle District, whatever…. I knew nothing about it until I went among the Scotch…some of them came by foot, and they just parked in with friends or relatives, or whatever.

Originally from Marsboro though for many years a resident of Lennoxville, Ferne Murray recalled what it was like to be at home when *na h-òrduighean* was held locally:

> ★I remember my mother would be cooking for a week in advance; it was nothing for us to have eighteen or twenty to dinner. And you always knew as children that you would be sleeping on the floor — there would be blankets and quilts put on the floor for us children, while the aunts and uncles and others would have the beds. At mealtimes there would always be three sittings at the table, and we would always be the third — you'd never *expect* to be at the first sitting; that was for the guests. And though the main purpose was supposed to be spiritual — and it was — mother would remark about the social side, how much they all enjoyed the visiting. They had a wonderful time together, and that was one of the things that made the Scotch 'different' from other English-speakers in the area, as it set them up with a family and community awareness we didn't find that incomers from the city had.'

While this religious observance was 'different' to Myrtle, to the 'Gaelickers', as she called them, it was simply taken for granted, as predictable as Christmas or Easter, and the very mention of *na h-òrduighean* provokes happy memories for those who are old enough to have attended. They tell of visits and conversation lasting for hours on end — theological discussions sparked off by the church services, the latest news of family and friends, or stories and reminiscences on whatever topic happened to be raised. They recall the pleasure of mealtimes with friends, and the spirit of hospitality that characterised every home. [19]

While the socialization was much enjoyed, the main focus of the five days was intended to be on the church events. The pattern was the same each time, as Maryann described:

> Well, every day Thursday, they call it *Latha na Taisg* [day for pledging] — they do yet, *Latha an Taisg*. And we just gathered there to read and pray. A man here and there getting up in church and praying...That's the way they were going on, opening the church in the morning. And — that was Thursday. Friday they had a *Ceisd* day [*Latha na Céisd,* the day for questioning]. Some putting out, you know, a verse, and all the others were reading out, and all that, and talking about it, and how they were converted, and all that — nice, nice, nice! Saturday, of course, there wasn't so much going on, but Communion Sunday — we had a school house near the church, and the English-[speaking] people from Megantic would be coming to Marsboro, and we had English church in the school house, but the Gaelic in the big church, you know, in Marsboro. And that's the way we were working it. Very good.
>
> Well, Monday was just any other ordinary day, praying, and reading the Bible, and...getting out, like that, you know, when the ministers [visited]. We always have two and three ministers coming from Montreal, and some from Ontario, and...of course we had to pay those people coming [from] far away.

Myrtle Murray also remembered that on Friday 'they had a question box, and the elders, along with the visitors, would take these questions out, and then have a conference and discuss some of them.' Her first impressions of *na h-òrduighean* remained with her well over fifty years:

> I stayed over [in Milan for one of the school holidays] one year to go, and I was amazed at the hundreds of people who went into the Gaelic service and came out. And if it was a fine day on Sunday, by this time they would have an English service in the sugar bush. English was being more spoken, but a lot of the elderly people just did not talk anything but Gaelic.[20]

When Muriel Mayhew, a former pupil of Myrtle Murray's, looked back on 'many a communion season', she especially recalled the predominant colour of dress worn by the congregation: 'Oh black! everything was black!' and the fact that there were very strict rules governing who was permitted to the Lord's Table. Communion Sunday was the day on which all church members partook of the Lord's Supper, and those going to 'the Lord's Table' for the first time marked the beginning of a public commitment to Christ and the following of His teachings as understood by the Presbyterian Church. This decision was considered a serious step in life, 'not to be entered into lightly,' but only after much soul-searching, then a statement to the minister to 'make known intentions' followed by a solemn examination by the Church Session. Members of the Session were at liberty to accept or reject the candidate, depending upon whether or not he or she was considered to have the required faith and devotion for such a commitment.

On Thursday, Friday, and Saturday, people were given the opportunity of taking this solemn step, and all new communicants were given a small metal token which would admit them to the Lord's Table on Sunday. Those who were already members also received tokens, so that only those considered worthy would gain admission. The Rev. Donald Gillies explained briefly: 'The Session was constituted on Thursday; you came before the Session, and the Session would examine you — regarding your faith, you know, and what was the reason that you were coming to the Lord's service. And if you were found worthy you were accepted.' Sometimes known as 'fencing the tables', as only those with tokens were admitted on Communion Sunday, Muriel recalled that 'Some of the [communion] tokens were metal; [in later years] some were card; you had to have one to take communion. If you joined the church you got one before communion,' And, emphasising how strict it was, she added with a smile, 'and if you had done something bad since the last one they would be taken away.' When I asked what sort of things would be termed 'bad', before she could compose a serious response, Duncan McLeod mischievously joked, citing the least likely scandal that he could invent — 'Oh, like going out with the minister's wife, or the organist, you know!

[laughs] I don't know when you got your card back!' — his point being that *any* scandalous behaviour was likely to come under the watchful eyes of the minister and the elders.

On the actual day, the Communion Table with the bread and wine was at the front of the church, below the pulpit, and although people talked of 'going to the Lord's Table', they were in fact served from it by the elders. The communicants sat in a designated number of pews at the front of the church, which were generally roped off ('fenced'). The back of the pews were covered with white cloth or sheeting, the 'tablecloths of the Lord's Supper.' The service itself was long, sometimes two or three hours, and was the high point of the five days, at times very emotional, and occasionally reducing some of the participants to tears.

On the final day, Monday, a morning service of thanksgiving was held, and *na h-òrduighean* was over. Those who had travelled prepared to go home, and the village returned to its former routine, all hoping to feel uplifted and fortified for the months to come by the inspiration, rest and pleasure of the five-day spiritual exercise.[21]

Onwards and Upwards

The traditional ways of the Presbyterian Church were not, however, to continue, for, suddenly, a major and drastic change occurred even while Gaelic, the language of Quebec Presbyterianism, was still fairly strong. It was initiated at a national level when plans were afoot among all the Protestant Churches to form what is now known as The United Church of Canada. Though there was a great deal of discussion at a local level, the very prospect of such radical change brought division within communities once firmly bonded by their Presbyterian faith. Comparing this crisis to what her parents had told her of the Disruption of 1843, Maryann Morrison lamented the turmoil as she felt that the split affected their beloved church so profoundly, that it never regained its strength:

> Well, people was upside-down, you know — very much. The Presbyterians at Megantic lost their church...to the Union. They had to build one, so they built one and we went over there. But it was a small one, you know, not a big, big church like the one they had.
>
> Oh, [according to some] they were no good! they were no good, Presbyterians, Presbyterians. The Union was for change...But they didn't change the Bible any, no. But there was the same thing in Scotland [during the Disruption] — sisters wouldn't talk to sisters. Brothers wouldn't look at brothers...Then it was the same at Megantic too.
>
> Well, now, the Presbyterians built a little church for themselves, and there's where our father was buried from...And when the Union was over [complete], and the people going to the other church, and us going to the [original one] —

oh, it was so funny. People you know, and you'd just pass them by and didn't say
'Good morning', or 'How are you?' Not a word. Well, they took our little
church and went with the Union to the big, big church. And then after years
and years, the [United] church got so small…there was nobody coming; people
was going away to Montreal and to the States from the farms, you know, left
the farms and go and live down to the States. And they couldn't keep the big
church up…And they sold the church to the Presbyterians for one dollar! We
got our big church back, and that's where Sam was buried from, but his father
and his other brother was buried from the little church, you know, the…
Presbyterian. But they turned Presbyterians, you know…gave the church for
one dollar! They come back, you know, they know that it was just as good as
the Union.

While those who decided to go with the union in Megantic eventually,
through lack of numbers, returned to the Presbyterian Church, the
congregations remained divided in Scotstown, where two separate churches
settled into harmonious co-existance

Naturally, changes bring new ideas, and before long some members of the
Presbyterian congregations began feel out of step with other Protestant
churches where an organ and hymn singing had become standard practice.
Initially this caused further discord, especially among the older generation
who wanted their form of worship to remain as it was. Not that the psalms
were antiquated, for they are timeless, but instrumental music was the fashion,
and as such was more attractive to the younger generation. As Maryann put
it, the older people 'didn't care for happy things, and happy songs, or anything,
just…to get the psalms…But, by the last of the time, they got used to it, and
they liked it. But they didn't like it first.'

The Quebec Gaels were not, however, the only Canadian immigrants who
felt pressured to forsake their much-loved style of psalm-singing, as this was
also the experience of the Russian group, the Doukhobors. Having lived
through and observed the decline of Russian psalm-singing in Canada, in
1975 a retired Doukhobor school-teacher offered this explanation which
might equally apply to the Gaels:

> Perhaps the old type of psalm-singing is doomed. Why? Because the old type were
> [sic] based on martyr-like suffering, sung by old-timers who actually suffered in
> Siberia and elsewhere. The style was melancholic. Now in a new setting in Canada,
> the young people have not experienced the same suffering and consequently, they
> will not be able to take over these psalms. [22]

And so, in line with the rest of the Presbyterian Church of Canada, the
organ and the hymns became standard, with the occasional psalm woven in
and sung in the new style.

Today, only the older generation remember the huge throngs of faithful
Presbyterians that once flocked to *na h-òrduighean and* filled every pew in the

churches. Old photographs taken after communion services, and memories, such as those recorded here, are all that is left of the old-style church gatherings. The custom of distributing communion tokens to the 'worthy' is now a thing of the past — there is a glass-case display of tokens and other items of historical interest in Scotstown church, dating back to the time of the first settlers who arrived in Winslow in the 1850s. Changes are inevitable, and, as several people would point out, they need not be for the worse. Today women play a more visible role and also have a voice in the concerns of the church.

Muriel Mayhew, a church elder and 'volunteer historian' for St. Andrew's Presbyterian Church, Sherbrooke, reflected on her lifelong association with the church. Having seen dramatic changes over the years, she felt that, apart from the poorer attendance, many had been for the better. From her youth, it had struck Muriel that the presentation of the gospel was generally lacking in joy and in the spirit of love:

> *Most of the old-style ministers preached sermons of *fear* — not the *love* of Christ. A lot of ministers came from Scotland, but it was The Rev. Malcolm MacDonald, born and brought up in Winslow, Quebec, who was the first I ever heard preach an evangelical message, based on repentance and the love of Christ.

She remembered that her 'mother was indignant' when Muriel commented on the stern, judgemental attitude that many ministers showed, and, using as one example her own mother's days as a 'thankless skivvy' to the minister, she suggested they were 'not above criticism themselves' as far as their own way of life was concerned. Then there was the indelible memory of a young woman (named) who married a man who loved to dance and she, though brought up by parents who frowned on dancing, went with him to the village dances. Tragically, she died in childbirth, and so did her newly-born infant. Naturally the funeral service was filled with grief for this beloved friend, daughter, wife, mother, sister, but it was made infinitely worse by the minister (named) who chose as his text 'The wages of sin is death.'

The numbness was unforgettable, and Muriel felt that there was a harshness in the attitude of some of the clergy. She reiterated that this 'lack of love' was a feature which seemed to go unnoticed by most her mother's generation who 'put the minister up on a pedestal'. Or, as the Doukhobor school-teacher suggested, that too may have been a reflection on a much more austere way of life.

The emphasis of the Presbyterian Church has shifted considerably since the days when the traditions brought over by the first Hebridean settlers were rigidly followed. One of the aims today is to re-examine the customs associated with Presbyterianism and to ascertain whether or not they are still relevant. In 1976, the Rev. Tony Boonstra put it this way in the sermon he delivered in Milan Bethany Church on the first Sunday in November:

And what about our traditions? Are we doing things a certain way because our forefathers did them in this way or because they are the most meaningful to us today?

How much do we rely on our tradition? If it happened to us as it did to the people of Eastern Europe, that there was a sudden change of government, and because of it we would be unable to worship as we see fit, would our faith be able to sustain the altered situation?

Are we able to say that in the last analysis it is not the faith of our fathers that counts, but it is my faith? What counts is my personal commitment to Christ. Our forebears only pointed us in the right direction. But it is for us to chart our own path. It is for us to search the Scriptures daily...Are you willing and able to say with Luther: I take my stand — not on the church, not on tradition, but on the Word of God...I will not let custom or tradition stifle the work of the Holy Spirit.

It would have to be said, however, that one of the strongest traditions of the Eastern Township Gaels was 'searching the Scripture' — the daily family worship. It has not totally disappeared, but it is the steady erosion of this very tradition that the Rev. Donald Gillies identified as the source of the drastic decline in church-going. Tradition cannot therefore be regarded as some general negative force of the past; it consists of a complex amalgam of practices; some, as Muriel pointed out, best forgotten; others so vibrant that if we abandon them the life-force that drives them eventually dies.

Over the years the changes within the Church have been reflected in the daily lives of the people. The older generation look back on the days when the Church imposed its strict rules on everyone, yet each one was filled to capacity. But, as Christie MacKenzie pointed out, those days were also characterised by a strong spirit of fellowship which united the community: 'There was wonderful feeling for one another...And that was the neighbourliness.' Asked if the old folk been too strict in their observation of religion she replied 'There might have been some, but oh my, I would give a lot to have it back to where they had it. Their standard of living [code of conduct] was so far ahead of ours.'

Notes

1. *John Ramsay of Kildalton...Diary*, p. 63.

2. Topics which people imagine to be 'in the Bible' but which, on further investigation, are not, are discussed by Lee F. Uttley in 'The Bible of the Folk', *California Folklore Quarterly,* Vol. 4, Jan. 1945.

3. The style is demonstrated on commercial recordings such as *Gaelic Psalms from Lewis,* (School of Scottish Studies). The singing of psalms was also traditional to Russian immigrants, the Doukhobors, who, like the Gaels, retained this church custom for the first few generations and then modified it. Koomza J.

Tarasoff, *Traditional Doukhobor Folkways: An Ethnographic and Biographic Record of Prescribed Behaviour*, p.63.

4.   Several people who have retained a link with Lewis have obtained copies of the cassettes *Gaelic Psalmody Recital*, 2 vols., Stornoway, 1978.

5.   See John S. Moir, *Enduring Witness: A History of the Presbyterian Church in Canada*; W. Stanford Reid, 'The Scottish Protestant Tradition' in *The Scottish Tradition in Canada*, pp. 118-136; and Alexander G. MacDougall's M.A. thesis, 'The Presbyterian Church in the Presbytery of Quebec, 1875-1925'.

6.   'Preaching for a call' in the Presbyterian Church occurs when the 'vacancy committee' of a church invites a candidate(s) to preach to the congregation as part of the selection procedure in choosing a new minister.

7.   Complete texts will appear in *An Axe, A Saw*…See also, M. Bennett, 'Gaelic Song in Eastern Canada', *Canadian Folklore canadien*,1992, pp. 21-34.

8.   Most services were in the Marsboro Church, three miles away, though some were in the old school, two miles from the Morrisons' home. Angus's wife Mary added that in her young day 'some of the French priests used to have long services too'.

9.   *Memoirs of Dell*, p. 24.

10.   Even in family worship, hymns did not come into the Presbyterian church till they started using English. In Isobel's youth her family would have sung psalms.

11.   Psalm 100.

12.   In *Stornoway 1858-1983*, p. 36, Guy Lalumière remarks on 'les Ecossais' and their strict observance of Sabbath.

13.   Deuteronomy 5, 12 — 14.

14.   Strictness is not exclusive to Presbyterians. See David Daiches's description of the Jewish Sabbath in Edinburgh in *Between Two Worlds*.

15.   At my grandparents' house we took it for granted that Saturday evening would be spent preparing the Sunday dinner, peeling potatoes, carrots, onions, turnips and chopping cabbage, bringing in extra peats and polishing all the shoes for church. If it happened to be too rainy to go out and play, Granny would start the chores after Saturday dinner (around 2 o'clock) and have us polishing the silverware and sanding the kitchen knives. (I silently wondered at the fact that we never peeled potatoes on the other days of the week.)

16.   *Annals of Megantic County*, p. 18.

17.   The text is from Matthew 12, v. 1; the discussion is summarized from a recording on Aug. 8, 1992.

18.   Simultaneous services in Gaelic and English are recorded in Norman MacLeod's late-nineteenth century description of Communion Sunday in *Reminiscences of a Highland Parish* pp. 304–14.

19.   My mother and her siblings always had to sleep out in the hay loft during Communions in Uig, as 'granny always had a houseful — but we loved it!'

20. This recording of Mrs Murray was made on August 18, 1982 by Isobel Loutit and Gladys Hutley. Tapes are in the Special Collections at Bishop's University.

21. Osgood Hanbury MacKenzie describes Highland Communions and notes that the 'tables were fenced' to any one who was a 'frequenter of concerts or dances'. *A Hundred Years in the Highlands*, London, pp. 156–158.

22. Recorded by folklorist Koomza J. Tarasoff and quoted in *Nothing But Stars: Leaves from the Immigrant Saga,* p. 50.

6

Traditions of the *Taigh Céilidh*

Visiting, usually referred to as 'going for a céilidh', or 'céilidhing' even when speaking English, was of central importance in the social lives of the Gaelic communities.[1] Possibly the earliest written record of the *taigh-céilidh* in this part of the Eastern Townships is by 'home-boy' John J. Mullowney who lived with the MacLeod family in their two-room cabin in Spring Hill from the mid 1880s to the early 1890s.[2] Though he started life in Liverpool, he had learned Gaelic with the local children, and quickly fitted into their way of life. As he was observing everything for the first time with the eyes of a nine year-old, his experiences may have made a more lasting impression on him than if he had been born into the lifestyle. Though he does not use the word *céilidh* (for he was, by that time, writing largely for an American readership), what Mullowney describes is a lively portrait of what once was characteristic of every village in the area:

> Occasionally, when winter conditions would allow, little Katie MacDonald and her brother Dan would come over to the McLeods' to spend the evening. Then, as the blazing logs chased Winter's cold away and the flames painted eerie shadowgraphs upon the walls, we would gather around the wood stove and listen, spellbound, while our elders spun their tales. Sometimes these tales would take on the guise of ghost stories, sometimes becoming so awesome that we youngsters would creep off to bed with our hair literally standing on end... The Scotch are rich in folk-lore and the most earnest believers in premonition...our elders, especially the women, were strongly possessed of the powers of divination or premonition...I could cite many incidents to attest to that statement...[He tells a story of Mary MacLeod hearing continuous unexplained knocking; she sent the children to the door; nobody there. The next day her husband was called to help a Frenchman who was snowed in; they carried him back to their house, almost frozen stiff. As they passed the door with him, they replicated the knocking sound of the door. He died shortly afterwards.]...Coincidence? Maybe. But I have seen so many similar incidents, so many like prophecies come true that it has often caused me to wonder deeply. It has made me, candidly, credulous.
>
> Night after night, during the long winter evenings, people would gather, first at one place, then at the other. Around a crackling brush fire they would congregate...and would swap stories, joke and sing the folk songs of their old

145

homeland. In the meantime the women would prepare vast quantities of food…[Some evenings] the women quilted…[other times] all the moveable pieces of furniture would be thrust out of the way, and, as the fiddlers ground out their gay Scotch melodies, all hands would temporarily abandon their cares to join in joyful dances.[3]

Well over a century later, Muriel Mayhew recalled her childhood memories of winter evenings when her father and some of the neighbours would enjoy the stories in a very similar setting: 'We sat in the kitchen by the stove…you could see the flames of the wood burning…that was before we had stoves that were entirely closed in. And I believe that before his day they were even more open in style.'

To anyone who grew up before the advent of electricity, memories of the old style *taigh-céilidh* are as familiar in this part of Quebec as they are among the older generations in the Highlands and Islands of Scotland. Muriel's neighbour of many years, Bill Young, gave a typical description:

Visitors were always dropping in. You never had to be invited, eh? The teapot was always on the stove. People'd just come and walk right in — there were no preliminaries, no…That was the pastime in the evening, you see. We had no TV or anything like that. We had to be quiet, of course. Children were to be seen and not heard in those days, and we were allowed out into the living room to sit. And of course visiting was a big thing, wasn't it? Everyone came around and visited…

Time meant nothing, really — quieter type of life, and us children'd sit around and the old folks'd tell these ghost stories. They didn't believe them, I suppose, but it used to scare us and we'd be afraid to go to bed, and — [laughs]…Oh, there were those that believed in the second sight.[4]

Telling stories was popular no matter whose kitchen offered hospitality, and an evening visit might be spent entirely on one subject, or, more usually, might cover a wide range of topics — emigration stories, historical legends, anecdotes or comical stories about local characters, ghost stories or other accounts of the supernatural. Some of the men would tell about their own adventures 'out west' or 'up north' and when they ran out of adventures of their own they would recount stories they had read. No two sessions were alike, and people never tired of hearing variations of a story they had heard many times before.

Sitting by the fireside in Milan on a winter's evening in 1976, it occurred to me that the small group that had called to visit me had probably had many a céilidh together in the past. There were my neighbours, Duncan and Kay McLeod, who had walked through the crisp snow, and Hilda and Harvey MacRae from Gould, who, along with Annie and Donald Morrison of Scotstown, had driven more than ten miles. 'Just like old times,' someone remarked, giving the perfect cue to ask the company about the *céilidhean*. Donald responded:[5]

It would depend on what happened. Probably one night they'd get into ghost stories a lot, and another night — I can just remember on the Red Mountain [where I was born and brought up], sometimes they'd get talking about the West. You know, they'd pick a different subject about — probably Donald Morrison the Outlaw story; and they'd probably get onto something that happened locally. Sometimes it'd be a comical thing, like when they caught the two robbers that supposedly robbed the bank in Scotstown.[6]

Hilda picked up from Donald's remarks as naturally as she would have done at countless *céilidhean* in the past. Close to eighty, she and her husband had a fund of stories about local characters, most of them 'long-since gone', whose wit and wry humour lived on in the spirit of the Township Gael. Eyes sparkling, Hilda began, oblivious of the fact that her own razor sharp wit mirrored the main feaature that made her 'characters' so memorable.

Do you remember Johnnie Norman who had the store, the grocery store right up above the Baw Baw's?[7]...And A.D. came in. And the very same thing, a great many people tried to make out he was rather backward, A.D. Morrison, but he was nobody's fool. But a lot of people would try and poke fun at him. And one of them was this smart-aleck traveller that came in. And he had seen him before, and he was asking him all sorts of questions to catch him out and make a fool of him. Finally, A.D. turned to him, and said: 'You know, we both made a mistake. When you came in, I took you for a gentleman. And when you came in, you took me for a fool. We were both mistaken.'

No sooner had the laughter subsided than Harvey, without introduction, picked up the thread:

The woodchucks were digging in the cemetery — there were thousands of them there, digging holes! Peter Buchanan was the mayor of the town, so the Baw-baw went to the council and he wanted them to buy some traps so he'd catch the woodchucks. And Peter Buchanan said 'No, we're not going to buy traps.'
'Alright then, we'll let the woodchucks eat your father!'

It was like unravelling a ball of coloured yarn as one story led to the next in what turned out to be a string of anecdotes. And, as with every successful céilidh, the dynamics of this one were such that participants created just the right amount of tension as they drew upon themes, expanded ideas and bounced quick retorts off each other. With split-second timing, they seemed to steer the evening's entertainment along its unique course, as stories, discussions, poems, sayings and songs elicited highs and lows of emotion, laughter, nostalgia, even sadness and regret.

Hilda remarked that, during her childhood and youth, virtually all the stories and songs she had heard were in Gaelic, her mother tongue. After she went to school she became completely fluent in English and French and was literate in all three. Although there was only ten years between Hilda and Donald, she considered that her seniority had stood her in good stead so far as language and culture were concerned. By the 1920s and 30s, people were beginning to tell the stories in English, as several families, including Donald's, decided that their children should speak English 'so that they would get on in the world'. Likewise, in Duncan's home, English was spoken to the children while the parents still carried on the family business in Gaelic to please their older customers. And when Duncan and his brother called at Muriel's home, just a hundred yards down the road, she and her parents thought little of switching to English. Just as in Gaelic Scotland today, both languages would be heard during house-visits, so that when there was a lull between stories, issues such as language-use were discussed along with the day's news and current affairs.

Songs, too, were an important part of the entertainment at the old-style *taigh-céilidh*, where old favourites such as *'Mo Rùn Geal Dìleas'* and *'Fear a' Bhàta'* could raise a chorus, and local compositions could evoke a range of responses from listeners.[8] As with the stories, themes covered a wide territory, though perhaps those of nostalgia for the past were most frequently sung. When Prof. Charles Dunn of Harvard University visited the area in the late 1950s he recorded singers with strong voices, surrounded by animated companions prompting them to sing this or that local favourite.[9] His invaluable collection is now in the Library of Harvard University but, sady, it has been many years since songs were an integral part of the activities of the *taigh-céilidh* in the Eastern Townships. Even in 1976, the only songs included at most of the house-visits I experienced were those I was asked to sing myself, for, once it was known that I had grown up in a family where Gaelic songs had been part of everyday life, it was naturally expected of me to make my contribution.

In 1991, the oldest Gaelic-speaking resident, Johnnie MacKenzie of Scots-town, in his hundredth year, spoke of Gaelic singing as a thing of the past:

> Oh I could sing — I didn't have many songs but I used to listen to a lot of them. There were some good singers in our class at that time [at the turn of the century], there were some very good singers, women and men. Oh I could sing a hymn, or sing a song, what little I know of them, but I wasn't keeping them in practice. [Were they all Gaelic?] No! Mostly all English. Years ago I guess it was, but it turned around to be English mostly. We had this fellow by the name of Johnnie Iain Mhurraidh [?] and he could sing any song or hymn or Gaelic song that he knew, and he was a good singer…He could sing any song or anything that he ever learned, he could sing it to perfection, Gaelic or English…[Johnnie then recites in an emphatically stressed rhythm:]

Guma slàn do'n rìbhinn òg
Tha tàmh an eilean gorm an fheòir,

'S e dh'fhàg mo chridhe trom fo leòn
Nach fhaod mi'n còmhnaidh fuireach leat —

Now that was one of them, but he had quite a few others.

Singing at *céilidhean* seems to have endured longest where people were most isolated, for example, in the outlying lumber-camps, such as those described by Donald Morrison and Alex MacIver. In Alex's experience, the songs in the camp bunkhouses were usually in Gaelic, with some in English, and a few songs a mixture of the two.[10] Though he protested that he 'couldn't sing any more', Alex could recall many locally composed songs that he first heard in the lumber-woods — some anecdotal and amusing, a few satirical, and others, such as *Oran Holeb*, nostalgic. Nowadays the title may seem confusing as the name 'Holeb' never appears at any point in the song. Alex explained, however, that it was composed in the lumber town of Holeb, where so many Quebecers worked all winter. 'At one time it was very popular — in the railway and lumber-camps and back home too.'

Oran Holeb

1)
Chan 'eil air an t-saoghal nì ri fhaighinn
Na rinneadh e feum bhith leum le aighear
Ach guthan bho nèamh gu sèimh a chanadh
A maitheadh dhomh peacannan m'òige.

2)
An uair bha mi òg bu luath a ruithinn,
Is b'aotrom a dhannsainn cluinntinn fidheal,
Tha abair leis [sic] leam bhith seinn na luinneig
Nuair bhith a gabhail nan òran.

3)
Cha dhean mi'n diugh danns' 's cha chluinn mi fidheal;
Is òranan binn cha sheinn mi tuilleadh.
Bhon tha mi gun sunnd, 's mo chairt-iuil air a briseadh,
'S cha chàilear dhomh tuilleadh ri m'bheo e.

4)
Mo Earrach air chall, mo Shamhradh seachad,
A Foghar air teanntainn rium am fagus,
A falt air mo cheann a' sealltainn abaich,
'S e 'g innse nach fada bhios beò mi.

5)
Nuair bhios mi leam fhéin bidh mo dheòir a sileadh
Mo smuaintean air tìm nach till rinn tuilleadh.
Gach nì dhomh ag inns' gu bheil an t-am ann fagus
San cuirear mi laighe nam ònar.

6)
Nuair a chluinneas mi eun an crann na coille
Na creutairean binn a' seinn an ceileir,
Theid m' inntinn 'na leum gu tìr mo bhreith
Far am bithinn ri cleasachd 'nam òige.

7)
Nuair a ruigeas i thall a nall air ais i
Le naidheachd am ionnsaigh leam nach taitneach
Gu bheil cuid ann dhe'n òige bh'ann an [?]Lagan
An diugh tha 'na laighe 's na fòdan.

8)
Tha cuid ac' 'sa chuan 'na ghrunnd 'nan cadal,
Is cuid mar mi fhéin 's an aois a' laigh orr'.
Gach nì dhomh ag inns' gu bheil an t-àm ann fagus
'S an cuirear mi laighe fon fhòdan.

9)
Nuair thig an aois le h-aodann frasach
Is crith anns gach ball is gann a sheasas sibh,
Sùilean ur cinn ri diùltadh faicinn,
'S ur fiaclan air caitheamh 's iad breòite.

10)
Sibhse tha òg thugaibh móran aire,
Is cuiribh gu feum ur ceudne [sic] maduinn,
Gheibh sibh gliocas on aird a dh'aireamh bhur latha
Ur grian mur laigh i 's sibh gòrach.

The Song of Holeb (Maine)

1)
There is nothing to be gained in this world
That would not make you jump for joy
But voices from heaven, singing serenely
That the sins of youth were forgiven.

2)
When I was young I could run so swiftly,
And lightly dance to the sound of the fiddle,
And I'd join in singing the choruses
When the songs were being sung.

3)
Today I can't dance, I don't hear the fiddle;
No more can I sing the sweet songs.

I feel pretty low, my compass [purpose] is broken,
I do not have any interest any longer.

4)
My Spring is lost, my Summer is gone,
The Autumn is now drawing near,
The hair on my head is looking ripe,
A sign that I shall not live long.

5)
When I'm on my own, my tears will fall
With my thoughts on a time that will not return.
Everything tells me the time is near
When I'm laid to rest on my own.

6)
When I hear a bird in the branches of the trees
The sweet creatures singing their song,
My mind swiftly leaps to the land of my birth
Where I used to play in my youth.

7)
When I get over there, it comes back to me
With news not very pleasant to hear
That some of the young who were in Laggan [?Dell]
Are today lying under the turf.

8)
Some of them are sleeping at the bottom of the sea,
Some like myself are showing thier age.
Everybody tells us the time is near
When I'm laid to rest in the ground.

9)
When age comes with its showery face
Every limb shaking, you can hardly stand,
The eyes in your head refusing to see,
Your teeth are worn out and brittle.

10)
You who are young, take much heed,
And put to good use the prime days of your life;
You will get wisdom from on high, according to your numbered days
Before your sun sets while you're still foolish.

Recalling the camp céilidhs, both Alex and Donald identified lumbermen who knew verse after verse of countless poems and songs. Some, including Donald, had phenomenal memories and could sing, or recite by heart, all 259 verses — 'eight-liners at that' — of *Donald Morrison, the Canadian Outlaw*, composed in the early 1890s by a local bard, Angus Mackay ('Oscar Dhu'). Originally printed in a book of the same name, Oscar Dhu's poem was so popular in the lumber-camps that hand-written copies of it circulated among the men. In 1976, at our fireside céilidh in Milan in the company of the MacRaes and the McLeods, Donald spontaneously sang 116 lines of it, and, laughingly drew to a halt by saying 'at one time I knew the whole book.' When I asked him if he systematically learnt it, his reply was animated and emphatic: '*No*, eh! I used to *hear* those songs when I was young, up here — father, Donald MacRitchie, different ones used to sing parts of 'em, and I'd listen; we'd *hear* them…' Considering the length of the entire song, little wonder that, in the setting of a more modern céilidh, Donald sang only a section of it. Back in the lumber-camp bunkhouses, however, the men enjoyed epic entertainment in the same way as today's camp-dwellers enjoy a two-hour film on video.

Hungarian-American folklorist, Linda Dégh, discusses the prevalence of long tales among the men of 'certain non-village communities' such as workingmen's hostels and barracks accommodating migrant labourers. She observed that 'men exhausted by a day's hard work find listening to [long] tales a welcome recreation…' By way of contrast, she observes that the same storytellers tell shorter tales at informal gatherings where 'the village young are too impatient to listen to a long-drawn-out narrative.'[11] Not so much impatience as time was the main factor in the Quebec village ceilidhs; one long story or song would have monopolised most of it, so there was a different etiquette at work which Donald automatically observed when he handed the floor back to Hilda and Harvey. Regrettably I did not manage to record the song in its entirety, but in 1993, almost two years after Donald's death, Alex confirmed that he had 'heard him sing all of the Outlaw song on a number of occasions…and there were a few of the men knew it in the camps.'

In the same way that a variety of videos are selected by the men in today's camps, the topics of choice in the old-style bunkhouses ranged across the spectrum of adventure, travel, romance, nostalgia, comedy, politics or a combination of all of them. A few of the men were quick to satirise social situations in song and their ephemeral compositions could tease, shame or ridicule anyone who stepped outside the line of behaviour acceptable to the majority. And, judging by a brief example of bawdry sung by Alex to illustrate his discussion, the lumbermen were no different from any other group of men in isolated situations — bothymen, oil-rig workers, or miners — all are familiar with a repertoire that weaves in a little thread of blue. But these ditties were strictly to remain confined to camp and definitely not intended to be aired at local céilidhs in the villages.[12]

Apart from the spontaneous gatherings in the *taighean céilidh* or lumber-

camps, there were organised concerts, usually referred to as *céilidhs*, held
regularly in the schools or village halls. According to Johnnie Bard, the heyday
of the 'Gaelic concerts' in the Oddfellows' Hall in Scotstown reached its peak
in the 1940s. Most of his generation loved the old songs, but as time went
past, those who did not speak Gaelic were not so keen on them. Though
Duncan McLeod now regrets the loss of the older traditions, he admits that
during his adolescence he did not appreciate the long Gaelic songs at the
Milan céilidhs:

> We used to have Gaelic concerts and those that could sing 'd be up on the stage
> — the building's gone now, but it was just beside our church — the
> Oddfellows' Hall — in 1959 it was gone…You know, when we were kids we'd
> go to these concerts, and that was one thing we got sick and tired of, the length
> of the Gaelic songs! [Some of us] didn't understand a word of it, and [some of]
> the singers weren't that good either!…The hall 'd be full — oh, a hundred and
> fifty, probably two hundred, that was in the 1920s, that's when I remember it.
> The building was built in 1915, and prior to that they used to hold them in
> other [places] in Milan — and in people's houses, but not on a large scale. [13]

Johnnie Bard's description of the entire evening is very much like the
céilidh-dance familiar to Gaelic Scotland, though the Quebec substance used
to treat the floor seems much more ingenious than the pre-packaged *Slipperene*
that was sprinkled on the floors of my teenage years in Lewis:

> When the singing was over, the rows of chairs were removed, placed along the
> walls, and the floor was scattered with cornmeal to prepare for the dance. The
> orchestra [or band, as it is called in Scotland] consisted of two local fiddlers and
> a piano-player who kept going for the rest of the night playing music for
> quadrilles, the Paul Jones, foxtrots and waltzes. And every occasion ended with
> 'Take your partners for the last waltz!' which was always to the tune of
> 'Goodnight Ladies.'[14]

Despite the demise of the village-hall céilidhs, the informal house-visits
still continue as an important part of the Quebec Hebridean culture. People
still céilidh, have a 'lunch' of tea and home-baking together, and enjoy
discussions on the everyday topics that always had a place at the old-style
céilidhean: current items of news, local gossip, genealogy, cooking, baking and
household management, knitting or any other needle-craft, hobbies, medical-
lore or recently publicised discoveries, weather-forecasting, farming, hunting,
fishing, gold-mining, politics, religion, travel, or whatever the moment
happens to bring. [15] And interwoven with the more serious exchanges there
are usually local anecdotes that have circulated in oral tradition for many years,
often with an amusing or poignant side to them, reminding the company of
their common background and of their forebears who once told the same
stories. Today, however, they are all told in English, and, though people still

listen to songs, they generally do so via the media as there is a radio in every kitchen, and often a cassette recorder and television too. Gaelic tapes from the Old Country are popular, and occasionally someone will bring out a treasured home-recording of local singers who were the star-turns at the céilidhs until the 1960s. Inevitably memories come flooding back and the voices remind the listeners just how much they have lost from a once-vibrant tradition.

Quebec does not have any monopoly on cultural nostalgia, for, in the closing decade of the twentieth century, tradition-bearers on *both* sides of the Atlantic hark back to the days of the *taigh-céilidh*, where, during the long winters' evenings the finest and best songs, stories, proverbs, riddles and tongue-twisters could be heard. They both have a common yearning for their traditions that have faded over the years, and for the way of life that produced them. There may be no Gaelic society on earth where 'times have changed' so rapidly and so drastically as in Quebec — language, population, house-types, farming methods and agricultural trends — yet, paradoxically, I would suggest that the little village of Milan is also one of the few places where, in the 1990s, the *taigh-céilidh* can still be found. Granted, the prevalence of house-visits is no longer in the winter — in fact it is in the middle of the summer. This is not just because road conditions are notoriously unpredictable, often with several feet of snow blocking roads, but because there is virtually nobody left during the winter except Ruth Nicolson. As any of the locals would quickly point out, the deep snow didn't stop them in the past, and it wouldn't stop them today; 'it's just that times have changed.' Even within the past two decades, a comparatively short association with Quebec, I have seen clear evidence of that for myself: when I lived in Milan for a year in 1975-76 there were still just enough people of Hebridean descent to make it possible to have a spontaneous *céilidh*. Nobody had to be asked; there were the McLeods (Duncan and Kay), the Nicolsons (Ruth and David), and Mary MacLeod, the MacDonalds, and the Rosses, who all lived in the heart of the village of Milan, and on the edges were the MacArthurs, the Shermans, the Morrisons, the Stewarts, and the Moulands, not to mention numerous families in the nearby communities of Scotstown, Dell, Gould, and so on. Today in Milan, apart from Ruth, the entire village is French, with a few 'mixed' houses where both French and English are known, but where most of the visitors are French, and where television culture has completely taken over. If one would wish to experience a 'real *taigh-ceilidh*' then a visit to Ruth's would perhaps be as close as any to be found on either side of the Atlantic.[16]

My two summers living with Ruth not only enriched my entire experience but gave me an insight I would never have attained otherwise. To refer to her house as the last *taigh céilidh* is no exaggeration. Scarcely a day passed but somebody, quite unannounced, arrived at her door to visit. Some days there were several sets of visitors, each welcomed and treated to characteristic hospitality. Baking was scheduled into most days, not as part of a plan, or even as a chore, but more a reflection of a way of life: it was exactly as it had been in 1975 when, on the many occasions I 'dropped in' she would be attending to something in the oven, or making tea. On snowy, winter days when I called in passing, Ruth was often at her baking-board, and even if she had finished, the smell of fresh baking was the first thing a visitor would notice the moment the main door was opened. She had no definite pattern that she could describe; as I observed her, she would make her decisions: today baking-powder biscuits [oven scones], tomorrow oatmeal scones, the next day cookies, brownies, or some other favourite recipe, and most days 'something for dessert' because the oven was hot.[17] Living with Ruth in the summer months when the kitchen was hot, the door was always ajar, and the smell of baking wafted through the screen-door so that all who approached the house would playfully remark upon the alluring smell. Often the visit would begin with good-natured teasing, suggesting that such a delicious smell was why Ruth had so many visitors in the first place. But of course that was not the case. Almost all of the summer visitors had travelled by car at least ten miles (Scotstown is the nearest village), and some even boasted several thousands of miles 'just to visit Ruth'. While the teasing always made her laugh and return some witty remark, for she knew quite well they had other friends and relatives to visit, Ruth would welcome each one into her kitchen. Rarely would the company get beyond the kitchen to sit in the living room, but would be invited to 'take a seat' as soon as they were inside.[18] The two wooden rocking chairs were usually favoured, unless guests were asked to sit round the table to eat, then any or all of the six wooden chairs would be occupied, and finally, the daybed would hold the remaining guests. In the course of an afternoon or evening I have seen all the seating filled, and Ruth bring some of her dining-room chairs to the edge of the kitchen. Only when everyone else was comfortably installed would Ruth sit down, often on a wooden stool near the stove, as she invariable needed to keep an eye on that side of the kitchen.

Before long, the kettle, which was always kept full on top of the woodstove, was brought to the boil, and, if Ruth felt comfortable enough to accept help from anyone else, (for example, her sister), she would ask her to fetch out the china cups and saucers from the cabinet to help set the table. Even if it did not seem very long since the last meal, guests were invited to a generous spread, consisting of an inviting array of home-baking, usually with a variety of jams that Ruth would identify individually — by the maker, 'that one is Noëlla's, Wayne's wife', or by the locality of berries — 'we picked these out by Dell cemetery', or by the season — 'that's some of last year's…' And so the socializing would progress, with all the company enjoying the 'lunch' and the visit. On many occasions the entire evening was spent around the kitchen table, long after the teapot had been emptied several times. The participants would remain there, like players in a serious game, where one conversational move would send the entire group into fast-moving exchanges and banter. All of a sudden, one participant might dart in and draw everyone to a halt with a long-forgotten local anecdote that immediately captured every imagination or set them all off again in another direction. The dynamics of one evening would never be repeated at another, even when the same players returned for a second round.

For example, though Ruth and her younger sister, Bernice, had a three-week reunion in Milan every summer, they would eagerly listen to all the local stories they had heard throughout their lives. A simple action like pouring out tea elicited a memory such as *'Do you remember, Ruth, Grandpa would get mad if he saw us asking for tea *'Oh, cailleach na té!'* Often the one would prompt the other into telling a favourite episode: 'Oh, tell the one about…' and so it would go, 'I remember the time…' There was often uproarious laughter, especially when their Aunt Ivy, visiting from Scotstown, would add her wry perception of a situation, or tease 'the girls' — Ivy is eight years older than Ruth — about some amusing incident. Over a number of these occasions a fairly detailed portrait of their family life gradually emerged, which included certain aspects that both of them claimed to have long since forgotten.

Since this was the setting for many of my observations, it would serve two purposes to piece together details from these *céilidhean* to form a composite account of Ruth's and Bernice's family memories: first, it will show how the interaction between the participants of the *céilidh* eventually builds up a picture of life; and secondly, perhaps more importantly, it will acquaint the reader with these lives that are so significant to the community of Milan and to this project.[19]

Ruth's and Bernice's father was known to everyone as Norman 'Doak' [MacDonald], and, since their mother died when the children were young, both sets of grandparents made strong impressions on the family. There was 'Little Grandma' with whom Bernice and her sister Alma, a year older, lived, and there was 'Big Gramma' who originally lived on the family farm in Milan (now owned by Peter Jort), who stayed there for the rest of her life, and who, from all accounts, was a formidable character. All of them were Gaelic-speakers, though 'Big Gramma' began to talk English to her grandchildren — not always quite grammatically, as Bernice recalled:

*'Big Gramma' used to say things like 'Get me the pan dog' for 'Get me the *dog-pan*,' to feed the dog. Well, she always said it the same and we never corrected her — she wouldn't have taken kindly to that! That was 'Big Gramma'; her name was Ishbel [MacDonald] — she was kind of stern; she didn't show much sympathy.

But she had had a hard life — her husband had been killed by a falling log at the age of 39, leaving her with six children to look after, including [our] Mother, who was four years old when her dad was killed. She had lost other children in infancy — they died very suddenly, with chicken-pox or measles. She was married to her first cousin. Her eldest son was old enough to take over the farm when his father died, but he also died as the result of an accident. On the way to church the horse kicked over the traces and he was found with a crushed pencil in his top pocket, as if the horse had kicked him in the chest. 'Big Gramma' lived with our father and his family because they actually moved into the old folks' farm. When our mother died, Ruth was eleven and a half, I was two and Alma was three. Momma was pregnant when she died, the baby had died in-utero, and though she went to the doctor, but — she hadn't been too well. The baby didn't abort, and Momma died. The older children stayed with their father and 'Big Gramma', who took over from their mother, and though she did most of the work she also taught Ruth to do house-work. Ruth used to milk the cows too.

Meanwhile, the two little ones, Bernice and Alma, went to stay with 'Little Grandma' (Mary) in Dell.

We went over there right away [after our mother died]. And we slept on straw mattresses — we liked that — Alma and I were real happy when we saw that…

Well, in looks 'Little Grandma' was very short, she was in her 60s, and so sweet and gentle, never angry. She talked Gaelic with Grandpa all the time, and would throw a little bit of English in when we were kids. And we had a hired man over there who was French then she'd go back and forth…[Then we would get confused because she didn't use one language at a time, and Alma] used to say things like 'Oh look at the big *cuileag mòr!*' [sic] And I always asked her 'Can I *sguap* the floor?' We swept it twice a day after meals and I liked to do it, so I'd ask…

Little Grandma was so nice, we just loved her. She was never angry — she was very special…Grandpa was a bit severe, and she'd say [loudly whispered] 'Wait till Grandpa goes to the barn.' But one time we had a [wooden, home-made] rattle and we never found it till years later [as one of them had hidden it to stop the children being so noisy]…And he would [play with us sometimes] and hold on to our hands and we'd be on his knee, [saying]:

Hob-ob aig an each a' dol asteach a Linwick
Bidh e turabaich 's a bramadaich
Gu ruig e taigh Iain ?Ruidhlear.

[The horse goes hop-op, going into Lingwick
He'll be swaying about, and farting
Till he reaches the house of Ian the Dancer (reeler).][20]

[Then when] I was five and Alma was six, and we went back home to the farm in Milan so that we could go to school. When we got home, we were with Ruth and Helen and Charlie but I don't think they understood Gaelic as much

as we did. Until then, I didn't know our other grandmother, 'Big Gramma', at
all, and she was living with us [on the family farm]. She was quite strict and she
didn't waste any smiles, she had a lot of hardships in her life. But she didn't
seem to have much time for children; if we ran around it irritated her and we'd
have to scurry out of the way.

The two girls shared only a short time together at the family homestead
before Ruth left Milan to go to MacDonald College, a teacher-training
college in Montreal. Shortly afterwards, however, their father remarried a local
woman, Marion Matheson, who, happily, was a good step-mother to the
family and could soften the influence of 'Big Gramma's' stern ways. Many
years were to pass before Ruth and Bernice could again share a home together
in Milan, if only twice a year for a holiday. Somehow, however, the daily
routine of Ruth's kitchen automatically takes them back to the family farm
in a way that no other event can. A simple operation like cleaning off the
stove after baking scones reminds them again of 'Big Gramma'. Suddenly
Bernice remembers:

Oh she was the one who had the feathers [for the stove] — I think they both did!
Just a lot of feathers tied up in a bundle with string, especially for cleaning off the
stove, after making scones.[21] Oh, there was a warming oven at the side, for water,
and we kept it filled to have hot water for the dishes, and you'd see the steam
coming up.[22] Gramma used to make barley scones, and she used to make 'water
barley scones' and they were very thin, but I didn't like the flavour of them.

It was the ordinary, everyday things of life that were woven into the fabric
of every *céilidh* — talk of how people lived and how they made a living, with
the occasional diversion of a story or a joke.[23] In such a setting, it is only in
the telling and re-telling of memorates and anecdotes that traditions of family
and community are valued and continue to be kept alive. Whether the
céilidhean are held throughout the winter evenings, as was the custom in Gaelic
Scotland, or in Quebec before so many people moved away, or whether they
are in summertime, around Ruth's kitchen table, scarcely matters. The
importance of these social events lies in the fact that they not only entertain
but they also nurture a closeness between family members and friends that
extends across time and distance to their forebears and kinsfolk in the Outer
Hebrides.

Notes

1. The function of the *céilidh* in a Gaelic-speaking community is discussed in *The Last Stronghold,* Chapter 3.

2. D. M. McKillop, a contemporary of Mullowney's, refers to the activities of the *céilidh* throughout his book, *Annals of Megantic County.*

3. John J. Mullowney, *America Gives a Chance,* the first paragraph is from p. 19, the other two from p. 25, re-ordered, my summaries within square brackets.

4. The question of belief is a delicate matter and since this recording was made the first day I met Bill, he was naturally quite cautious. Later, he was more open with his opinions and told several stories which confirmed widespread belief in supernatural phenomena. See 'Folkways and Religion of the Hebridean Scots in the Eastern Townships' in *Cultural Retention...,* pp. 91 — 127.

5. Though I had not intended to record this visit, I quickly switched on my machine (without external microphone). The entire sequence was recorded Oct. 27, 1976.

6. The stories I recorded in 1976 are in *Cultural Retention,* pp. 91 — 127. Others will appear in my forthcoming collection, *An Axe, A Saw and a Bible.*

7. There was a Donald MacLeod in Lingwick, regarded as being eccentric, who was nicknamed 'the Baw-Baw. The same nickname turns up in Mull, usually as a 'frightening character' threat to children.

8. M. Bennett, 'Gaelic Song in Eastern Canada: Twentieth Century Reflections', in *Canadian Folklore canadien,* pp. 21-34.

9. Over a dozen of these songs formed the core of a Ph.D thesis by Dunn's student, Nancy Rose Dunkley, 'Studies in the Scottish Gaelic Folk-song Tradition in Canada', (1984). All the texts and melodies in the thesis are fully transcribed and discussed.

10. A fuller discussion of Gaelic songs in the Eastern Townships, along with examples of texts, is contained in my paper 'Gaelic Songs of Quebec', given at the Conference on Folksong, *Association for Scottish Literary Studies,* in Aberdeen in August 1993. I have discussed the occurrence of macaronic songs in 'Gaelic, French and English: Some Aspects of the Macaronic Tradition of the Codroy Valley, Newfoundland' in *Regional Language Studies...Newfoundland,* pp. 25-30.

11. Introduction to *Folktales of Hungary,* pp, xxxiii-xxxiv.

12. Hamish Henderson refers to the North-east bothymen as having a staple diet of 'brose and bawdy ballads'; see sleeve notes to the record, *Bothy Ballads,* School of Scottish Studies, 1973.

13. The Milan church, which held regular weekly services when I lived in the village, was demolished in the early 1980s. It was not a very old building and was in fairly good condition, but the members preferred to 'take it down' rather than see it sold for a secular purpose. [Duncan McLeod, in conversation.]

14. Op cit. p. 125.

15. Since the appearance of Bill Lawson's *Register* in 1988, the interest in genealogy has greatly increased. Enthusiasts will tell their 'Q number', point out connections to other families, and reconstruct complicated genealogical networks. According to one passionate enthusiast, [1992] it is 'not so much a hobby as a disease'.

16. To my great regret, I have come across just as much, if not more, evidence of the take-over of television culture in Hebridean homes which were, within my own lifetime, well-known for *céilidhean*.

17. The recipes are discussed in greater detail in Chapter 6.

18. There were two exceptions during my stay: one when the daughter of a local man who had moved to Ontario over thirty years ago brought a visitor from Scotland; and one when a friend, originally from Montreal though living in Milan, came to call. Although this room has a television, we only watched it once, when there was a programme about the Loch Ness monster.

19. This account is based on notes in my Fieldwork Notebook (re-ordered) and a short recording of Bernice, Aug. 14, 1992.

20. Dwelly gives *turabal* = oscillating; *turraban* = constant rocking motion of the body; and *bramadaich* = state of being swelling.

21. All the croft houses in the vicinity of my grandparents kept a *badag*, as it was called, for cleaning the *grate*, (in my childhood, the Rayburn), or the top of the griddle. Every time they killed a hen Granny would keep the tail and/or wing feathers to make a new *badag*.

22. Before most homes had hot-water plumbing, a fairly common design of kitchen range was one that incorporated a small water-tank, which Bernice calls an 'oven', attached to the side of the stove. When water was needed for dishes or washing it would be ladled out with a 'dipper' or small saucepan that was usually kept on a hook nearby. Since the stove was almost always lit for cooking, there was seldom a shortage of hot water.

23. In his quest to define what evokes a 'sense of belonging', Anthony P. Cohen suggests that people employ 'whatever means come to hand: the use of language, the shared knowledge of genealogy or ecology, joking...the aesthetics of subsistence skills...[all are] processes which occur close to the *everyday* experience of life, rather than through rare, formalized procedures.' Op cit, p. 6, his emphasis.

7

Foodways of Yesterday and Today

And bless the hands that prepared it...[1]

A Well-Stocked Larder

Tha sinn a' toirt taing dhuit, a Thighearna, air son na cothraman prìseil so tha thu buileachadh oirnn. Cuidich sinn air son a bhith dèanamh féum dheth. Cuir sinn air do chùram 's math ur peachdaidhean. Tha sinn toirt taing dhuit an diugh [bhith] comhla ri chéile...Air sgàth Chrìosd, gu sìorraidh, Amen.

[We give thee thanks, oh Lord, for these precious gifts [opportunities] thou hast bestowed upon us. Help us to use them to thy glory. Keep us in thy care, and forgive our sins. We thank you today for [the blessing of] being together. For Christ's sake, forever, Amen.]

[Alex MacIver, August, 1992]

With heads bowed and eyes closed, familiar words of thanks were solemnly spoken at every table, before and after the 'breaking of bread'. The custom for generations, even when there seemed little for which to give thanks, 'asking a blessing' is, among the Eastern Township Gaels, an integral part of mealtimes to this day. As the twentieth century draws to a close, very few tables are blessed in Gaelic, and no table is, by any stretch of the imagination, lacking in the gifts for which they duly give thanks.

After the unforgettable first winter of potatoes and oatmeal, the diet of the settlers improved greatly. Preparation of food continued to be based upon traditional Hebridean practices, with modifications and inventions made out of the necessity to adapt to climatic and agricultural conditions in Quebec. As already mentioned, fields and gardens were planted every spring with staple crops, and farmers relied upon their own livstock for dairy produce, eggs and meat. All summer and autumn they had plenty milk, cream, butter, cheese and eggs, but, as winter approached, the supply gradually diminished, with cows going dry and hens moulting. Maryann Morrison remarked, 'They were laying eggs; but not too much in the wintertime. We had ducks, too.'

While most families could get by in winter with what milk they had, there was never any surplus that could be made into cheese, or, more importantly, separated for butter-making. Although it could be bought at a general store, if at all possible families liked to have their own butter. Russell MacIver's family farm at Victoria was typical:

161

Well the most we ever milked was seven, but we had a few young stock…We used to churn and make the butter and put it in the pound mould, push it in, put the wrapper on, [and sell it] sometimes. That's 25 cents a pound. What is it now, three or four dollars?…Oh! It was the very best. They had a [cream] separator. Sometimes if we didn't have enough milk [to make it worth using the separator] we'd skim it, put it down in the cellar in a pail and skim it off, then churn it. [Then] oh, a little bit [we'd keep for winter],…yeah, just salt it to taste. Of course it'd keep a lot better, and then they'd have a big crock and they'd put some in there for the winter.

Summer was always punctuated with references to the long winter months when there would be no cream to churn. And so families would try to preserve a reasonable amount, not only for the table, but also for baking. 'No margarine in those days, only the good butter.' The women, responsible for all household concerns, would therefore try to make more than they needed during the summer's frequent churnings, to save a portion for the winter's supply, as Christie MacKenzie explained:

Oh, that was put away in stone crocks, you know, just packed in…it had to be salted to keep…Towards fall, you know, when the cows would be practically going dry, [there would never be enough cream to churn], but there'd be crocks of that butter. But what we used in the summertime, when they were making butter just to use, it was made into prints, like. But we couldn't keep it like that; it had to be, eh, [salted in crocks]. Oh, about twenty pounds, like. They were big…So the oldest was on the bottom, but it always kept. 'Course it was saltier than you'd have it if you were just eating it right away. But it [kept fresh]…we never had any of it spoil.

Storing butter in this way was common practice long before the emigrants left Lewis, as Hugh Cheape of the National Museum of Scotland explains in his article 'Pottery and Food Preparation, Storage and Transport in the Scottish Hebrides'. Illustrated by photographs, he catalogues the earthenware crocks, *crogain*, from the nineteenth century, used to store surplus butter during the summer months at the sheilings in Lewis. Furthermore, Lewis writer James Shaw Grant confirms the Islanders' taste for butter as he notes that merchants in Stornoway bought in supplies of salted butter which could last much longer than a year and still taste like 'good butter'. [2]

In the Eastern Townships. farms where more than one or two cows a day were milked also offered an opportunity to earn a little extra cash as farmers could sell either the butter or the cream to one of the two commercial creameries in Stornoway or Milan. Ruth Nicholson and her sister Bernice Laurila, whose father, Norman MacDonald, owned and operated the Milan creamery, recalled aspects of this small business.:

Ruth: *Everybody around brought cream to the creamery and he made the butter, Mondays and Fridays. And it was open to the public where they could go and buy butter.

Bernice: ★And on Tuesdays he had to be there himself for the testing of the cream. He had to take a sample of every cream that came in. He took a special course for this in Montreal — while our mother was still alive. He did this himself with a special machine; a round machine that held about forty-eight of the little testing bottles, and it spun round really fast; he read the scale on the neck of the bottle. He had about fifty customers from the area. People used to come from all over, from the States they'd come up and buy butter because they said it was the best tasting butter you could buy. Most of it was packed in 56 pound boxes and sold.

For the Morrisons in Cruvag, the closest creamery operator was in Stornoway. The owner used to drive out to farms in Marsboro and then up the track to Cruvag to buy surplus cream from several branches of the family. Angus recalled that they used to keep it fresh by submerging the crocks in the 'ice-cold brook down below the house.'

Nobody considered the refrigeration of milk as crucial as that of cream, however, as there was always the morning and evening milkings so that a fresh supply was never more than a few hours away. In those days families were not concerned about keeping it 'ice-cold' as today's taste dictates. If it turned sour during hot, humid or thundery days of summer, milk was never wasted, as it was easily turned into *gruth* ('crowdie', similar, though not identical, to cottage cheese). The method is well-known among Scottish crofters as the simplest and most straightforward way to make cheese since it does not require the addition of rennet: [3] A big pot of the sour, usually thick, milk is set on or near the coolest part of the kitchen stove where it gradually warms to blood heat. In the course of a few hours it separates into curds and whey, and is then poured through a muslin-covered strainer or colander to catch the curds and let the whey drain into a second container. Just as it was in my grandparents' house in Skye, the whey was put aside as a refreshing drink, or, if nobody wanted it, then it was fed to the dogs or pigs. After the curds are completely drained they are usually transferred to a bowl, a little salt is added to taste, then enough thick cream mixed through the dryish curds so the *gruth* can spread easily without being runny. Again, lack of refrigeration was not a problem, for, although *gruth* can keep fresh for a few days, more often it would be eaten with that day's batch of freshly-baked scones.

Gruth was the only cheese described to me, though the techniques of cheese-making well-known in Lewis and Harris before the emigration, may have been used in earlier days. [4] A strong possibility is that most people began to rely on a cheese factory set up earlier this century by a French family, Les Dumoulin, at St Léon, nine miles from Milan. It supplied the local merchants with huge 'rounds' of white cheese, similar to cheddar, which Duncan McLeod recalls cutting into wedges to be sold by the pound at the store. By the 1930s the St Léon factory had closed, and until another French family in Megantic began to operate a *Fromagerie* known as *La Chaudière* in the 1960s, storekeepers imported cheese. The speciality of *La Chaudière* was, and still is, a mild curd cheese, which appeals to the taste of most Eastern Townshippers and is often chosen as a gift for former residents returning home for a visit — it has become the 'regional cheese' of French and Gaels alike.[5]

Not all commodities could be home-produced, everyone relied on the village store for certain basics such as tea, sugar, salt, spices, and items they could not grow or raise for themselves. There were several general stores in the villages which kept a stock of supplies to meet the modest needs of the settlers.[6] Since the days of buying and selling wood ashes, virtually all of them operated a barter system — storekeepers would exchange or give credit on certain goods for which they in turn had another market.[7]

In most towns and villages, family-operated businesses were established during the early years, with Stornoway, Marsboro, Scotstown, and Milan being the main centres for obtaining supplies. The names of their owners became synonymous with local merchandising, and, until the summer of 1993, Milan had the longest-lived family-store in the area — the well-known 'McLeod Bros', latterly owned and operated by Duncan McLeod.[8]

> Well, the store was started in 1877 by my grandfather. He had been in business over in the Winslow area, and when he heard that the Trans-Continental Railway was being extended from the Sherbrooke area east to [?this part] and when he knew that they were going to come through some area in the Milan area, he and another man went over there and staked out a claim to some land. He built a store and he built a home for his family, and also it was used for a number of years as a hotel and public rooms in Milan. That's when there was nothing but the railway going through there.

The McLeods were an enterprising family who served the community in various capacities for well over a century. In the late 1800s and early 1900s the part of the building that operated as an hotel was vital to travellers, as Milan was the only place for miles around that a visitor could find lodgings for the night. Duncan, who took over the store after his father's death in 1967, recalled that 'there were two hotels — 'McLeods' was the temperance, and the other one, MacIvers' had a license…it burned down just after the turn of the century.' It is as a general store, however, that the sign *McLeod Bros.* is known to Eastern Townshippers, Scotch, French or incomers alike.

In his book, *The Milan Story*, Duncan tells the history of the family store and the village of Milan. One aspect of the store's work which is not recorded in the book, however, is the meticulous book-keeping that characterised the entire operation. Since Duncan himself was very much involved in this, he no doubt took it all for granted. He regarded it not just as part of the day's or week's work, but expected every store to operate with the care that was built into his own business. It is not surprising, therefore, that he skimmed over the details which still serve as a record, not only of the running of a village store, but also of many aspects of the lives of members of the community.

On August 12, 1992, I accompanied Duncan McLeod and his nephew to the store for the last time. It was the day they were making the final clearance of the last few items that had not already been removed on one of their numerous clearances prior to the sale of the building.[9] Although the 'regular stock' had long since been dispersed, there were several articles which, at the very last moment, still told part of the story of the country store. Among the items lying on the original, forty-foot-long shop counter were a couple of bags of oakum once used to caulk between the logs of buildings, a few boxes of iron rock drills, pegs and wedges for splitting quarried stones, a baking-board and an old, cracked, wooden ox yoke (both of which he gave to me), a fly-swatter (which he humorously gave Ruth), old signs that had once been nailed above the shop door, an even older railway sign, **MILAN STATION**, which once hung on the platform nearby, and two coats, made of thick buffalo skin with felted hair and wool-quilted flannel lining, so heavy I could hardly lift one by myself. Last to be removed were two enormous ledgers, divided alphabetically with the biggest section under <u>Mac</u>, and showing three generations of hand-writing which followed the same pattern of book-keeping. About to burn them in a bonfire, Duncan offered me the chance to leaf through the two tomes, suggesting I 'might be interested in having a look.'[10]

Since the contents of these invaluable ledgers could form the basis of a thesis on economic history, I have selected only a few items to indicate prices of provisions in previous years, and to complement the oral tradition about the exchange or barter system which operated.[11] While customers paid cash whenever possible, credit was given at the store to most families who, in turn, redeemed the debt as soon as they could. According to the entries, there was a seasonal pattern to the exchange of commodities such as pulp-wood, butter or eggs. From the householder's side, Christie MacArthur regarded specific goods as being important to their household: 'We used to exchange butter and eggs, and even we used to pick strawberries [to bring to the store]…well, butter and eggs went in exchange for tea, and sugar and things like that.'

While money was scarce, the exchange system was part of the way of life. It seemed to work well, and people considered it to be fair. As Christie MacKenzie put it:

> We were very well off; we were getting money for what you sell, you know… but everything was cheap. A pound of butter, when I was making butter, [years ago] I was selling it for ten cents a pound. It wasn't much going like now. Eggs, fifteen cents a dozen, or something like that. But we managed to live very good.

The following brief excerpts from McLeod's accounts ledgers give an idea of some of the items bought and their prices at the time:

1927

15 lb salt	30 cents
cake of cooking chocolate (8 oz)	30 cents

1928
| 1 pr mitts | $1.00 |
| 4.75 lbs haddock | 48 cents |

1936
1 lb butter	28 cents
5 lbs sugar	30 cents
1 pr shoes	$1.85
1 pr rubbers [overshoes]	60 cents
half pound tea	33 cents
3 glasses [i.e. tumblers]	48 cents
1 cigar	10 cents
1 bag oats (one bushel)	$1.35

The inclusion of the cigar is a reminder of 'a certain fondness for tobacco' which has been commented upon over the centuries, since the days of Martin Martin.[12] While it is possible to grow tobacco in this part of Canada, the climate is not ideally suited to cultivation on a commercial scale. Nevertheless, several farmers managed to raise a few plants for their own use, which they harvested and hung in an airy barn to dry. As and when the tobacco was needed, it was cut with a tobacco-cutter, an implement, which, to this day, can regularly be found in Eastern Township homes or at auction sales. Since the stores sold unprocessed tobacco, imported from Virginia, more people kept cutters than grew tobacco.

So memorable was one man's addiction to tobacco, that his grandson, Alex MacIver, told this story which influenced his own decision not to smoke:

*My father, [nicknamed 'the Bugler'] and his brother had to go after tobacco for the old man — his father, *Iain Dhomhnaill Bhàin*. He used to smoke, and he said 'chaidh e mach as a cheann' [*he went out of his head*] without a smoke, so he sent the boys seventeen miles for tobacco, walking through the snow to Cailean Noble's store in Winslow — he kept it. The Bugler said they used to carry it half a mile and then stop. It was the leaf tobacco; people would cut it with a tobacco-cutter at home. And none of them ever, ever smoked since.*

Within his own life, Alex's only dealing with tobacco was during a brief episode when he worked with the Railway company on a job where 'they were ripping up floors and I had to chew tobacco on account of germs.'

As Alex's story points out, only those who lived in towns or villages could enjoy the convenience of being near a local store, and while a day's outing to the merchant may have been pleasant in mild weather, in the depth of winter it could be positively dangerous. People knew only too well that there could be as much as eight months of snow, several months of deep drifts, and a perpetual threat of 'white-outs' from blizzards. Even towards the end of winter the risks were high, with thaws followed by sudden freezing temperatures

1. George N. and Annie MacDonald with daughter Muriel (Mayhew), 1916.

2. Angus Morrison with family portrait: the Morrisons from Geocrab, 1880s. L to R, Mary (age 18), Donald, Lexie, Samuel, Maryann (age 16).

3. Label of the trunk brought by the MacRae family from Galson, Isle of Lewis, 1880s.

4. John D. MacLeod, Milan (c. 1920s). As child of six, he sailed from Lewis with his parents in 1850. [collection of Kay Young]

5. Some of the emigrants were given a cast iron pot for making maple syrup when they got to Quebec...A reminder in Miriam's garden, 1995.

6. Squared-timber log house built by Lewisman, Donald MacRae. [Collection of Miriam MacRae Holland]

8. Detail of joint on a squared beam, hand-hewn with broad-axe.

7. Miriam MacRae Holland with Donald MacRae's broad-axe, 1993.

9. Victoria school, Cruvag, late 1920s.

10. A bear killed on the MacIver farm, is carried out by Murdo Beaton (front) and Big Neil MacIver (Russell's father). Malcolm Morrison follows, holding a fox he has just killed, 1912. [Collection of Russell MacIver]

11. Marsboro Church Communion service, 1914.

12. Ministers and precentors outside St. Luke's Church, Milan, na h-orduighean, 1940.

13. R.E. and Maryann Morrison at Cruvag, Marsboro, 1940. [collection of Angus Morrison]

14. Communion tokens and a communicant's card.

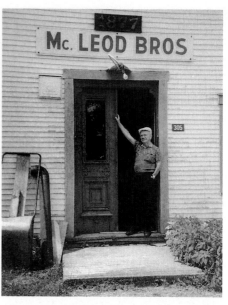

15. Bill Young, Scotstown, Royal Canadian Artillery, 1939. [collection of Kay Young]

16. Duncan McLeod outside the family store (1877), Milan, 1992.

17. John MacKenzie (Seonaidh a' Mhuilleir) and Christie Murray on their wedding day, 1920.

18. Dam constructed by Scotch settlers, near site of a mill at St Leon.

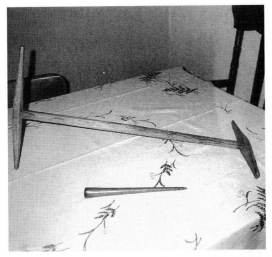

19. *Crois iarna* and *dealgan* on Ruth's hand–embroidered tablecloth. Local chairs.

20. Woollen blanket, hand–woven in Milan, early 20th century.

21. Duncan McLeod holds one of the wooden chains hand-carved by Murdo Matheson.

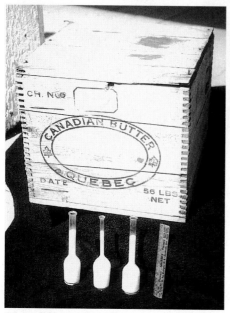

22. 56 lb butter box for export; bottles for testing butter fat in cream; from Norman 'Doak's' Creamery.

23. Home-made wooden mould for one pound of butter.

25. Tobacco cutter.

24. Buckwheat in flower.

26. Preparing for a Quebec winter, 1930s: hay at Harvey MacRae's in Gould. On the back of the photo is: 'Stack is 23 feet high, 18 feet wide and 40 feet long.'

27. A lumber camp in North Whitton, c. 1923.

28. Fox-farming at Harvey MacRae's, Gould, 1930.

29. Winter 1912, the MacIver family set out in their cutter; Russell and his sister Annie are the two children.

30. The MacIver family, July 1916. Annie (left), small girl at back is Christine, Gordon at front, and Russell is to the right of his mother.

31. 'And some of them went out West…' Post-card from McLeod's Crossing sent to Saskatchewan in 1912.

32. 'One time I could stand on my head; now I can scarce stand on my feet!' Russell MacIver reflects on farmlife in the thirties.

33. Bedroom in Muriel's house; patchwork quilt and braided rag rugs made by her grandmother, mother and aunt.

34. Log-cabin patchwork quilt by Muriel's grandmother, c. 1900.

35. Reverse side of 'Dresden Plate' patchwork quilt showing detail of quilting techniques, late 1940s.

36. Eastern Townships' cotton batting factory, 1881.

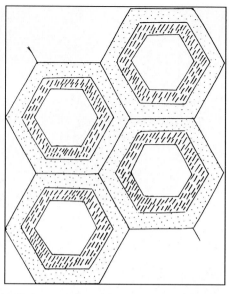

37. Diagram of Mrs Matheson's rug design.

38. 'Fieldwork': the author interviewing Ruth Nicolson in her kitchen.

39. Ruth Nicolson making buckwheat slaps.

40. Muriel Mayhew baking oatmeal scones.

41. Angus Morrison and his bride, Mary, on the Morrion's farm, Cruvag, 22 August 1940.

42. Angus and Mary Morrison on the site of the family farm, 1992. 'It breaks my heart to see how it's all growed over…'

'43. & 44.Scotch' houses, now abandoned, with rowan trees that live on.

45. Interior of Miriam MacRae Holland's log house, 1992.

46. Donald Morrison, the 'Megantic Outlaw', became known as 'Canada's Rob Roy'. In 1889, when this picture was taken, he was in his early thirties. Shortly afterwards he was sentenced to prison. [Special collections, Bishop's University]

47. Welcoming notice at the town line of Stornoway.

adding to the dangers. Since the vast majority of farms were relatively far from the stores, little wonder, then, that towards the end of autumn one of the main concerns of every household was to obtain provisions for the winter. All had to be stocked with basic supplies to feed large families through more than half of the year, a situation which prevailed until the appearance of snow-clearing equipment after the Second World War.

In Cruvag, the Morrison family prepared each year for a major expedition, as Maryann recalled:

> We'd go to the store that was ten miles from us. My husband had team of horses — we had a car [in later years], but when we first went there [it was always horses]…He'd go to Megantic in the fall, you know, before the winter sets in, and he would buy about, oh, about ten or eleven bags of flour — that's a hundred pound bag. And we raised buckwheat on the farm. They never saw buckwheat here in Montreal [where Eva and I live], they don't have it. We made pancakes like Jemima's.[13] But it's not the buckwheat that we used to have. We had barley flour; we had oatmeal flour; we had buckwheat flour…and beans, lots of beans. We used to buy beans by the bushel.
>
> Well, we had to have a — we had a closet in the house — it was for flour, and there was a — oh, the house we had at Marsboro there, it was a beautiful house; five rooms — my husband built that himself, five rooms upstairs. There was one closet for flour, bags of flour.
>
> [And we'd buy] a bag of sugar, a hundred pounds; but we used to get more than that, because you could go to Megantic with a — little sleighs, you know, horses and sleighs, and get what you wanted [if you ran out of anything]. And there was always a road across the way to Megantic.
>
> And molasses, great big jugs of molasses. They used to love the molasses — with beans. A gallon, but we didn't use it all but just on beans, that's all.
>
> We bought raisins, tea, sugar — a box of raisins, wooden, oh yeah, nothing but wood, and twenty pounds apiece.
>
> Tea — a box, wooden box. Oh, I suppose there would be ten, fifteen pounds [in it]. But we'd drink a lot of milk, you know. The children was all milk drinkers.
>
> But when we'd get out of little things like raisins, and tea, and sugar, they would go with a team, a little team, anytime.[14/15]

It might have been a slight exaggeration to suggest they could go *anytime*, for, even when a cautionary eye was kept on weather conditions, things could go suddenly wrong. In 1992, when well into his hundredth year, John MacKenzie from Marsboro recounted an unforgettable experience of one such trip he had made as a young man:

> In the narrows between the two lakes, that's where the ice usually broke up in the winter. It would heave up in the middle, in the narrowest place on the lake…I remember going to Megantic with my mother…my father used to have some young horses, and one by the name of Polly, and he used to keep her in colts all the time…He was working, and I was driving one of these colts, and

my mother was going over, and we were going to bring my father home that evening. So when we got to the narrows in the lake, the ice had bursted up in the middle. So [in order to get through this], I'd have to get out of the sleigh and just hold on to the sleigh until the horse would break the [surface]. I'd have to get out and raise the sleigh out of the [hole and onto solid] ice [again]. I had my feet soakin' wet and it was, oh, about three miles from there, till when we used to get to Megantic. And Malcolm Smith who was running the store in Megantic at that time — he had a game leg and he never kept any help in the store — and he never had anything in the store more than he had to. When we got there my feet were freezing in the wet socks. Of course I wrang them out, or my mother did, but they were frozen, still wet — they weren't dry! We got to Malcolm Smith's and he didn't have a stocking I could buy to put on dry. He just had the necessary things, just groceries and things…But that day, oh boy, did I suffer with cold feet! And all I could get [by way of relief] was get them off, wring them out, and put them back on. But before I got to Megantic on the sleigh and horse…boy, did I suffer with cold!

After he and Christie were married, they shared the winter food-shopping expeditions, no doubt taking care not to repeat John's unforgettably cold feet. As Christie and John recalled the sort of list that formed their essential winter supplies, they reflected the universal roles in every household, with the wife as home-maker and her husband as provider. I have tried to recreate their spontaneity and interaction by including Johnnie's comments in italics. Christie began by contrasting today's diet with that of their first forty years of marriage, when all the Scotch people 'used to buy a lot of herring, you know, the salt herring.' Two thousand miles from the sea, and more than a century away from their crofter-fishermen forebears, the Quebec Gaels still regarded salt herring as an essential part of their diet.[16] For the MacKenzies' comparatively small household of five there was always a keg ordered and occasionally they also had salt cod from Newfoundland. Most of the list was 'dry ingredients', and despite having taken their own grains to the grist mill, they still had to buy the flour they could not produce:

We never raised wheat — *you wouldn't raise wheat in this part; the season's too short.* In the western provinces they raise it. Oh…we used to buy the wheat flour…I think a barrel. *Oh, it would hold two hundred, and two hundred and fifty pounds.* It would last the winter, with the barley and the buckwheat — *with other things.* The rest of the winter's supplies consisted of — not any more than tea and soda, and different things like that, you know. Oh, yes, and that's one thing they used to have in them years — green tea. I hated the taste of it! I do to this day, but some women were crazy about green tea. Oh the regular black tea, oh, five-pound packages would do us. We didn't use coffee as much as we did tea, but we used to have some. We used to have molasses. We used to have a, like, a twenty pound pail, wooden pail, a keg, they called it. We used to get that full of molasses. And oh, we used to get that full twice in the wintertime, in the stores in Milan. Raisins, once in a while, but they were a luxury. Sugar, yes, we used to have sugar, oh, ten pounds at a time when I was growing up. 'Course when I was grown up, we used to buy a hundred pound bag.

A shopping day such as this was a major event in every household and the children were expected to do their share of carrying in the supplies and helping to store them. Having listened to the tapes of his mother I had sent to him, Angus Morrison noticed that she had forgotten to mention a barrel or keg of fish — 'Of course that was so long ago' — and added that 'salt herring and salt cod were pretty important' to their diet. Maryann did, however, say that they were always glad to have fish, and they occasionally caught local trout, although apparently not as often as she would have liked 'because it was just little rivers, you know. But it was nice trout, they called it 'lake trout'. But they were small, but very sweet when you cook them.'

In the 1990s, the Morrisons continue to have trout on their weekly menu, as Angus and Mary's brother are now able to fish regularly from a well-stocked, artificial pond which the two families created a few summers ago. The fabrication of man-made ponds has become a fashion of the 1990s, almost entirely carried out by French families, except for Angus who shares the hobby with his brother-in-law. He remarked how drastically times had changed, and, returning to his mother's winter shopping list, Angus smiled at her inclusion of beans among the staples; the very mention of them evoked memories of working on the farm and in the woods with his brothers. And whatever they ate for breakfast, dinner, or supper, there was always tea[17]:

...barley flour — min eòrna, *and oatmeal*, and pònair — *beans* — *gee whiz!* [laughs] A h-uile làtha! Biodh sinn ag obair anns a choille, ceithir bràithrean, trì bràithrean 's mi fhéin. Agus bhiodh sinn a' toirt ar dìnnear, dhan a' choille, ann am poca, 's mu mheadhon-làtha dheanadh sinn teine anns a' choille, agus dheanadh sinn peile té —...Oh, bha i math, an té; chuireadh sinn siucar innte, cha robh bainn' againn, oh, bha i math...Oh bha i laidir, bha i dubh.

[...barley flour — *barley flour,* and oatmeal, and *beans* — beans — gee whiz! [laughs] *Every day! We would be working in the woods, four brothers, three brothers and myself. And we would take our dinner in the woods with us, in a bag, and about mid-day we would make tea in the woods, and we'd make a pail of tea —...Oh, it was good, that tea. We'd put sugar in it, there wasn't any milk, and oh, it was good...Oh, it was strong, it was black!]* [18]

Tea is still the popular drink, and, just as in the Highlands and Islands of Scotland, it is offered whenever visitors call. While the outdoor brew in a pail has lost none of its appeal to woodsmen, the tea-pot is still a feature of most kitchens, and often 'loose tea' is used, even though short-cut methods of tea-bags in mugs has taken over as the prevalent method with the majority of North American tea-makers. The social aspect of tea-drinking has retained its significance, and an occasion does not need to be 'special' for china cups and saucers to be used. Many of the women regularly serve tea in the china cups, reserving their very finest bone china 'for special'.[19] Most homes I visited had china imported from Scotland, many, though by no means all, with tartan, clan crests, thistles and/or heather featured in the patterns. Not only is their fondness for china a reflection of 'old world taste', but the actual choice of pattern continues to speak of Scotland to those who share in its use.

Angus Morrison's mention of beans as a regular part of the diet speaks for all households in the area, as both Scots and French alike regard them as a staple. Preparation is more-or-less standard throughout the area as the Milan 'bean feast' demonstrates each autumn, when, just after harvest, individual householders bring earthenware crocks of baked beans and hot, fresh rolls to the community hall. Apart from minor individual differences from one cook to the next, the methods of cooking are basically the same: a quantity of dried 'navy beans' are put into the bean crock and soaked in cold water overnight. (About two cups would serve a family of four to six people, and although that would be considered small, it will be used here to give an estimate of proportions.) In the morning, the swollen beans are rinsed, and covered with fresh water, or stock, and baked or simmered for about an hour. When they begin to get tender, the other ingredients are added: salt fat-back-pork (c. 6 or 8 ounces, diced finely), molasses (c. 4 tablespoons), mustard (c. 2 teaspoon), and in more recent years, a tablespoon or two of tomato puree. The mixture is stirred thoroughly, more liquid is added to cover the beans, and the crock is returned to the oven and baked slowly for another six to eight hours. It must be checked every so often to add a little water if the beans show any signs of drying out.

Home-baked beans are regarded as 'local', and in every sense that is true, as they are recorded in the observations of Jacques Cartier who reported luxurious crops grown by the Indians in the sixteenth century.[20] Nowadays several varieties of beans are grown, such as string or runner beans (set beside a frame to support them during growth), French or kidney beans (free-standing, like small, low bushes), and, to a lesser extent, broad beans, all of which are usually eaten fresh or bottled, (nowadays frozen) and are never referred to simply as 'beans'. That term is reserved *only* for baked beans, while other varieties are always described with an adjective, such as 'green', 'yellow', 'waxed' or whatever is appropriate to the legume.[21]

The assimilation of dried beans into the diet undoubtedly dates back over many years, probably to the first generation of settlers who found that they were readily obtainable, kept well, were relatively easy to prepare, and, served with fresh bread, made a nutritious, economical and complete meal for the family. There seems little doubt, however, that around the turn of the century this item of food was still regarded as 'outside' the food repertoire of the Gaels, and more characteristic of their American neighbours in the New England states. It was not uncommon for young people to venture into this part of America to look for work — for example, Christie MacArthur went as a teenager, responding to a relative who knew someone looking for young women to work 'in service'.[22] Very likely recipes were brought back from the States, and became established in the food patterns of the settlers. This idea is also suggested by Eastern Township poet and satirist, Angus Mackay ('Oscar Dhu') whose song, 'Guard the Gaelic' laments the loss of his mother tongue:

> Lads and lasses in their teens
> Wearing airs of kings and queens,
> Just the taste of Boston beans
> Makes them lose the Gaelic.
> They come back with finer clothes
> Speaking Yankee through their nose
> That's the way the Gaelic goes,
> Pop! goes the Gaelic.[23]

Written in the first decade of the twentieth century, Oscar Dhu's song had a prophetic quality in its amusing rhyme. The idea of young Gaels leaving for a short time and returning with no pride in their mother tongue was of deep concern to Mackay. He sensed that language loss was not far away from a people who, in their attempts to better their situation might embrace aspects of other cultures, such as food, fashion and language, without considering the effect of subconsciously denying their own. Today the language is all but gone, and beans are so characteristic of 'local food' that when absent members of family return home on holiday, at least one day's menu will be reserved for home-baked beans. A visit 'home' would be considered lacking without the foods assiciated with family roots in the Eastern Townships, for these familiar meals have taken on importance as symbols of identity.[24]

Baking

Apart from Sunday, the day of rest, almost every day was baking day, especially in larger families which, in days past, were not unusual.[25] In the Murray household in Milan, (Christie MacKenzie's folk), there were seventeen including the parents; at the Morrisons' in Cruvag there were fifteen, and, as Angus confirmed, the kitchen was always busy:

> Bha trì duine deug againn…bha teaghlach mór aca — chan eil iad mar siud an diugh…Nam biodh aon *cent* agamsa airson a h-uile sgona a dh'ith mi, bhithinn beairteach; bhiodh airgead gu leòir agam a' dhol dhan t-Seann Dùthaich deich uairean sa bhliadhna…Oh bhiodh gu dearbh! [laughs] Cha robh mo phàrantan, mo mhàthair a' ceannach bid aran; bha i a' dèaneamh briosgaidean, sgonaichean, sgonaichean aran flùr gheal, sgonaichean aran eòrna, sgonaichean — A h-uile làtha.

*[There were thirteen of us [children]…they had a big family — not like people today…
If I had one cent for every scone I've eaten, I'd be rich; I'd have enough money to go to
the Old Country ten times a year…O yes indeed! [laughs] My parents weren't, my
mother didn't buy any bread whatsoever; she was making biscuits, scones, white flour
scones, barley flour scones, scones — every day.]*[26]

Angus's wife, Mary, who still makes scones frequently, recalled her mother-in-law's kitchen, and remembered that Maryann 'had the knack of getting them to help her'. The oven was in use daily, some days with scones (though most were made on the top of the stove), other days with bread, for it was all part of the week's work, as Maryann recalled:

I made plenty of bread, kneading it with my hands. But one of my boys, [Roddy] — oh, he died a long time ago — when he got up in the kitchen he was making the bread for me. He wasn't married then — I have his picture right here. We had yeast, Royal Yeast; it was sold like that, in a box.[27] Just, well, put it in the water, let it melt, and put three or four quarts of water in that, and lots of flour. But that was twice a week.

The bread was left to rise overnight, and in the morning — many's the time I got up through the night to turn it down. Well…the house was warm; we had three stoves in it, that house. Very warm…Covered with a blanket, we could keep everything warm like that. You have to let your yeast get up. Turn it in the morning, and then you can turn it in your pans after. I used to make big pans of them, buns…My husband took the measure of the oven I had to the tinsmith, and he made pans big enough for my oven. So that would be quite a big pan, just one pan. I had everything very comfortable.

The tinsmith, who lived in Megantic, was French-Canadian, while Gaelic was, of course, the language of the Morrison home. The term 'language barrier', so frequently used today, was unknown to them, as the Gaels and French dealt with each other quite naturally. Both groups learned words and phrases as they went along, indicating that communication was not a problem. In a case such as Maryann's bread pans, the measurements and monetary amounts were written down to avoid confusion: 'What he would do, you know, he'd wait for figures he wanted, and they'd copy them. My husband could understand a little French, but not much.'[28]

Quebec's Hebridean kitchens are renowned in the Eastern Townships for turning out a variety of scones — white flour, whole wheat flour, rolled oats, oatmeal, or a combination of any two. Some are made in the oven, though most are made directly on top of the stove or occasionally on a griddle. Although individual recipes vary, the basic ingredients are flour, salt, a small amount of sugar, baking soda, and sour milk. If fresh milk is used, the baking soda is replaced by baking powder. Most recipes are not written down, though in recent years a number parish cookery books have included scone recipes contributed by women of various church groups.

At one time a daily feature of every table throughout the Highlands and Islands of Scotland — I.F. Grant notes that 'all self-respecting housewives became expert in baking scones'[29] — not surprisingly, scones are considered to be the most characteristic food of the 'Scotch' in Quebec. To anyone brought up on scones in the Old Country, however, there are notable differences: the local terminology varies from that used in Scotland, and, almost without exception, the Eastern Township scones are much thinner than the ones baked in Scotland. Even a more recent immigrant, such as 'war bride' Annie Morrison from Lewis, has adopted the Quebec style of making scones. She no longer makes the thicker ones her mother made, for, as she pointed out, people *expect* them to be fairly thin, (about the thickness of the coarsest oatcake in Scotland) — otherwise they would resemble what Canadians call 'tea biscuits' or 'baking-powder biscuits'.[30]

There is also the question of differences between Canadian and British flours, clearly, if accidentally, demonstrated to me by my mother who lived in Canada from the mid to late 1960s. Brought up on a croft in Skye, where scone-making was very much part of the day's work, she took for granted her successes in the kitchen, regarding the skill as 'second nature'.[31] I recall her dismay in Canada, however, at her repeated 'failures' — batch after batch of scones, each made more carefully than the last, 'exactly as Granny made them'. They turned out flat no matter what she did, and my assurance that they were just as tasty seemed more irritating than convincing. Eventually, on a visit home, she mentioned her lack of success at scones, which she attributed to 'losing her touch'. Her father, a crofter all his life and a keen reader, told her she should not expect family recipes to have the same result unless a similar sort of flour was used. When she insisted she was using 'ordinary flour' he pointed out that Canadian wheat has a higher gluten content than British and advised her to ask the local women, or buy a Canadian recipe book, which would give suitable proportions of flour to raising agents and ensure success.[32] She also needed to learn from the local women that her recipe would be found under 'biscuits' in the index — another strange idea to the immigrant who used that term the hard, crunchy, sweet treat occasionally eaten in her youth, but which has now taken over from the daily scones. Biscuits, we quickly learned, are 'cookies' in Canada — yet another example of the continuous process of acculturation.

In 1976, during one of my visits, Harvey and Hilda MacRae's home in Gould, Hilda was comparing observations she had made while on a visit to the home of her forebears in Lewis. Since her mother tongue was Gaelic, visiting Lewis was like going home, and Hilda took every opportunity to get to know her third and fourth cousins. While she was talking about her trip of a lifetime, Hilda was setting the table for tea and scones, standard fare for all visitors for as long as she could remember. She expressed surprise, however, that most of the homes she visited in Lewis relied on the local baker, or even supermarket, for their scones, and was dismayed to discover that the pattern of frequent baking that characterised virtually all the Scotch homes in the Eastern Townships was almost extinct in Lewis. Hilda spoke of language loss in Quebec, identified symptoms in Lewis which raised her anxiety, and remarked upon the fact that modern times very rapidly and insidiously change traditional ways. Hilda was not, by any means, stuck in the past; she very much believed in progress. She was quite clear in her mind, however, that the Isle of Lewis was not immune from the sort of drastic changes in native culture which had hit the Gaels in Quebec: one need only spend some time in a Lewis kitchen, and compare the food preparation of today's generation to that of their parents. As far as Hilda could see, Lewis had undergone a culinary revolution which made her contemplate the possibility that Quebec might follow suit. As far as world affairs are concerned, the subject of home-baking which initiated the discussion may be regarded as relatively insignificant. It was not simply the item of baking, whether scones for the Scots, soda-bread for the Irish, or croissants for the French that was the issue here. It was, rather, the value of the accompanying time and effort required to retain that item as an aspect of tradition. Astutely observant and analytical, Hilda's example of this one issue, and her ability to relate it to the rest of her traditional heritage, sums up the essence of the work of the folklorist:

> The study of folklore is not the study of the past, though it necessarily includes it; rather it is as much the examination of the operations of tradition, from historical development of items, the stability and change they demonstrate, to matters of transmission — of items, of course, but especially of their meaning, [and] of the values they purvey...[33]

Hilda considered the baking of scones as an aspect of traditional culture which characterised Scottishness to most of her generation, and found it unthinkable that perhaps the younger generation in her native Quebec would also give up. Had she lived long enough to see the 1980s and 90s, she would have been heartened to find that there are still no 'boughten' scones served, as most of the Scotch women, including her daughter, Miriam, have stuck with the traditional ways.

Conscious of it or not, the preparation of food is one of the few remaining aspects of community life over which descendants of the Hebridean settlers still have control. For, in cooking and baking according to traditional 'Scotch' recipes, they assert a form of ethnic and cultural identity easily recognised by all members of the community, both inside and outside the group.

The choice and preparation of food is also extremely important in every social situation: household visits, quilting bees, church socials, communion seasons, harvest or other calendar celebrations, to mention some of the list.

As Zofia Szromba-Rysowa suggests:

> In every society diet fulfills many functions and serves, among other things, to establish and preserve social relationships; it was governed by customs and...had a significant social aspect as it played an important role in hospitality, [and in] the strengthening of social position...[34]

In 1976-77, and during the summers of 1991 to 1995, I enjoyed the products of several kitchens, in particular those of Muriel Mayhew in Lennoxville, and of Ruth Nicholson in Milan (my bases for more recent fieldwork).[35] I found out, for example, that baking scones needed no special occasion — 'there's not too many left' was enough of a prompt. As is the case with most home-baking, however, the anticipation of visitors was an added incentive to have 'freshly baked' ones for that day. In neither house was I the 'visitor' as I was staying there, but could observe the everyday planning of household activities.

Baking scones always began with routine kitchen preparations, such as making sure the surfaces were cleared, then getting out utensils and the baking-board, usually referred to as 'breadboard'. In Scotland I had considered this to be a feature of pre-war households, for, within my own lifetime, only my grandmother in Skye, and our school cookery classes in Stornoway, used baking-boards. The modern kitchen, with its emphasis on counter space with clear surfaces, has largely dispensed with the need for them. It was interesting to notice, however, that although Muriel had lived in a modern house in Lennoxville since the late 1940s, the baking-board was still regarded as part of the procedure, and was placed on top of the kitchen counter. Ruth's house, however, was built at the turn of the century and (until very recently[36]) retained most of its characteristics; her kitchen featured hand-made pine dressers, a stone sink in the corner, a wood-stove, a day-bed, two rocking chairs and table and chairs in the centre of the room. Ruth placed her baking-board on top of the table, the traditional site for all her baking activities.[37]

The women display the same 'second nature' attitude to baking which was once common in every Hebridean home. They use traditional family recipes which are written down only if someone asks for them, and although it would be a straightforward matter to formulate recipes according to the standard technique of recipe books (a list of <u>ingredients</u> followed by the <u>method),</u> for the purpose of this book I will give only two examples set in the normal context in which recipes were traditionally learned.[38]

Having watched her on many occasions, I tape-recorded Ruth immediately after two baking sessions in July, 1992. Apart from the addition of titles, and minimal addition of words and phrases for clarity [in square brackets], the recipes are presented in Ruth's words.

Wholewheat Scones

The recipe? Well, I used two and a half cups of whole-wheat flour and one and a half cups of white to make four cups — that makes it easier for me to measure the soda and my salt. I put two level teaspoons of soda and maybe oh, a teaspoon of salt, and I put about three tablespoons of shortening and rub it in…No [special kind — any] lard would do, you know, just what makes them tender…And I put about a tablespoon of sugar in — it takes [away] the strong taste of the wholewheat. Then around two cups of sour milk; if you have buttermilk or sour milk — I use the powdered milk for two cups [nowadays] and I pour vinegar in [to turn it sour]…[When we were up at the farm] we had our own cows then, and I'd have my own sour milk then, or sometimes I had buttermilk, 'cos I made butter too then…Oh, the *bainne goirt*, [sour milk] yeah, I haven't thought of that for a long time, the *bainne goirt*. But anyway you put all that in and just mix it up till, you know, not too soft, and not too stiff, and I put the whole thing on the breadboard, and I don't know if I can describe it — [But you floured it first?] Oh, yes, you have to, yes, and roll out. You cut off [a portion from the mass of dough] and you'd roll out. [Kneading it is] not necessary if you haven't got it too soft. And you cut a strip off [the rolled out portion] about three inches, and then I roll it out to flatten it out and cut it into various sizes, square, whatever.

[How thick?] Oh, for wholewheat, a little bit thicker than other things, [about one third of an inch] sometimes — this is through experience. And then…I put them on the [top surface of the wood-]stove, but not too hot, as flour burns so quickly, and I turn them over and get them browned on the other side, and then I can put them [further] back so I can get more [to fit], so I have the whole batch on the stove, on the top of the stove.

[Making scones was learned at home, but] not from my mother; I don't remember her making them, [because she died when I was thirteen] but my grandmother — it would be my grandmother…Well, I don't know if she hit them with the knife to see if they were cooked. [Ruth always tapped them with the blunt side of a knife to hear if they made the 'right" sort of noise, indicating that they were cooked — a more hollow noise than if raw inside.]… [And they were always baked on the top of the stove], oh, of course…and it keeps me warm. [You could bake them] on the electric griddle; it's slower, 'cos you haven't got the space, [and you also have to bake] them a little bit longer.

Even on a hot summer day, Ruth bakes on top of the wood-stove. She opens the outside door that leads from her kitchen onto the verandah, and the back door into the wood-shed, leaving two opened, screened windows, and the airy, screen doors shut to keep out the flies while allowing a cooler air to circulate and cool down the hot kitchen. Nevertheless, the temperature rises considerably, and Ruth is more likely to make jokes about people who 'can't stand the heat in the kitchen' than take out her electric frying pan.

Baking day seldom means that only one item will be made. More usually a contrasting batch of scones, such as oatmeal, will be turned out, along with 'something for the cookie-jar.' Oatmeal scones, which I had never tasted in Scotland, are highly popular. They are made with a combination of oats — 'rolled oats' or 'porridge oats' in Scotland — and white or wholewheat, in a similar method to the one above, but rolled slightly thinner than other scones. Again, they are baked on the top of the stove or on a griddle, cooled on a rack and served with fresh butter and home-made jam. [39]

While wheat, barley flour, and oatmeal were used in scones, buckwheat flour was generally made into two varieties of pancakes. The Gaelic-speaking Scots had their own name for them, *slapaichean* in Gaelic, and buckwheat 'slaps' in English. Only one kind of them was categorized as 'baking' while the other, which will be discussed separately, is more in the category of cooking as it is part of a main meal. Christie MacKenzie learned both kinds in her mother's kitchen. The first method she described produced a thick pancake which would be eaten for breakfast or a small meal. (She also describes the second type but they will be dealt with after the activities of 'baking day' have been completed.)

> We always made the slaps, you know — the buckwheat slaps [directly] on top of the stove. And some make them with sour milk in the frying pan; sort of a cake, like, and cut it in four. Well it would be eh, thicker than a pancake, and it would be the size of the frying pan. Then you turned it out on a plate and you cut it in four quarters.
>
> Well, there's the soda, and the salt, and the sour milk. By golly, I don't know how much buckwheat. It would be according to the amount you were making! [My mother] used to make a stack like that [about nine inches] on the plate. There was eight or nine or ten of us around the table for every meal, you know. We used to have them for supper, mostly. Well, sometimes we used to have maple syrup, and sometimes molasses.

As far as cookie-jars and cake-tins are concerned, most of the women keep recipes which have become favourites over the years, such as those from a recipe book, magazine article, newspaper feature, radio programme, or from a friend. An impressive variety of such goodies appear at most social gatherings, and usually they are regarded the way a dessert might be — to be eaten after sandwiches and/or scones. Of these, the only recipe to be considered 'Scotch' is shortbread, which has a similar range of individual differences, just as in Scotland. Basic ingredients are flour, butter and castor sugar, and local experts will discuss the merits of using all butter, as opposed to margarine or half-and-half, and despite the extra expense, will opt for butter if their recipe calls for it. Although shortbread is the only item in this category to be regarded as 'traditional', it is true to say, however, that serving a lavish spread on social occasions is considered characteristic of the Scotch hospitality. [40]

Buckwheat Slaps and Pork

In any discussion remotely connected with food, it is almost inevitable that the subject of buckwheat slaps will come up. In this conversation with Russell MacIver we had been talking about hunting, then crop farming, when suddenly he lit up with enthusiasm:

Russell: Buckwheat pancakes, that was a great feed! Did you ever have any?

MB: I did. I had them at Ruth Nicholson's. She'd cover the top of the stove with them.

Russell: Yeah. My, they're good. My father was a crackerjack at making them. He'd make, he'd fry up pork steak and venison steak together. And that gravy, you can't get that taste any more; I don't know why, but you don't get it.

MB: And you'd have that with buckwheat pancakes?

Russell: Yeah. You'd have two plates on the table stacked this high [indicates c. 4 inches high] and stacked that high. Oh, some of the fellows could eat an awful pile! [laughs]…'Course my mother was, I suppose, just as good as him, and my two sisters; Gordon, my brother, is good; I'm fairly good myself at it.

The buckwheat slaps eaten as part of the main meal, were different to the ones Christie first described, and were always eaten with fried pork, or, as Russell said, pork and venison. Usually there would be no potatoes with this meal, as the buckwheat slaps were eaten in place of them. [41] Christie continues:

You make them with water — the soda, and the salt, and water instead of sour milk. And you cook them like a couple of tablespoons on top of the rim of the stove, you know. You turn them…And with pork chops they are delicious.

To describe the recipe out of the context of the actual situation does not, however, give any real impression of the production of *slabaichean*, as the older people call them. Had I not watched the procedure, I would have had no idea of the agility required of a cook who has to co-ordinate his or her work while making such a meal for family or friends. This was demonstrated for me by Ruth whom I watched several times. [42]

Preparation and accurate timing are crucial, for once the slaps are ready to be made, there is not a moment to stop for anything else. The pork is cooked first, usually in a frying pan, then the wood-stove is fired up for the fast, alert cook to pour onto its smooth, hot surface enough thin batter to make slaps about the size of a saucer or small tea-plate. Having covered the complete stove, about thirty inches in width, the action then starts to look like a relay race, as it is time to go back to turn the first one immediately after pouring the last one. No sooner is the last one turned than the first one has to be removed. With the family or guests seated at the table, the cook stands at the stove, and occasionally darts towards the table to replenish the serving plates. The work of pouring, turning and removing continues with perfect co-ordination until all is complete, and several piles of buckwheat slaps and a large platter of fried pork grace the table. Only then can the expert sit down and join the company whom she has encouraged to 'start before they get cold!'

Recorded on July 29, 1992, after she had cooked and served a meal for four guests, Ruth herself describes the procedure. At this point, a complete transcription of the conversation is given so as to give the clearest impression of what took place. The reader may notice that the order in which the stages of the procedure are discussed is not in the exact order that they took place; rather than a step-by-step set of instructions, they represent a re-tracing of the steps with some comments given along the way:

MB: Ruth…we've just eaten the most delicious meal of buckwheat slaps and rinds of pork. [We also had fried pork-chops.] What do you call the salted fat-back pork when you cut it up and fry it up?

Ruth: *Cnaoiseagan* is what I call them…I think that's what the old people [called it], well there was such a thing, and I always think that's what the *cnaoiseagan* was.

MB: They cut up the pork fat and fried it till it was all rendered?

Ruth: Hm hm.

MB: Delicious.

Ruth: Yes, it's good.

MB: Now, the buckwheat pancakes, or *slabaichean*, how did you make them?

Ruth: Shall I give you the amount I made tonight? [Yes] Well, I used two cups of buckwheat flour and, oh I put a heaping tablespoon of white flour in, I don't know if it's necessary, but I used to put it in the other kind of buckwheat, and salt…maybe salt to taste, you know.

MB: About a quarter, or less than a quarter teaspoon?

Ruth: Oh, it was more than that, for that amount.

MB: More like a teaspoon [from what I noticed].

Ruth: Yes, and I can't tell you how much soda because I added some soda to it because it didn't have the green tinge to it, so…Yea, at first, almost [a teaspoon] anyway, and then a little bit more, but not too much because then you taste the soda. [You begin to see the green tinge] after you put it on the stove…

MB: And then when you mix up the flour and the soda and the flour and the salt — and you did this in a[n aluminium] pan with a handle on it

Ruth: Well, it's easier to handle, unless you had it in a pitcher; I never do, but —

MB: And then you can just pour it directly on to the stove?

Ruth: And I've got the sink right there, so I can lay it [down].

MB: Into your dry ingredients, then, what did you put?

Ruth: I just put quite hot, not boiling water, but good and hot, and stirred it up to make a thin mixture. A very hot fire.

MB: That was really hot, I could see.

Ruth: Yes, I don't know if you could do it on a, I suppose, on a griddle, you could.

MB: Is it hotter than for pancakes?

Ruth: I suppose. This would stick, this kind of buckwheat would break up if it isn't cooked quickly enough.

MB: Well, I've seen you prepare the stove, but maybe you'd like to tell how you did that?

Ruth: Oh! [laughs] I fried the pork on a fair fire, but then I added small pieces of wood, kindling, or whatever I have to make a really hot fire. And if the stove is hot enough it doesn't sizzle, but if it gets cool the buckwheat will start sticking to it.

MB: I like the way you cleaned off the stove.

Ruth: Oh! [laughs] I used [newpapers first] then paper napkins or something over there, or a cloth.

MB: Do you put any oil or anything on the stove?

Ruth: No, no. When it's hot enough you don't need to. Still, on an electric frying pan you don't need any either. It's hot enough — you don't need any grease.

MB: So you just put the mixture directly on the stove?

Ruth: And then it forms, it's all little bubbles, and when, what'll I say — when, the holes, they become holes [burst] you turn them.

MB: They're like little volcanoes, aren't they!

Ruth: Yeah, yes.

MB: And when these little bubbles have burst all over, you turn them.

Ruth: Yes, so that it's firm enough so that you can handle it to turn it.

MB: You have a real production line going there. [Ruth laughs] That's why I see that you have to prepare the pork in advance. And the gravy — ?

Ruth: Yeah, well I did pork pieces, scraps of fat, so that I would have enough fat in it to make a, you know, a fair gravy, instead of just plain water.

MB: Yes. The essence of the pork is still in the cast iron pan and you add boiling water?

Ruth: No, I put cold in, because it doesn't spatter all over but it just —

MB: And is that it? Nothing else in it?

Ruth: Well, salt, a little salt.

MB: And a good hot bowl on the table.

Ruth: Yes, and your guests should be eating as soon as there's enough to get going.

MB: So I saw.

Ruth: That's the way to do buckwheat, though.[43]

No food can monopolize a conversation like buckwheat and a discussion on its importance can find its way into a conversation at any moment, as people never tire of talking about it. Every participant will be firmly convinced by personal taste of the right and wrong way of milling it, and of the best methods of cooking with it. In his droll way, Russell MacIver joked that when one local character of his youth got married, 'she said the only thing she took on her honeymoon was her fiddle and a barrel of buckwheat flour!'

Once commonplace on every farm, in every country-store and every household, buckwheat has become much more difficult to obtain since the Legendre mill ceased operation. Individuals regret that they now have to search in healthfood stores in Sherbrooke or Montreal, or ask relatives to try to obtain some from country stores in Vermont or New Hampshire.[44] As often as not, however, they find a product that does not seem to measure up to the buckwheat that they used to obtain at the Legendre mill at Stornoway. When anyone finds a new source, there are telephone calls between friends, often long-distance, to pass on information of the new find. Generally the call concludes with a promise to 'ring back if it's any good' or 'no good' depending upon the context of the conversation. For example, in 1992 I brought some 'across the line' from Vermont, and while it was judged to be 'fairly good' and 'worth buying again', nevertheless, it had too many little black specks in it to meet the former standards of milling. In 1993, on my way to Quebec from North Carolina, I visited a rural water-mill in the Appalachians which still ground locally-grown buckwheat, so I bought a quantity to bring to Ruth who examined it enthusiastically. As it appeared to have fewer specks than a previous batch she had obtained in Megantic, I was asked about the plants, the mill, the mill-stones, the people who ran it, and so on. Once again buckwheat was the subject of several conversations, some in Ruth's kitchen, others on the telephone, or when friends called to visit. Word got around that perhaps this 'new source' might be worth following up, so that a week later, and ten miles away, while visiting Mary and Angus Morrison, I was asked for the address of the mill. [45] The most notable feature of all of these discussions is that over and over again they reaffirm close ties between the Scotch and the French that go back to the 1850s when the Legendre family opened the first mill. 'Oh they were real nice people, and they could talk Gaelic' is repeated, giving the impression that there is a longing to have the community spirit restored. Thus, 'the real buckwheat' becomes a symbol of a cherished past.

Preparing and Preserving Meat

In those days, people looked forward to a special 'feed of buckwheat and pork' when a pig was slaughtered during autumn or winter. Fresh meat was enjoyed just after an animal was butchered, and then the rest of the carcass was preserved fresh-frozen (in the depth of winter), salted or cured. Bill Young recalled that in his family 'the pork was salted in barrels or anything other than that. They smoked the hams; and the bacon sometimes was smoked, and sometimes was salted down and eaten as green bacon — it wasn't cured.'

At a ceilidh in Ruth's kitchen in 1992, she and her sister, Bernice, discussed the subject with Isabell Beattie (née MacArthur). Bernice described how their family made hams after they had butchered a pig:

*[The meat] was soaked in brine for so many days before the smoking — it was a special kind of a smoke house, seven or eight feet high; the smoke would go out the top. The fire just smouldered with wood chips of a special kind, or sawdust, so that it wouldn't burst into flames. And for about two weeks they'd build fires like that. Not night time, just in the days.

Isabell recalled a similar process at the MacArthur's farm, less than a mile away from the MacDonalds, and added *'we hung them up from the rafters in the barn after they were smoked.'[46]

While their forebears in the Outer Hebrides had relied on fish and mutton as their main sources of protein, the settlers in Quebec relied more upon pork and, to a lesser extent, beef, which was generally kept in barrels in a briny solution, with saltpetre added so that the meat would retain its red colour. Most people were of the opinion that the Scotch settlers, apart from a few families, ate little or no mutton. Bill Young remarked: 'I don't believe the people were much eaters of mutton...we never ate mutton at home. Well, there were sheep — we weren't, they weren't great on sheep — only for wool.' Bill's wife, Kay (née MacLeod) also shared his opinion, as did many others, with the exception of Isabell's mother, Christie MacArthur, who dispelled my suspicion that the sheep were allowed to die of old age. She said that they ate mutton occasionally, always fresh or from the cold-shed, as they never salted it. No one today seems to have heard of the dry-salting of mutton that was once so common throughout the Highlands and Islands, although the dry-salting of other meats was practised throughout Quebec. [47]

The local diet was also supplemented by fish, and whatever wild game they could get. Christie MacKenzie, born in Milan in 1897, recalled:

> [We ate] deer meat…Oh yes, we used to have rabbit; oh, yes, rabbit stew was quite a thing…[father and] even the boys used to set snares for them… Partridges, well, as I said before, there wasn't too many that had guns, but those that did used to kill some partridge.

For hunting enthusiasts, such as Russell MacIver's family, the area was a sportsman's paradise. Russell recalled his father coming home from the nearby woods with 'a whole bunch of partridge tied to his waist…' and added that there was always 'plenty to eat then'. His own favourite meat was venison, and, as the following conversation shows, Russell was expert at preparing and preserved it:

MB: Would you have it often?

Russell: Hardly any time through the year that we didn't have some. He was as bad at killing deer out of season as anybody! [laughs] Lucky. Through the summer, just for ourselves, just for a treat, cut it up — we had a well down in the swamp and the overflow, that was better than any fridge you ever saw. And anybody coming around he'd go and get one of them jars, quarts, two quarts and that was pretty good meat!

MB: Did they bottle it — the meat?

Russell: Oh, sometimes like that in the summer as we didn't have a fridge at that time — we didn't have no electricity.

MB: How would they do it?

Russell: Oh just cut it up and put it in the jars.

MB: And boil it? [That's the way the Gaels did it in in Newfoundland.]

Russell: No, it went in raw — bring it home to cook it…It was put up raw, but it was air tight…They had a rubber [seal] on and it was air tight. If you could see a bubble in it you'd have to fix it up again.

Duncan: And you'd keep it cool in the water.

MB: They were full of inventive ideas.

Duncan: Well they didn't have one of these [points to the fridge] so they had to have next best thing.

MB: Did they use salt?

Russell: Oh they used to use salt to preserve the meat too — put it in a crock and cover it up and put it in the cellar. It'd keep pretty good, because there's some cellars that are pretty good.

MB: Would it have a layer of salt, a layer of meat?

Russell: Yeah, or in brine.

MB: In an earthenware crock?

Russell: Yeah.

And without giving any indication where the conversation was ultimately headed, Russell told his story about the hens dying after they drank the brine (Chapter 3).

Whenever an animal was butchered, none of it was ever wasted. The hide was put aside to be cured for leather, the meat kept for the table, then the internal organs, head, trotters and offal were all used and indeed relished for a variey of local delicacies, such as head-cheese and *maragan*.[48] Families had their own favourite way of making them, with variations from kitchen to kitchen. For head-cheese, the head of a cow or pig was skinned and the ears, and sometimes the brain, were removed. The head was then boiled in a very large pot for several hours, till the meat, mostly from the jowls, was tender enough to fall from the bones. The pot was removed from the stove, and all the bones were taken out, paying careful attention to the smallest ones. The meat was then put through the meat grinder (mincer), and returned to the liquid in which it was boiled. Salt was added to taste and the mixture then poured into dishes and left overnight to cool and set, just like a jelly.[49] Knuckle bones were sometimes boiled with the heads which imparted a distinctive flavour, and increased considerably the gelatine content to ensure proper setting.[50]

Butchering an animal also occasioned the making of a second specialty — *maragan* (puddings). Among the Gaels of the Eastern Townships, the word always denotes a *white* pudding (*marag gheal*), the only kind made by them, although the French appear to favour what is known as *marag dhubh* (black, or blood pudding) in Gaelic Scotland.[51]

Despite the fact that making *maragan* involved considerable work, so popular were they that the effort was considered worthwhile. Girls would help their mothers, and learn as they went along, just as Bessie (MacIver) Smith did in Tolsta (Quebec) where she grew up. Even after she married and moved to Scotstown, she made *maragan* for many years, and, at the age of eighty 'had done her share':

To fill them casings was a job — an awful job. Well, we'd wash them to death, you know, you'd have a big tub. Kill an animal, and you'd have that [intestines] in a tub, you know, and you'd have to clean all them *caolanan* [intestines] out, you know, from the animal, and wash them. And from this animal that they'd kill there'd be suet, and she'd have this suet, and barley flour, and salt, and pepper, and onions. And all that was worked together. And the filling them *caolanan*, you know, was a job. But they wouldn't break, like the casings you get today.

The *maragan* made in Quebec differed from those made in the Scotland. as the latter are made in sheep's casings, and a mixture of oatmeal and wheat flour provides the cereal in the recipe. Although Bessie had heard of using Scotch oatmeal, she had always used barley flour because her family grew oats only for cattle feed, not for cooking. As far as she knew, casings were now unobtainable in the Eastern Townships so she got hers from Vermont, where, she said, 'you could get the real oatmeal too.' Bessie added that the area of Graniteville, Vermont, had so many people of Scottish origin, many from the Eastern Townships, that some of the food stores began to cater for Scottish taste and recipes. And so popular are *maragan* there that Bessie's relatives send her a box of pork casings in salt, ready to use, and even the barley flour which can no longer be obtained in Scotstown. Furthermore, a small funnel-like device has been specially designed for filling the casings, and anyone who makes *maragan* in Quebec today seems to have acquired one of these American-made gadgets. With the pre-cleaned casings and the miraculous filling device, much of the hard work and frustration are eliminated.

Bessie Smith has collected two other recipes in addition to the one she has been using for some seventy years; while there is a similarity between the one from Vermont and the one from Quebec, both are worth recording, along with Bessie's added advice.

The first, which she calls 'Maggie's Recipe', is from Bessie's cousin who was 'born and brought up across the line' in Vermont. She gew up with the Gaelic traditions of her Eastern Township parents, however, and being an enthusiast of traditional recipes, she sent the following to Bessie, along with the pork casings, barley flour, oatmeal, and casing-filler:

Maggie's Recipe

3 cups ground oatmeal (our mothers used graham or whole wheat flour.)
2 cups ground suet — don't skimp.
3 or 4 medium sized onions, ground.
1.5 tablespoons salt (or to taste.)
c. 1 tablespoon pepper.

Mix ingredients in a large bowl with your hands. Cut the dry packed in salt casings to yard lengths. Place casings in water. Open the end and feed on to the funnel. Blow air into it and fill with the dry ingredients. Tie both ends. Use casings enough to take all the mixed filling. Bring the water to boil in a large kettle. Put in prepared *marags*. Prick frequently with a darning needle. Don't cook more than two or three at a time. Boil gently for 20 minutes…Remove to cool, and add more until all are boiled. I have an old fashioned hat-pin I use for pricking the casings to release the air.

To this Bessie added two hints from her years of experience: 'No, not *boiling* them for twenty minutes, but *simmering* them, because if you boil them they break.' Also, add a teaspoon of sugar to the ground onions because 'If you're making a dressing, or anything, and you're frying onions, you put a couple of teaspoons of sugar on them and they won't repeat — and the same thing with that.'

Bessie's daughter-in-law, Evelyn, who was born in Stornoway and is a sister of Kay (MacLeod) Young, also had a recipe. Although she and her husband, Raymond, had long since left the Scotstown area and live several hundred miles away in Cornwall, Ontario, she continued to use family recipes and to make maragan. I visited her in Scotstown in 1993, when they were on a visit to their summer home. Evelyn said she had altered her mother's recipe for maragan because she could not find all the original ingredients. Interestingly, she incorporates Bessie's 'onion hint' in the recipe:

Maragan: Evelyn's Recipe

3 cups Scotch oatmeal.
4 cups barley flour.
8 medium sized onions, ground fine.
Add one tablespoon sugar to onions and stir well.
1 tablespoon salt.
1 tablespoon pepper.
2 teaspoons ginger.
2 lbs. ground suet, very fine.

Mix above ingredients in a large bowl. Work well with hands until mixture is like fine crumbs. Place casings in water. Open end and ease on to the funnel. Blow air into it and fill with the dry ingredients. Bring water to a boil in a large kettle. Put in prepared *marags*. Cook gently until done. Prick with a pin to let the air out of the casings.

Bessie suggested that traditional recipes are an important way of keeping in touch with family, as her cousin in Vermont had written to say that it was Thanksgiving, 'a big celebration in the States', and although they had long since adopted American holidays, they insisted on serving *marag* (not stuffing) with the universal menu of turkey. The local butcher supplied the casings every year, and as far as they were concerned the preparation and eating of *maragan* celebrated their link with Quebec. In much the same way these recipes were part of Bessie's Lewis heritage which she, in turn, has left to her children.

Preserving Fruit and Vegetables

Ever mindful of keeping a daily supply of vitamins through the long winter months, families relied upon preserving wild berries and fruit from the summer and autumn harvest. Nature has conveniently arranged their growing cycles so that strawberries, gooseberries, raspberries, blackberries (brambles), blueberries, choke-cherries, cranberries, and finally apples, ripen in succession and do not flood the kitchens with a sudden, overwhelming glut. In July, everyone welcomed the first fruits of summer — wild strawberries — and, despite the fact that they are minuscule compared to cultivated ones, the effort required to make a quart was well worth the reward of their sweet taste, the family's delight in a dessert of strawberries and fresh cream, and the assurance that winter would not be devoid of the occasional treat.

As settlers expanded their kitchen gardens and began to gain access to plant nurseries, some set aside an area for cultivated strawberry plants, a row or two of raspberry or blackcurrant canes, and a few crowns of rhubarb. The task of picking was often assigned to young children accompanied by a grandparent, or older sibling, while the women were responsible for preserving the berries and fruits. Recipes were well known in the community, seldom written down, and followed standard practices of measuring a cupful of fruit to one of sugar, or a little less, according to the desired sweetness. In more recent years pectin was added (except for blackcurrants which never need it) and recipes followed according to those 'on the label of the bottle'. Many a hot day saw the large pot on the stove, preparing for the next batch to be jammed and bottled, then stored in the cool cellar until needed.[52]

Although crab-apple trees grow wild in the region, many families preferred to cultivate a small orchard of one or two chosen varieties. Now well over a century old, the names of the varieties are not known locally, but are referred to simply as 'good for eating' or 'good for pies'. After the harvest, clean apples were carefully packed in boxes and stored in a cool cellar where they would keep for approximately three months. If there were any left after that time (and there usually were), they could be preserved as apple sauce, or air-dried, a technique which the Gaels learned in Quebec. Christie Mackenzie, like most of the women, recalled spending many an evening preparing apples for drying:

> We used to peel the apples, and cut them up, and put them on strings, and dry them…around the stove, oh a couple of weeks anyway. Then we'd put them away, in boxes…Well, they required a lot of cooking, you know, to soften them, and so on. Any they didn't make the pies that fresh apples would make; they didn't taste as good.

Once a familiar sight in most kitchens, strings of drying apples are no longer part of autumn's annual cycle, as freezing has taken over. An occasional reminder can still be seen in some kitchens, such as Ruth's, where a rod once used to suspend strings of apples above the stove has been adopted as a general drying rail.[53]

Isobel Stewart, a contemporary of Christie's, who grew up in Tolsta, looked back over the years which, paradoxically, have somehow been labelled 'fairly poor' in today's terms. She considered the community to have been blessed with a plentiful store of food, and a great deal of incentive besides:

> When we were kids we had apples, all kinds of apples, [?pears], plums, and rhubarb. And when I think of it, my grandmother was the first woman in Tolsta that ever grew tomatoes! Now where she got the seed I'll never know. But anyway, I remember one time when some *cailleachs* came to the house one day and they were invited for supper, so she had some tomatoes. They wouldn't touch them for anything! 'Don't touch that! You're going to kill yourself eating that!' because they thought it was just something she'd picked up somewhere and she shouldn't either. She just laughed at them, but she was the first woman in Tolsta grew tomatoes. [Did they catch on after that?] Oh, not too much, there was a lot of them that never cared for them anyway. It was just really, everybody'd just mostly *snèapan* and *buntàta,* you know, [turnips and potatoes] just the very [?basics], but grandmother, she'd a beautiful garden. And I remember, oh when *we* got tasting the tomatoes — she slept downstairs; our house is still standing in there — and we use to go down and sleep with granny, one on either side of her, and we'd a big tall sack[54] and we'd take it and hide it under the pillow when the tomatoes were half red and half green. And she'd put us to bed and go out in the kitchen. And we used to slide this window up and we'd slip out in the garden and get a big tomato and get the sack in and eat it. [laughs] [55]

Isobel's comment about the conservative attitude towards her grand-mother's innovative gardening practices could just as well be describing the Highlands of Scotland. Having discussed the importance of potatoes, and to some extent kail, in the diet of the nineteenth century Highlanders, I. F. Grant remarks upon the prevailing attitude she observed in 1961:

> ...the modern Highlanders are not, as a rule, great vegetable eaters. If they have a garden, and the habit is on the increase, little is generally grown beyond cabbage, curly kail and, in sandy districts, carrots. I have seen very tired looking lettuces imported from Glasgow to the Islands to be eaten by visitors.[56]

While fruit preserving occupied most of the time allocated to bottling and canning, there was usually a day or two set aside for vegetables. Turnip greens or spinach could be kept in sealed jars for the winter, by boiling them in a large pot for a few minutes, or just long enough for their springy, bulky leaves to collapse into the familiar form of 'cooked greens', then compressing them into sterilized jars which are vacuum-sealed when hot.[57] Carrot thinnings, now called 'baby carrots', were also boiled and bottled, as were beets (beetroot), though the latter were generally preserved in a pickle of vinegar, sugar and spices. It need hardly be said that autumn was an exceptionally busy time in the kitchen.

In more recent years, housewives have increasingly experimented with recipes for pickling and preserving fruit and vegetables. Ingredients such as apples, onions and tomatoes are combined with recent introductions such as squash, and favourite recipes which include sugar, vinegar, cloves, allspice, and various other spices and herbs are exchanged, as are jars of newly-made jams and preserves. Aside from the original practical and economic reason for preserving foods for the winter, there is now a more social aspect. Housewives are rarely compelled by economic circumstances to take out the jam or pickling pan; the prime motivations are taste and the pleasure of sharing the products in the social setting of family and community. This shift in emphasis is not by any means confined to the Eastern Township Gaels; more generally, it is a feature of modern Quebec.[58]

Maple Syrup and Sugar

A favourite emigration anecdote that comes up from time to time concerns the Lewis people who 'were told all they had to do was tap a tree and they'd get sugar.' It is never attributed to anyone in particular, but is told to illustrate the fact that the new settlers had huge adjustments to make, and many new skills to learn in Quebec. They soon learned how and when to 'tap' the maple trees for sap in spring, by drilling a small hole through the bark and inserting a spike or spigot into it, to allow the sap to drip into a bucket suspended below; at the same time they learned how to use the big cast iron kettles (pots, in Scottish terms) to boil up the sap to make the syrup — forty gallons is boiled down to one gallon of syrup. As far as I can ascertain, there are no memories of who learned first, or from whom — 'Oh, just learned it, I guess' — but rather vaguely the French and/or Indians are credited.[59] Uncertain also is the source of the recipe for maple sugar, which is the next stage of production after the syrup.[60] This kind of sugar is made by boiling a quantity of syrup till it reaches what is known as the 'soft ball stage', that is, when a spoonful of boiled syrup dropped into a cup of cold water will form a soft ball, as opposed to dispersing if it has not been boiled long enough. (The expression is well-known to toffee-makers.) After that stage is reached, the contents of the pot are either poured into moulds to make maple-sugar loaf, or are whipped to add air, and then poured out to set on 'cookie sheets' or trays. Stories of 'sugar growing in the woods' could only come true after a great deal of effort.[61]

Since most 'lots' of land granted to settlers had enough maple trees to provide syrup for a family when the sap began to run in April, it was a pretty busy month for all concerned. After a few decades of land-clearing, they discovered in some areas that second growth woods grew into extensive groves that could yield enough sap to produce syrup on a commercial scale. For most of this century, therefore, farmers were able to supplement domestic income by canning or bottling their syrup and selling it. As time went by, they also kept up with new techniques that were developed, though Russell MacIver was of the opinion that this sweet harvest from the trees brought mixed blessings:

> We used to make maple sugar too. We had a sugar bush, I suppose it was tapped for about seventy-five years, and you'd see all the different kinds of holes, and different kinds of makes and spouts, and they'd come out with another invention, you could tell what it was on the bark. [Enjoy sugaring time?] Huh! [Laughs!] I didn't like it too much. It was awful hard work and it was awful wet work — out in the wet snow, soaked all the time, and it was hard work too... Oh, we sold some. And we'd first have the kettles, the big kettles, and boil it in the woods, but then we got an evaporator, and boy, it used to take a lot of wood.

Nowadays, some of Quebec's biggest producers are in the Milan area, where sugar-houses can be instantly recognized by their large metal stove-pipe chimneys, and by the enormous wood-piles that stretch several times the length of the house. The maple groves nearby are no longer tapped with spigots and buckets, but have an intricate system of plastic tubing running from tree to tree, with the taps running directly into it, and the entire yield running straight into the condensers. Gone is the sound of the drip-drip-drip in the spring, and no longer is there a need to stand with wet feet for hours on end. Usually the producers run family businesses, many of them on farms that were once cleared by Hebridean settlers, and now bear French names, or simply a notice saying *Syrop d'érable*. Even farms which have retained arable land, cattle and crops of vegetables and grain, can find that their main income comes from shipping canned syrup to Montreal and New York where it can earn an instant profit.[62] There is nothing instant, however, in the months of cutting wood, the long hours in the sugar-house fuelling the stove and attending the condenser, or in the sterilizing of cans or bottles, or in the filling, sealing and labelling. It is still hard work, regarded today as a major part of the Quebec economy.

Taste and Tradition

In the 1940s, aided by a grant from the American Committee on Food Habits, Professor Kurt Lewin examined several questions surrounding *why* people ate what they ate. Apart from concluding that food habits are not based on a biological need for nourishment, his report highlighted the cultural and psychological aspects involved in the complex patterns that exist. He referred to those who prepare the food as 'gatekeepers' who control these patterns, and who, at any moment, could prevent certain foods from reaching their destination. From all accounts, it is the women of the Eastern Townships who have been the 'gatekeepers' of food traditions, and, as such, have also been careful custodians of part of their Hebridean culture and identity. [63]

Over twenty years ago, when many folklorists were primarily concerned with the study of stories, songs, and objects of material culture, American folklife specialist, Don Yoder, drew attention to the strong connections between *food* and its central role in maintaining culture. [64] Among the Eastern Township Gaels, the preparation and presentation of food retains a vital role in reflecting Scottishness. In any social situation, even if the participants were to remain silent — a most unlikely occurrence — the food served would speak of cultural retention. In the closing years of the twentieth century, when the mother tongue of the first settlers is fading towards extinction, the strongest indicators of culture are now reflected the foodways of the Eastern Township Hebrideans.

Notes

1. I often heard this phrase repeated by guests at Ruth's table in Milan.

2. Hugh Cheape, Food in Change, pp. 111–121; James Shaw Grant, *Stornoway Gazette*, Nov. 1993.

3. F. M. McNeill gives a 'cottage recipe', *The Scots Kitchen*, p. 212; I.F. Grant refers to instances where rennet was added, and heat was not, therefore, necessary for crowdie. Op cit, p. 218.

4. I.F. Grant states it was 'universally carried on' in the Highlands; see also, drawing of a cheese press, *Op cit,* pp. 216–17; F.M. McNeill gives recipes, *Op cit, p. 212–14.*

5. Göran Rosande discusses visits 'home', suggesting that after many years they reawaken latent local or regional identity. See 'The 'Nationalisation' of Dalecarlia' in *Tradition and Cultural Identity*, p. 96.

6. J.I. Little gives useful details of the history of merchants in this area in *Crofters and Habitants*, pp. 166–171.

7. This was common in most rural communities. For a comparative account of the Gaels in the Codroy Valley, Newfoundland, telling how 'the shopkeeper used to mark it down...' see *The Last Stronghold*, p. 85.

8. In August 1993 Duncan McLeod sold the property which consisted of a large country store, the top floor of which was the McLeod home. While I lived in Milan in 1976, Duncan was reducing the stock to wind down the business, with the aim of retiring. An active, energetic, and enterprising individual, he then began trading in antiques, which not only kept him in business with fewer demands on his time, but also allowed him to combine his interest in 'old things' with his expertise in commerce. As part of the process, outdoor auctions were

held to dispose of the stock. I recall seeing a bi-lingual auctioneer standing on a platform outside the store, and crowds from all over the Eastern Townships in attendance. Not surprisingly, Duncan McLeod is known the length and breadth of the entire area.

9.   Photographs of the store and the last of the contents are now in the Photographic Archive of the School of Scottish Studies.

10.   Duncan may now deposit them in the Special Collections of Bishop's University Library, Lennoxville, as they are relevant to the economic history and sociology of the Township of Marston.

11.   I have chosen to ignore all names attached to records as there is no point in exposing family debts from another era.

12.   Martin Martin, *Description of the Western Isles*, p. 91. See also, Donald MacDonald's more up-to-date reference to a fondness for tobacco, *The Tolsta Townships*, p. 26.

13.   Maryann jokingly refers to the widely advertised pancake mix, 'Aunt Jemima's Pancakes', which has taken over from home-baking, especially in modern, urban homes. In 1992, it had not, however, gained any credibility in the Marsboro home of Maryann's son, Angus, as his wife still baked all their supplies from traditional recipes.

14.   There were many similarities with settlers elsewhere in Canada; see, for example, *The Last Stronghold,* pp. 84–85

15.   I.F. Grant refers to the 'monotonous diet' of fish and potatoes, including herring, as being characteristic of the nineteenth century. op cit, pp. 299–300. Most islanders would extend that statement well into the twentieth century, though far from regarding it as monotonous, they now lament the fact that herring is difficult to get, and 'good salt herring' even more scarce. During my own childhood and adolescence on Skye there was always a barrel of salt herring in my grandparents' house, and it was still regarded as a staple in the 1950s and early 60s. Despite the drastic decline in the Scottish herring fishery, in the 1990s my mother and uncles still eat herring or mackerel once or twice a week.

16.   I.F. Grant emphasises the importance of tea in the Highlands, 'a universal drink' by the nineteenth century, and 'in spite of the dire poverty of some of the crofters…they managed to buy and drink it.' Op cit, p. 305–6 (erroneously cited in the index as p. 205).

17.   Similarly in Scotland, roadmen and other manual labourers talk of using syrup or treacle tins for tea-making, and Marie Salton tells me that in her youth (the 30s) hill-walkers and campers used Lyle's Golden Syrup tins with a wire handle fixed to the rim for tea-pails. It is not simply the need for something to drink that is central to these practices, otherwise water would suffice; there is a significance in having *tea*.

18.   Typical of their generation, my grandmothers were of the opinion that tea is at its best served in china cups.

19. Vicki Peterson, *The Natural Food Catalogue*, pp. 72–73. For an informative, general discussion of legumes, see pp. 66–84. Tinned beans in tomato sauce, so common all over Britain, are *not* part of the regular menu — most have never tasted them, and express an aversion to trying, seeing no point, when the 'real beans' are readily available.

20. For an brief, comparative discussion on methods of cooking beans, see Maria Kundegraber, 'Plants and Herbs as a Food of the People: An Example from West Steiermark, Austria' in *Food in Perspective*, p. 174. Very few Scottish texts appear to discuss the cultivation or preparation of beans. A. Fenton refers briefly to Lord Belhaven's 1699 description of Lowland gardens that included 'a few 'Turkie beans' and ordinary beans and peas to go with pork' but gives no indication what either variety was, nor how they were cooked. See *Scottish Country Life*, p. 72. Reference is also made (p. 179) to beanmeal in Scotland, though I did not encounter it in Quebec.

21. This was very similar to the pattern established between the Highlands and Islands of Scotland and the cities of Edinburgh, Glasgow, London, etc. when a large number of young women spent several years 'in service' as domestics in 'big houses' before returning to their native area. Some inevitably remained in the city, only to return home on holiday.

22. Recorded from Donald Morrison, Scotstown, who sang fourteen verses, and told me the song, also called 'Oscar Dhu's exortation to the Gaels', was published in *By Trench and Trail* (pp. 114–115). In America Boston is known as 'bean-town'. Traditional stories credit the Indians with introducing the Pilgrim Fathers to beans during their first winters in the New World and acknowledge that without the kindness of the native peoples who gave them dried beans, many would not have survived.

23. Göran Rosander discusses the question of 'territorial identity', op cit, p. 96, and suggests that in all probability it is possible to have two or even more regional identities.'

24. See also Bill Lawson, op cit, which gives the list names of children in all the emigrant families, confirming that large families were the norm.

25. Angus is referring here to what Canadians call 'baking powder biscuits' which, in Scotland, are called 'plain scones'. The other scones he mentions are, as will be described later, much flatter than those they call 'biscuits'.

26. Maryann's description of the use of yeast indicates that local merchants kept supplies. The Gaelic settlers in the Codroy Valley, Newfoundland, however, used a leavening mixture of hops and boiled potatoes, as they had no yeast for baking (or brewing) until well after the First World War. *The Last Stronghold*, p. 87; the recipe is very similar to the method quoted by C.P. Traill, *Backwoods*, p. 256 (new edition).

27. The tendency today is to assume that English was the common language in every aspect of commerce; this was not the case, as a large proportion of the Lewis, Harris and Uist immigrants were monoglot Gaelic speakers. Throughout

his book, *Crofters and Habitants*, J.I. Little seems unable to deal objectively with the question of language, as he makes frequent references to Gaelic as foreign while French is assumed to be acceptably native. It is unfortunate that a book which is presented to the reading public as a seminal work on this part of Quebec displays such language bias. Having chosen to present his text in English, Little includes quotations in French *without* English translation, yet he uses *only* English translations from Gaelic originals, creating an impression for the reader that Gaelic is foreign while English and French are not. Most unfortunate of all is the fact that he projects a personal prejudice against the Gael, which is not only patronising to the subject and irritating to the reader, but reflects very poorly on the writer.

28.   Op cit, p. 306. See also F. M. McNeill, 'Bannocks, Scones, and Tea-Bread, *Op cit,* pp. 169–185.

29.   Peggy O'Hara discusses the experiences of Canada's 'war brides' in *From Romance to Reality*. She notes that most women had to make enormous and wide-ranging adjusstments, from the smallest domestic details to major social changes that were suddenly expected of them in the new land.

30.   In a discussion about cooking and baking, Marie Salton remarked to me that the English girl is a 'good, plain cook', whereas the Scots girl is 'born with a rolling pin under her oxter [armpit]', that is, a baker by instinct. [Dec. 1993.]

31.   The leading flour companies produced their own recipe books, and in some areas sponsored radio programmes, which gave a range of recipes while encouraging home-bakers to use their recommended product. For example, *Cream of the West* and *Robin Hood* flours both produced 'tested and tried' recipes that remained popular for decades.

32.   Gerald Thomas and J.D.A. Widdowson, introduction to *Studies in Newfoundland Folklore: Community and Process,* p.xxii.

33.   Zofia Szromba-Rysowa, 'The Social Aspect of the Popular Diet in Poland with Special Consideration of Eating Customs and Nutritional Prescriptions and Proscriptions' in *Food in Perspective*, p. 267.

34.   Lennoxville which adjoins the town of Sherbrooke is regarded as the main centre for English-speakers of the Eastern Townships. Since my first visit in 1976, much has changed; very little is visibly 'English' since the enforcement of Quebec's language policy. The village of Milan is approximately fifty miles away.

35.   In the winter of 1992–3, Ruth's son who lives with his French family in Montreal began to make 'improvements' to his mother's kitchen, modernising it to the sort of standard expected where he lives. He removed the sink and pine surrounds and replaced it with a stainless steel one, sunk into a counter-top.

36.   A series of photographs of both women is deposited in the School of Scottish Studies Archive.

37. Ruth keeps a small file box of 3 x 4 inch cards, and writes down new recipes in the standard way. Although she knows many of them off by heart, she still brings out her box when making cookies, brownies, or puddings, as a checklist to make quite sure she has them correct. On the cards she also notes modifications, such as 'use less sugar'. For a broader discussion on the subject, see Edith Hörandner, 'The Recipe Book as a Cultural and Socio-Historical Document' in *Food in Perspective*, pp. 119–144. Ruth's recipe box, by way of contrast, may give very little evidence of her ethnic origins as she mainly records non-traditional recipes. It does, however, confirm the importance of food preparation in her household, as many of them have evidence from the baking-board on them, testifying to their frequent use.

38. I have asked several people about oatmeal, and to make certain they knew what I was describing, brought some medium cut and fine oatmeal from Scotland. Only the very oldest people were familiar with it; Christie and John MacKenzie had seen it, as had Christie MacArthur, all born towards the end of the nineteenth century. They were also familiar with *aran coorce* made from the Scotch oatmeal, but had not seen it in Quebec for many years. To everyone else, 'oatmeal' meant rolled oats. In the Codroy Valley, however, the winter's supply list included a 'hundred-pound sack of coarse Scotch oatmeal.' See *The Last Stronghold,* p 85.

39. See also Z. Szromba-Rysowa, *Op cit.*

40. Just as in Scotland, so it is in Quebec: dinner is not dinner without potatoes, as far as 'Scotch' are concerned, but this is the *one* exception

41. The issue of *context* in folkloristics has been widely; see A. Dundes, 'Texture, Text, and Context', *Southern Folklore Quarterly*, 28 (1964), pp. 251–265.

42. At Ruth's these meals have always been very jovial, with teasing at the table, challenges as to who could eat the most and anecdotes told about individuals who could eat twenty or thirty, then a triumphant moment when Ruth finally manages to sit down and join the company. Fieldwork notes, Aug. 1992.

43. Healthfood stores in Canada, America and Britain nearly all carry buckwheat. Contrary to some of the earlier notions circulated via British herbalists, it is not only a good source of protein, but is high in iron and contains most of the B complex vitamins. See V. Peterson, *The Natural Food Catalogue*, p 30.

44. V. Peterson explains the difficulties involved in removing the hulls which form the little black specks, an operation which tends to add expense to the production of flour. See *The Natural Food Catalogue*, p 31. See also 'Pit' Legendre's comment in Chapter 4 which indicates the family's mastery of the skill.

45. Edith Hörandner discusses salting, pickling and curing meat in 'Storing and Preserving Meat in Europe: Historical Survey' in *Food in Change*, pp. 53–58.

46. Salt mutton was standard fare during my own childhood and adolescence. (See M. Bennett in *For What Time I Am in the World,* edited by Bill Usher and Linda Page-Harpa, p. 133.) Bearing in mind that refrigeration did not become

commonplace till the 1970s, more than twenty years after the coming of electricity, it is understandable that the older methods prevailed in the Hebrides.

47. *Maragan* is the plural of *marag*.

48. This is more or less the same as 'potted heid' which is common all over Scotland. For a more detailed discussion, with recipes for bottling and preserving, see *The Last Stronghold,* p. 86–89.

50. Bruce Walker discusses the common method used to collect blood for the making of puddings or *maragan*. See 'The Flesher's Trade' in *Food in Change,* pp.127–137. See also my brief description in *For What Time I Am in the World,*, p. 131. For a Canadian comparison of practices among the French and Gaels, see *The Last Stronghold,* p. 86–87.

49. The Jubilee Guild in Canada gave out jam recipes to encourage good practice so that by the 1940s most traditional recipes had been substituted by standard ones. See also *The Last Stronghold,* p. 94.

50. Photograph in the School of Scottish Studies Archive.

51. The word 'sack' is used loosely for any cloth bag, small or large, such as a flour sack, and not, as is generally the case in Scotland, a standard sized jute or hessian bag used for coal, potatoes or peat. (In Canada, this is a burlap bag.)

52. In a study of vegetable gardens in two Quebec communities between 1935 and 1965, Michèle Paradis records the introduction of tomatoes in the late 1940s and suggest that their long-term influence on eating habits was considerable. 'Du jardin à votre assiette…le jardin potager en milieu rural', *Canadian Folklore canadien,* Vol. 12, No. 1, 1990, p. 95. His comment would also hold true among the Scotch population; consider, for example, the addition of tomatoes or tomato paste to the recipe for baked beans (quoted above).

53. I.F. Grant, *Highland Folk Ways,* pp. 296–299 and p. 300. Thirty years later, visitors still complain about the lack of variety in the fruit and vegetables they can obtain in Hebridean shops, though the situation has improved since I.F. Grant's observation. The complaints are as much a reflection of the visitors' inability to acculturate as they are of the Islanders' resistance to change. Similarly, in rural Quebec until approximately 1955, most vegetable gardens had potatoes, carrots, turnips and cabbage. Michèle Paradis, op cit, p. 87.

54. Preserving turnip greens by this method is common in other parts of Canada. For example, in Newfoundland I recorded descriptions from settlers in the Codroy Valley; see *The Last Stronghold,* pp. 93 — 93.

55. For an interesting discussion on this subject in the wider context of Quebec, see Michèle Paradis, 'Du jardin à votre assiette…le jardin potager en milieu rural', *op cit*, pp. 83–98.

56. Darrel D. Henning discusses techniques of making maple syrup in 'Maple Sugaring: History of a Folk Technology', *Keystone Folklore Quarterly,* XI:4, pp. 239–274.

57. Maple sugar is very popular all over Quebec; see Marius Barbeau, 'Maple Sugar', *Canadian Geographical Journal*, 38, Apr. 1949, pp. 176–189.

58. C.P. Traill writes of her experience in 1836 of collecting sap and making maple sugar; see *Backwoods* pp.155-8.

59. For example, Paul and Julia Doerfler who own and work an 'old Scotch' farm on the Tenth Range keep cattle, goats, and poultry, and produce a wide variety of grain crops, fruit and vegetables. Nevertheless, their main source of income is maple syrup, when, two or three times a year, Paul loads a truck with home-canned syrup and drives to New York to sell it.

60. Kurt Lewin, *Field Theory in Social Science*, pp. 170–187.

61. Don Yoder, 'Folk Cookery' in *Folklore and Folklife: An Introduction*, edited by Richard Dorson, p. 325. Despite the fact that Richard Dorson's book, *The Handbook of American Folklore*, was published much later (1986), unfortunately he does not heed Yoder's advice, as he only includes *food and festivals*, with no study of food as part of daily life.

8

Mostly Women's Work

Soap-making

Whenever a domestic or wild animal was butchered, there was always more fat than could be used for cooking.[1] Most of it was from the suet, with some from layers of fat, depending on the condition of the animal. While there were a few families that kept a small amount aside to make ointment for medical use, most people used the remainder for making soap.[2] In between times, housewives would save the fat drippings from day-to-day cooking in a jar or crock, so that when soap-making time came around it could be added to the basic supply.

To prepare for soap-making, all the suet and fat was slowly rendered down in a very large pot on the stove. When it had melted, all the pieces of tissue and other impurities were skimmed off, or caught in a sieve. Sometimes, if it was more convenient, this was done days or even weeks before hand, and the fat left to harden in a block. Not only was it ready for use, but the rendering also prevented it from becoming rancid as quickly as fresh suet.

The soap itself was generally made out of doors over an open fire in a very large cast iron pot, such as the one given to the first emigrants for maple syrup.[3] While many of the older people mentioned soap-making in passing, the most detailed account was recorded in 1976 from the late Isobel Stewart of Dell, then in her sixties. Though a commercially available product, Gillet's Lye, became available after Isobel was married, during her childhood and adolescence, she had often helped her mother and grandmother 'start from scratch' with their home-produced lye.

The local knowledge dated back to the early days of land-clearing, when the settlers used to burn the wood and sell or exchange the ashes to be used for commercially produced potash. They also learned how to use wood ash as part of the domestic soap-making process, so that long after the commercial venture folded, they used the ashes from their kitchen stoves for the extraction of lye, as Isobel described:

> I can remember my mother, and my grandmother — everybody — they used to put all the wood ashes in a barrel, and they'd have it up on a little table, like, made outside, and they'd make a hole in it, and have a bucket underneath. And every little while, you know, [water would be poured on it] — if it rained, that

was even better; rain water's beautiful! Put that in, and soak down the ashes. And the lye would come out of the ashes, just in this pail, and you used whatever amount you wanted, and made your soap. [4]

This process, known industrially, though not locally, as 'lixiviation', leaches the ashes to make a lye solution which is then evaporated to make crystals for the potash market.[5] For domestic use, however, this reducing stage is not necessary, as it is just as effective to use the liquid collected after percolating water through the ashes. With the two basic ingredients ready, the soap-maker would begin by lighting a good fire on which to place the pot of fat, then when it had completely melted, the liquid lye was added and the mixture stirred thoroughly to produce the soap.[6] While in this liquid stage, it was poured into moulds that had already been prepared. Isobel said that they frequently used small cardboard boxes for moulds, and would line the bottom and sides with paper, just like preparing a cake-pan, so that the soap could easily be removed when set.

No two people turned out identical soaps, and indeed no two batches made by the one person would be the same either. Weight, colour, and smell varied according to the kind of fat, the amount of lye, and the presence of additives. The natural colour of the soap usually varied from light to dark beige. If ammonia was added, it would produce a much lighter colour, and would also increase the dirt-removing properties of the soap. Isobel recalled one amusing incident when she added so much ammonia that she produced a pure white soap, just to tease a neighbour who had never heard of this method but always wished to have white soap. Some people used to add perfume or cologne when they wanted to make a fragrant toilet soap. A very light soap could also be made by whipping the mixture with a whisk before pouring, so that air was trapped in it. This was simply a matter of choice, however, as there seemed to be no particular advantage in doing so. The strongest soaps, such as those used for housecleaning and heavy laundry, were the ones with the most lye added. After the use of commercial lye became more common, the user had to be careful not to add it indiscriminately, as it could produce a soap which was very harsh on the skin.

And it would really take the dirt out; and of course we had the old scrub board, [and on laundry day we used the bar of soap like that]. Oh yeah! We didn't know what soap powder was in our day; maybe some people had it, but we didn't, but oh, it did a beautiful job. [It was a lot stronger than the soaps you buy] Oh, yes. Sometimes your hands would be really sore and cracked afterwards, but of course that depended on how much lye they put in it, I guess, but it took the dirt out, I can tell you. Yeah, and we used to have our Saturday night baths in it too, I've seen us — but I remember my mother used to get Baby's Own soap, and oh, that was really something. And that was kept in a little corner by itself so it wouldn't be used. But just washing our hands at the sink or something we had to use this.

Wool Working

Kay Young (née MacLeod), who was born after the First World War, and brought up on their family farm in Milan, was one of the few women of her generation whose mother, 'even in her day, did the complete job from the sheep to the bed.[7] When the subject of wool comes up, most of the women still talk from personal experience, although theirs is now confined to knitting and crocheting.[8] Nevertheless, Kay's generation is still familiar with the wool-working traditions that were part of the everyday life of their forebears.

As already mentioned, many farmers kept between one and two dozen sheep, more than enough to provide the wool needed for one family.[9] Since there was generally no need to process the entire number of fleeces, any surplus could be sold to a neighbour, bartered for goods at the local store, or exchanged for other wool products such as machine-carded wool.

Shearing in the early summer was 'men's work', and was followed soon afterwards by washing, generally 'women's work'.[10] Since all the washing was done outdoors, a suitable place to build a wood-fire was chosen by the older women of the household, then, helped by the teenage girls, they would begin the day's work by lighting a fire to heat up the water in big pots. Families who lived near a river would take their wool there, as it was much easier to light a fire by the river that than to carry all the water needed to fill the wooden tubs. The fleeces were washed in warm water lathered up by homemade soap, and, employing the same method used in the Scotland for generations, the young girls gently tramped the raw wool. Maryann recalled the carefree atmosphere of her younger days, when her mother was in charge of the procedure:

> She'd wash the wool in tubs, and I for one would go into the tub and wash the wool. And talk about nice clean feet when we'd come out of the tub! That was the best way to wash the wool — and that was our shower![11]

Afterwards they would either rinse the wool in the river, or, if it flowed too quickly, in tubs of fresh water. Then, having squeezed out as much water as possible, they would take the fleeces home and spread them out to dry, in the traditional manner that long pre-dates current garment labels dictating 'Wool: Dry flat'. Young girls learned simply by watching their elders that woollen fibres can easily be over-stretched and damaged by hanging, and that flat stone surfaces are preferrable to grass, which may itself be damp, or may stain the wool.[12] As the years went by, the young men of Angus Morrison's generation began to help with the wool washing, and though his father might have adhered strictly to the traditional division of labour, all his sons willingly helped when asked.[13]

Although washing the wool removed dirt, grime and much of the excess oil from the fleeces, it did not get rid of the little twigs and burrs that tend to stick to sheep. This task usually required more time and patience than the women could afford so it was done at home with the help of the children, as Isobel Stewart recalled:

> Then, in the evenings, we kids had to help. After the wool was washed, it was full of little bits of hay and twigs, and all. I remember evenings we used to have to sit and pick this wool…Kids all had to do that. I had six sisters.

Dyeing

Although some of the wool was used in its natural shade, generally for blankets, and some was turned into grey, (either by carding the black and white fleece together or by twisting it after it had been spun), there was always a quantity to be dyed in order to meet the requirements of weavers and knitters.[14] Christie MacArthur grew up in a household where everyone was familiar with the range of work surrounding wool:

> My father always kept twenty [sheep], shear in the spring, and then if there was a black sheep [you'd] keep the wool from the black sheep and p'rhaps two of the white ones. Then take it to the mill and it was made into rolls. Well, now, if the black sheep was quite black it was all right [??]. Black, and mix it in with the white which also made grey, and other times they'd dye the wool…Yes, yes, they used to make it out of goldenrod, the flower in the wild…but as far as I can remember they bought [a lot of the dyes].

The newly washed wool was usually dyed before carding and spinning, although it could also be done at a later stage. The techniques and skills involved were undoubtedly part of the traditional knowledge of the first immigrants, who adapted them to suit the availability of materials in the New World. Of the many Hebridean recipes that use plants for dyeing, only a few appear to have been retained in the Eastern Township.[15] The first generation women favoured the use of the most common Hebridean dye of all, crotal, which is the name given to the russet-brown colour produced by the lichen, stone parmelia, *Parmelia saxatilis*. Their method for dyeing raw wool was fairly straightforward, and very similar to one known throughout the Highlands and Islands of Scotland and among Gaels in Nova Scotia and Newfoundland: a layer of wool, a layer of lichen, alternating till the pot is almost full. Water is then added to cover the wool (which then reduces in bulk so that it no longer reaches the top), and then it is slowly simmered on the open fire.[16] When the wool has taken on the desired shade, it is removed from the pot, rinsed in clean water with salt in it, and, as before, squeezed gently and dried flat.[17] Maryann Morrison, who had gathered lichen with her mother from the rocks in Harris, was pleased to be able to do the same in Quebec:

Och, yes, all the crotal we wanted.. Well, they had a big pot, you know, to dye
in…and my mother used to be outside with her fire on under it and…poke the
clothes [blankets] down there, and the yarn that she wanted to dye. Oh, she
made all the dye she wanted…[18]

Although crotal may have been the favourite in Maryann's day, as far as
wild plants and flowers are concerned, goldenrod is best remembered by most
Quebec women, Scotch and French, as their most popular for the dye-pot.[19]
In her comprehensive study of the use of Scottish plants in dyeing, Su
Grierson records that 'wild goldenrod', *Solidago vigaurea*, was used for dyeing
in the Highlands, and although she notes that it grows in Lewis, finds no
reference to its use.[20] In either case, the use of the plant, or absence of use, is
more reassuring than surprising, as it points to the practical approach adopted
by the women no matter which community they inhabited.[21] In Lewis, the
plant is comparatively scarce, and there is a profusion of others to choose from,
whereas in the Eastern Townships goldenrod grows in such abundance that,
no matter where one lived, it could be easily obtained from roadsides, pastures,
and waste ground.[22] As a young woman in the 1930s, Isobel Stewart had seen
it used for dyeing in her family:

My grandmother used to [dye the wool], but I don't remember just how much
of anything she used. She used to use the goldenrod.[23] That was a very
prominent colour, it was a kind of a, och, a *mì-chàilear* [unpleasant] kind of a
colour! [laughs] Kind of a golden colour. And they used other herbs and things
I don't remember what they were, but goldenrod I remember.

Since colour is a matter of taste, it is quite likely that the youthful Isobel's
preferences did not agree with her grandmother's. Goldenrod remained
popular as a dye, and, depending on the method used, it produced a range of
shades, from pale lemon to a brownish-yellow.

As with all dyeing, the work was done out of doors on a fine day in summer,
and the same large pot was again used on the open fire. It was more than
half-filled with water, as large a quantity of goldenrod plants that could fit
were pressed into the pot, which was then brought to the boil and simmered
to extract the dye. The plants were then skimmed out of the liquid, or it could
be strained, though this was not usually practical. Next, a quantity of alum
(according to Scottish home-dyers and spinners of today, about four ounces
to every pound of wool[24]) was stirred into the dye to act as a mordant or
'fixer' so that the colour would not fade.[25] All additives were obtained from
the general store, and according to local merchant Duncan McLeod, alum
was the most common, which was also the case in Scotland.[26] The addition
of mordants was especially important because of the unstable nature of most
of the dye pigments.[27] Finally, the wool, already wet to obtain the best results,
was added to the solution. The fire was kept stoked to keep the contents of

the pot simmering, but never boiling, as too much heat spoils the texture of wool. From time to time it was stirred and the wool pressed right down into the solution with a stick to make sure all fibres were dyed evenly. As with other dye recipes, the length of time taken depends on the depth of shade required: the longer it remains, the darker the shade becomes. At last, it was taken out, squeezed to remove excess moisture, and dried in the air and sunshine (again, preferably on stones or dry wood, and not directly on the grass). The pot on the fire was then ready to accommodate the next batch, which would be paler in colour than the previous one. Even if a new dye-pot was prepared using exactly the same recipe, as every woman knew, the resulting colour would never be identical to the previous one, no matter how closely she followed the method.[28]

In *Crofters and Habitants* J.I. Little lists commodities available at Leonard's Store in Stornoway and includes venetian red, cochineal, madder and copperas among the commercial dyes. From this list he comes to the conclusion that 'Scots clothing would not be entirely drab, despite their church's fulminations against the vanity of colours.' Unfortunately Little has no appreciation of the fact that centuries of Gaelic poetry and song records the Gael's fondness for bright colours.[29] Observing Highland women in the early nineteenth century, Mrs Grant of Rothiemurchus recorded that the women were 'all in home-spun, home-dyed linsey-woolsey gowns...The girls who could afford it had a Sabbath day's gown of like manufacture and very bright colour...generally ornamented with a string of beads, often amber...they all wore the plaid, and they folded it round them very gracefully.' Her description leaves no doubt as to the Highlander's fondness of colour.[30]

McLeod's Stores in Milan kept popular brands such as Sunset Dyes or Diamond Dyes for strong colours that not be easily produced with natural ingredients. Indigos were the most popular for men's suiting and women's skirts while scarlets had a range of uses that included coverlets and petticoats.[31] While the directions on the packets were usually followed fairly closely, the procedure was basically the same as for natural dyes. As far as the women were concerned, they had at their disposal the means for producing wool in any colour of the spectrum, and, aside from preparing wool for spinning and weaving, their skill with the dye-pot was also used creatively in home-crafts. For example, in 'Aunt Annie's' house, the patchwork quilt on the day-bed had a predominance of vibrant scarlet pieces cut from various fabrics which had been dyed especially for the quilt, and I have also seen home-made rugs with splashes of bright colours that turned out to be old longjohns and other underwear dyed purple or red. Even if the homemaker had used the standard navy-blue dye for many of the original items of clothing, she could use these dark shades creatively by placing beside them a range of colours dyed specially for the purpose.

Carding

Whether the raw wool was dyed or natural, carding was the next stage of the process.[32] The first settlers spent many a long winter's evening at this task, and while they enjoyed the comfort of the wood-stove, the scene was familiar enough to those who had known the same routine beside the peat fire. The men might be occupied at an indoor task such as mending boots, or sharpening tools, while women and girls worked at their wool. And no matter what the activity, they could all take an active or passive part in the stories, anecdotes, riddles, weatherlore, medical knowledge, songs, or whatever aspect of oral tradition happened to arise. As discussed in Chapter 6, it was very much in the pattern of the *taigh-céilidh* especially if a neighbour or two happened to come by for the evening.[33]

Before the carding began, the fleece was teased out manually by pulling the closely clinging fibres apart. It was then combed out, a small piece at a time, between the metal teeth of a pair of hand cards, so that the fine fibres were separated, all running in the same direction and ready for spinning.[34] These pieces of soft, carded wool, rolls or *rolags,* as they were called, [the Anglicized plural of *rolagan*] were then laid aside in a basket till there was enough to begin spinning. Carding requires repetitive, hard work, and although it may appear to be as simple as using a hair-brush, it takes considerably more skill to get into the rhythm and to assess how much resistance of the fine metal teeth is needed on the various parts of the fleece as each one consists of many different grades — for example, wool from the belly is much softer and an entirely different quality to that from the flank.[35] Maryann Morrison recalled that 'Many's the time I was very tired carding wool.'

There were times, however, when this work took on a completely new aspect and the tediousness and monotony seemed to disappear when a number of women organized 'carding bees'. Isobel Stewart looked back to when she was a girl in Dell and the times when the whole kitchen floor seemed to be covered with wool to be carded. With the help of willing neighbours, however, the work was much more enjoyable:

> We used to go when they'd have bees, like, at different places. And I remember being at Murdo A.'s, that's one of the places I really remember best — Murdo A. MacDonald's. They were neighbours of Danny's. And oh gosh, it seems to me there was tons of wool! We were little kids, but they had it in the kitchen, on the kitchen floor, like. All the women were round like this, and they had the — I've got a pair of them — cards. And we were down in the middle of the floor, having a ball, pulling this apart, and they were all sitting here, gabbing away. Mrs. Murdo A., she was Scotch, but she went to the States when she was young, and she didn't talk Gaelic. But the rest were all gabbing, something else! And someone else would break into English every little while because she didn't

speak it. We were having a ball, we were enjoying it all! And of course they'd
have lunch, and she was a beautiful cook, Mrs. MacDonald was. And she'd have
all kinds of goodies. And we used to like to tag [i.e. follow] our mother round
[to different carding bees].

The opportunity to socialize was a welcome break from household routine,
and no doubt the special treats were an added attraction. As already mentioned,
'bees' (such as barn-raisings) were a common feature of pioneer life, and food
was an important part of these events. The pattern was well-known to many
European immigrants before they ever emigrated, and, as Zofia Szromba-
Rysowa points out in her article, 'The Social Aspect of the Popular Diet in
Poland...', this type of 'neighbour's work' was a common feature of early rural
communities in Europe. Referring to house-building, mowing, threshing,
spinning, and stripping feathers, she observes that:

> this work...was always connected with hospitality, and usually with the
> consumption of alcohol. This was the only pay for the work, which was dependent
> on neighbourly help...People who were invited to do communal work were
> received as guests. The value of the food, which was significantly better than
> everyday fare, often exceeded the value of the help.[36]

While the women at the spinning, carding or quilting bees drank tea or
coffee, with absolutely no question of alcohol being served, they prided
themselves in serving their best home-baking, which always included a variety
of kinds of scones made freshly that morning. As a child, this was no doubt
the highlight of Isobel Stewart's day out with her mother: 'But I can remember
that, and oh my, that wool was so beautiful and white.'

While most of the wool carded in former times was destined to be spun,
occasionally some of the women would card it as a quilt-batting.[37] Ruth, who
was about fifteen years younger than Isobel, remembered helping her
grandmother who had bought a neighbour's wool for this purpose:

> Oh I've done a little bit of it, of the carding...Now what it the world do you
> call that? [Already carded, fluffed up — *rolags?*] No — you just...take it up of
> this lump of, pile of, ehm — [Ruth suddenly remembers the word] — a *peard!*
> A *peard* is when you take the cards and card the wool. They would be 8 or 10
> inches by 3 and a half or 4 inches wide. Oh I've done a little bit of it, of the
> carding...[In my day] nobody spun it, because we [carded] usually with Mrs
> MacArthur's wool, to make quilts — the batts. [By yourself or with another
> group of women?] Oh no! I never did that by myself; there'd be two or three
> get together because it's a long tedious job, and you have to work against the
> little needles that are on them.[38]

Such a practice was a matter of economics, however, as Isobel recalled:

> I've seen them [card for batting], but we never made any ourselves. Well we
> didn't have the wool — everybody didn't have sheep, and the ones that did,
> they'd either sold it or keep it for *stocainnean* or *miotagan* [socks and mitts] and

all that stuff. We considered it a waste [to use wool for batting] but there was a few that did, that had enough of it or that could afford to make it. Oh, they were beautiful and soft.

As the years went by, almost everyone who had wool to card began sending it to one of the carding mills. La Patrie was convenient for those who lived in Scotstown, while the people of Milan, Dell, Marsboro, and surrounding areas took theirs to the Legendres at Stornoway. The carding mill was even more convenient for families who did not keep sheep, as Ruth's remembers 'Oh as far back as I remember we never had sheep, so they must have bought the wool. We'd go to the the mill, to the carding mill, you know and we'd buy, the long strands — *peards* — in strings, like, you know, about that size — [about an inch in diameter].' And, as Christie MacKenzie concluded, 'It was fun to spin it after being at the carding mill, because it was always so nicely done. 'Twas much less work.'

Spinning

The spinning wheel was already well established in Lewis and Harris long before most of the emigrants left home, as it was introduced into Lewis by Lady Seaforth in the 1830s.[39] Although the hand spindle was in use until much later, according to the Crofters Commission, most women had adopted the spinnning wheel by 1884.[40] Maryann Morrison remembered it was among the few household items brought over from Harris in 1888, and remarked that this was the case with many of the first settlers. Thus, the treadle spinning wheel became a common feature of Quebec homes, and to this day is valued, though it is no longer in use by the descendants.[41] Many of them have remained within families but been moved out of the area as the population dispersed — for example, one woman said that her daughter had taken their wheel to Montreal, while another added that her grandmother's wheel had 'gone to the States with one of the girls.' Occasionally a spinning wheel is brought back into use when it is bought at an auction by a keen craftsperson, as there is still a strong interest in spinning and weaving in the surrounding areas.[42]

The treadle-style spinning wheel was not, however, the only kind in use by the Gaels, for, according to various descriptions, they also used the 'walking wheel' (in Lowland Scotland known as the 'muckle wheel' and in the Codroy Valley, Newfoundland, as the 'French wheel').[43] This type has no treadle, and is used standing up, with the spinner stepping back a pace or two every time the fibre is drawn out, then going forward again to let it run back on the spindle. Since there is no record of anyone bringing a this kind of wheel from Scotland it is most likely that the settlers who arrived in the 1830s may have been introduced to them in Quebec. Though Isobel Stewart, whose family had had both kinds, attributed this to intermarriage between a Gaelic and a French-Canadian family, there was no intermarriage in the MacDonald family in Milan where the walking wheel was frequently in use. Ruth continues:

> Oh well, my grandmother used to spin...Ishbel MacDonald [was her name] — she came from Lewis — I guess likely up around Uig that she came...she was about nine years old when she came —
>
> And she had a large wheel, you know, the great big wheel, and she used to do a lot of spinning when I was quite young. [Walking back and forth?] Well, you pull the yarn away, way back, 'cause it's the spindle is up that high, you know — you can't get that on tape! [laughs, as she demonstrates with a hand] [About four feet off the ground.] And she'd stretch it, and then it would go back as it spun around, and you do it —...Oh yes, standing up![44]

Ruth agreed that 'You'd be on your feet a lot to do it,' and her close friend and aunt-by-marriage, Ivy MacDonald remembers Ruth's grandmother working late into the evening:

> She had a big family of boys, and she used to have the wool sent to a mill and make these, what do you call them, strings, you know — and she never had time to spin that wool while they were awake, you see, and so when all the children went to bed she'd spin.

When asked Ruth if her grandmother had ever given her or her sisters a chance to spin, her immediate response was similar to that of other women of whom I have asked the same question: 'Oh no! That was a no-no for us, for the kids. Oh no, we weren't supposed to touch that. But she had it out in the shop, what we called the shop.' So important was it to keep the spinning wheel in good working order, that many of the girls who wanted to learn felt they were not encouraged to do so. Although the reason was seldom, if ever, given, is was probably the fact that any slight adjustment in the tension of the spinning wheel can cost the spinner a great deal of time trying to regain the most suitable setting for her wheel.

Christie MacArthur (born 1888), had similar memories to Ruth's, although though both her mother and mother-in-law used the treadle wheel:

> Oh, I suppose I tried it a lot of times, and my mother always told us — she didn't allow us to use it, we'd always upset it...It was after I got married that I was spinning...my mother-in-law did hand spinning...and after she died I had to, I did it for myself. [We used] a small spinning wheel...[you sat down to do it] Oh yes.[45]

Women of Ruth's and Ivy's generation considered the older women such as Christie MacArthur and Maryann Morrison to have been among the last of the traditional hand-spinners. Considering that Christie was thirty and Maryann in her early forties at the end of the First World War, they were, as far as today's women are concerned, of another era. For them, such work was all part of the household routine, time-consuming and demanding, though generally made lighter either by singing, or by working communally, or both. Isobel Stewart recalled that her grandmother 'used to hum tunes when she'd be [spinning] — all the time they used to sing hymns, she'd be humming hymns when she'd be spinning.' And although Maryann admitted that it could be very tiring, she also recalled that it could be very enjoyable, especially when one of the women organized a spinning bee.

These were usually planned when someone wanted to weave a length of tweed, or blankets, which required 'too much wool for one person to spin.' On the appointed day, neighbouring women would bring their spinning wheels to the house, usually travelling by horse and cart, and, in the company of friends, would spend the day spinning. Rather than being looked upon it as a day's work — which it was — it was regarded as one of the rare opportunities of socializing enjoyed by the women. And once again the preparation and sharing of food played an important part in the day's enjoyment.[46]

Looking back over her long life and all the changes she had seen, Maryann found it difficult to understand why crafts she had enjoyed had disappeared. Certainly, times and technology had changed, but Maryann knew that the coming of electricity did not affect spinning in any way. 'They got lazy; they wouldn't spin, and they wouldn't card,' she concluded, forgetting for a moment that the women of the following generation — Mary (Angus's wife), Ruth, Muriel and Ivy — were anything but lazy. Nevertheless, there were other significant factors which brought about changes in the lifestyle of the second and third generation of Scotch settlers.

From 1915 onwards the Eastern Townships played a very significant role in Canada's woollen industry, as the Canadian Co-operative Wool Growers Association, a nationwide organisation, was first established in Lennoxville. It began with the founding of the Sherbrooke County Sheep Breeders and Wool Growers Association and continued to be a centre for woollen products until 1993 when wool prices dropped to their lowest level for fifty years, and the Co-operative closed its outlet wool shop.[47] With the centralization of wool production and the standardization of quality, it appears that small producers, such as the Hebridean settlers and their families, gradually began to rely on factory products and on mechanised spinning. From all accounts, it was in the 1920s and into the 30s that hand-spinning went out of favour.[48] By the 1940s, the hand-spinner was the exception rather than the rule, and, just as in the Highlands and Islands of Scotland, several decades were to pass before the craft was revived, generally by 'outsiders' attracted by idealized images of the traditional way of life.[49]

Twisting and Winding

The spun wool could be destined for several uses, depending on the needs of the household. If intended for weaving, the bobbins could go directly to the loom as they came off the spinning wheel; for knitting or crocheting, however, two or three strands had to be plied together to prevent the wool from losing its original twist. There were two methods for doing this, depending on how busy the women were at the time. If one woman was working alone, she would generally use the quickest method and twist the newly spun wool on her spinning wheel, with two or three spools making up what then became know as two-ply or three-ply wool. Or, if two women were working together, such as Christie MacArthur and her mother, one would carry on spinning while the other would use the hand-spindle for plying together strands of the spun wool. The two-ply wool was generally used for mittens, socks, while the three-ply was made into winter sweaters:

> The spindle — I did it myself…After my mother was spinning…she'd be busy spinning and I'd be twisting it for her…we used the spindle…There'd be two businesses going on together…you know, I have one at the house, some place…It's just a stick, and you wound it around this end…at the big end. And you could have it around the loom…on here. And then you twist it…And you'd wind that on, and start all over again…We had a pan or something to put it in; if not, just let them run, and see that the cat wouldn't get after them! I never used it till after I started spinning…And my mother died…and afterwards we used to twist it on the spinning wheel.[50]

Though it is many years since they have been used, several homes still have hand-spindles, either displayed as a relic from the past, or, like the one Christie spoke of, 'it's somewhere yet.' In the summer of 1992, Ruth Nicolson brought out one that had been her grandmother's, a tapered piece of wood, approximately 3 cms at the base 'formed as to make the use of a whorl unnecessary' as Arthur Mitchell wrote of the ones he saw on a visit to Lewis in 1875.[51] Ruth, who had never used it herself, called it a *'dealgan'*. 'I used to hear them talking; I think it was my step-mother's brother, probably. I don't know where I heard it…I don't believe [I ever saw anyone using it]'.[52]

If the wool had been twisted on the spinning wheel, then ply on the spools had to be wound into hanks using a *crois-iarna*. Maryann pointed out that there was no need to bring this simple winding device from the Old Country because a *crois-iarna* could easily be made: just take a stick about eighteen inches long and attach two shorter sticks to each end, at right angles to the longer one, but not parallel to each other; viewed end on, the two shorter sticks form a cross. To wind the wool into hanks, the long stick was held in the middle, and with a deft movement of the wrist and forearm the wool was wound round and across the end sticks to make a hank. The person winding could count the turns if they wished to have hanks of standard measurement, usually to the nearest ounce.

Until well into the 1960s store-bought wool came in only in hanks, which cannot be used without re-winding. And so for years after hand-spinning had gone out of fashion or favour, youngsters were asked to hold a hank of wool to be wound into balls for knitting.[53] Nowadays, however, the knitter has a choice of buying wool already in balls, or, less commonly, in old-fashioned hanks.

Knitting

Partly because it became part of the school curriculum, and partly because people still valued home-knitted garments, knitting was one of the crafts that most girls learned at an early age and still practise today. When homespun wool was common, most women made mittens and socks for the entire family, many knitted sweaters and the older generation even knitted winter underwear. Grey wool, spun from a mixture of black and white carded together, was most commonly used for socks, with two-ply for everyday wear, and three-ply for winter boots. The common feature of modern sports socks with a stripe or two of a different colour was long established by traditional knitters who usually added matching stripes of bright red or blue round the ankle or at the toe so that the washday task of mating large numbers of laundered socks would be slightly easier.[54] Because knitting is a task which can be done intermittently, work in progress was always kept handy in the kitchen for spare moments between other chores.

Although I watched my grandmother in Skye hand-knit long underwear in the early 1960s (using four needles and off-white or pinkish 'wheeling', two-ply-wool, which she got at the Portree mill in exchange for fleece), according to Isobel Stewart (forty years my senior), very few of the Scotch women knitted winter longjohns by the time she was growing up:

> The French women used to; oh, yes, they made underwear. My gosh, we had a neighbour, she had a knitting machine and…she'd knit the stocking legs, you know, and then she'd knit the foot [by hand]…Oh, heavens knows [where she got the machine] — I guess her mother had it. They had it on a table. Of course they had those things, that you could make it small or bigger, you know…She'd knit big round tubes, you know, for underwear…She was French, but some of the Scotch, I guess, had them too. But not so much the machines, they used to [hand]knit them, underwears, a lot of them — That's all they had, they didn't have any of the fancy stuff they have today.[55]

The changing customs in knitting closely parallel the situation in Scotland: until the 1950s, necessity came before pleasure and practicality before fashion;

the dye-pot dictated the colours; and availability of wool, time, and traditional skill determined if a garment was to be made in the first place. In the sixties, seventies and into the eighties, most girls and women had 'something on the needles', and even among professional women, it was common for part of the office or staff-room lunch hour to be spent knitting. Gradually the 'perpetual socks' were no more and fashion garments held the attention of enthusiasts. Now, in the 1990s, staff-room knitting is a thing of the past — 'paper-work has taken over every spare moment' — while home-knitters, though fewer in number, continue to show creativity in their use of colour and patterns, both store-bought and invented.

Weaving

Compareed to knitting, considerably fewer people learned the craft of weaving, and although the equipment required is much more elaborate and expensive than a pair of knitting needles, even the families that did have looms ceased to use them by the end of the First World War. Although the majority of Quebec Hebridean homes have blankets that were woven by Gaels in Quebec, when I began fieldwork in 1976, Maryann Morrison was the only person I met who had learned to weave at home. Of course she had seen plenty of it in Harris before her family emigrated, and remembered the loom that had come over on the 'Siberia' in 1888.[56] Although she said that the same loom also produced a good many yards of cloth in Marsboro, her son, Angus can just barely remember it being used.

Kay Young's mother, born before the turn of the century, was probably among the last of her generation to weave, as others of the same generation (such as Christie MacArthur and Christie MacKenzie) grew up as the craft was dying out:

> She used to make all her own [blankets]. She used to make all her own wool — for the blankets it was the natural colour except for contrasting threads. They dyed that in blues and reds. They were done in squares [rectangles, usually two strips], the most of the ones here.

There was a great variety of blankets woven, and though most were the natural wool colour, with a coloured stripe or two at the ends for decoration, some were woven with dark shades such as natural blacks, greys, crotal browns, or mixtures of bright reds and blues. The coloured ones were of the heaviest homespun yarn and were usually known in both languages by the Gaelic word *cuibhrig* [a coverlet].[57] In 'Aunt Annie's' house, the bedding was as it had been for decades, with some of the blankets woven in Quebec, and some from Lewis. Her daughter, Muriel, recalled the bedding that had been in use as far back as she could remember:

She brought a *cuibhrig* [from Lewis, in 1910, that] my grandmother had woven, or my grandfather, I guess, for he was a weaver…Some of those blankets were from the house in the Middle District that they had; probably some that my grandmother had — my Canadian grandmother. That grandmother was three months old when they came over — Annie MacDonald, her people were from Bernera…Oh yes, they spoke Gaelic. Strange, you know, there are so many questions I would like to ask today —

Close inspection of some of the blankets reveals a whitish cotton warp, scarcely noticeable against the natural shade of the homespun weft. Apart from the blankets Maryann's family brought from Harris, which, she said, were woven in 'the double yard', the rest of the blankets were made in two strips and joined up the middle with a neat herringbone stitch. This type of seam is also characteristic of the Scottish blankets woven in Cape Breton and Newfoundland, though some women used a simple overstitch, which is equally serviceable though not so flat to the touch.[58]

While I cherish the luxury of sleeping under these blankets at Muriel's and Ruth's, I discovered that the continuation of a tradition has more to do with general preference than one person's appreciation of fine craftsmanship. Remarking to Ivy MacDonald on the 'beautiful hand-woven blankets' on my bed at Ruth's — 'I just love them' — I detected a hint of reservation in the tone of Ivy's reply:

> Yes, they are, they're awfully heavy, but they're beautiful, aren't they?…I had a couple that I bought from an old lady and they'd never been used, but to put them on the bed they were too heavy even without anything else on the bed, you know. They were lovely, white…They'd keep you warm, but they're too heavy — I can't stand anything heavy [laughs].

Similarly, when writing of the Highlands and Islands, I.F. Grant also comments on the weight of the hand-woven bedding and suggests that is one of the reasons why they lost popularity. Though she makes no mention of the current preference, or fashion, for the easy-to-make, lightweight down, feather or synthetic 'downies' which were emerging at the time, Dr Grant could well be writing on Ivy's behalf: 'The old blankets, although warm, were very heavy and they, and the bed-covers, are now little esteemed.'[59] Even master-craftsman Norman Kennedy who dyed, handspun, and then wove a special pair of blankets for a niece's wedding in Aberdeen, was dismayed to find that, in spite of his efforts, the exquisite gift was never used.

The general demise of traditional weaving has not, by any means, been confined to the Eastern Townships, though naturally that was the only area that Maryann Morrison had in mind when she regretted the loss of interest in the craft: 'Well, there was nobody wanted to do it.' In spite of the passing of so many years, Maryann could still remember her mother weaving *clò-mór* in Harris. Not only did she weave for their own family in Marsboro, but managed to meet a local demand, and help supplement the family income besides:

> Oh, the house was big enough. She was weaving for very little [money]. She would…make articles — the double yard, that she was making for twenty-five cents for a double yard — the big, big yard. I used to work the loom myself, oh yes. And spin, and card, and do all that work, yeah. Oh, it's a long time ago! You know, nobody has been talking to me like you, that would keep my mind so clear. They never ask anything here about what we had in the old country. They don't care if we had anything or not!…[Eventually] she sold the loom.

As anyone who knew Maryann would confirm, her mind remained quite clear till her death in her hundred and eighth year. At the age of a hundred and one, she went on to explain how they used to weave cloth in two thicknesses, according to their needs. There was the all-wool *clò-mór*, the heaviest tweed, which was used for winter coats, jackets, pants, and heavy blankets; and there was the lightweight material, sometimes with a cotton warp and a single-strand woollen weft, which was used for skirts, dresses, men's and boys' warm shirts, and even petticoats. Christie MacKenzie, whose aunt used to weave, said she called this lightweight material 'flannel':

> She used to weave flannels that made underskirts, and different things like that…I think her husband made the loom, Uncle Murdo. I think he made it; he was very handy as a carpenter.

In the days when the stores did not carry a wide range of materials or ready-made clothing, housewives had to plan carefully to meet the needs of their families .[60] Ivy MacDonald recalled Ruth's grandmother speaking of the days when she had to make just about everything they wore:

> She had a loom — now I never saw this, but she said that when she was married first that she used to make cloth and then make little pants [trousers] and things for the boys. I bet you [said with laughter and a hint of sarcasm in the voice] they were snappy-looking, you know, but they were pants anyway!

In these modern times when the choice of ready-made garments extends far beyond actual needs, it would be easy to imagine the past as an time of widespread deprivation. From the point of view of the Hebridean settlers in Quebec, however, it was a time of plenty in comparison to what their people had left behind. Granted, they worked extremely hard, but they could look back over their years in Quebec, to the first winter when the snow drifted in through the walls, and be absolutely certain that never again would they know such cold, hunger, or deprivation; nor would they have to use every single blanket in the house unless they had a houseful of visitors during Communion season or holidays.

Fulling

After the *clò-mór* was woven, it still had to be 'finished' at the *luadh*, known in English as 'fulling' or, when referring to Gaelic Scotland, as 'waulking', and known in Cape Breton and Newfoundland as 'milling'.[61] The function of the *luadh* was to make the cloth thicker, warmer and more wind-proof, by repeatedly pounding it on boards; technically, the action re-orders the arrangement of the minuscule particles, which become interlinked like little hooks, and make the cloth thicker than the stiffer fabric that comes off the loom. The end of a long process, the *luadh* was happily anticipated not only by the weaver, but also by the rest of the family and neighbours who would be taking part. In Gaelic Scotland it has always been associated exclusively with women, but it is clear from descriptions from Nova Scotia and Newfoundland that very soon after their arrival in the New World, immigrants began to share the work between men and women.[62] As far as I can ascertain, one of the earliest accounts from Quebec is from Megantic County's Arran settlers in the 1830s. Not only were men taking part but the operation described what is usually known as the *luadh chas*, the 'foot-waulking', which died out in Scotland before the hand-waulking.

Writing in the 1880s, Dugald McKenzie McKillop described previous decades of communal work activities, all known as 'bees', in Megantic County. Logging, quilting, spinning fulling, each 'bee' had its own characteristics, though none, apart from the *luadh,* left the same impression of amazment on him that he records here:

> Perhaps the oddest kind of bee was a fulling bee. There was a great deal of kicking done in this matter. I have myself watched with wonder the antics of the young men carrying out this process of thickening the web. Perhaps some survivor might write an essay for the local papers on 'A Hard Way to Make Thin Cloth thick'.[63]

By the mid-1970s, only a few of the oldest Quebeckers had ever heard of the *luadh,* which for some reason had died out even before the weaving did. Although Isobel Stewart had seen as much wool-working as anyone of her generation, she had never heard of it. Bill Young, who grew up in Scotstown, could remember hearing his grandmother sing waulking songs, although the work in which the songs had their origin had become extinct. The significance of her songs interested Bill, and after he was married, he discovered more about their context from his wife's grandmother whose people settled in Milan, where Kay herself grew up, just 'two doors down from Aunt Annie's...French people have it now.':

> Now it seems to me that I've heard her explaining that they all sat around and they put their feet on the [cloth]...And eh, I know my Grandmother MacDonald sang a waulking song and a spinning song — I used to hear her sing them.

Not surprisingly, Maryann Morrison was the only one who had ever participated in a *luadh*, and while she had memories of both Harris and Quebec, she remembered best the *luadh* of her childhood. She immediately recited a ditty she had heard around the boards:

Oh, na luaidh! Tha cuimhne mhath agam ..Bha òran ann a bh' againn —
'S na Hearadh fhuair mi m'àrach;
Chan eil nàir' orm ga ràdh,
Cha dheanadh an clò àlainn seo
[...?] còta-bàn Shasainn.
Girls used to sing…Oh, it would be lovely to listen to them, girls
singing…Wasn't it good? But it went out…

[Oh, the waulking! I remember well…There were songs we had —
In Harris I was reared;
I'm not ashamed to say so.
This beautiful tweed would not make
[...?] an English petticoat.]

When asked if she had any more songs, Maryann replied, 'No, she sold the loom...,' suggesting that, for her generation, the two activities of singing and working were inseparable. Then, casting her mind back over ninety years, Maryann gave a description based largely on those she had seen in Harris.

To prepare for the *luadh*, the woman who owned the cloth invited neighbouring women and teenage girls to her house on an appointed evening, usually in late autumn or winter. A 'table' for the *luadh*, was set up in the house using either three or four planks of wood, about ten feet long, or an old door, across trestles, then chairs or home-made benches were placed along both sides, and a chair at each end. The roll of cloth, which could be as long as twelve yards, though often it was approximately four times the length of a blanket (enough to make one pair when pieced together) was placed on the boards. It was then opened out and the two ends either tied together by knotting the yarn from the surplus warp , or tacked together with a darning needle, thus forming a large loop. Maryann continued '[You] saved all the pee you could...' and when the women arrived they took their places and the work began. 'Just dip [the newly-woven cloth in the urine, squeeze it out to remove excess], and put it on the boards. But it was a dirty work for girls, wasn't it?'

The cloth had to be 'good and wet' so that with the constant beating on the boards it would shrink and become thicker. Traditionally, urine was favoured for wetting because it had the added advantages of removing excess oil from the wool and of setting any dye that had been used. It is interesting that the Cape Breton and Newfoundland Gaels adopted the practise of dipping their cloth into warm, soapy water, a procedure that eventually took over in the Hebrides, whereas in Quebec the settlers retained the old custom. The lifespan of the *luadh* in Quebec was considerably shorter than that in the two other areas where there are still people in their fifties with first-hand accounts of milling.[64]

Maryann remembered that in Marsboro they used to have the *luadh* in what they called the 'summer kitchen'. Apart from this, her description is mainly what she remembered from Harris:

> It was in a little place back of the house, but it was attached to the house. You could come in on that door and walk up like you do here...to another place... Apron? Oh, no, I don't think so. I don't remember an apron at all...But they were nice big girls, healthy looking too. Oh, there would be...six or seven on each side...And they were singing to beat the band, there.

As much as two hours later, after many songs, the cloth reached the desired texture and width, traditionally measured with the joints of the middle finger. It was then rolled up on a board (about three feet wide) to the singing of a slightly quicker song, and set aside till the first dry, sunny day, when it was washed, stretched out, and dried in the fresh breeze.[65]

Although everyone at the boards had to work energetically, yet it did not feel like hard work in the light-hearted company of the other women. The memory of their singing remained with Maryann for the rest of her life, and, reflecting on the very earliest ones she had experienced, she seemed to imagine the entire scene in her old age: 'I never saw anything [so] beautiful like we have in Harris.'

Their home in Quebec was bigger and better equipped for the women to get washed and changed into other clothes if they so wished. They were then ready to relax when the men joined the company for a meal and the evening's entertainment — usually stories, songs, music, and maybe a dance on the cleared floor, depending on how strict the family: 'We used to have dances, you know, in houses, *some* people — but my father would never allow a dance in the house, and he wouldn't allow me to go to a dance.' Since it could not be regarded as an organized dance, if the occasion to dance arose, then it was all the more enjoyable for the young people who were forbidden to go to the village dances.[66] The evening's activites were characteristic of the *taigh-céilidh*, which, fortunately for younger generations, had a much longer life-span than home-weaving.

Although the traditions of the *luadh* lasted much longer in Nova Scotia and Newfoundland than they did in Quebec, only in the Eastern Townships is it reported that men did not join in, that only urine was used to wet the cloth, and that only Gaelic was sung.[67] The French settlers could also weave, and in the days that Maryann spoke of, it was quite common for neighbours, Gaelic or French, to share skills such as weaving or tailoring to do a required task. Muriel Mayhew, whose mother emigrated to Quebec in 1910, was of the opinion that weaving was more common among the Hebrideans in those days, though the situation became reversed shortly afterwards when 'the French people did more weaving than the Scottish people. The first generations may have done it, and I imagine they did, but not by the time my mother came to Canada.'

Similarly, in Newfoundland, while the Gaels brought their weaving skills with them, it was the French that took over and became the more expert weavers.[68] Today, the only weavers in the Eastern Townships are French, but judging by the number of 'revival' craft set-ups and summer courses in spinning and weaving, few, if any, of them have learned through family tradition.

Maryann's earlier comment that 'they got lazy; they wouldn't spin, and they wouldn't card' might raise a few objections, for the women in the succeeding generation were, and are, anything but lazy, if we judge by today's examples — her own daughter-in-law, Mary, or Ruth, Muriel, Kay or Ivy. The decline must, rather, be attributed to a complexity of reasons, domestic, local, regional, and national.

As years passed, and houses were built with better and more efficient heating, people no longer needed to have such heavy blankets. At the same time, lighter-weight materials were becoming available, as factories produced cheaper synthetics with fashion appeal and twentieth-century lure. There was also the fact that, after mills were established (around the First World War), women had the choice between doing all the stages of the work themselves or of taking advantage of time-saving machines. There was also the stark reality that war changes community life and though Maryann's family in Cruvag did not seem to be affected by the First World War, there were few in the Eastern Townships that could say the same of the Second.

Between the wars, the younger generation of women were leaving home, some to be college-educated, an entirely new idea, hitherto reserved for young men training for the ministry or medicine. Times *were* changing: with young women earning a living, there was more money and less time for the older crafts. For example, Ruth and Muriel and several of the other 'girls' trained as teachers, while Ivy trained as a nurse, and though they returned 'home' to work, and later to marry, by 1939 they were again faced with the fact that Canada 'was involved in a war.' In exactly the same way as entire villages in Lewis or Harris still look back on those years, two generations of their kinsmen in Quebec were also actively or passively involved.[69] The young men either volunteered or were drafted into the Canadian regiments and and sent overseas. For six years the division of labour was redefined; women did men's work as well as their own, while the men for whom they had once woven *clò-mór* were clad in uniform. Not surprisingly, by the end of the war, changes had taken place that were to remain part of a new lifestyle. Those who had served in the forces were eligible to apply for new land and housing grants in Lennoxville; thus several young families moved out of the rural homesteads and into the suburbs of the town, where they were closer still to modern amenities and completely out of range of rural activities such as carding or spinning bees, even if they had continued. Of all the wool crafts, only knitting and crocheting survived, and continued to be practised for economic and practical reasons, though less so as each decade went by. Nowadays women knit and crochet for pleasure and recreation, or simply 'to pass the time'.

Home Crafts

Sewing

Family photograph albums record several decades of clothing styles, many of which represent the skill of the local tailor or home-sewer. For example, a professional portrait of Maryann's family, taken by 'one of those photographers who used to go around', shows the group who left Harris and settled in Marsboro, wearing their Sunday. Some of the clothes may even have been made in Harris, as Maryann remembered there was a tailor in Geocrab who made men's trousers, while the women did the sewing for the rest of the family. In Quebec, however, the women had to make all the clothes as store-bought goods were not readily available during the early years. Winter coats, jackets, trousers, and skirts were made from the *clò-mór* while shirts, dresses, and petticoats were made from flannel, the lightweight material. There was no need for paper patterns, as the women were well practised in cutting their material, and if there was any doubt they could always rip the seams of an old garment, and use the pieces as a pattern.

With all the sewing that needed to be done, a hand-turned or treadle sewing machine was part of the furnishings of nearly every home, a feature still retained by the older houses today. Like all the women of her generation, Maryann spent many hours at the machine making clothes for her thirteen children, her husband, and herself:

> I've had two sewing machines in my life. The first one was Ben Hur. And —
> oh, the boys started to use — to fix horse-blankets on it and that was too big
> and rough. And then that machine went out of use, and I got another one. Oh,
> well, it's [advertised] on the television all the time, Singer sewing machine, that's
> it! I did all the children's [clothes, you] couldn't get any school [clothes] when
> my children were small. You had to make everything. And going to school, I
> was making overall-pants for them and a jumper [usually known as pinafore-
> dress, in Scotland] like a coat, and blouses — print like that, you know. Print for
> blouses, and a [draw]-string in the middle, and tie it in here [at the waist]. That's

what we had — no style [by today's standards]..They looked very good in it to me.

One of the more recent photos the Morrisons' collection shows a family group photo taken during communion season, when Maryann and R.E.'s children were ages ranging from toddlers to teenagers. Angus remarked that the family would have spent Thursday to Monday going to church, four days dressed in their Sunday best instead of one. During his childhood and adolescence, he recalled that their parents kept them all very well dressed, especially on Sunday, the only day of the week they wore shoes:

Bha sinn a' coimhead glé mhath le deise bhrèagha 's brògan, ach bhiodh sinn a' dol dhan sgoil air ar casan rùisgte — cha robh brògan againn…Dìreach ach Là na Sàbaid!

]We were looking very good with beautiful suits and shoes, but we would be going to school on our bare feet — we didn't have shoes {on us then}…Only on Sundays!]

Families that did not have their own hand-woven fabrics could either buy from the merchant or exchange wool for them. For example, Christie MacArthur spun only enough wool for knitting, and kept the rest of their raw wool to exchange for cloth when a peddler came around. Similarly, Christie MacKenzie explained what her mother used to do:

If she had a surplus of wool, she'd sell it to the peddlers that came around, you know, and get — in repay she'd get cloth material. And she used to get some flannel from them for the men's shirts. And then she'd get some cotton for our dresses and things like that…They used to come from Coaticook. There was a fellow by the name of Armitage, and there was three generations of them, Armitages at a woollen mill there, used to come around with a couple of horses and a sort of van — oh, he'd have lots and lots of material. Some people that had small families, you know, would sell all their wool to him and get material…Oh, he'd sell too, but it was mostly for wool, because he took it in and it was made into these flannels.

Former school-teacher, Myrtle Murray (b. 1898), who came to Milan from Birchton when Ruth, Muriel, Kay and Duncan were all at school, could look back to her first memories of moving into this area of 'Gaelickers', as she called them. Because of the fact that she grew up in the predominantly English and Irish area of the Eastern Townships, she saw everything with fresh eyes. At the age of ninety-four she could remember the very oldest women wearing bonnets 'of white cotton…the old ladies wore a — I can just remember certain women could launder these *curracs*, say. And they came down [under the chin] and had a frill like this, and these frills had to be ironed. They'd stand out, they had an iron that made it.'[70] As far as their clothing was concerned, 'well, a good deal of it was in wool, but no, they weren't backward.'

Myrtle remembered the women wore fairly long woollen skirts, with flannel petticoats, 'they wore them for warmth…whatever they needed for heat.' The men wore woollen trousers, usually home-made, and 'in the winter they were heavy.' For lighter garments 'they went into Sherbrooke and got print, and made it,' just as Maryann had done with the cotton she bought in Megantic. Myrtle felt that not only was the clothing practical but there was also an interest in the fashions of the day, as can still be seen in many of the older photographs.

Naturally, the Quebec winters required more protective clothing, and though it was unheard of for women to wear trousers in the Hebrides till the 1950s, I wondered if the harsh conditions might have influenced styles in clothing. Myrtle's first-hand account recorded the reaction in the village to a woman breaking with tradition:[71]

> MB: Did you ever, in those days, see any *women* wearing pants [trousers], like you do now?
>
> Myrtle: Oh, no! I remember our old neighbour, he was *shocked* when I wore knickers [knickerbockers].
>
> MB: To your knees?
>
> Myrtle: You know, knicker-pants.
>
> MB: When did you get them?
>
> Myrtle: Oh, I got them the first or second year I was teaching.
>
> MB: To keep warm?
>
> Myrtle: Well, no, It was just because it became the fashion…they were just comfortable.

While others may not have been quite as keen to keep up with fashions as Myrtle was, eventually the styles did change. One of the biggest influences on this was the fact that young women left home to go into service in the States, usually the Boston area. Occasionally a special gift would be sent 'home', such as the one shown in a studio portrait of six-year-old Muriel MacDonald (now Mayhew) in 1920, wearing her best woollen dress in MacDonald tartan with tartan taffeta sash, sent to her by her father's sister, Aunt Mary Belle, in Boston — 'I can still remember that dress' which was to be Muriel's first of many tartan garments.

The girls 'in service' would send surplus clothing home to members of their families.or they would bring back new fashions when home on holiday. Then, women skilled at sewing would copy the styles and produce clothing that kept them abreast of the fashions of their day. For special occasions, such as weddings, fabrics could be bought from stores in Megantic and Sherbrooke, as Christie MacKenzie recalled. Shortly after she and John and had celebrated their seventy-first wedding anniverary, Christie insisted that I should see her wedding dress, made for her by her sister. Her daughter, Jean, showed it to me, while remarking that 'no doubt she'd have told you she wants to be buried in it.' The following fieldwork note accompanies my photo:

> Christie's wedding dress is ivory silk and quite beautiful. Her sister, Kate (2 years older), made it; she was a seamstress 'she did it for a living'. The fabric is very fine, so also the stitching, especially the hand-sewing which is *incredibly* delicate. On the bodice is a design in tiny marcasite beads, interspersed with pearls, some of which have a marcasite knotted on top of pearl, like a tiny crown. (The marcasites are so tiny that when Jean tried to sew one on after the dress was at the cleaners, she could hardly find a needle fine enough — no wonder!) Along the neck, sleeve (armhole), and down the side seams are little pearls which also serve as buttons along one shoulder and down one side. The buttonhole loops are minuscule and the dual function of the pearls is almost invisible. The style is mid-calf, and has a neat sash with silk fringing. A remarkable example of exquisite needlework.

Christie's dress was, just as she said, the 'last word' in fine tailoring.'

Quilting

The first thing that struck me about the bedrooms in 'Aunt Annie's' house, was that every bed was topped with a homemade patchwork quilt. All of different patterns, they dated from the end of the nineteenth century to the first half of the twentieth, though I was soon to discover that the craft of quilting has carried on into the present day. Over the heavy wool blankets, the quilt, which tended to be much lighter, made sure that the sharp night-time drop in temperature would not chill the family even after the stove had burned down.[72]

Today, almost all homes still keep a wide variety of quilts of various designs and fabrics. The very oldest are not usually the ones that are on display, as they were pieced at random from unmatched fabrics, often of various qualities, as utility items and are less valued than the better planned ones. Furthermore, they tended to wear out after years of use, and, like most worn goods, lose value.[73] Quilt-making was once very common throughout Scotland, though compared to North America there is very little evience of it today, and most Highlanders summarise the demise with an account similar to my mother's — 'in our childhood, the twenties and thirties, all the beds had home-made quilts but as we left home and started bringing home presents of bought bedspreads from Glasgow, Granny threw out the quilts — sometimes as bedding for the dogs — by that time they were so old-fashioned.' By the 1950s there was not one left, and during my teens in Lewis (1960s) I saw no patchwork in the homes of any of my friends, as 'candlewick covers' had completely taken over. And so, living in Aunt Annie's house gave me the pleasure of turning back the clock and enjoying the original context of this, and other, traditional crafts.

The oldest quilts were pieced together from whatever material was available — scraps left over from sewing, or re-cycled material from outgrown or worn clothing. The under-side was always less decorative, as it made use of pieces of sheeting or 'plain cotton'. Then in between was the 'filling' which, as Ruth mentioned, was carded wool or cotton 'batting' which could be bought from the local merchant.[74] They were then completed with 'tags' or 'tacks' to keep the batting in place. Christie MacKenzie recalled that 'it was just odds and ends of your dresses and aprons, and so on. They never had material enough of one kind, like. Just hit or miss. And tacks, you know, the old tacked quilts made — instead of *quilting* them, they were tacked.' Nevertheless, most were artistically done, and very decorative, as many of the women had the knack of combining thriftiness, born out of necessity, with originality and creativity.[75] Closer inspection reveals waistcoat and jacket linings; old suiting; 'saveable' parts of old skirts, jackets, coats, shirts, dresses, blouses and even longjohns that had seen better days — all could be pieced together in a pattern with colours and textures complementing one another. As already mentioned, the underwear was brightly dyed for a more decorative effect that was also more serviceable than the original lighter colour.

Although there were established patterns which had names, such as the log-cabin, the Dresden plate or double wedding-ring, no two quilts were alike. Some women also invented a pattern as they went, while others preferred 'crazy quilts' of random-shaped and -sized pieces, stitched together and afterwards embroidered along all the seams, usually with 'feather stitch' in embroidery silk. Specially prized were crazy quilts of velvets and/or silks, and women who managed to gather enough scraps of these materials were considered most fortunate.

After the patching had been completed, the actual quilting was done on a large wooden frame consisting of two long 'poles', and a pair of frame-ends. The poles, which are set across and pegged into the frame-ends to form a large rectangle, are usually bound with muslin so that fabric can be stitched to them. The width of the rectangular formation can be adjusted as required by means of wooden pegs set into holes on the frame-ends, thus, when the quilters, who work from the outside edges inwards, need to move towards the centre, they pull out a set of pegs, tightly roll the quilt on the pole, and secure it again by pegging it into the frame-ends.[76]

To begin quilting a new quilt, the 'backing' is stretched across the frame, ('right side' facing downwards for fabric that is printed, pieced, or with a 'nap'), then nailed, tacked or stitched to the frame. The backing is then completely covered with batting — either raw wool (common only in the oldest quilts), placed evenly in soft, brushed-out fluffs, or store-bought batting (which came in foot-wide rolls) laid out in strips until the entire area is covered. The pieced 'top' is then laid over the batting, right side up, and stretched until taut in all directions. This is then tacked to the frame — I have seen 'thumb tacks' (drawing pins) used — to keep the material in place. Careful preparation is crucial, as the whole point of quilting is to secure the warm 'fill' so that the finished product has an even texture, with no 'thin spots' that would defeat the purpose of the quilt.

Seldom would a busy housewife quilt an entire coverlet by herself, as it takes countless hours to hand-sew every single seam in a fine running stitch.[77] Once again, bees enabled the work to be completed efficiently in a few afternoons while providing another opportunity for the women to socialise. Although the bees were all held in the home for many years, in the 1960s a group of women in the Scotstown Presbyterian Church began to organise quilting bees in the church hall, mainly to raise money for church work by selling handmade quilts. During my fieldwork in 1976, I was able to join this weekly quilting bee in the hall, a much more practical place to erect a frame, leave it overnight, or even over a week, than one person's kitchen. While the setting had altered from earlier times, the method of quilting remained the same, as did the social aspects of meeting friends, catching up on news, and sharing tea and home-baking together.

By the 1970s, there were a few modifications in the craft as the women could afford to buy new fabric of their choice and to experiment with pattern books from other parts of Canada and America. Thus new designs were added to the repertoire, such as the intricate and challenging pattern the 'Texas Star', and all the quilts were filled with modern polyester batting. When I returned in 1990, the regular quilting bees I had known, and which I had seen as part of the 'Scotch identity', were a thing of the past. The wheel of life had turned another part of its circle with the few women who still quilt setting up the old frames in their homes.[78]

In 1992, I asked Ruth Nicolson, whose home has generations of quilts on the beds, how she experienced this traditional craft. Again, to retain the context and as much of the atmosphere as possible, and not merely to elicit facts about quilting, I will keep the interview intact. The conversation carries on from the point where Ruth spoke (above) of hand-carding in her grandmother's day:

> Ruth: You just take…a *peard*. — they would be eight or ten inches by three and a half or four inches wide…Just fit them side by side, you know, and close enough so they wouldn't separate after they were quilted…You put the backing down on the frames, and then lay the *peards* on top, and then the top, whether it was a plain piece of material, you know, or sometimes you'd put the designs on, or even appliquéd them on.

MB: You've used both [hand-carded] wool and store-bought [cotton or polyester] batting — how does the one compare to the other?

Ruth: Well, I found that one with the [hand-carded] batting was pretty hard quilting.

MB: Do you mean hard to put your needle through?

Ruth: Well, not so much that, but it's so thick that it makes a large stitch — I'd rather just the cotton batting, the 'queen bat'.

MB: The stuff you buy?

Ruth: Yes, that's much easier to quilt.

MB: It was the old-fashioned kind, the hand-carded wool that wasn't easy to quilt, then?

Ruth: Yes. And it wasn't everybody who wanted it, but our houses were never too warm away back then, you know, and they needed the hand-made quilts, were nice and warm and not heavy.

MB: How about washing them?

Ruth: Well, I think that wasn't always so successful, but they did it; but sometimes it would separate and mat, you know, if there wasn't enough quilting. That's the secret of keeping a quilt in good shape, and when you wash it, if you have enough quilting close enough together to keep the bats, whatever, they wouldn't separate and bunch up.

MB: You also went to quilting bees?

Ruth: Oh, yes, quilting around here, oh, many the one! Huh! Many the one I did help with.

MB: How would they arrange that?

Ruth: Well, it was the ladies, maybe it was the 'Carry On Society' or the 'Ladies Aid Society' would announce that they were quilting. Somebody would let everybody know that we were going to quilt. And we would take three or four days to make a quilt...
    At first when there was room [around the quilt] there was four on each side, and even one or two at the end to begin with, [because we'd work inwards from the edges]. But then you'd narrow it down where there would be p'rhaps two on each side, and the ends would be done. And very often to finish it off there was just two, one on each side to finish it.

MB: There's always a problem when you're quilting that there may be one woman in the village whose stitches you wouldn't want on your quilt — what would you do?

Ruth: Well, I don't know. I think maybe some have been corrected, perhaps ripped out if the stitches were too drastically wide, but it was really just the better quilters that would come.

MB: You wouldn't send one out to make the tea, would you?

Ruth: Well, maybe that would be a good way to ease off the large stitches, but we didn't have much trouble with that. Everybody seemed to be pretty good quilters.

MB: I used to go to quilting bees in Scotstown [in 1976].

Ruth: Yes, I suppose; I never went in Scotstown, just two or three times. By then I thought we'd done enough. We got fed up; we'd done enough on the quilts up here [in Milan].

MB: When the women got together like this in the old days do you think that this was an opportunity to talk and socialize that they wouldn't otherwise have had?

Ruth: Oh, yes, sure, they wouldn't meet any other way maybe all week, and — oh, they'd meet in church on Sunday maybe — but I think that was a good [opportunity to get together] — and tell stories too! [laughs]

MB: Did anybody ever sing?[79]

Ruth: No, not really. Nobody was that much of a singer.

MB: It's not something you need to do to music — but you could talk and converse. I guess the men called it gossip?

Ruth: No doubt! Though, eh, I suppose there was gossip sometimes too. But we used to have fun and have our tea-break, which was very nice.

   Somebody'd bring — maybe each one'd bring something, or else someone would announce today that they would bring the lunch [home-baking] tomorrow.

MB: It wasn't usually the woman whose quilt it was who would provide the food, then?

Ruth: Not too often, no, because, eh, whether she would have anyone for dinner that day, I don't know, but — [pause]

MB: You need quite a space to put up a quilt.

Ruth: Yes! I've had it in the dining room here, but it's hard; you're having to walk around, no, *crawl* under the quilt to get to the bathroom, because it takes quite a space for a quilt.

MB: Did you keep your own quilt frame?

Ruth: Well, at last we had a frame that went around [from house to house], but many people had their own frames. I had frames too, they're still here — or they should be! [laughs]

MB: Where did you get it?

Ruth: Oh my grandmother had it — yes, I'm pretty sure it was my grand-mother. They used to tie quilts too, [an entirely different technique] way back — I had one or two of those.

MB: The frame is in four pieces, isn't it?

Ruth: Yes — and each piece had holes bored every, maybe every three inches apart, and we used to sew the lining on that. Then we got more sophisticated and had the thumb-tacks to punch in on [the frame], to tie it on, which was less work.

MB: And then you didn't have to unpick the stitches?

Ruth: No, but you had to pull all these tacks out, though. Except the end — as you turned the end you'd have to take the tacks out as you rolled up the quilt and you finished that row, whatever width. Some [of the women] could reach in, oh, 'way far, and others couldn't. I could never reach very far. But there were some good quilters here!

MB: Yes, Duncan's sister, Jean, was a wonderful quilter.

RN: Yes, his mother too, and Ivy. They were especially good quilters. I wasn't but I used to quilt just the same!

When the quilting was completed and the women at the bee had gone home, the quilt-maker still had to finish off the edges at her leisure. She usually did this by machine-sewing a self-coloured binding all around, then hand-hemming the inside face. Most were square cornered, though occasionally an expert sewer would tackle a mitred corner.

The 'tied' quilts Ruth spoke of took much less time than quilted ones, and were, therefore, regarded more as utility. Instead of stitching along all the seams — 'real quilting' — these are made by stretching the same components over the frame (as above), then selecting points at regular intervals, say every 6, 9, 12, or 15 inches, and securing the quilt with 'ties' made from thick strands of wool or cotton sewn through from the front to the back with a big needle, leaving a few inches of 'loose end' at the beginning. The stitch is repeated over the selected point, then the strand is cut to leave a second loose end facing outwards. The two ends are then tied together and clipped, thus leaving a 'tie' as a feature of the quilt.

The scope of this book cannot extend to tracing the changes in materials and patterns of quilts, or to studying the less obvious features attached to the craft, such as sense of value and attitude.[80] Even in the relatively short time-span I have looked at all of these aspects, however, I sense changes: Now that there is no longer an economic need to piece together left-over or recycled fabrics, as everyone can afford to buy, the circle is coming around full swing. Old dresses or overalls are again being considered, whereas fifteen years ago they had a certain stigma of poverty attached to them. Women can also afford to spend more time dabbling in new patterns than they could in the past, when they had neither the extra cash to buy the books nor the spare time to browse.[81] Although the emphasis is no longer on the practical use of the quilts but on the decorative effects, I notice a change in value when it comes to choosing between old and new. Only fifteen years ago, the 'best quilt' was likely to be one made with new cotton or polyester materials, neatly quilted with polyester batting. The fabrics in it would have been carefully chosen to suit a particular pattern such as the 'Texas Star', either pieced in the exact colours of the pattern book or in fabrics that demonstrated the quilt-maker's own imaginative sense of colour. For example, in one such quilt made by Jean Murray, the star was made from all the gradual shades of the spectrum strikingly arranged with every single piece matching perfectly — a considerable test of skill, as there are well over 300 pieces in one star.

Returning to the Scotch homes in 1990, however, I noticed that the 'best quilt' is now more likely to be one that was made by a grandmother; for example, in 1991, the one on my bed at Muriel's house was a log-cabin design, made by her paternal grandmother, Anne MacDonald who died in 1948. The strips, salvaged from old clothes, were only about half an inch wide, and the seams were hand-quilted through carded wool 'fill' that had stood the test of time and the wash-tub.[82] The colours did not come from a pattern book but are the product of the artistic qualities and care of a traditional craft originally practised out of necessity by women who believed that if a job is worth doing, it is worth doing well. Furthermore, it gave these women one of the few opportunities they had to get away from the ordinary, hum-drum, repetitive daily chores of home and farm. The planning and piecing allowed them to express their creativity, and to use moments of relaxation in a rewarding and satisfying way, while, as already stated, the communal work of quilting created a welcome opportunity to socialise. From time to time, when today's elderly people talk of the function of work-bees, they clearly appreciate that the importance of these social occastions was far beyond what they imagined at the time. And only now, when they reflect on the past, do they realise what a vital a part their communal work played in holding their community together.

Rug Making

If quilting made use of re-cycled materials, then rug-making could use up even scraps that were too worn or unsuitable for quilts. There were two basic types — braided or hooked rugs. The former needed no equipment, and any member of the family could, and did, join the activity, either by helping to cut strips or by joining ones already cut, or by doing the braiding. There was no need to match quality, thickness or colour, as any fabric could be cut up, though it was more practical to do so, both from the point of view of convenience and decoration and design, which was limited to concentric patterns of colour.[83]

Before the braiding began, used clothing was cut into strips — about one inch wide for thick material, and up to two inches for thin fabric. If the rug-maker wanted uniform bands of colour around the rug then strips of the same colour were then sewn together. Next, three strips were braided together, and then, before the braid grew too long to handle, it was either wound into a circle and stitched together, or the end part was bent back on itself and the two edges sewn together to form the centre of an oval rug. As new colours and fabrics were joined on and braided, this sewing was continued, with the braid placed on a flat surface to keep it from warping, then wound around, forming the chosen oval or circular rug. There appears to have been no standard method of joining new colours or of sewing up the rug; some women sewed new pieces together, while others cut a diagonal edge and cleverly twisted the ends together to hide the unsewn join. To sew the braid, some did it with a sharp needle, overstitching the edges at the back of the rug with strong cotton, while others used a bodkin to weave a strong thread back and forth through the loops on the edges of the braid, making an invisible join and a rug which is as neat on the back as it is on the front.

Even within families there were different styles. Muriel's mother 'Aunt Annie' made the little braided bedside rugs out of scraps — practical, utilitarian and decorative — while an aunt who had gone to live in the States emulated the local people she had seen dyeing rags for rugs by buying ready-made balls of self-coloured rags, factory-cut by an enterprising company in America who cashed in on the revival of interest in traditional crafts. The result is an enormous carpet, rather than rug, which covers most of the floor [see Plate]. Muriel, for whom this masterpiece was made, remembered how it came about:

> *Aunt Helen was the one who made the big braided rug upstairs. I can still see her sitting on the floor upstairs sewing the braids around the edge becasue it was too big to hold. She used to buy mill ends at the store, make the braids at home into great big balls and then make the rug. She made most of it at home, then when it got so big she brought it up here in the car and she'd bring the balls to the house — she finished it here.

Mat or rug hooking was probably just as common as braiding in former days, though it was, for a time, replaced by ready-cut wool rug-hooking kits. Usually fairly small, rarely measuring more than 36 inches by 24, colourful, well-worn, hooked mats can still be seen, often used as a door-mat at the entrance of older homes. Aside from the purely practical, favourite hooked mats are generally kept out of the way of the main stream of household traffic to prevent the design from being obliterated.

Both women and men were skilled at this particular craft, which could make use of the tiniest scraps of fabric, even ones rejected for braiding. Despite the thrifty use of fabric, this was not its greatest attraction, as these mats were often works of art.[84] The base required was usually made from an old hessian bag, such as a washed, opened-out potato sack, generally called a 'burlap' bag.[85] The rug-maker would sketch a design or picture on this material, and then stretch it across a small homemade wooden frame. For example, in 1976 Muriel's husband, Herbert Mayhew, gave me one he had made with the picture of a favourite horse on it (now in the National Museum of Civilization). The burlap could be either attached to the frame with small nails or sewn on with strong yarn to keep the material rigid throughout the hooking. The frame was usually placed across the knee, or resting on the edge of the kitchen table while the rug-maker sat about two feet away, or just the right distance to be able to rest the frame on the lap. The work was then ready to begin: small strips of material, of any length and about half an inch wide (or less if a very thick material was used), were held in the left hand underneath the frame, and hooked into the hessian from above, using a small mat hook which resembled a short wooden screw driver or awl handle with a hook in it. Sometimes the hook was homemade from a three or four-inch nail. Little by little, the pattern was hooked, using colours to correspond with the plan of the design.

Patterns on the hooked rugs varied widely. Many had broad coloured borders with a few flowers inside; some were geometrical; others had a theme which was designed for a specific reason — for example, a child might wish to have a bedroom mat with a picture of a favourite animal. It was also possible to buy a commercially pre-stamped hessian backing to be hooked in the same manner as the others. No two alike, the results depended on materials available, and the skill of the maker. When the picture or design was finished, the mat was removed from the frame and finished off by sewing a 'backing' of strong material, and an edging of fabric, or braid.[86]

There was one other method of rug-making, much less common than braiding or hooking, which made use of recycled felt from old or unwanted hats, cut into hundreds of pieces. The idea may have been the innovation of a very creative Scotstown woman, Mrs. Matheson, whose daughter, Margaret, had several examples of her mother's handiwork, including cushions, rugs, a variety of quilts, and a unique, much-admired, velvet embroidered crazy-quilt.

These unique rugs were made by cutting up felt hats into three sets of hexagonal shapes — the first set about two inches across; the second, an inch-

and-a-half; and the third, an inch across.. Then a great deal of sewing had to be completed before the rug could be made — first of all, the one-inch pieces were centred and finely hemstitched onto the inch-and-a-half pieces; then these were centred on the two-inch pieces and hemmed in place. Only after all the sets of hexagons were sewn could they be stitched together to form a pattern like a honeycomb [see Plate 37]. Finally, the rug was backed with a strong material or burlap and bound around the edges. Though there were several examples of this type of rug in the Matheson home, I have not seen it elsewhere. Not only was it extremely time-consuming, (perhaps an elderly woman's pastime), but also very few people had the large amount of felt needed to make such a mat. Because of her local reputation as a fine craftswoman, however, Mrs. Matheson's neighbours and friends would save felt hats for her as they knew she would put them to good use.

Quilts and rugs were made long before anyone had heard of 'recycling'. The word may not even have existed, but the concept was certainly part of the local value system. Regardless of who made use of hand-me-downs or the worn-out clothes, it was pleasing and satisfying to know they were not wasted, for the older generation abhorred waste of any kind. Occasionally the women joke about being 'Scotch', meaning thrifty, although they would quickly correct anyone who confused thriftiness with meanness. The very suggestion would be enough to chill the atmosphere, for their entire approach to home-making is also characterized by hospitality and generosity.

Not much has been said about the role of men in all of these crafts, for they were largely the work of women. From time to time, however, comments from the local men can be overheard, usually in the form of a compliment *about*, rather than *to*, one of the women — wife, mother, grandmother, sister, aunt, daughter — praising her skill and creativity. Sparing as such comments might seem — for the Scotch in Quebec are no more given to gushing compliments than their counterparts in the Old County — a strong sense of appreciation of the women's role within the home is still very evident.

Notes

1. A. Fenton notes that tallow was a 'frequent export item' from the butchering trade but does not say if it was rendered from suet, how or where it was exported, or for what purpose. *Country Life in Scotland,* p. 163.

2. Apart from incoming 'crafts people', I encountered nobody who saw candles made from fat, though there is evidence that the first settlers did so in Annie Isabel Sherman's *History...*, p. 31.

3. C.P. Traill gives a brief account of soap-making by a servant whose method was similar to the one recorded here. See *Backwoods,* Appendix A, pp. 259-259, 1989 edn.

4. According to Marjorie Plant, ferns and bracken were used in preparing 'salts' for soap in Scotland. 'Other possibilities were oak, ash, beech, thorns, juniper, whins, nettles, thistles, 'stinking weed' [ragwort?], hemlock and seaweed.' See *The Domestic Life of Scotland in the Eighteenth Century*, pp. 148. Soap-making became much easier in Quebec since the kitchen stove burned suitable fuel for potash-making.

5. For commercial production see *The Harmsworth Encyclopaedia*, vol. ix, pp. 448-450.

6. Marjorie Plant quotes five pints of lye of the ashes to four pounds of tallow. Op cit, p. 148. Though she writes that 'the entire operation was unpleasant', this was not the opinion of Isobel Stewart or any of the other women who made soap. See also J. Dunbar, *Smegmatalogia; or the Art of Making Potashes and Soap, and Bleaching Linen*.

7. Copies of photos from the Kay's family collection are deposited in the archives of the School of Scottish Studies.

8. From 1990-93, recordings on the subject were made of Ruth Nicolson, Muriel Mayhew, Ivy MacDonald, and Kay Young. The 1976 recordings from Christie MacArthur, Christie MacKenzie, Maryann Morrison, Isobel Stewart, Jessie (MacLeod) Turner (Kay's sister, unrecorded interview), Bill and Kay Young and Muriel Mayhew were included in 'Folkways and Religion of the Quebec Hebrideans' in *Cultural Retention* pp. 72-81.

9. In Scotland sheep are numbered by *scores*, not *dozens*. Though nobody named a specific breed, by the time Belden & Co. pubished their *Illustrated Atlas* of 1888 'breeders of Cotswold sheep' were established in the Eastern Townships, outwith the 'Scotch area'. Johnnie 'Bard' confirms that they kept the stock good 'by the pure-bred ram bought from a breeder in Canterbury.' *Memoires*, p. 151.

10. Since women in the Highlands and Islands often 'kilted up' their skirts to tramp washing, especially woollen blankets, men were not welcome on such occasions.

11. Descriptions of washing clothes, wool or linen in the Highlands are mostly by English visitors, surprised, or even shocked, to see how the women tramped their washing. For example, see Capt. Edward Burt, *Letters from a Gentleman*, Vol. I, p. 47.

12. See also Margaret Fay Shaw, *Folksongs and Folklore of South Uist.*, p. 6.

13. This was very close to the pattern in the Codroy Valley, where in the 1970s the task was done by men or women; see photograph, *The Last Stronghold*, p. 148.

14. Judi Palmer, *Dyeing with Natural Dyes*, pp. 9-10.

15. Margaret Fay Shaw has twelve recipes for plants, and one for commercial substances. Crotal comes first and others state ' same as you would for crotal.' See Op cit, pp. 53-55.

16. Maryann's recipe for crotal is very similar to Margaret Fay Shaw 's *Op cit*, p. 53. See also Hetty Wickens, *Natural Dyes for Spinners and Weavers*, pp. 31-33.

17. Two photos from the Werner Kissling collection (1930s) showing women washing and dyeing a fleece using crotal are published in Su Grierson's *The Colour Cauldron,* p. 122. For an earlier account see also N. Morrison, 'Vegetable Dyeing in Lewis', *Scottish Field,* June, 1929, p. 28. Though russet is the most common shade, some lichens produce reds and purples; see Jean Fraser, *Traditional Scottish Dyes,* pp. 41–46. Neither red nor purple seems to have been made from lichen in Quebec.

18. In Gaelic Scotland, Maryann's word 'clothes' commonly denotes 'bed-clothes'.

19. From recordings of Christie MacArthur and Isobel MacIver in 1976, and from a number of older women in 1992-93; both groups favoured goldenrod.

20. Su Grierson, *Op cit,* p. 114.

21. M. Bennett, 'Plant-lore in Gaelic Scotland' in *Flora of the Outer Hebrides* pp. 56-60.

22. Margaret S. Furry and Bess M. Viemont compiled a list of plants adopted for natural dyeing in North America for the United States Dept. of Agriculture in 1935 (*Home Dyeing with Natural Dyes*).

23. Violetta Thurstan, *The Use of Vegetable Dyes,* pp. 21-22 and Hetty Wickens, *Natural Dyes for Spinners and Weavers,* p. 46.

24. Though the Quebec women did not quote a specific quantity, four ounces is the consensus of the references cited here. (My thanks to hand-spinner Jean Burnard for showing me her wool samples from Highland dyes.)

25. A change of mordant results in a change of shade. V. Thurstan suggests chrome and cream of tartar for goldenrod (*Op cit,* p. 22) but I did not record any mention of chrome.

26. J. I. Little suggests that 70 lbs of alum listed in Leonard's stock was for medical purposes (*Op cit,* p. 167) but according to Ivy MacDonald (1992), though small quantities were used as an astringent a quantity as large as 70 lbs was more likely to be destined for the dye-pot than the medical cabinet. Alum has been used as a mordant in Scotland for several centuries; see Clow & Clow in *The Chemical Revolution.* Their earliest reference is 1702, W. Petty's 'An Apparatus to the History of the Common Practices of Dyeing' in *The History of the Royal Society of London.*

27. Hetty Wickens, *Natural Dyes for Spinners and Weavers,* pp. 34-43; J. Palmer, *Op cit,* pp, 11-14; S. Greirson, *Op cit,* pp. 46-52, and J. Fraser, *Op cit,* pp. 8-16.

28. This is common knowledge in dyeing. Knitters are also cautioned to obtain all their wool for a garment from one dye lot, whether home-made or commercially produced.

29. Little does not give brand names He also lists sulphur among the dyes, though I found no reference to it except as part of a spring tonic (mixed with treacle). *Op cit,* pp. 167-68.

30. *Memoirs of a Highland Lady: The Autobiography of Elizabeth Grant of Rothiemurchus...1797-1830,* 1911 edition, p. 206.

31. There were various recipes using indigo and other natural ingredients, (e.g. stale urine). See Margaret Fay Shaw, *Op cit*, p. 55.

32. Margaret Fay Shaw describes carding in the late 1920s and 30s, *Op cit*, p. 6.

33. See also *The Last Stronghold*, pp. 55–81.

34. Patricia Baines has a step-by-step description with photographs in *Spinning Wheels: Spinners and Spinning*, pp. 193–198.

35. See diagram of wool grades on a fleece, Patricia Baines, *Op cit*, pp. 229–231.

36. A 'lunch' could be served at any time, from mid-morning till late at night, and generally consisted of sandwiches, or rolls with a variety of cold meats, homemade scones, oatcakes, butter, jam, cakes and plenty of tea.

37. There are parallels in Scotland; when neighbours helped with sheep-clipping, carding or planting, they would be offered food and hospitality.

38. See Zofia Szromba-Rysowa, 'The Social Aspect of the Popular Diet in Poland with Special Consideration of Eating Customs and Nutritional Prescriptions and Proscriptions' in *Food in Perspective*, p. 268-269.

39. The 'fill' in a quilt, whether sheep's wool, commercially fluffed cotton, or polyester, is referred to as 'batting'.

40. The word that Ruth remembered using is given by Dwelly as *peurda*, 'first card in carding wool' and *peurdan*, 'the first tufts of wool off the cards in the first carding. Ruth pronounces it with the *'a'* sound, *peard*.

41. D. MacDonald, *Lewis*, p. 63. I. F. M. Dean discusses spinning wheels in Scotland and the teaching of home-spinning (from 1633) in *Scottish Spinning Schools*.

42. *Crofters Commission Report*, 1884, Vol. I, p. 145. In his *Guide to the Highands and Islands...*, P. Anderson reports that Hebridean women used the hand-spindle in 1850, (p. 645). In the 1870s Arthur Mitchell collected examples of two types (now in the National Museum, Edinburgh), one requiring a whorl and one (most common in Lewis) 'formed as to make the use of a whorl unnecessary'. *The Past in the Present*, pp. 1-24.

43. While visiting Maryann in Montreal I showed her G.B. Thompson's *Spinning Wheels*, so she could identify the type brought from Harris. See also Dorothy K. Macdonald (Royal Ontario Museum of Archaeology) *Fibres, Spindles and Spinning Wheels*.

44. Quebec spinning wheels turn up 'across the line' in Vermont, and are highly valued. At his Spinning and Weaving School in Calais, Vermont, Scottish master-craftsman, Norman Kennedy has several which are over a hundred years old.

45. I. F. Grant, *Op cit* p. 224 and *The Last Stronghold*, pp. 150-151. This type is listed as the 'Great Wheel' in Mabel Ross's *Encyclopedia of Spinning*, p. 93.

46. Recorded Sept. 1991, transcription re-ordered.

47. Similarly, Newfoundland spinner and weaver, Lucy Cormier told me that her mother wouldn't allow the girls to touch the wheel — 'they would spoil the tension' — thus Lucy did not learn till after she left home. (Memorial University Folklore Archives, 1971.)

48. Spinning bees were common among Gaels in Canada. See *The Last Stronghold*, pp. 150-152 and the photograph from 1898 of a 'spinning frolic' in Florence M. MacKley's *Handweaving in Cape Breton,* p. 21. The main difference between the Quebec and Newfoundland events was that in the Codroy Valley the meal was in the evening, a sit-down dinner that included the husbands, brothers, or fathers of the women, followed by music, singing and dancing. I came acorss no similar reports in Quebec possibly because music and dance were discouraged among the Presbyterians whereas they were part of most social gatherings among the Catholic Highlanders in Newfoundland. In Gaelic Scotland older generations recall getting together for carding rather than spinning.

49. The shop closed on June 26, 1993, when the world prices of wool dropped. See 'Lennoxville: Wool Shop latest victim of the Times', in *The Record*, Sherbrooke, May 19, 1993. (The price drop also affected Scotland, and many crofters sold no wool in 1993 while they still retained a backlog from 1992, hoping for a market recovery.)

50. While none of the women blamed the foundation of the co-operative for the decline in spinning, the dates given suggest some connection between the two.

51. Norman Kennedy's School of Spinning and Weaving testifies to an enormous interest in the United States and Canada. (While in his teens, in the 1950s, Norman learned from traditional craftspeople in Barra and elsewhere.) In Scotland the situation is similar as nearly all the prominent spinning teachers are revivalists — e.g. my spinning teacher was from England; and one of the best-known teachers and authorities, Patricia Baines, was a professional oboist who took it up as a second career. (P. Baines, *Op cit.*)

52. Christie was recorded while in hospital in Megantic (hence the extraneous noise on the tape.) This passage is re-ordered for clarity. Nobody I recorded had any personal memories of spinning with the hand-spindle. See Mabel Ross, *Encyclopedia of Handspinning*, , p. 175, and P. Baines, *Op cit*, pp. 41-44.

53. Arthur Mitchell, Op cit, pp. 1-24, in particular, Figs 8 & 10, which are closest to Quebec hand-spindles.

54. Dwelly's *Dictionary* states: 'dealgan, s.m. spindle, *Bible.* Used in ancient times for spinning thread.' (The word is still used.)

55. This was also the case in Scotland — winding the wool was a job that called for a pair of free hands to hold hank after hank to help the knitter.

56. Also in the Codroy Valley, Mary MacArthur, who reared a family of six boys, explained the advantage, especially when there were only minimal differences in the size of feet for that number of children. (Recorded 1971.)

57. In Quebec the only knitting machine of this kind that I saw was in the folk-museum in St. Romain, the former house of the Curé. In the Codroy Valley, I saw one in use, a small circular device with needles and hooks, on which Mary MacArthur made socks, sleeves for sweaters, legs for longjohns. She showed

me how it worked, how to increase and decrease by removing needles, and said she bought it via a mail-order catalogue from the States. (Fieldwork notes and tapes for *The Last Stronghold*.)

58. I. F. Grant discusses weaving in Harris in the 19th century, *Op cit*, pp. 238-239. Mary Gladstone gives details on the types of looms used in 'The Big Cloth': *The History and Making of Harris Tweed*, p. 12.

59. Donald MacDonald, *The Tolsta Townships*, p. 160.

60. When Codroy Valley weaver, Lucy Cormier, won the all-Newfoundland prize for weaving in the early 1920s, she was told that it was the neat herringbone seam on her blankets that swung the judges' final decision. (Fieldwork, 1972) See also Harold B. Burnham and Dorothy K. Burnham. *'Keep Me Warm One Night': Early Handweaving in Eastern Canada*, and Dorothy K. Burnham, *The Comfortable Arts: Traditional spinning and Weaving in Canada.*.

61. I. F. Grant, *Op cit*, p. 233.

62. J. I. Little notes the stock of clothes in Leonard's Store; according to the inventory, there were no women's dresses, skirts, or men's shirts or trousers. *Op cit*, p. 168.

63. Margaret Fay Shaw describes the *luadh* in the 1930s, *Op cit* pp. 6-7. See also John L. Campbell, *Hebridean Folksongs*, chapter 1, and M. Bennett, 'A Codroy Valley Milling Frolic' in *Folklore Studies in Honour of Herbert Halpert*, pp. 99-110.

64. John L. Campbell describes men at a luadh on a visit to Cape Breton in 1937 in *Songs Remembered in Exile*, p. 43. See also *The Last Stonghold*, pp. 154-156.

65. D. G. McKillop, *Annals*, p. 73. I do not know if men took part in the *luadh* in the Eastern Townships though, so far as I can tell, there is no record of them being excluded.

66. The last *luadh* in the Codroy Valley was in the MacArthur household in the 1950s, much later than most places in the Hebrides.

67. The little fragment remembered by Maryann, recited rhythmically without a tune, is the only waulking song I came across in all my fieldwork in the Eastern Townships. I got no information on 'rolling' or 'clapping' songs (*òran basaidh*), such as I recorded in Newfoundland (*The Last Stronghold*, pp. 174-176). See also *Folksongs and Folklore of South Uist* pp. 226-268.

68. Folklorist Olav Bø encountered a similar attitude to fiddle music and dancing in Norway: both were regarded as part of local tradition, yet frowned upon by the church as un-Christian. See 'The Role Played by Tradition in a Local Community Today and Earlier' in *Tradition and Cultural Identity*, p.146.

69. I have tape-recorded Gaelic, French and English milling songs in the Codroy Valley, MUN Archives, 1970 — 92 and CBC film, 1975, and M. Bennett, 'Scottish Gaelic, English, and French: Some Aspects of the Macaronic Traditions of the Codroy Valley, Newfoundland' in *Regional Languages Studies... Newfoundland,* May 1972, pp. 25-30..

70. For example, Allan MacArthur's grandmother and mother could weave, but did not learn; he acknowledged Lucy Cormier to be the best weaver and Lucy, in turn, said that the French learned from their Gaelic-speaking neighbours. Fieldwork, 1971 — 72.

71. Most of the men I interviewed were involved in the Second World War. Bill Young was in Italy; Herbert Mayhew was overseas, two of Christie MacArthur's sons were in the Far East (one returned 'wrecked from years in a Japanese prisoner-of-war camp'); Russell MacIver was exempted, but had family stories to tell.

72. In Plate 2, Maryann Morrison's mother is wearing a *currac;* Frilled bonnets or 'mutches' were commonly worn by older women in Scotland until the 1920s. Their significance is discussed by I.F. Grant who also mentions the use of goffering irons to launder the frills; *Highland Folkways,* pp. 330-331.

73. See also Annie Blake in Labrador, 'No Pants in My Day' (transcribed from an interview by Elizabeth Goudie and Doris Saunders), *Them Days,* 3, 1, (1977), p. 13.

74. See also Ruth McKendry, *Quilts and Other Bed Coverings in the Canadian Tradition,* and Mary Conroy, *300 Years of Canada's Quilts.*

75. Kay Young gave me a quilt of very oldest utility style, quilted with local wool, made by her MacLeod grandmother in Milan; now in the National Museum of Civilization, Ottawa.

76. Belden's pictorial *Atlas (1881)* shows the cotton-batting factory.

77. See Ruth E. Finley, *Old Patchwork Quilts and the Women Who Made Them* (1929).

78. As with most home-made gadgets, there are variations on construction and method. See photo in Dorothy Brightbill's *Quilting as a Hobby,* p. 28.

79. The only woman I met who did this, Duncan McLeod's sister, the late Jean Murray, in Scotstown who was a very enthusiastic quilter. After her family had grown up and left home, she used to have a quilt on a frame in a spare bedroom 'to pass the time'. She also attended quilting bees.

80. Lauri Honko discusses the 'process of ongoing identity negotiations' in *Tradition and Cultural Identity,* p. 9.

81. There was no singing at the quilting bees I attended in Scotstown.

82. For a community case-study of comparative quilting practices, see Mary I. Gullick, 'The Historical and Social Context of Quilt Make-up in Weardale'.

83. Books of patterns and instructions were available in Canada long before they caught on in the Eastern Townships. For example, in 1928 Marie D. Webster published *Quilts: Their Story and How to Make Them.*

84. The log-cabin patchwork quilt on a box-bed in the Highland Folk Museum in Kingussie is very similar to this one .

85. See also the 1927 book by Ella Shannon Bowles, *Handmade Rugs.*

86. Marius Barbeau, 'The Origin of the Hooked Rug', *Antiques*, (Aug. 1947), pp. 110 – 113.

87. In Skye (as in many places in Scotland) my grandmother used opened out potato sacks made of jute (burlap) to back home-made rugs.

88. See Ramsay Traquair, 'Hooked Rugs in Canada', *Canadian Geographical Journal*, (May, 1943), pp. 240-254.

9

Customs

The Cycle of Life

Early Infancy, Baptism and Naming

Babies were all born at home, and in the early days it was not unusual to have more than ten children. Christie MacKenzie, who was one of fifteen of a family, described the usual set-up in Milan, with parents in the downstairs bedroom and 'whoever was a baby at the time' in the home-made rocking-cradle beside them — 'just a very plain cradle, well, there wasn't a hood [like you see in pictures of ones in the 'Old Country'] but there was ends, like, that came up higher than the sides.'[1]

In virtually all the old kitchens there was also a rocking chair, where, by the warmth of the stove, the baby could be lulled to sleep to the sound of the mother or grandmother singing. It was quite usual to have a grandparent or two in the home, and, with infants to be nursed, an extra pair of arms was welcomed by many a busy mother. Often the senior members of the family were given the important spiritual role of leading the family worship morning and evening. Most families respected their long-standing religious traditions and automatically continued the practice of infant baptism. The ceremony was conducted by the minister, usually in the home, and although there was no special age at which it took place, parents would often wait till the summer months, as they generally liked to be able to take the baby out of doors for the occasion. As a result, the baby might as old as eight months before (s)he was christened. Christie pointed out that 'if the baby was well, there was nothing to hurry it out, you know, but if it was a sickly baby, they were on edge to get them baptised as quickly as possible.' In her day people generally referred to the ceremony as 'baptism' though the word 'christening' appears to have been more common with the next generation. Interestingly, the circle has come round again, as Muriel Mayhew remarked: 'Nowadays you seldom hear the word *christening,* which is what it was in my day, as people refer to it as *baptism* and today it is always in church.'[2]

Muriel recalled that 'nobody made a big fuss in those days — there wasn't the money to do that.' The baby was usually dressed in a long dress, preferably one that had been in the family and handed down. There were no god-parents and the ceremony was held in the presence of the immediate family and close friends.

Afterwards the baptism tea was served, with the 'usual scones and oatcakes' and perhaps a cake. So seldom did any family neglect to have their children baptised, that Christie recalled the only family she knew:

> This [man in Milan] hadn't seen to it that they'd get baptised and it was working his wife into a frenzy, you know that she wasn't getting him to do it. And I think the first four were [eventually] baptised together…I remember the oldest one, [about eight years old], when the water was put on him, he [commented out loud!]

Nowadays, with the frequent Scotch-French or Presbyterian-Catholic marriages, and the major decline in the birth-rate, families still respect the tradition of baptism though not 'as the old people knew it'. There has been the addition of god-parents, special gift-giving, the inclusion of the Catholic and Anglican churches, and a selection of names that were never heard of in any Gaelic society.

Traditionally, names were chosen in the old Highland way, with the eldest child being named after a paternal grandparent, the second after the maternal side, and so on, turn about. If, for example, both grandfathers happened to be called 'John', the name would usually be chosen but combined with a second family name. And so, names such as John Norman, John Angus, John D. or Catherine Mary, Catherine Ann, Mary Kate, or simply two initials, such as J.D. were just as common among siblings in Quebec as they are in Lewis. The individual concerned would know whom they were named after, and so would the family.

Throughout the Gaelic settlements a system of patronymics was commonly used to identify individuals and the family to which they belonged. In one small community such as Dell, out of twenty-five families before the Second World War, eight went by the name of Morrison and five by the name of Murray. Some were related, though not all, and there were a number of children in all of these households. With the most common Christian names being John, Angus and Murdo, there were several Morrisons and Murrays who appeared to have the same name on the baptismal and census rolls. Locally, however, there was no confusion whatsoever, as their patronymics, naming the Christian names of the father and grandfather, instantly identified the family to which each belonged. So efficient was the system that it could range across all the villages and hamlets in the entire Gaelic community, as Angus Morrison from Marsboro explained:

> [Is mise] Aoghnas — Aoghnas Ruairidh Eoghainn. Now, if you say, if you're talking about Aonghas, which Aonghas are you talking about? Well Aonghas Ruairidh Eoghainn, [Angus, son of Roderick, son of Ewen] — you wouldn't just say Aonghas Moireasdan. My father was Roderick Ewan, Ruaridh Eoghainn [Roderick, son of Ewen].

'Where you going?'

'Well, we're going to *Ruairidh Eoghainn's*.

Sometimes a person who had been of great importance to the family was honoured by having a child named after them, such as in Muriel Mayhew's case. Her mother, Annie MacDonald had been 'in service' in Glasgow before she emigrated, and one of the women in the household was particularly close to her:

> She was named Muriel Mitchell, and I was named after her.. [My mother] liked the family very much, and when she first went back to Scotland she visited them, and this lady was a doctor…That's where I got the name Muriel! Everybody thought it was very odd to be called Muriel in that community! [laughs] My father wanted to call me Lillian too — my grandmother was called Lillias — no, my *mother* wanted, but my father wouldn't have it because the only Lily he knew was [a certain eccentric] and she wasn't quite bright!

And so she was christened Muriel Florence MacDonald (after another relative). Nevertheless, it did not save her, nor her father before her, from being known by a local nickname that came into being long before she was born:

> My father was George 'Deacon', 'cos my grandfather was called 'The Deacon'…[It happened that] once he got dressed up when he was going to church and his mother said to him 'Oh my! You look just like a deacon!' And still it stuck to him, so my father was called it after that.

Even marriage outwith the community and the legal adoption of the name Mayhew had no effect on the nickname, for, to this day, Muriel is known by her close friends as Muriel Deacon.

Nicknaming

Just as commonly as in Gaelic Scotland, both nicknames and patronyms could (and can) operate simultaneously Angus continued:

> Everybody had a nickname, the family, I mean. Oh, it was something…

Where are *you* going?'

'Well, we're going to John the Colt's.'

> When I think of it, it makes me laugh!…We had a neighbour, MacDermitts — well I told you about him — and d'you know what they called the old man, Mr MacDermitt? 'The Colt!' [spells out] C-O-L-T. *Seonaidh* the Colt, *Niall* the Colt. Well they had to or you wouldn't know who you were talking about… Everybody had to have a different name, or we wouldn't know who we were. If I talk about the MacDermitts to you, if I didn't say *Seonaidh* — Johnny — *Seonaidh*, 'Well, which Johnny?'

'Well, John the Colt' — [you might mistake him for] *Seonaidh Moraistean.*

Kay McLeod (Duncan's wife) remembered 'there was a man called *John the Horse* because he had the first horse in the Middle District, and he couldn't stop talking about it.'[3] Russell MacIver' referred to his Great-Uncle Alec as *Wild Alec* — 'they called him *Alex Fiaich,* Wild Alec...Oh he was a hunter and a trapper.' Russell's father was known as *Big Neil,* then there was *Big Donald MacDonald* who had the threshing machine (and these men *were* big); Russell's old friend John Nicholson was simply 'Nick', (or Nick Nicholson), while a family who lived near Big Neil's were known as the *Spurrags.* (Possibly from *speurag,* a sparrow, as Russell joked that they 'weren't quite right'.) Then there were the *Queue girl',* one of whom became Mrs Duffy. And long after he was dead, Donald *Slick*'s family, the Grahams, still kept the name because, as Russell remarked, 'pretty near everybody had a nickname to tell em apart'. Without any doubt he enjoyed the colour and wit of many of the names, as Russell applied the system far beyond the Townships. When he spoke about Canada's Prime Minister, Mr Maloney, for example, he had no need to explain that they seldom agreed on political matters: 'I always call him *Baloney.*'

There was a John MacArthur in Milan, who, as a young man, went to Boston to work around the turn of the century. When he came back everyone called him *John Boston,* partly because it was unusual to go there in those days, but mainly because his real name, John MacDonald, was so common. To this day, regardless of whether or not they have ever left Milan, the rest of the family have been nicknamed *Boston* — even his brother became known as *Alex Boston,* and his children and their children were also tagged with the name. Then there were the *Cyclones,* Smiths, who were never allowed to forget that they, or their relatives, survived being inside the house that got turned upside-down in 1917.

And if there was one John MacDonald, there were dozens of them, though probably the best remembered was John *Dodge* MacDonald from Dell, so-called because he was said to have deserted from the army during the First World War. Although 'old Dodge', as he was later known, died many years ago, the nickname has been carried by the rest of his family to the present day. His wife, Annie, who was eighty-eight when I visited her in 1976, was born and brought up in Lewis and had been a herring-gutter with the Lewis fisher lassies, following the herring fleets from Stornoway up to Lerwick, down to Peterhead, Aberdeen, and right down to Yarmouth. She emigrated to Quebec as a young woman and settled in Dell when she became *Mrs Dodge,* much-beloved throughout the villages.

The MacDonald's neighbour, John A. McLeod, was known as *Johnnie Bard* because of his inclination to verse-making. When citing local examples, neither he nor anyone else makes a distinction between patronymics and nicknames — they are all referred to as *nicknames.* In his *Memoirs of Dell*

Johnnie Bard notes that John Morrison was *Iain Aoghnais Uilliam* [John, son of Angus, son of William]; Norman Morrison was called *the Stump* and his son was A.D.; Donald M. Campbell went by *Malavy*; Donald Murray was *Big Dan*, 'nicknamed on account of his physical smallness'; John D. Graham was *Iain Domhuill Aoghnais òg* [young John, son of Donald, son of Angus]; John K. MacLeod was *Iain Coinneach an t-saighdear* [John, son of Kenneth the soldier].

No matter where they went within the Townships, or even to the quarries in Vermont and the woods in Maine, the men found that the system of naming went with them. As Donald Morrison (of Red Mountain, later Scotstown) pointed out, it was essential: 'And talking about, Murdo, my Uncle Murdo [who worked in Vermont], there were so many Murdo Morrisons there that every time they'd have a Murdo called there'd be fifty or sixty of em look up.'

Donald remarked that 'around every area there were characters' who were known by an odd assortment of names. There was Donald MacLeod in Linwick who was known as *the Baw-baw* (nobody knew why) and in North Hill there was another old wit they called *John a' Mogais* [John the moccasins]. Nobody ever spoke of Ann MacKenzie, 'but we always knew her as old *Anna Sheumais* [daughter of James] and *Bob a Sheumais* was her son.' They lived in Donald's local community of Red Mountain as did the more famous *Oscar Dhu*, the poet and writer Angus MacKay. He was probably one of the few to choose his own nickname, based more on his knowledge of Highland poets than on his familiarity with Gaelic orthography.

Nobody seem to have any idea why Donald himself was known as *Domhnull Pudlean* and unfortunately I was too late to ask. Nevertheless, his friends still affectionately refer to Donald by that name several years after his death. I did, however, ask others, such as Duncan Mcleod, who explained why he goes by unusual nickname of *Pope*:

> My father was nicknamed *Pope*. Not *THE* Pope, but *Pope*, after the politician. When he was a little boy about five or six years old somebody saw him up on the [station] platform following in John Henry Pope's footseteps. John Henry Pope was walking back and forth waiting for the train to come and my father was behind him. And somebody said *'Oh, seall, seall sud! Pope!'* That's the story I heard — we were Duncan Pope, Robert Pope, etcetera.

Though Alex MacIver left Marsboro as a teenager, he still bore his grandfather's nickname, *Alex Bugler*, more than a century after it caught on: 'They called him the Bugler because he used to play the bugle in the army…There were four brothers in my grandfather's family: *Iain a' West* — John, and the others had nicknames too — *Bréun* [Boisterous], *Suaine* [Sleepy], and the Killer — and the Bugler.'

Neighbours of the MacIvers was a family of MacAulays who went by the patronymic *Sgaire*. 'They called the older fellow the Sgaire and he had quite a

family, and they lived out on the Bosta Hill there. There were a lot of
MacAulays there and those Sgaires now are all over, and a lot of them French
today.'[4] Though there was a second family who went by the name *Sgaire,* the
ones near Alex's people were from the family of a Malcolm MacAulay who
composed *Oran Chaluim Sgaire,* the well-known love song. Muriel Mayhew,
whose father's people are related to the girl in the song, takes up the story:

> My grandmother's ancestor — I suppose my ancestor too, as far as that goes —
> and it was her aunt who was the Margaret in the story. Anyway they were
> lovers and they were supposed to get married and he was much beneath this
> family and [her parents] didn't want her to marry him because he was a sailor
> [fisherman], I guess. And he had come home, he had come back to get her, and
> they would go away together. And they had decided or planned to meet one
> particular night and she went out to meet him on the moors and a fog came up
> and she lost her way, and he thought she had decided not to come, and she, I
> guess, thought that he hadn't come to meet her, and then he made up the song
> after that, was what I was told. And his name was Malcolm and her name was
> Margaret, and he was *Calum Sgaire* [Malcom, son of Zachary]. And in the end
> they made her marry a person they had chosen for her, [the local merchant, an
> older man, with whom she would have a more prosperous life]. And she
> married him with her hands behind her back. She wouldn't give him her hand
> in marriage, and I think it was a few months or a year later she died. She was
> supposed to have died of a broken heart. Now isn't that romantic?
>   Later on I think he came to Canada [Quebec]. If I'm not mistaken, he
> married somebody else anyway — but he had made this song for her… [Now
> the name *Sgaire* is very common around here], the MacAulays…the
> descendants of *Calum Sgaire*…My mother was related to them somehow.[5]

Interestingly, the name *Bosta,* identified by Alex as the hill where the
MacAulays settled, is also mentioned in the song from Lewis:

> Ged is math a bhith seòladh
> 'S olc a tha e 'gam chòrdadh
> 'S mór gum b'fheàrr a bhith 'm Bòsta
> Cuir an eòrn' anns an raon.

[Although it is good to be sailing/It doesn't suit me at all/I would far rather be in
Bosta/Planting the barley in the field.]

Alex MacIver considered one of the more unusual references in his area to
be a family, whose people had left Ness in the 1850s, who all went by the
name of *Sgoth.* Although he did not know why, it seems to me very likely
that, being Ness-men, their livelihood would have depended upon fishing
off the Butt of Lewis in a locally-built *sgoth,* a vessel that is distinctive to Ness.
And even after several generations the family would keep the name used by
their forebears who left Ness.

In Milan were Ruth's family, MacDonalds on both sides, the *Doaks* on her father's side and the *Laoichean* on her mother's. While Ruth is called *Ruth Doak*, taking the name from the male side, the *Laoichean* [possibly meaning 'little heroes'], the female line, is still referred to in discussions about families. For example, when both Russell and Duncan were explaining how they were [distantly] related to 'Ruth's people, the *Laoicheans'*, Russell commented: 'I come in on that, because there was one of them married to my great-grandfather Angus MacIver, and she was a *Laoich*…And I think Leslie Allan, [i.e., Leslie, son of Allan MacLeod of Milan], his mother belonged to the *Laoichean*.' Duncan added: 'They're the ones that we were related to — And it's mainly *Laoichean* that Ruth was visiting in Lewis last summer, [1990, when we were in Lewis].' There was a timespan of a century and a half and they were instantly connected to the island their forebears had left. Not surprisingly, nobody knew why or where either of Ruth's grandfathers had acquired the nicknames that are still continued to the present day.

Next door to Norman Doak's creamery were the MacLeod family who are probably quite pleased that one of the few nicknames to have been dropped within a generation was that of the grandfather, the *Buffalo*. According to his grand-children, Evelyn Smith and Kay Young, he was so-named because he was the first in Milan to have a buffalo-skin robe. Not far from them was the MacKenzie family, whose son John, *Seonaidh Tharmaid* [John, son of Norman] was also known as *Seonaidh A' Mhuillear* [John the miller] though he had never worked in a mill in his life. It scarcely needs mentioning — 'everybody knows his grandfather was a miller.' Just as in Gaelic Scotland, acquiring a nickname is the easiest thing in the world, but getting rid of it again is next to impossible — you can move a thousand miles away, become a cowboy out west, a financial adviser in Toronto, a prisoner of war in Japan, an automobile worker in Detroit, but the name will be there waiting as soon as you step off the train in Milan, Scotstown or anywhere near home.[6]

Childcare

The code for bringing up children was based on a combination of common sense, Gaelic tradition, and Biblical knowledge. Fresh air and exercise, good wholesome food, a share of the day's labour, a good night's sleep, and sound spiritual guidance from the Bible and the Catechism were considered standard requirements for life. And, since parents and grandparents were responsible for the upbringing, children were reminded of the Fifth Commandment (*Thoir urram do d'athair agus do d' mhathair*: Honour thy father and thy mother…[7]) as often as any child in Gaelic Scotland.

Christie MacKenzie recalled her childhood:

We, as little ones, had to be in bed by daylight because there was only a few lamps — there wasn't enough to go around. Besides, a grown-up would have to carry the lamp for you; they wouldn't trust them to children. [Even in the long summer evenings there were few concessions]. Well, not very often — no later than what's good for you! [laughs] Maybe till seven o'clock or something like that.

They were very serious people [laughs] My grandmother didn't tell many stories when I was a little girl. No, it was more how I should behave and what I should do and shouldn't do, and all this, you know — they were always sort of bringing us up. And we were told to look out for things that might hurt us, you know…[I don't remember any word of the *each-uisge* (water horse) but there were other warnings to keep us safe.] Oh yes, oh yes. Of course we didn't have any water around us like that, like there was any danger. But *'Mach as a' choille!'* you know, [get out of the forest] for fear we got lost, because there was wilderness all around us.

Like most of his generation, Donald MacLennan grew up in the 1920s listening to 'all kinds of stories' — historical, amusing, frightening, terrifying, sad, even tragic.[8] While storytelling was one of the main sources of entertainment, especially during the long winter evenings, Donald suggested that most tellers had certain stories which were intended to teach young, impressionable children various lessons — never steal, lie, cheat (or, for that matter, break any of the Ten Commandments).

The most terrifying of all was about a well-known criminal in Lewis, *Mac an t-Sronaich*, who was also notorious in Quebec. The children would listen in suspense, almost frightened to breathe, to stories of the evil murderer who was eventually hanged for his crimes. Donald's mother used the stories of *Mac an t-Sronaich* as a lesson of what might happen if any of her children ever committed a crime infinitely smaller than the horrors they were afraid to imagine:

It was said that he had said: 'If my mother had made me go back with the first jack knife I ever stole, I wouldn't be here today.'[9] That was drilled into me about not stealing — what would happen to you if you stole.

Donald then recounted one of his father's amusing stories, originally told in Gaelic, as was the message — you shouldn't ever tell lies and you shouldn't be deceitful or mean either:

In some community over in Scotland, in Lewis there, when they used to kill their pig and they had no refrigeration. And so they'd have fresh meat, they cut — the family'd kill a pig this week, and they'd cut it up and divide the pieces amongst the whole community. And the next week somebody else'd do the same, and they'd have fresh meat all year round. But this year there was a disease, or an epidemic that killed off all the pigs but two. And there was a fellow there, he was very, very tight, and didn't like to share with the others; and he went to the other fellow that had the live pig, and he told him: 'You know,' he said, 'it's not going to be fair for us — we've got the only two pigs, and when we kill them and divide them up amongst the people we're not going to have enough for ourselves.'

'Ah, well,' the fellow says, 'keep it then.'

'Oh,' he says, 'we can't do that. They'll think we're awful stingy. Well,' he says, 'I don't know what to do. What would you do?'

'Oh,' he says, 'I thought of an idea. You kill your pig, and hang him up, and announce you're going to cut him up in the morning, and,' he says, 'some time during the night hide him, and you can have the meat to yourselves.'

Well, he thought that was a good idea. But this other fellow, he went and he told all the neighbours what he was going to do. And after he had gone to bed, he went, and all the neighbours went and they took the pig, cut him up, and handed him around.

And anyway, early the next morning the fellow got up and he was going to go and hide the pig, and he went and his pig was gone! Now he was in an awful stew, and he ran over to this fellow that had advised him to cut it. 'You know,' he said, 'somebody stole my pig, during the night.'

'Oh,' he said, 'that's a good story,' he said, 'you keep telling that and people are going to believe you.'

'Oh, yeah!' he said, 'but they did! They did!'

'You just keep on telling it just like that,' he said, 'people'll believe every word you say.'

My father always used to use that expression when he'd catch us telling a lie, or when he thought we were — he'd say in Gaelic *'Cum sin a mach, agus creididh daoine'* Tell it like that, people will believe it!

Aside from the basic rules of the Ten Commandments, there were several 'worldly' activities that were ruled out by most of the early settlers. Among them was card-playing, as Kay (MacLeod) Young recalled:

My father, that I know, wouldn't touch a deck of cards…[But] we played cards in the house; we were kids, and my father wouldn't touch them. He didn't approve of us playing with them, and as we got a little older he used to tell us a story.

He used to play cards. He used to play around the table, and one night they were playing, and apparently a card or more would drop. And the men went to pick the darned cards that were under the table, and they saw the horse's hoofs, the devil's hoofs.

That card game was never finished, I don't imagine. After that, my father would never play cards…I think, possibly, he had played cards when he was younger [and that was taboo] — his conscience always bothered him, and maybe it was easy to see the devil under the table.

Kay remarked that 'it was always a bit of a joke in our family' though her husband, Bill, did not entirely agree; he considered the old man's attitude was very much in keeping with that of most of the Presbyterian community.[10]

Not all children's stories had morals attached, as Muriel confirmed when she spoke of her very happy childhood memories:

I can remember when I was about six, and we sat in the kitchen by the stove, my father would open the damper and you could see the flames of the wood burning and that would make shadows all round. And he used to tell me stories about when he was young, when he was working away, out West, Montana mostly — working in the woods or on a farm — anything he could find…He was quite adventuresome…I can remember some of the stories but not really in detail. But I do remember he used to tell me stories of books that he had read — *The Sky Pilot* for one, and *The Man from Glengary* — Art Conway stories. He used to stay home from church, when my mother would go, and he'd tell me stories in front of the fire.

In the wider community, George 'Deacon' was also regarded as a good storyteller. Duncan added 'And I remember he was a great reader, because there was always books up at the store, and when one book came in he read it ten or twelve times!'

In general, great importance was placed upon reading, at home, at school and in church. Muriel recalled how, as she grew older, her father used to encourage her to read independently by reading aloud to her all but the last page of a story and then asking her to finish it herself. As she looked back she was amused at how often she would be so engrossed in the story that she would 'just have to finish it.'

The books most often read were, without doubt, the Bible and the Catechism. Even though family worship was the norm in most homes, not a day went by in school without reading or committing to memory a portion of Scripture. Not surprisingly, the teachings of the church had a major influence on the conduct of the community. Nobody had other expectations, as Christie MacKenzie remarked: '*Agus Latha na Sàbaid, cha robh spòrs idir ann!* [And on Sundays there were no sports whatsoever.] — You know, when I think of it today, Sunday is the *day* for sports — No sir!' In 1976, when I asked Christie if she thought the old people had been too strict, she admitted she used to feel 'they were too much down on the dancing,' but she repeated her yearning for a return to the old-fashioned code of conduct: 'I would give a lot to have it back to where they had it.'

Courtship and Marriage

Village schools, churches and local halls were the most common places for young people to meet. Many of the older couples relate to one of these as the place where they first met or started going out together. Much the same as in Scotland, courtships were only as private as any small community would allow — going to church together, to a concert or dance (if the family approved[11]), and walking out together, but without the public display of affection that is much more common today.

Very little was made of betrothal or engagement until after the First World War when it became increasingly common to follow the fashion for buying a ring and getting engaged. Although the first settlers would have practised the betrothal custom traditional to Gaels, the *réiteach,* I have not heard of anyone holding one in Quebec.[12] Until the 1920s, marriage ceremonies were usually conducted in Gaelic by the minister, not in church but in the home of the bride or, less frequently, that of the groom.

The earliest personal account of a marriage which I recorded was from Maryann Morrison who, by that time, had been widowed for many years. She had grown up with her future husband, Roderick Morrison (*Ruaraidh Eoghainn*), in Geocrab, Harris. They were cousins, and when their families emigrated to Quebec in 1888 she was twelve and he fourteen: 'We were on the same ship coming over and on the same place. When we came to Marsboro we were in the same place, and we followed one another.'

Maryann and 'R.E.' were married in 1894 and, despite the fact that everyone had so much to do with land-clearing, cultivating, building, and raising animals, the family still took time to prepare for a fairly elaborate celebration. Although all the women were accustomed to making their own clothes, Maryann had her wedding dress made by a dressmaker in Lake Megantic, and, judging by her detailed description eighty-four years later, it was a very special dress:

> There's where I got my wedding dress made. I got the cloth from the one that we used to buy groceries from. And I took the cloth to a dressmaker. That's the way it was — you had to make it yourself or else go to the dressmaker.
>
> It was light blue, like…oh, it wasn't thick, you know — I don't know what you call [the material]…Well, it was long, like your own, and there was pleats… and a…frill, down [the front], and…two pleats like that, and then this was turned down with a little pink ribbon.. I can't make [describe] it for you, but it's nice. Like that, and then this way, and when the two pieces were getting together on the pink ribbons., small ribbons…bows, in between every [button]…Oh, it was nice, nice. And oh…it wasn't a new coat I had at all, but, it was a good coat — and a nice little hat with a veil on it. So, I was in the style.

The wedding was held at home in Cruvag, and Maryann's parents saw to it that all the guests, mostly relatives, were generously fed:

> Well, we had a good roast beef and, put on it — you get it in the store, you get it today too, caraway seed, coated caraway pork. My father had enough meat, you know, of his own. It was in March…the twenty-eighth of March is my anniversary. So we had beef, pork, and sheep. But we didn't eat sheep [at the wedding] but just pork and beef…
>
> My mother was making cookies and cakes, and I didn't make the wedding cake myself. I had a good friend that was working in the States, and she come to the house and I wanted her to make the wedding cake, so she made the

wedding cake…[It was] a good fruit cake [which is the tradition at all Scottish weddings] and it had a lot of frosting on it. And when the frosting was done, you know seed[13] — and it was sprinkled with that. That was the frosting. But the fruit cake was very good. Then you cut it and pass it around; it would go very quick, too.

Although the caraway used to decorate Maryann and R.E.'s cake was store-bought and sugar-coated, her son, Angus, remembered that his mother 'used to put that in cookies, and pastries, anything. And [my wife], Mary, puts it her baking — and carrot salad. It grows like a wild grass around here. We had it up Cruvag.'

After the meal everyone enjoyed the customary get-together, the old-style *céilidh,* where they exchanged news, stories and a few songs. Since the Morrisons adhered strictly to what they considered to be the proper code of behaviour for practising Christians, there was no instrumental music or dancing, and certainly no alcohol.

The young couple were given gifts by the family, and Maryann could still recall in some detail what they included. All of the presents were of a practical nature and Maryann and R.E. were very grateful to receive them:

My father gave me two cows; this was my wedding present. My father gave me two cows and one sheep — *two* sheeps. And his father gave him one cow and two sheep. So we had four sheep and three cows. So we were very rich, mind you. It isn't everyone that got that much in those days. So, we had that to start with.

A cousin of mine gave me one sheet, and another one gave me a pair of pillow cases. That was all — except my grandmother, blankets, of course, that she made herself. Oh dear! But it wasn't rich people then, like today. I'm just telling you the truth. Oh, it was a poor, poor place when we got married — very poor. But it's not that today, oh, no.

In those days, Maryann added, there was no such thing as a honeymoon for newlyweds to look forward to:

Go away, no, but stay at home and work, and work, and work! No, there was no such a pleasure as that, dear. There was no money, no money to go. Working right through when you get married, that's what it is.

But I enjoyed it. We were a happy couple. If we didn't love each other we couldn't live so long together…Today they go and leave you and they go and do this and do that…It isn't the same world we have today, as the old.

In the next generation, the old homestead at Cruvag saw several other marriages, including that of Angus Morrison and his bride, Marie Claire (Mary) Martin on August 22, 1940. The young couple met in Marsboro, very close to where, over fifty years later, they live in their retirement. Mary was from a close-knit French-Catholic family with a long connection to the area:

I was born in Stornoway — [and] where I was born we were across from some
Morrisons who [spoke Gaelic] When we went to Stornoway it was all Scotch
development in Stornoway [because these people] came to Stornoway before
they came to Marsboro…[Then when my family] came to Megantic I was six
or seven — eight. And then we came here [in Marsboro] when I was fifteen. I
lived right beside the church there [across the road from our present home]
until I was married. [So Angus and I met here]…I didn't speak English much
before I got married.

Angus and Mary were among the first to marry across religious, language
and cultural boundaries. Apart from the fact that their marriage ceremony
was held in the church in Lake Megantic, there were many similarities
between the two generations. Mary's cousin made her wedding dress, though
during the first part of the day she wore a less formal outfit: 'Well, because,
that was early in the morning when I wasn't going to go to church in the
long dress, as it was just a small wedding. But for the dinner at the house I
wore the dress.'

Dressing up in Sunday best was common, indeed expected, among the early
settlers. As Mary observed from looking at the Morrison family photographs:

Even when they came here they were well dressed. [Like that picture of the
whole family — they all had their suits on.] Oh yeah. Nobody dresses like that
[nowadays] — not too many dress [for church] like that today [i.e. to the high
quality, as opposed to fads, fashions, or casual looks.]..In those days you couldn't
go to church dressed [in casual clothes] like these days. [Angus: Oh, today, they
even wear shorts!]

Maryann was just as keen that Mary and Angus's wedding cake would be
as special as her own, so she baked it herself: 'She made the cake and frosted
[iced] it. Oh she was a good cook, Mama, Number One! Maybe Lexie helped
her — and she [Mary] could do the same [as she's also a wonderful cook].'

A local woman was hired to come to the house while the wedding party
was at church, and she took over the dinner preparation which Maryann had
already begun. In this way, the meal was all ready to welcome them when
they returned to Cruvag: 'And [the dinner] was in the house — it was a big
house — a big table, and it would hold, oh, twenty, twenty-five people. They
had roast, I think roast beef, potatoes, and vegetables, and wedding cake.'

Since the wedding was in the middle of summer, the guests were able to
enjoy the day both inside and outside of the house, and, much like any social
occasion at Cruvag, they talked, reminisced, laughed and sang a few songs.
Nevertheless, consistent with the religious views of their elders, there was no
instrumental music or dancing.

After their wedding, Mary and Angus lived with the Morrisons for three
years. Angus recalled that in those days 'there was around fifty-six all Scotch
Gaelic families' in the community so although Mary was French, Gaelic

remained the language of their home. When talking directly to her, English was used, and Mary did her best to learn some Gaelic: 'Sometimes I could follow what they were talking about; I couldn't understand much, but sometimes I could know what they were talking about.'

Though there were common elements in all the old-style weddings, there were individual differences from family to family, and village to village. John Norman MacKenzie [*Seonnaidh Tharmaid*] married Christine [Christie] Effie Murray in Milan on March 31, 1920. More than seventy years on, their daughter Jean remarked 'they were married at Mom's home in Milan, in the Yard'. The framed photo, displayed for decades in their family living room, had been moved to her bedside when Christie recalled their wedding day at *Yard na Féidh.*:

> Oh, [John] had a black suit and a white tie — a white tie, that was funny? [And you've seen my wedding dress, ivory silk. My sister, Katie made it. She was two years older than I am and she was a seamstress.] She did it for a living.
>
> [After the marriage ceremony] we had a supper. My sister baked for that supper too — Rolls, oh she had bushels of rolls; I don't remember that we had [a wedding cake], but there was plenty of other stuff to eat. Oh, the poor girl, she worked for our wedding...Katie, the little one...she baked at home and it was taken down to the hall in the town — in Milan [with the snow on the ground and all, to] the Oddfellows' Hall.
>
> [And we had] a dance after the supper...Oh, I just loved to dance! We hired an orchestra that played. Planche's Orchestra — he had an orchestra and he used to play at dances in Cookshire; John hired them — there was a violin and a piano...We had square dancing — I don't remember the names of [the dances] but Angus Kenny, the one that called the changes...you could hear him anywhere...'Set to your corner, do-si-do...'

Christie's contemporary, Myrtle Murray, who was the local school teacher, also loved to dance, and in her ninety-fourth year she remembered the dances they used to do in Milan. They were the same dances as they had done at Myrtle's own wedding, when she married local man Albert Murray:

> The two-step, one step, barn dance, waltz — anything you want to do. [And square dances, sets] oh, yes, oh, yes!...They were different [to the dances I had grown up with in Birchton, among the English setttlers]...they were dances that came along with the people [who settled there], the Gavotte, and all the rest of it...Well, it didn't matter if the Gavotte was French!...[sings] do-dle-do-dle-do-dle-do...[I just loved to dance.] A good way to meet people... And Johnnie MacKenzie was a good-looking man. [At the local dances] he always had a blue suit, and he'd have a good haircut.

While Myrtle confirmed that 'a lot of people in the early days just were married in the home,' she added that the season of year could make quite a difference to the set-up:

I went to Christie Bella's wedding, anyway, out in the country. She married Angus Doak. [she was a Nicolson], David's cousin, I guess, [and he was a MacDonald, one of Ruth's people]. Well, it was a lovely day, and people gathered *outside* in the sunshine. Oh, the minister came, and she was dressed in a pretty dress — she was a pretty girl...That was on the lawn...it was a beautiful day.

Impressed by the beauty of the outdoor ceremony, Myrtle and Albert decided that they too would hold their wedding in the open air. They chose late summer, and, following tradition, held it at the bride's home, forty miles from Milan:

When we were married we lived over here [she demonstrates with a little map drawn on her lap with her finger], and here was a little meadow, and here was a sugar bush. And we came out from here [the house], and walked over [beside the sugar bush] about three o'clock and took our vows facing the sunset, [close to my family home].

[There were flowers] oh yes — you had your own and your friends had flowers too...And I had a veil.

My father built a big table outdoors by the house [for the dinner] and I suppose there were 50 or 70 there. And then he just took this table down and he made a platform [out of the same boards] and we danced on this. And my father fiddled — I don't remember if anyone else fiddled or not. And it was a lovely day. We had supper and then we danced by the moonlight.

There was a sunset, and every year, as long as we were able, we went back and stood there and [I wore the same dress each year]. Those were the fond memories we had.

After their wedding Myrtle and Albert returned to Milan — 'work couldn't stop just because somebody got married' — though, unlike most couples, they were able to begin their married life in their own home. It was much more common for newly-weds to spend the early years of wedlock with a set of parents. Christie remarked that 'practically everybody' did, and when the wedding was over, everyone would go back 'to his own place':

And we went back home to our parents — to *my* parents, yeah. And I think it was the next day we went to Sherbrooke to have our photo taken. [We weren't in Milan] very long, I don't think...and [then] we went to [live at John's] home in Marsboro from our place. I don't know how long we were married when we went out to Marsboro where he came from.

Within a year or so they moved to Scotstown where there was work for Johnnie and an opportunity to build a home in which to raise their family. I visited them in that same house first in 1976 and Christie 'put on the kettle' as she had done for countless visitors over the years. She had seen two more generations since they moved in, and a good many changes in customs besides.

Local weddings had become more commercialised and new ideas had come in from 'across the line'. Pre-wedding showers, for example, began to be organised for every bride-to-be:

> We didn't have a shower — we were married in 1920. The first wedding shower that I ever knew of in Milan was the one for Cousin Margaret MacNeil, at our place. That was in 1925…At first, when the showers started, you know, there'd be dish cloth or some simple thing like that…But today, shower gifts are [like] regular wedding gifts, beautiful things. [It's gone out of proportion], oh, I think so, now…and it makes it hard for some because some can afford it and a lot can't. But they try to keep up with the Joneses.

And of weddings in general, Myrtle concluded that 'today it's overdone.'

Death and Burial[14]

'Death comes to us all,' is the minister's reminder at funerals, and although not everyone receives a warning or a premonition, these are still accepted as part of tradition.[15] Nobody likes to hear a dog howling at twilight as 'everybody knows' it means there will be a death in the vicintiy. More specific to individuals are tokens, such as A.D. Morrison seeing a halo of light around a head or Muriel Mayhew smelling flowers. Such warnings are by no means peculiar to the Gaels, however, as they shared by many cultures and may be as common in the New World as they are in the Old.[16]

At the approach of death, it was usual for members of the family to gather, for, as Christie MacKenzie pointed out, 'when there was anything serious the family wasn't really left alone, like, there was always someone,' at least one person who 'would generally stay up with them':

> One or two of the closest friends or relatives, like uncles and aunts, or something like that. Yeah…[And] there was another thing that's, oh, it's so different now — when somebody in the community died, there wasn't a hand's turn lifted by anybody — only just the chores that had to be done, until after the funeral. Regardless — even haymaking time. Everything would [come to a standstill.]

Just as in Lewis and Harris, so it was in Quebec, various individuals in every community took over specific responsibilities attached to the entire process. Often the same woman who was called upon in childbirth would arrive, and, helped by family or neighbours, would begin the process by washing the body. Duncan Mcleod : 'The neighbouring women came over and dressed her up, and she was on the sofa in the front room until the undertaker came, and then she was placed in the coffin…it was the women of Milan, or Victoria, or wherever it happened to be.'

Muriel recalled that her mother used to keep a special pair of linen sheets for laying out the dead. When called upon to help, she would take them to the home of the bereaved, and when the funeral was over the sheets were laundered and ready for the next occasion. Muriel noticed that when the sheets were no longer needed by any of the local families 'because the undertakers did all that,' her mother 'put them in with the rest of the household linen'. Though it seemed pointless to comment at the time, Muriel 'didn't like that — I didn't ever want them on *my* bed.'

The question of dress is one that is often settled before death and it is common for individuals to let their next of kin know exactly what they wish to be dressed in. Usually the deceased are attired in their best clothes, though some, like Christie MacKenzie, who said she didn't 'know of anybody that was buried in a shroud' had a more unusual request: the silk wedding dress her sister had so lovingly stitched more than seventy years before. 'And I'm going to be buried in that dress — ask Jean to show you it,' she said when I visited her in her ninety-sixth year. It was a topic that was openly and naturally discussed, during a visit with friends or, as Russell MacIver recalled, among old pals, over a beer in the hotel:

> It seems to me I saw a shroud once, but I don't remember now who it was. But they used to put them in their best clothes…Yeah. You talk about best clothes! You know, some people would buy clothes just for the funeral and never wear it, but a fellow in town here, Nicholson — they call him Nick — he didn't believe in that. He always used to wear a shirt like this and pants — brown shirt and brown pants, nothing fancy — that's what he wanted to be buried in, so they buried him like that. And I thought it was a very good idea. So I told my nephew that's what I wanted too. Of course I haven't got a suit anyway, and certainly I wouldn't go and buy me one! [laughs]

Since most men in the community were skilled in woodworking, the making of coffins was not confined to a certain carpenter as was more common in Scotland. Christie recalled

> Whoever was the handiest person in the community, and whoever had decent lumber [would make the coffin]. And the women used to line it with whatever they could get to line it with…well it was usually something white if they could get something white. There wasn't always just what they'd like, but they did the best they could with that. Some of the coffins were quite crude but they did the best they could…well, sometimes they used to have planed boards, you know…Just line it — they used to varnish or paint the outside, as best they could. There wasn't always the paint either.

Nevertheless, when given enough time to prepare for the inevitable, there was always a pride in fine craftsmanship, as Russell recalled:

> I remember an uncle of mine, Donald Graham, he made a casket for his step-mother, and my, now, it was a good casket. And my aunt she lined it and it was just as nice, you know. [They used] pine — well, if they had it — any lumber;

mostly it would be pine. [In those days they didn't paint it —] well, they'd cover it with cloth, black cloth outside usually. Then in the old days they used to have a glass, something like that, you could look in [the lid]. Yeah. [She lined it] with some kinda stuff, then, maybe satin, and made a little pillow and stuff. Did you ever see any of them caskets with glass on them?…It was flat all the way, you'd see them, [head and shoulders, through this little window] and, you'd see their hands. I remember my grandfather, Donald McIver, and his sister Mary, that's the kind they had. But that's all they had then, at that time. [All the same. you would have to be pretty skilled to make one with a piece of glass in it.] You would just fit the glass in, like a frame, like a mirror.

Duncan added that some men, such as Donald MacInnes, who were accustomed to dealing with funerals, even prepared for their own by having the right size of coffin ready-made: 'He always had his own casket in the shed at home in Milan. I remember as a kid we'd go in there…It wasn't fancy, but it was well wrought, well made.'

On the lid of the coffin was usually nailed a silver-plated metal plaque with name, age and date of death of the deceased. Just before the burial it was removed and retained by the family as a keepsake.

When the body was encoffined, copper coins were placed on the eyes and hands laid across the breast or by the side. The 'remains' were set on chairs or trestles in the best room, usually with the lid of the casket open, ready for visitors to pay their last respects. News of the death would rapidly go round all the neighbouring communities by word of mouth, while those who were 'away' had to face the heart-sinking 'letter edged in black' which did not always arrive in time to allow the recipient to attend the funeral.

Having seen many changes in the traditions during her life, Christie preferred the days before modern funeral parlours took over all the arrangements:

And then they would hold a wake, like nights — but the remains would be in the house. They'd have a service, it was like a [regular church] service — they'd have singing, and they'd have reading of scripture, and prayer. That would go on from after supper till bedtime, like. [And some of the people would stay up all night], well, relatives, or uncles, aunts or cousins, or somebody like that — it was usually the relatives, like, sometimes friends — not very often though…

When the neighbours arrived they would bring gifts of food to the family, then, after a brief word of consolation, would proceed to the room to 'view' the body. Johnny Bard recalled that 'in between the viewings the face would be covered with a napkin saturated with some concoction containing camphor which was supposed to preserve the natural look'.[17] Around nine o'clock in the evening the prayers would begin, solemnly thanking God for the life, acknowledging His will (no matter how difficult to understand), and asking for comfort for the bereaved. At no point would there ever be any mention of the soul of the departed, for that concept has no place in the doctrine of the Presbyterian Church. Psalms were sung, led by one of the group appointed to precent, then the minister or elder would bring that part of the evening to a close with a short benedictory prayer.

A 'lunch' was then served in the kitchen or dining room, after which some of the visitors would leave. Those who decided to stay would gather near the kitchen stove and 'visit', talking in low voices, reminiscing, remembering 'the good times,' sometimes laughing and remarking how the deceased would enjoy the yarn. Silently, almost unnoticed, an individual would leave kitchen, return to the 'room' for a moment's contemplation by the remains, then come back to the company. Thus the night would wear on, punctuated by visits to the 'room', a lunch around midnight, another one at 3 a.m., and the group talking in hushed voices till the appearance of the first member of the family in the morning. A dignified departure allowed the bereaved the privacy of their home until the next night when the wake would continue.

Despite the solemnity of death, it was not necessarily without light-hearted moments, especially if the deceased had had 'a good innings'. Though it had been many a long year since Russell MacIver had seen a wake, with characteristic wry wit and deadpan expression he continued:

> Oh yes, yes…Oh, usually all night, and one or two would stay a couple of nights. Well they used to do that a long time ago but they don't now…Oh they'd visit and they'd sing — they didn't want them to mourn too much, I suppose. I remember a story told one time, 'bout a fellow who was almost dead and his wife was cooking, you know, for a wake. And he could smell the roast pork, and oh! It made him hungry — oh he was pretty near dead, and he wanted a piece of that. 'Oh no,' she says, 'you can't have any of that; that's for the wake!' [Laughs]

Funeral traditions, rehearsed for generations, appeared to fall into place just as they did in Lewis or Harris.[18] As soon as the exact place of burial was confirmed, neighbours would dig the grave, at times in the harshest of weathers. Sometimes the ground would be frozen so hard it was impossible to sink a pick-axe and in such cases the body would be stored in an out-building until the first thaw. No matter how much effort was involved, 'in those days nobody paid for this — it might be your tragedy next.'[19] In every village there were individuals the community could rely upon, for example in Milan Christie MacKenzie recalled that 'in those days they had undertakers. Around here it was Donald MacInnes — he had a black team and he had a hearse. He could put it on runners or wheels. I remember a few of them. [He had] two black horses.' A few miles away in Dell, Isobel Stewart recalled that her in-laws, the Shermans, had a horse-drawn hearse:

> Oh, yes, and they had the black, you know black [?housings?] on the horses — did you ever see that?…they had covers to put over the horses, all in black, and

everything, long tassels. Oh yes. [In the old days — it wasn't like it is now], no, it was a very sombre [occasion]. Och! It was just terrible, you know, you could hardly breathe at one, you'd be so scared someone would make you laugh; you're not supposed to smile, or anything.

Whatever else these horse-drawn funeral processions may have lacked, it was certainly not dignity or the importance of paying last respects. Some of them were so impressively large that 'children liked to count the buggies,' as Johnny Bard recalled, though they were told by some of the adults not to do so 'as it was a bad omen.' Despite discouraging his own children from counting, Johnny's father told him of one funeral procession he had attended with a hundred and thirty horse-drawn vehicles.

Bereavement and mourning were taken very seriously and protocol was followed according to tradition. Most people died at home, and when a death occurred the door of the house was draped in crêpe to announce the bereavement to the community. If the deceased was elderly, black crêpe was used, if middle aged, the colour was purple, and if it was the death of a child, then white crêpe was draped on the door. While everyone wore black or dark grey to a funeral, the community expected the bereaved family to dress in mourning clothes on an everyday basis. Widows dressed all in black, while widowers, whose workday clothing would have to remain serviceable for manual labour, wore a black crêpe armband on the left sleeve for a year. If the deceased was an elderly parent or grandparent, then six months was an acceptable time to dress in mourning colours. The black could also be substituted by grey and later purple as time went on.

Over the years the customs related to death and burial have changed considerably, largely due to the universal takeover of big businesses. Christie MacKenzie looked back over the years of her long life when there were no such things as funeral parlours and concluded 'No, no, but here was a closeness between people that isn't at all any more.' Times had certainly changed when she herself died in 1995, but not so much as to deny the old lady her wish to be buried in her wedding dress. And that same spring, when Russell MacIver died after a hard winter of illness, he was laid to rest in his familiar 'brown shirt and working pants', with 'no fuss', just as he would have wished.

Visitors to the Eastern Townships are generally struck by the neatness of the graveyards in the area. A visit to one of them or a tour round all of them is a favourite Sunday afternoon or fair-weather outing. When family, friends or newcomers are taken for a drive in the area it always includes the cemeteries. There is a visitors' book at most of them, signed by folk from near and far, many 'home for the summer', having long since moved out west or to one of the big cities. They all pay respects to their families and forebears whose epitaphs now tell more of the history of the area than most of the residents of the nearby towns and villages.

Calendar Customs
Hallowe'en

October 31, *Oidhche Shamhna* or Hallowe'en, has a long history among all Celtic peoples.[20] In ancient times celebrated as the Celtic New Year, no reference to the origin of the festival comes down through oral tradition among nineteenth and twentieth century Gaels on either side of the Atlantic. Throughout Gaeldom it was celebrated by dressing up in disguise and by carrying out various deeds of mischief in the community.[21] Variants and combinations of these activities have taken place for countless centuries; for example, my grandparents in Skye recalled their adolescence in the 1890s when, after dark, local boys with blackened faces would climb up on the thatch of the house and drop a turnip down the chimney, causing smoke and complete chaos within the house. During my own adolescence on the Isle of Lewis in the early 1960s, when there were no thatched houses left in our village,[22] we kept the night of the 31st for guising and another night, usually the following Friday, for mischief, though we did not actually call it 'mischief night'.

The first settlers also kept Hallowe'en, and for the first three generations the emphasis was clearly on the mischief. Johnnie 'Bard' McLeod described one memorable Hallowe'en of his school days in Dell, when he and some of friends got six hens 'from DA's place', carried them off in a potato sack, then took the 'buck sheep' and, under the cover of darkness, let the whole lot loose in the schoolhouse. When the teacher came in the next morning she was met by the assembly of animals, with droppings everywhere, and, predictably, she was furious. 'We all got into trouble,' and the whole day was spent cleaning the entire school, including the walls, windows, stove and all its pipes. The distraction from the day's lessons turned out to be 'a blessing in disguise' for the school, though Johnnie was later punished by his father for his part in the mischief. He makes no mention of guising, though his contemporary, Christie MacKenzie, remembers that it played a small part in the custom in Milan:

> [We celebrated Hallowe'en, but] not until we were pretty well grown up. And *then* it was exchanging animals, you know. You'd go with one cow to a farm, and…replace it with another animal; sort of take one farmer's cow to our place and ours to their place, and different things like that. Nothing harmful at all…
>
> And we used to try and camouflage [chuckles] a little bit…We used to have a sort of a scarf around our face and, so that we could see through it. But that was about all, because we didn't have many clothes to choose from. [I would have been], oh, nine or ten, I guess. 'Twas after I went to school…oh, we were allowed to do it. Kids before us had been doing it and we went along with it.

The participants in the more daring Hallowe'en feats were usually adolescent boys. From her teaching days in Milan in the twenties and thirties,

Myrtle Murray took delight in remembering the sense of humour that was attached to another Hallowe'en episode:

> Duncan D.L.'s grandfather, also D.L., who had the store, was a very devoted temperance man, and, one Hallowe'en, a number of the young men, including his own son, Pope, took tar and oil — black. And on the side of the store, next to the station — just across from the station, tracks in between — [they painted] D.L. McLEOD, SELLER OF LIQUORS. Well, it raised D.L.'s Scotch temper, and almost every year as long as he lived, he painted it; [but] that black oily paint would come through![23]

Over fifty years later, Duncan confirmed Myrtle's story, adding that the graffiti outlived both his grandfather and his father and could still be seen when, finally, around 1992, Duncan himself had the old store torn down.

Muriel Mayhew, who was a pupil of Myrtle Murray's in Milan, recalled being drawn into one of those pranks played by the boys:

> *My mother had the key to the church which was just next door to us in Milan — she always kept it on a special nail just by the door, ready for whoever needed to get into the church. And one Hallowe'en, Freddie MacKenzie prevailed upon me to the get the key — it was really pretty easy as the women were all at some gathering that night, and Freddie and the boys would have known that. So of course, the key was back on the nail long before mother got home. And that night, at a time when nobody expected it, they rang the church bell, and of course everyone in the village would be alerted, and wonder what was happening.
>
> The next day the custodian accused my mother of giving out the key to someone who shouldn't have had it, but my mother vowed it never left the nail — she was sure of that, I didn't tell her any different!

One of Isobel Stewart's anecdotes suggests that Hallowe'en presented the ideal opportunity for prank-playing as it validated occasional outbursts of mischief. Not that pranks were out of the question at other times of the year, as some people knew only too well. A few of the young fellows in Dell, including Isobel's own nephew, seemed all too ready to seize an opportunity of tormenting their good-natured neighbours:

> Johnny, the oldest boy, oh he was full of the *Satan* [Gaelic pronunciation], and he used to tease the Dodges [MacDonalds] awful, you know. And I don't know if it was Hallowe'en or just any old time, but they had a pig. And Johnny was a demon, of course, and he had to start it, to play a trick on them. They went out and they got the pig, and they held its nose so that it would squeal, and they were running down back in the field, and Annie comes down, and John comes down, and I believe Annie said she was on her bare feet, because she mentioned stepping in the *sgaird* [dung]. She said, '*Oh, tha iad thall an siud* [They're over there]'.
>
> And they'd hold the pig's nose, and they'd run somewhere else. '*Chan eil, tha*

iad thall an seo [No, they're over here].' And they kept them up for about an hour, running after that pig!

To the boys it was all fun, with no harm intended, though Annie and her husband may not have thought so at the time. In fact the boys knew there would be no repercussions from this family, who were held in great affection throughout the community, whereas they would not have dared to try the same prank on any of the more austere members, including their own parents.

Only a few miles away, on the other side of Milan, where Ruth grew up, she recalled that when Hallowe'en came round they *'didn't do much up at the farm but in Milan they used to.' She recalled some of the pranks that were regularly played in her youth:

*Like, they'd carry off your steps [if they were loose] and put them somewhere else; or maybe the chairs on the front porch would disappear; they'd turn up again, and wherever they landed they would know who they belonged to. Or one time they put a buggy on top of the roof of a shed — that was the big boys — it'd have to be the big boys to handle that.

Some years later, after young women such as Ruth and Muriel had gone to college in Montreal and young men again served in the army during the war, a transition began to take place. By the time Ruth married and had children, the community was beginning to replace their old ways with the Hallowe'en customs that have now become standard throughout North America:

*Years later, in the forties and fifties, I used to go with my children when they were small. Some would have black on their face, some had these awful masks, others with just a bit of rouge on. [This was also the custom in 1976 when my five-year-old son and I visited Ruth and David. Ruth gave him a choice of peanuts, apples and store-bought Hallowe'en candies in black and orange wrappings covered in pumpkins and witches].
Today [in the 1990s] the kids come dressed up for 'Trick or Treat'— they're in and out the house before you know it. Oh, they have fun, you have your treats for them, and the mothers are waiting outside near the house for the little ones. And sometimes they carry a pillowcase to carry the 'loot'. They even come from Springhill [Nantes, where all the children are French-speaking].

Since factory-made masks and elaborate costumes fill every department-store window in North America, not surprisingly they are now an establised part of the festivity in the Eastern Townships — indeed, they are fast catching on in Scotland, where even the turnip is being replaced by the American pumpkin. At the same time, there are still parents who create outfits with and for their children. Today, much of the fun now associated with Hallowe'en begins in the school, where, under the direction of the teacher, young children make paper witches, cats and pumpkins to decorate the classroom walls and windows. It's still fun, though quite different from the sort enjoyed in Johnnie Bard's day.

All Saints' Day

Since Hallowe'en was regarded as a pagan festival by the early Christian church, in accordance with their policy the actual day of celebration was kept and invested with a new Christian significance. Thus, two feast days were established in the church calendar, All Saints' Day on November first and All Souls' Day on the second. These are generally thought of as Catholic holy days, with little or no significance to the Presbyterian Churches. Nevertheless, Christie MacKenzie said that at 'one time we did have a church service and that was November first, All Saints' Day. We always had a service on All Saints' Day.' I have not come across anyone in the next generation (to which Ruth, Muriel and Duncan belong) with any memory of such a service, or reference to it.

Christmas

Much the same as in the Scottish Highlands, the celebration of Christmas was, in earlier years, 'nothing like it is today'. It is most unlikely that the first settlers celebrated it at all, for, even well into the twentieth century, Presbyterian Highlanders adhered to the idea that there is no Biblical evidence to suggest that Christ's birth should be celebrated on December 25, or any other day, for that matter. But by the turn of the century the custom had caught on, and Christmas celebrations became part of everyone's winter activities.

Children of Christie and Johnnie MacKenzie's generation believed in Santa Claus who 'came down the chimney' after they had gone to bed on Christmas Eve. Christie recalled:

> We hung our stockings up the night before, and we'd get an orange and an apple and a few peanuts, and — that was just about it. [Oh, yes, we believed in Santa] and it was a sad day…when we got wise to [the fact] that there was no Santa Claus…Oh, it was after I went to school. I must have been nine or ten, or there[abouts].
>
> The next day nobody worked, only just what they *had* to, like chores on the farm and that. [There was always a special Christmas dinner], and my mother used to have a chicken as a rule — there was no turkey — most always had chicken for dinner…[And] oh, potatoes and dressing; she used to make dressing…Sometimes turnips, not many more than that. [Then dessert], oh yes, we always had a sort of a raisin thing with molasses…a pudding, like…I don't know if you'd call it a Christmas pudding today; there wasn't much in it besides

the raisins, but it was good for us anyway. We enjoyed it…She used to make a
sauce, like vanilla, and sugar and butter and that — just a sort of creamed sauce
to put on it.

A Christmas tree, now such an integral part of the festivity, was the
exception rather than the rule in those days:

Oh, *some* used to [have one] at that time, when we were growing up. But
we didn't…it was the ones who were — better fixed, you know — that used
to have them. Of course they used to trim them with something, and so on. We
didn't have much but the bare necessities.

In Dell, where Isobel Stewart lived, things were much the same:

We never had a Christmas tree when we were kids. We used to hang our
stocking at the foot of the bed and that was it! Oh, we'd get an apple and an
orange and a handful of peanuts and a handful of candy, and maybe a little
white ball stuck on the top. And we'd be pleased!

By the time Myrtle Murray settled in Milan as the schoolteacher, there
was a special Christmas event for the entire village. Myrtle recalled that it
was held in the Oddfellows' Hall:

We had a Christmas tree party in the hall. The children all sang — had
entertainment. And they had a tree…Youngsters probably went and [cut] it.
[They decorated it], well, they had tinsel, and put gifts under it…As I
remember Milan, they didn't give a lot of gifts. Oh, a [wooden] spinning-
top, maybe one made of a [cotton] spool [and the children would still be
delighted]…They used to have a real community spirit, but now it's
commercialised.

This fairly moderate celebration of Christmas lasted until after the Second
World War, and by the sixties and seventies most families had adopted what
the old folk now regard as a more Americanized attitude to the festive season
— every home has a lavishly decorated tree; houses, front porches and gardens
are brightly lit with coloured lights; tables groan with excesses of food; and
there is always a super-abundance of presents. Peanuts and candy are everyday
fare, and, as Isobel wistfully reflected, 'today the kids are always looking for
more.'

It is not only the children who expect more, however, as Christmas has
become big business for a number of entrepreneurs who, since the 1980s,
have bought up farms and turned the land over to commercial Christmas
tree-growing. There is a certain irony in looking at so many carefully tended
crops of perfectly formed conifers, acre after acre destined for the Christmas
markets of New York, Boston, or Montreal. For the old-timers it is a painful
reminder of their forebears who laboured so tirelessly to clear this same land
to grow food. As the century draws to a close, the new harvest yielded by

these fields will still help feed the land-owners; it will also keep many of them in a style unimagined by the Gaels who first cleared the land.

New Year

Although most Scots would expect Christmas to have been a very low-key event among emigrants, we invariably expect to hear that New Year was the main focus of celebration. Regardless of the big night in Scotland, there is no parallel tradition to Hogmanay or New Year's Eve in the Eastern Townships. Even *Oidhche Challuinn,* observed all over Gaelic Scotland until after the First World War and in parts of Nova Scotia and Newfoundland until the 1960s, had been totally forgotten.[24] Lewis historian and writer Donald MacDonald from North Tolsta, who was known to many of the Township Gaels, described it as one of the most vivid traditions of his youth, yet his Quebec contemporary, Christie MacKenzie, whose people originated from the same village, seemed puzzled to be asked. She summed it up briefly: 'I don't think there was anything different from any other day for that [and they didn't have a church service].'

To mark the beginning of a new year on a very small scale, however, some families began to take the opportunity of having a get-together over dinner. As Ruth explained, 'it might be our house one year, and Ivy's the next — we'd take turns.' Since it was a public holiday for everyone, a similar arrangement was followed in most families though I asked a good many before I found one where a celebratory dram was part of the enjoyment. Muriel recalled her father raising a glass with neighbours who visited, and even though her mother was a strict Presbyterian there was no discord as that had been an established tradition before she left Lewis. A few miles away, in Marsboro, however, the Morrisons had no such custom as it had not been part of their very strict way of life in Harris.

Candlemas Day

Candlemas appears on the church calendar as the Feast of the Purification of the Virgin Mary, but not surprisingly it has no religious significance among Presbyterian Gaels. Regardless of denomination, however, Gaels in Scotland regard *Latha Féill' Brighde* (*An Fhéill Bhrighde*, St Bride's Day), the first of February, as the first day of spring, and though the term is still used among the older people in Gaeldom, it has long since died out in the Eastern Townships where winter conditions can last until May.[25] In both Scotland and North America the second of February, Candlemas Day, survives as a day for predicting the weather and, while the term is still used in many parts of Scotland,[26] it is now known all over Canada and the U.S.A. as 'Groundhog

Day'. As Christie MacKenzie explained, 'We used to have Groundhog Day — if the sun would shine it went back into its hole, wasn't it?' Her husband Johnnie continued:

> For another six weeks. [That meant you were going to have colder weather for another six weeks], yes, winter until then. [If it was a dull day] I guess it was supposed to stay out if it was warm enough. *I* don't know — it never worked out! [Laughs]

Easter

Although nothing remains of the traditional link between Candlemas and the calculation of Easter,[27] and most of North America has now been taken over by chocolate eggs and bunnies, youngsters in Christie MacKenzie's day kept the most popular Easter custom known in Scotland:[28]

> [Eggs from our own hens —] Oh yes, as many as you wanted…Well, mother used to save them, you know. For weeks before she used to save some, in a cool place where they'd be all right, and Easter morning you could have as many as you wanted…Easter Sunday [they were cooked] in boiling water…ah, not hard-boiled. Well, the one that wanted them hard-boiled, they were left in a little longer…No, we never coloured them, no we never did that. [and we didn't roll them either] Oh, we'd just eat them at the table…yes, as many as you wanted, and that was a treat…No there was never a story connected with it.[29]
>
> [In church there was] a service, like a singing, appropriate to Easter Sunday…Well, once in a while they used to have a Friday evening service on Good Friday, but not always.

In those days 'work on the farm went on as usual on Good Friday,' even though their Catholic neighbours kept it as a holy day with no work whatsoever. Differences between the two religions, such as this, were very distinct until the 1940s and 50s when intermarriage became increasingly more common. Now, as church elder Muriel Mayhew points out, the Presbyterian Church not only observes Good Friday but the entire Easter season is highlighted on their church calendar. Lent, once regarded as Roman Catholic, is now observed with regular home Bible studies and church services that acknowledge the Five Sundays in Lent leading up to Palm Sunday, Good Friday and Easter Sunday, the final celebration.[30]

St Swithin's Day

'If it rains on St Swithin's Day it'll rain for forty days.' is a folk-belief that seems to have been well-known among Eastern Townshippers throughout the twentieth century.[31] Like most weatherlore, it turns up when conditions fit the saying — in this case, on July 15, if there happens to be a sudden cloudburst. And so it happened in 1994, when a small group of friends had chosen July 15th to celebrate two special birthdays that fell on either side of that date — Muriel's eightieth on the 14th and Ruth's eighty-second on the 16th. The party was held at Duncan's summer cabin on the shore of Lake Megantic and I had been invited to the 'pot-luck' picnic. Around 4 o'clock, not long after the two birthday cakes had been cut and distributed, the sky clouded over and darkened suddenly. Tables were quickly cleared, dishes, food, chairs and people were rushed inside just before the heavens opened. Looking out of the cabin window at the rain, Ruth's aunt-by-marriage, Ivy MacDonald, immediately recited the saying to Ruth who added: 'And I remember one year when it rained on St. Swithin's Day and it took us till September to get in the hay. Now that's a good forty days.'

So began a discussion of wet summers related to rain on St. Swithin's Day, though nobody seemed to know where the saying came from in the first place. I had never heard any tradition about St. Swithin while growing up in Skye or Lewis, but it does exist in Scotland, in the North-east[32] and the Lowlands, as my friend (and proof-reader), Marie Salton, has a traditional Scots rhyme from Edinburgh:

> St Swithin's Day if it be fair,
> For forty days twill rain nae mair;
> St. Swithin's Day if it be wet,
> For forty days will be raining yet!

The weather is always a topic of conversation when neighbours meet, however, and quite possibly the saying was adopted from English-speaking settlers in nearby East Angus or Canterbury. It dates back to the ninth century, to a legend about Saint Swithin, then Bishop of Winchester. He was known for his charitable work, especially in building churches, and, when he died in 862, had apparently requested that he be buried in the cemetery outside the Old Minster at Winchester. This was done, but over a century later it was decided to move him inside the cathedral — probably as a mark of great respect. On July 15th, 971, when the removal was carried out, cloudbursts and heavy rain apparently marked the occasion, and, ever since, it has been claimed that if it rains on St. Swithin's Day it will continue for forty days.[33]

Local Events and Organizations

Box Socials

One of the most enjoyable social events in the community was the fund-raising Box Social. Though nobody seemed to have any idea of their origin, Christie MacKenzie explained how these evenings were organized:

Anything happening, like the barn burning or the house burning or something [disastrous] — *everybody* pitched in and did what they could with the work and if there was anything they could give, they gave…it was just some way to help people…Oh, [the Scotch and French] they'd hold together just the same.. getting up box-socials to help. You know, selling the boxes and the proceeds going to a family that was destitute.

These socials were usually held in the school, though sometimes in a neighbour's home. There were clearly defined roles for men and women as Christie's husband, Johnnie, pointed out when he teasingly reminded that 'the women made the boxes and the men were bidding on them — to get the women!' She smiled as she went on to explain:

It was an evening thing, and it would be all free, [no admission charge] for the neighbours…Yes, it was fun…And some of them boxes would be regular shoe-boxes, you know, all trimmed up. Some of them would be beautiful! Oh, yes indeed! And as a rule, the best trimmed ones brought the most money [regardless of what was inside] [laughs]. Well, of course, they wouldn't know what was inside till they were too late anyway — they'd have bought it!

[In the boxes would be] a lunch for two people. They'd go on sale…[A typical lunch in a box might be] sandwiches and a cake and cookies, and sometimes fruit — whatever you could get. In the country store there wouldn't be too much variety…And they made tea or coffee [in the hall] — that was extra.

And you ate your lunch with your partner. Sometimes some had a mark on the box, you know, for their own girl, and the rest would make him pay for that box — they'd bid it, and bid it, and bid it up until — ! Yeah, it was [fun], and it was very interesting.

[As for disappointments —] oh, sometimes, sometimes. I remember my brother-in-law, Allan — the one in the picture with my daughter there — he was going with a girl from Boston. She used to come to her grandparents' place for the summer. He was going with her and my sister was home from Springhill, Mass., with her two girls. And the oldest girl wanted to go to a box-party, but she wanted Uncle Allan to buy her box because she didn't want a stranger to get her box. So Allan promised to do that, and when he started to bid on her box, everyone thought he had a mark on this Margaret MacIver's box, and they [pushed up the bidding as hard as they could] — he paid thirteen dollars to get that box! And it was his niece's box! [Laughs] [That was a lot of money in those days] but he wouldn't let her down, you know. He had promised to buy her box, and they kept on bidding against him…[The average price of a box would have been] oh, two and a half or three dollars, or so, I think…that was since I can remember, until, oh, until after we were married…Oh, yes, [it was a lot of money] but if somebody was in distress you gave what you could…Oh, yes, the money went to them.

[Occasionally a young man might even buy two boxes —] oh, sometimes, sometimes. The bunch would eat together, yeah. Yes, that was very interesting.

When the picnic-style meal was over, the rest of the evening continued like a village-hall céilidh with plenty of songs, stories and recitations in both Gaelic and English. Then, depending on who had organized the social, there might also be a dance, which, as far as Christie and Johnnie were concerned, was the ideal way to complete the night's entertainment:

> Once in a while they'd have an orchestra [to play for a dance]. The orchestra in them days was a violin player and a piano player, or an organ player. And they'd give them ten dollars — five dollars apiece for playing. Well, that came out of the proceeds, but the rest [went to the night's cause].

Fresh in her memory as though it had only been a week or two ago, Christie wistfully recalled that 'the last box-social I was at was in 1923.'

Sugaring-off Parties

According to Mary MacLeod of Milan, Gaelic speakers referred to the month of April as *mios an t-siùcair,* [sugar month]. After the syrup season was over, there was a special celebration, a 'sugaring-off party', similar to a 'harvest-home', which is held in many farming communities. Families would gather at the Oddfellows Hall in Milan on the appointed evening, and bring a sample of their season's syrup. They would then would boil up the new syrups, and, when the experts judged it to be ready (the 'soft-ball test' in cold water), everyone would go outdoors and gather round the area of clean snow, (usually near a fence where nobody had trodden) designated for the highlight of the night. The air filled with excitement, the spectators would 'hold still' and 'keep clear' while the boiling liquid was carried out of the hall to be poured into the fresh snow where it immediately turned into a kind of toffee. Still outdoors, with fork in hand, everyone would tuck in to the hard-earned treats. After the feast, as many 'as were allowed' would return to the hall for a much-enjoyed dance.[34]

Like every other dance in the community, however, this one was also regarded with strong disapproval by a stalwart core of Presbyterian church-goers. At the very mention of a dance, almost everyone has memories about how strict some of the older generation were, and how they frowned upon such frivolity. As already mentioned, Maryann Morrison's father would allow no dancing whatsoever, for in his generation they were under the impression that Christ Himself preached against it. Though references to 'King David dancing before the Lord' can be found in the Bible, it is quite another matter finding a text to support Christ's alleged condemnation of dancing.[35]

Looking back to her parents' and grandparents' generation and to her own youth, Muriel Mayhew attributed the austere, judgmental attitudes to the powerful influence of certain ministers whose interpretation of the scriptures

ruled the congregations: '*I can remember a minister who said if you went
to a dance and you thought the Lord was with you He'd leave you at the
door! So much for *I will be with you always, even unto the ends of the earth!*'

The Oddfellows Hall was demolished in 1959, and though syrup and sugar
are still made domestically and commercially, many years have passed since a
community sugaring-off party was held.

Agricultural Shows

Reflecting on the annual activities of summer, Duncan Mcleod remarked that
'there were a lot of fair days in those days. And as one fair dropped out, others
took over.' The first one of the year was run by the Agricultural Society of
Compton — 'that was Number One and it was held in Cookshire,' still home
of biggest annual fair of the Townships. 'Then there was the Scotstown Show'
which was closest to home for Milan folk. As years went by and transport
became more readily available, people would usually attend more than one
show, and plan their summer accordingly.

Much like the Royal Highland Show, or any of the smaller shows
throughout Scotland or North America, these events were, and still are, set
up to bring together the best of the area's produce and, in an atmosphere of
festivity, help foster pride in the quality of livestock, agriculture, horticulture
and home-crafts. The tradition dates back over a century, when several of the
townships organised Farmers' Clubs to help disseminate information and
technology between farms while, at the same time, facilitating various social
occasions. Among his old books Duncan Mcleod has a notebook from the
1890s of the minutes of the Milan Farmers' Club. In the records there is a
note of the fact that the government made local provision of a Township bull
to service the cattle and help keep the stock healthy.[36]

For the ever-busy farmers and their families, the Agricultural Show is a
day out, a welcome break at the busiest time of year with a chance to meet
up with friends and relatives, get to know newcomers, exchange ideas, catch
up on news of every kind, and indulge the children (and themselves) in special
treats that take their fancy. The organisation of each show, which has changed
little over the years, centred on three main activities: competitions,
merchandising and entertainment. For the competitions, various categories
were established: farm and domestic animals, vegetables, fruits, flowers, and
all their produce, such as butter, cheese, pickles, jams and other preserves. There
was a domestic section where 'the ladies displayed their cookery, baking,
artwork, and needlework,' and where you could find every kind of scone,
oatcake, cookie or cake, and some of the most colourful and magnificent
handmade quilts stitched locally. Each category was suitably displayed and the
competitions were judged and prizes awarded.

Ruth recalled how, every spring, the school-children were given flower-seeds to plant which they then nurtured over the summer, aiming to show their results at the September 15th show. Fondly remembering how her own children had carefully tended the flowers on the front porch, she laughingly remarked that 'you could be sure the first frost took the blooms before the show.'

Booths and stands were set up by merchants from near and far, all displaying and selling farm machinery, household appliances, and any new invention likely to make an impression on the farmers and their wives. This might be the only day of the year when everyone had plenty of time to consider the merits of new-fangled ideas. Cream-separators, for example, made their first appearance at one of the shows, and, after the coming of electricity in the 1940s, refrigerators, deep freezers, and other appliances made their début. The Annual Show was also the ideal place to introduce prefabricated sash windows, a boon to farmers racing the good weather to fix up the house as well as get the harvest gathered.

Over the years the attractions of the shows have remained fairly constant, as my own day at the Cookshire Fair in 1976 had the same features that Duncan recalled from his youth. Now, twenty years on, they are still part of the Show: side-stalls selling knick-knacks, candies and other treats; travelling salesmen with stalls of practical items and gadgets ('they've been coming here forever'); newcomers testing their fads and fashions — today, trendy Tee-shirts and aromatherapy oils, yesterday, remnants of calico and bottles of liniment; bingo booths and coconut shies; dartboards and targets to test skill in marksmanship. Everyone strolls from booth to booth, greeting old friends, laughing, gossiping, eating and spending money — they're all part of the fun.

Without a doubt, however, the most exciting events of the day are the horse and ox 'pulls', which display great feats of strength by magnificent animals. A team of two, sometimes four, beasts harnessed or yoked together, draws the heavy weights prescribed by the competition rules. Led by their trainer who shouts 'Pull! Pull!' they haul a sledge with over a ton of concrete blocks on it. 'Heats' are held, gradually increasing the weight for each round, till, panting and snorting, teams are eliminated. Finally, when animals in the last round cannot pull another inch, distances are measured and the winning team announced. Farmers take great pride in owning horses or oxen of such phenomenal strength, and although 'everyone ploughed with oxen at one time,' Duncan remarked that nowadays, 'the only ox I see is at Brome Fair' or at Cookshire (where I saw them myself). Heavy horses still pull the plough on a few farms in the area, now owned by French.

Agricultural Shows remain a big attraction in the Eastern Townships, and Cookshire draws an even wider public than ever it did. There are very few entries from 'Scotch' farmers, however, and those who attend nowadays do so with much nostalgia for days gone by. None of the schools that 'gave out flower-seeds' exist in the 1990s, and, although the onset of summer is still marked by a blaze of colour all along Ruth's front porch, the seeds are planted and tended by Ruth herself. Year after year her pots of petunias contrast with the bright white paint with red trim, and the colourful display still catches the eyes of passers-by.

The Annual Picnic

As seen in Chapter 5, the church was the centre of every community in the Eastern Townships. Not only did each one meet the spiritual needs of the congregation, with weekly services, prayer meetings and the twice-yearly communions, but the church also had an important social significance. It drew people together, and, for some families, the only outings they had were to the weekly services and church-related events, such as the annual picnic. According to Johnnie Bard, the picnic held every mid-summer at Hampden Church was the highlight of the church year for the people of Dell and the nearby hamlets.[37] As youngsters, Johnnie and his contemporaries were quite content with the wholesome fare of the farm kitchen, but they all looked forward to being treated to 'every variety of food…especially the home-made ice-cream.' It was a community effort, made on the site 'with cream from Norman Doak's creamery in Milan' The ice-cream machine and all the ingredients would arrive, and after the rock salt, ice, and cream were in place, 'folk took turns to wind the handle of this obstinate mechanical contraption.' Nevertheless, the end product was worth waiting for, as ice-cream was a very special treat in the days before refrigeration.

After the picnic (and perhaps a little rest), the remainder of the day was spent playing sports. Johnnie recalled highlights such as tug-of-war, hop-step-and-jump, and weight lifting, and remarked that 'everyone joined in, even the minister.'[38]

By the 1990s, the annual picnic had evolved into a rather different event. The small communities now join forces to organise one big picnic for the entire area, ('it makes more sense…'), held on a farm at the edge of Scotstown. Each July, the area becomes Mecca for returning Townshippers of Scottish extraction. They are warmly welcomed for the four-day reunion and programme of social events, which include a ceilidh, a dinner-dance, a church service and a picnic. In sharp contrast to Johnnie Bard's day, however, the vast majority of those in attendance are between the ages of sixty and ninety; most of the sporting events have been replaced by side-shows and nostalgic photographic exhibitions; more relaxed games (such as horse-shoe throwing in a long sand-pit) are available for anyone willing to have a go; and pipers, dancers and singers are imported from Montreal and the Maritimes.

The final celebration of the four-day event is held on the Sunday, when the ceremony known as the 'Kirkin' of the Tartan' is combined with a religious service. When I attended in 1992 there were approximately two hundred people from all over Canada and the USA, all gathered to celebrate their forebears. At the entrance of the ground where they all assembled was a huge banner proclaiming a hundred thousand welcomes in Gaelic: *CEUD MILE FAILTE* — the phrase may be common enough at Scottish events the world over, but, in Quebec, such a banner contravenes the official language policy. My fieldwork notebook recorded my impressions of the day:

Led by a piper, the procession advanced onto the ground set aside for the the Kirkin' of the Tartans — first the Saltire and the Maple Leaf flags, then a parade of over forty tartan banners on long flag-poles, each carried by a member or representative of the clan, many dressed in tartan, some in shorts and sandals. They stood in an impressive line, a blessing was said, and when they were all seated, the service began. Guest minister was an elderly Scot (?Ayrshire) who had been minister of Scotstown church (c. 1962?) He was a very good speaker, though the amplification/P.A. system that had been set up via a car battery increased the volume somewhat at the expense of the clarity. (Is nobody else nostalgic for those powerful voices that relied upon good projection? He could have done it, I'm sure, but the P.A. was all set up, and that's the way it is these days.) His short address to the children was especially engaging — the story of Bruce and the spider.

In his sermon, he began by emphasising the rich heritage of the Scots, then stated the characteristics of the early settlers — God-fearing people with clear values; strict adherence to Sabbath observances; etc. 'They reared their families on the Word of God, the Shorter Catechism, and the 3Rs.'

He spoke of their high moral standards, (with more than a hint of contrast to today's lack of them), and so on. It was a good, old-fashioned sermon, (complete with hell-fire and damnation) — well over half an hour, and though nobody could make the usual church complaint about hard pews, some began to feel uncomfortable in the hot sunshine.

Meanwhile, even as he spoke, there were small children and young people bathing in the river behind him — quite a contrast (I thought) to those very days of which he spoke and to the early photos I had seen of sombre outdoor services. After the sermon there was congregational singing and a solo by a guest singer from New Brunswick — a Gaelic version of Amazing Grace to a bagpipe accompaniment. After the benediction, the religious part was over and the picnic began.

People sat around in groups of families and friends, shared picnics and visited each other in a relaxed, friendly atmosphere. Part of the field had been set aside for a pipe-band recital and display from the 78th Fraser Highlanders who had come from Montreal. They are well turned out in their 18th century uniforms, (swords, pistols and all) and they practise tight discipline which is reflected in their band playing (including harmony sets and quartets), Highland dancing (especially the broadswords), and their displays of weaponry with a demanding rifle-loading routine. They were very well received by the crowd.

Around 4 p.m. people began to drift away and to say 'Goodbyes' to friends, some of whom had travelled hundreds of miles and would do so again 'next year, God willing.'

We went home with Ruth to Milan; so did her son, Wesley, her sister Bernice (home from Ontario), Bernice's son Norman (from New York), a friend Charles (home on holiday from Ontario and New York), and cousin Shirley MacAulay (from Saskatchewan, of Milan parents and with very strong kinship ties to the place) and Duncan McLeod. Quite a houseful, and Ruth wouldn't have had it otherwise — her kitchen full, one last tea together before the first visitors headed for home.

The Annual Church Picnic has turned into the Annual Scotstown Reunion, planned well in advance by a hard-working committee. New features have appeared, notably the *Kirkin' of the Tartans* which is gathering its own mythology not only in Quebec but in many parts of North America.[39] The original idea dates back only to the Second World War when members of the St. Andrew's Society of Washington, D.C. brought tartan banners to church for a ceremonial blessing by the Chaplain of the U.S. Senate, Peter Marshall. About twenty years later, an enthusiastic member of the organising committee of the Grandfather Mountain Highland Games, Murvan 'Scotty' Maxwell, organised a similar event in North Carolina. First held in 1968, the *Kirkin' of the Tartans* was based on the ceremony held in Washington Cathedral. Not only has it become an established part of the Grandfather Mountain Highland Games but it has been adopted by Games and Gatherings all over the United States and Canada [40] A creative blend of tartan and Presbyterianism, the ceremony undoubtedly fulfils the function of affirming Scottishness to the Scots overseas — surrounded by representatives of every clan and sept in the district, individuals can remember their roots, offer a prayer of thanks for Scotland and feel proud of their connection to it.

Old Home Week

Changes in the 'old ways of doing things' are not a recent phenomenon, as customs have been gradually changing ever since the first settlers arrived. By the end of the Second World War it was quite evident that the Gaelic community was rapidly declining and, while nobody could turn the clock back to the time when the area was peopled by Gaels, there was a consensus of opinion that those who remained could at least hold a celebration and invite former residents to come 'home'. And so, early in 1949, a committee was set up to plan for 'Old Home Week' which was to take place 'the last few days of July and the first few days of August', as Harria MacLeod recalled:

We sent out invitations. I was the secretary and I sent out fifteen hundred letters…We had a committee and they brought me names of all the people they wanted to invite to come for Old Home Week — people who were in, or came from, Scotstown, Milan, Gould, Marsboro…or whose family had come from there…originally Gaelic-speaking families. They took a photo of the Gaelic-speakers, about two hundred people, though a few like Kenny were included since they were involved with the organisation.

Since it was decided to hold it on the fairground in Scotstown, residents such as Harria and her husband, Kenny, worked together to prepare for the big event. One committee was responsible for arranging accommodation for visitors, while another planned the entertainment. 'There was a bandstand on the fairground where performances were held. We had bagpipers, dancers, singers…and dancing soirées.' And, as if it had been only a summer ago, Harria and Kenny laughingly recalled how much they had enjoyed the dances: 'Waltzes — and the Military Shoddies [?Schottische] — you trot, take three steps and a hop, three more steps, and a hop, and then you'd gallop around.'

But not everyone considered the *soirées* to be the most memorable aspect of Old Home Week; for some, the main focus was on the church activities. One of the visitors to 'come home' for the week was the Rev. M. M. MacDonald from Ailsa Craig, Ontario, who wrote a long (if sermon-like) letter to the *Sherbrooke Record* (Aug. 24, 1949). After acknowledging the hard work of the committee and the hospitality of the local people he wrote:

> Most gratifying to all concerned was the fact that these Committees gave place on their programs (sic) to Prayer Meetings on Thursday evening and brought their celebrations to a close on Sabbath with services in their churches.
>
> Another feature worthy of mention was the spirit of decorum and respect manifested by one and all, visitors as well as residents. Not one instance of rowdyism or drunkenness did we see during those seven days. It was evident to all that the whole assembly looked upon the occasion, not as a time of boisterous merry-making, but rather an event that called for cool serious reflections…

If the minister could attend the reunions of the 1990s he might be just as gratified to see similar levels of abstemiousness today. Nevertheless, it would not do justice to the spirit of the Gael or the Townshipper to deny that many a friendship is enhanced by the glow of a dram in a glass during the four-day event.

Harria conclude that 'It was the only Old Home Week ever held and it was just in the nick of time because within the next year there were so many people that passed away.'

In 1976, the same year as Harria and Kenny were recorded, Ellen Legendre reflected upon the questions that came up during my visit to her home in Stornoway — not just the ones I posed to Ellen and her brother, P'it, but more importantly the ones that she, in her old age, would have like to have asked her father. Ellen's words summed up the sentiment that so many of her 'good Scotch neighbours' expressed as they attempted to piece together a portrait of Quebec's Gaelic settlers: 'When you're young, you're not so curious and when you grow old, it's too late to enquire.'

Notes

1.   For example, I.F. Grant, *op cit*, p 176.

2.   I.F. Grant, *op cit*, pp. 361 — 62.

3.   BEK 4:B; Kay died in 1978.

4.   Dr Donald MacDonald in <u>Tales and Trad. of the Lews</u>, says the name Zachary [*Sgaire*] is peculiar to the MacAulays of Uig; see p. 58. He has a story of a Zachary MacAulay, tacksman of Valtos, 1712, see pp.42-3; much earlier generation,

5.   A version of the story of Margaret MacLeod and Malcolm MacAulay was recorded by Francis Collinson in Bernera Lewis, in 1954; see *Tocher*, 9, pp. 34–35. There is no mention of Malcolm going to Quebec.

6.   Elizabeth Brandon notes comparisons in French Louisiana; see 'Nicknames' in R.M. Dorson, *Buying the Wind,* pp. 272–73.

7.   Deuteronomy 5, v. 16.

8.   For stories I recorded in Quebec in 1976 see *Cultural Retention,* pp. 93–124.

9.   Interestingly, the term 'jack-knife' does not exist in Lewis, though the object does.

10.   My grandmother told a similar story set in Uig Hotel, Skye, about the devil-with-hoofs playing cards. In his article, 'The Bible of the Folk', Lee Francis Utley discusses a range of secular subjects which people commonly (but erroneously) claim as having Biblical origins. *California Folklore Quarterly,* 1945.

11.   Dancing was (and still is) frowned upon in Lewis some members of the church; Donald MacDonald, *Tolsta Townships*p. 28.

12.   M. Bennett, *Scottish Customs from the Cradle to the Grave,* pp. 98–101; I.F. Grant, *op cit*, pp. 362–64.

13.   By today's standards this may seem unusual, but coated caraway seed, sometimes called *carvey*, was common for cake decoration in Scotland until the 1950s (at least); see Bennett, *op cit*, p. 71.

14.   M. Bennett, *Op cit* , pp. 173–270.

15.   Calum MacLean, 'Death Divination in Scottish Folk Tradition', in *TGSI*, 42(1953 -9), pp. 56–67; John Shaw, *Sgeul gu Latha*, pp. 416–19.

16.   Vance Randolph, who first visited the Ozarks in 1899 and lived there from 1920, recorded many tokens of death among the descendants of pioneers; see *Ozark Magic and Folklore,* pp. 301–310. Equally wide-ranging is the

Newfoundland collection which forms the basis of Violetta Maloney Halpert's article, 'Death Warnings in Newfoundland Oral Tradition', in *Community and Process*, pp. 78–108.

17. *Op cit*, p. 132.

18. Donald MacDonald discusses Lewis funerals in Tolsta Townships, pp. 67–73.

19. Johnnie Bard, op cit, p. 132.

20. F. Marian McNeill, *Hallowe'en: Its Origin, Rites and Ceremonies in the Scottish Tradition*.

21. M. MacLeod Banks, *British Calendar Customs: Scotland*, vol. III, pp. 159–163.

22. The village of Gearanin was, however, almost entirely composed of thatched houses in the 1960s. They were occupied until 1973.

23. Johnnie 'Bard' MacLeod, op cit, p. 164.

24. Special Collection, Bishop's University, Aug. 18, 1982. Sheet 7.

25. 'Tolsta bho Thuath', *The Stornoway Gazette*, 21:9:51 and tape-recording in the School of Scottish Studies Archive, 1978; I.F. Grant, *op cit*, pp. 360–61; M. Bennett, *The Last Stronghold*, pp. 115–117.

26. The term Quarter Day is widely applied to the first day of every *raithe* (season), thus bringing Gaelic Scotland into line with the rest of the United Kingdom.

27. M. Bennett, 'Weather Sayings from Banffshire', *Tocher*, 47, p 310; Robert Chambers, *Popular Rhymes of Scotland*, pp. 365–67; Banks, *op cit,*, vol. II, pp. 157–58. Other variants, see Roy Palmer, *Britain's Living Folklore*, p. 157.

28. Scotland has variants such as 'First comes Candlemas, Then the new moon, The next Tuesday after that is Fasterne'en' (Shrove Tuesday).

29. Banks, *op cit*, Vol. I, pp. 40–46.

30. As children we were told that rolling our eggs was a symbol of the stone that was rolled from Christ's tomb.

31. The Presbyterian church does not generally observe the five Sundays after Easter that lead up to Ascension Day and Whit Sunday.

32. Since people generally do not believe all the so-called 'beliefs' about the weather, folklorist Carl W. von Sydow proposed they should be labelled by the term *dites* (*Selected Papers on Folklore*, pp. 106–126). See also H. Halpert's discussion in *A Folklore Sampler from the Maritimes*, pp. 113–116.

33. *Tocher*, 47, p. 310; Robert Chambers, *Book of Days,* Vol. II, pp. 61-64.

34. Roy Palmer, *op cit* p. 156.

35. From various conversations and Johnnie Bards *Memoirs of Dell*, p. 127.

36.   Lee F. Uttley, 'The Bible of the Folk', *California Folklore. Quarterly*, Vol. 4, Jan. 1945.

37.   In Scotland the Department of Agriculture operates the same principle in the crofting townships.

38.   *Op cit,* p. 125.

39.   Gerald Redmond illuminates the place of sport among Scottish emigrant communities in *The Caledonian Games in Nineteenth-Century America*. Since the 1850s, all of the sports remembered by Johnnie Bard were established in the official programmes of events at Caledonian Games across Canada and the U.S.A. (e.g., Montreal, in 1857; Redmond, p. 59) Furthermore, it was not unusual for ministers to have a keen interest in these sports, as the Presbyterian College in Princeton, N.J. (training base for many of the Quebec ministers) had a Scottish president who, with Scottish gymnast George Goldie, held Caledonian Games and encouraged training in athletics (*op cit*. pp. 16–17).

40.   At one Highland Games in the U.S.A. I heard someone say that the ceremony dates back to Culloden (1746) . I also received a letter of enquiry from Ontario asking if I knew how soon after Culloden the first ceremony took place — over two hundred years is the accurate (if disappointing) reply.

41.   From conversation with Donald MacDonald (Edinburgh and North Carolina) and the official programme *Grandfather Mountain Highland Games and Gathering of Scottish Clans,* July 1996, pp. 23 and 43.

10

Conclusions

At the start of the First World War, when there were approximately two thousand five hundred Gaels in the Marsboro area, Angus Morrison was four years old. At that age and at that time, it was not unusual to be 'quite unaware that there was any other language in the world but Gaelic'.[1] Today, Angus is the only Gaelic-speaker left. His children and most of his grandchildren are bi-lingual in English and French, yet, when he visited Harris a few years ago, Angus was just as fluent in Gaelic as anyone on the island.

While 'céilidhing' with the Morrisons in August, 1992, I was taken for a drive by Angus and Mary to the site of the old family homestead at Cruvag settled by the family in 1888 — the same farm where, in 1942, Angus and Mary had begun their married life. 'Oh! We worked hard, and we were as happy — we were happier, I think, than the people today.' I had already been privileged to record two generations of Morrisons, to see photographs of five generations, and thus the drive to Cruvag would complete the picture. The main road through Marsboro (renamed Marston in 1997) is wide and paved, so the real 'tour' began at the turn-off into the gravel road:

Angus: [driving along] Now this is the road going to Cruvag. That was our neighbours, [he points to the place] the MacDermitts [nothing but thick woods to be seen].

Mary: That's where he went to school, up there, on the right hand side. [more thick trees; but we have not yet reached the place]

Angus: No, we didn't come to it, Mary. [pause — no wonder she doesn't recognise it; I can't see anything but trees] Now when my father went to Cruvag there was no road here; there was nothing, right through the woods. But the woods weren't so thick as they are now…bigger trees and fewer. [We drive on] Now that's the hill, see. See the hill? Now, the schoolhouse was in here.

MB: Oh, my, you can't see a thing today…If you went in the woods there would you find the foundation?

Angus: Yes, yes, I could…I think we'll do that. [we stop, get out, and find no trace of it in the thick bush. We resume the drive]…Now, just look at this hill — see? [we come to the bottom of a straight, very steep hill]…Imagine! My

father going to Cruvag and no road or nothing. Oh, it took them a long time
[to make the road]. ... Imagine! Just imagine the people that came out here; no
road, no animals or nothing. And believe me — [aside] that's going down to a
lumber camp — coming out here with nothing to work with. You had to go
where they [sent you] — they got this farm for nothing, so they had to go
where they'd sent you...they wanted the good old Scotch people...When we
lived in Marsboro, before we sold the farm, there was around fifty-six all Scotch
Gaelic families...And [now] there's nobody living on this road. Look how nice
it is...That's a steep hill, eh?

MB: You can say that again! In the winter time it must have been something.

Angus: *Ooooh!* We had to climb a long, very steep hill, steeper than this...You'd
go in the bottom, then you'd go into a gully, and in the winter, the first of the
snow, it was all piling in that gully, and we had to give it up, and we'd go
through my cousin's [farm]. My cousin lived up here. [Pause; we drive on]
Look at the hills! [Laughs] See the woods they're going through!...It's a big
lumber company, got it now, they make paper — And in the winter we used to
roll the road with the big roller. And it would take four horses...Just the width
of a horse and buggy. When we left the farm [in 1943] it was just wide enough
for a car. You'd be lucky, if we'd meet another car on the road, well, you'd
maybe have to back up half a mile to go by.

MB: But it's a pretty wide road [nowadays] for a dirt road, isn't it? Two trucks
could easily pass now.

Angus: It is. That's why it's so wide, the Government made it wide enough so
that two trucks if they'd meet — they were hauling gravel to make the road —
See how nice and wide it is — the nicest road in the Eastern Townships. This is
better than the highway to Montreal, because the highway to Montreal is all
full of cracks and holes!

MB: [Looking round] It's all woods now, and it was fields one time...

Angus: Yeah, there was a house in there [he points as he drives on] and now
here, we used to have two — no, *five* mail-boxes, right here, one after the other,
and that mail would come from Nantes [Spring Hill] by horse and buggy, in
the olden days, when people didn't have any cars. But in the olden days, they
come from Nantes, right up, this was the end of the road, there was three
families up here, we were in Cruvag, an my cousin, we're going by — I'll show
you where my cousin lived. See! [the 'opening' off the road is almost
indiscernible, it is so overgrown; I ask his name]...*An greusaiche!* yeah, the
shoemaker's house. And there was a road going up here, there was three families
living, about a mile from up here...it's closing in now...[We drive on; noise of
gravel road on tape; finally we stop and get out at the old homestead,
completely overgrown with trees] No, you can't see nothing...
  It breaks my heart to see this —

When we stand at the edge of what was once a huge hayfield, Angus explains that 'in 1943 we sold the farm...We sold it to a woman for lumber... She cut all the lumber off. She had hired men, and they cut the lumber, and when she took all the lumber off the farm she sold it to somebody else.'

Every 'Scotch farm', every 'Scotch community' has a different story to tell. Again and again people ask 'But why? Whatever happened?' And, having discussed these very question among themselves on countless occasions, the ageing Scotch population wearies of trying to explain. They usually begin by emphasising how strong the Gaelic language once was — and, surprising as this may now seem to an 'outsider', Gaels instantly recognise the 'opening line', having used it themselves in Skye, Lewis, Barra, Mull, Cape Breton, Queensland or wherever the language is, or was, to be found. Next comes reference to the culture that went hand-in-glove with the language — the songs, stories and general way of life. Nowadays, however, fewer and fewer people can comprehend how much their forebears valued Gaelic culture and, surrounded by a world of materialism, may ask the question 'What do we mean by culture?'

Scottish historian and literary critic Angus Calder begins his insightful collection of essays, *Revolving Culture,* by stating that 'all culture derives from place...All culture derives from people'.[2] In the context of Quebec I would agree with Calder and reiterate my own introductory remark, that the mosaic of culture that makes up modern Canada cannot be understood without a knowledge of the place that gave birth to the culture of its first settlers. While Calder does not define the concept, Anthony P. Cohen, Professor of Anthropology at the University of Edinburgh, summarises several decades of debate among anthropologists seeking to clarity the meaning of culture. In Cohen's essay, 'Belonging: the experience of culture', he concludes that even the most prominent participants were 'not very helpful' in producing an accurate definition of 'culture'. He himself suggests that it is 'a field of meaning' of which individuals may not even be aware until they come up against a culture that is different from their own.[3] Each one of us, then, has a choice: to explore the meaning of culture for ourselves, or to look no further, contenting ourselves with the modern values of homogenised consumerism. Fortunately (from my point of view), the avenues of discussion remain open.

Angus Calder poses the question 'How did a country [Scotland] which apparently stood on the periphery of European culture contribute so much to Europe's Enlightenment (and to the diffusion of it in America)?'[4] As he implies, we must look outside of our immediate environment before we notice that, on a national and international level, we are surrounded by reminders that *culture* is highly regarded, and deemed to be universally desirable. Though it is almost impossible to define, perhaps, as in the case of love, if we have to ask what it is, we may never recognise it in any case.

In his introduction to *Scotland: A Concise Cultural History,* Paul Scott considers Scotland's contribution to European culture, thus world culture, and, in so doing, sharpens the focus on images of culture itself. Citing several examples from Scotland's impressive range, he observes: 'This is a very diverse culture with great strengths in many fields, from engineering to folk song, or from philosophy to dance.' Examples could fill a hall of fame — James Watt, John Logie Baird, Robert Burns, Donnchadh Bàn, David Hume, Scott Skinner, Robert Adam, Charles Rennie Macintosh, Dancie Reid and so on. Just as important to Canadian culture, however, are the less well known facts from Quebec: there was Dòmhnuill A' Mhuilleir, whose extraordinary skills as a millwright were of crucial importance to the development of the Eastern Townships; there were Murchadh Buidhe and Angus MacKay whose songs and poems expressed the tender love for an infant, the pain of parting, and man's inhumanity to man; and there were the fireside philosophers and the village-hall dancers whose names are remembered only in local anecdotes. They may lack world fame, but each holds a place among the 'cultural greats' of this part of Canada, where the Gaelic language was once the vehicle that transported their cultural values from one generation to the next.

In attempting to analyse the dramatic shift in language and culture in the Eastern Townships, I would suggest that, expressed in the most simple terms, there were forces exerted from two separate directions — first and foremost, *internally* (from within the community), and secondly, though eventually far more powerfully, *externally* (from outwith the community). Often there were several factors operating simultaneously, making it impossible to discuss each point in exact chronological order.

From the outset, the education system mirrored the deliberate policy enforced in Gaelic Scotland of employing English-speaking teachers for all schools. Not surprisingly, therefore, even before the turn of the century, there were clear indications that, within the group, Hebridean culture was not valued as highly as the Anglo-centric culture that pressed in upon them in the guise of 'Progress'. By the late 1800s some of the Gaelic poets were composing in English, partly because they had had no education in Gaelic literacy, and partly because English could 'speak louder' and claim a wider audience.

When Township bard Angus Mackay (Oscar Dhu) published his epic, *Donald Morrison, the Canadian Outlaw: A Tale of the Scottish Pioneers* in 1892, he wrote in the preface that 'The orthography of the [relatively few] Gaelic words...may be defective from a literary standpoint as I have followed the style of the late Josh Billings', (a Canadian humorist of the time who had a reputation for writing in dialect and spelling phonetically).[5] Included in MacKay's collection of poems *By Trench and Trail in Song and Story*, published in 1918, was his composition 'Guard the Gaelic: An Exhortation to the Gael'.

In 1976 Donald Morrison of Scotstown sang it from memory, introducing it with 'Oscar Dhu also wrote a song to the Gaelic language — Oscar Dhu's Exhortation to the Gaels'…My uncle was the publisher's agent…and Angus Mackay, Oscar Dhu, was one of the big sellers. And [my uncle]'d sell amongst the Scotch people that went to Vermont.' [Donald begins to sing]:

Is it not our bounden right
To uphold with all our might,
And with tongue and pen to fight
For our native Gaelic?

Guard the language known to Eve,
Ere the Serpent did deceive —
And the last one we believe,
Mellow, matchless Gaelic!

Pity the disloyal clown
Who will dwell a while in Town,
And returning wear a frown
If he hears the Gaelic.

'Tis amusing to behold
Little misses ten years old,
When they leave the county fold
How they lose the Gaelic.

Some gay natives of the soil,
Cross 'the line' a little while[6]
And returning, deem it style
To deny the Gaelic.

Lads and lassies in their teens
Wearing airs of kings and queens —
Just a taste of Boston beans
Makes them lose their Gaelic!

They return with finer clothes,
Speaking 'Yankee' through their nose
That's the way the Gaelic goes —
Pop! goes the Gaelic.

Though the so-called 'Tony set'[7]
Teach them quickly to forget,
They will all be loyal yet
To their mother Gaelic.

Then abjure such silly pride
Cast the ragged thing aside —

Let your mongrel 'English' slide
Rather than the Gaelic.

What a dire calamity
And how lonesome we would be
If our honoured Seannachie
Failed to charm in Gaelic!

Better far the 'mother tongue' —
Language in which mother sung
Long ago, when we were young —
Ever tender Gaelic!

And Buchanan[8], how could he
Sell his soda or his tea
On the side of 'Talamh a' righ'[9]
If he lost his Gaelic?

Also Merchant Edward Mac
Would not sell so much tomac[tobacco]
If his stock was found to lack
Lusty Lewis Gaelic!

And Pennoyer[10], what would you
At the Gould post office do
When you'd hear from not a few
'Ciamar a tha thu fhéin an diugh?'[11]
If you lost your Gaelic?

Little Donald with the plaid[12]
O'er his burly[13] shoulder laid,
Would go dancing in the shade,
And his glory soon would fade
If he lost his Gaelic.

From O'Groat's to Land's End too
What would brother Scotsman do —
But a single language know,
If they lost their Gaelic?

What would then become of those
Poems grand in rhyme or prose,
Which in stately measure flows
From Beinn Doran's spotless snows!
'Cabar Féidh' — the best that grows — [14]
'Fhir a bhàta' — how he rows!
What, I ask, would happen those
If we lost the Gaelic?

Then uphold the magic tongue
Which through mystic Eden rung
When Creation still was young —
Language in which Adam sung
To his Eve, Earth's first love song;
When the morning stars were flung
Into space, where since they've clung —
Ancient, Glorious Gaelic![15]

Since it was natural for Donald to use his song as a focus for discussion — indeed that was the point of singing it in the first place — in the style of the old *taigh céilidh,* he gave his opinions on the subject of language-use. His experience had been typical of most of his generation: born to Gaelic-speaking parents and brought up a very small community, where, despite its remoteness and cultural cohesion, his parents were of the opinion that their children would 'get on better in life' if English were their first language. And so they spoke English to the children and Gaelic to each other, a pattern which became as familiar to Donald's generation in the Eastern Townships as it was to many of my own generation in Gaelic Scotland.

A widespread change in attitude to traditional language-use began to emerge when, as in the Highlands of Scotland, nagging doubt threatened many families where Gaelic had been the mother tongue. Parental concern may well have been expressed in terms of 'progress', for, by that time, the second generation had succeeded beyond the prime concern of the first settlers, whose aim was not so much 'getting on in the world', as surviving in it. The sweat and toil of traditional practices had stood them in good stead in the past and so had their language; all were taken for granted as they had been for generations. It was not until attitudes began to change that anyone seemed to comment on language-use, such as Johnnie 'Bard' MacLeod in his *Memoirs of Dell*: describing a neighbour of his, John J. MacDonald (born in Tolsta, Quebec, later moved to Dell), MacLeod remarked that he 'spoke Gaelic better than English…Years later he journeyed to Lewis and brought back Annie' who became his wife, and 'fitted into the life of Dell like a pocket in a shirt…together they raised an entirely Gaelic-speaking family.'[16] To Annie and John MacDonald, speaking their mother tongue was the natural thing to do; there was no question of having to learn English to operate the family farm in Dell, for, when the children went to school, they would (and did) 'pick it up with the rest of them'. Of their generation, it appears that Annie and John MacDonald (born before the turn of the century), along with a few families such as the Morrisons at Cruvag, the MacDonalds in Milan (Muriel's people) and the MacKenzies in Scotstown (Jean MacIver's people), were becoming the exception rather than the rule.[17]

Looking back over half a century of language shift, Donald Morrison, like most of his contemporaries, firmly believed that the decision taken by his parents' generation was one which not only deprived them of a birthright, but actually disadvantaged them in life. Though he married a Gaelic-speaker from Lewis, Annie Burnside, Donald's experience of adult learning did not make up for the lost opportunity of childhood, and, even more seriously, it forced him to speak English to his own children. As Russell MacIver, another victim of language shift, put it, 'Well, that was a mistake; a bad one too! We'd learn English, [when we went to school] I'm sure!'

Abandoning the mother tongue was, and is, the most drastic example of 'undervaluing culture'. Nevertheless, there were other signals which indicated the emerging attitude to the traditional culture of the Gael. Taken individually, one small example may seem insignificant, but taken collectively, they are symptomatic of a lack of confidence:

> [Muriel's mother] brought these wooden egg cups [when she came over] from the Old Country, from Keose, and they smelled of peat. And she used to scrub them to get the smell of peat off them. It was awful [that she used to do that]! I'd like them to have the smell of peat on them today!...She just didn't like the smell or perhaps everybody else didn't like the smell!

'Aunt Annie's' loyalty to Scotland, Gaeldom and Lewis was never in question — she was enormously proud of all of them — but it was important to her how others perceived her cultural origins. Thus, for Aunt Annie's generation, the preferred choice of items characteristic of Hebridean homes might be fine bone china, embroidered table-linen, woollen sweaters, tweed blankets and books. Similarly in Gaelic Scotland, in my late teens, I had Gaelic-speaking friends of my own age who, when they left home for college, seemed embarrassed to be viewed as Highland, Gaelic, or crofting. Today, thirty years on, they assert all of these images, now that it is more desirable to be from a Highland-Gaelic-crofting background — there is even prestige attached to being any or all of these, and, for some, there is employment. Unimaginable as it was during the sixties, now in the nineties Gaelic has 'made it' to the Big Screen, the disco floor, the night club and even the Opera House. Having watched the dramatic shift of attitude through the 60s, 70s and 80s from another viewpoint, Angus Calder observes that the 'Gaelic revival was not exceptional in a Europe where Basques and Sardinians were asserting their linguistic peculiarity...But the stature of Sorley MacLean, the Gaelic poet...became quite extraordinary, as Lowlanders, taking note of his international fame, honoured the major living exponent of a dying tongue which they had often been brought up to despise.'[18]

In Quebec, however, it was not until it was far too late, and the situation had changed irreversibly, that an entire generation of partial-and non-Gaelic speakers could see that in this 'language game' their parents had actually scored a series of 'own goals'. Not that their French neighbours insisted that they should speak English — far from it. The Gaels made the initial move themselves, ensuring that the 'other team', the French in this case, would eventually win, hands down. Little did anyone realise at the time, that the Gaelic language would slide into such decline that there would be no going back. Furthermore, those who denied their mother tongue in favour of English, never imagined that it would not be that language which would ultimately take over the region. That fact was not to dawn upon them till much later.

Aside from language, the major factor that set the Hebridean settlers apart from their French-Canadian neighbours was Religion, but, despite all the theological and social differences between the Presbyterian Gaels and the Catholic Québecois, these differences cannot account for loss of language or culture except in cases of intermarriage. According to John L. Campbell, whose research in Nova Scotia focused on a similar issue sixty years ago, a more significant cause of language loss was the split within the Protestant church itself: 'I was told many times in 1932 and 1937 that the formation of the United Church of Canada had been a severe setback to Gaelic, as Gaelic congregations had joined [the Union] and were then without Gaelic ministers, while Gaelic ministers had refused to join and were left without congregations.'[19]

Inevitably intermarriage became a fact of life for both the Scotch and the French, requiring both sides to make enormous adjustments within families and communities. Only Maryann Morrison's generation saw the beginning of the ongoing process, when, in the 1890s, there were very few French-speakers in her home community and each accepted the other as good neighbours do: 'We didn't notice no difference. They were very nice. When they would meet a Scotchman on the road they'd tip their hat for them…which was very nice.' Maryann based her regard on personal qualities, irrespective of language or religion and, in a sense, was put to the test when her own children became adults — she and her husband 'R.E.' were among the first generation to face the issue of intermarriage, as two of their sons married French Roman Catholic girls. Maryann remembered when she first had to consider this possibility:

> When Sam came home from Montreal to Megantic — you know, they always take home their girlfriends…and Sam came home with this girlfriend, and in the morning we were talking like this, and he said: 'How do you like my girlfriend?'
> 'Is she French?'
> ''Se gu dearbh,' he said, ''se gu dearbh.' [*That's for sure.*]
> But we didn't find no difference. She's just like yourself and myself, and she likes to go to meetings and attend all the meetings. But she goes to her own,

she keeps her own [religion] in her mind. I don't blame her. She was brought up to it. But she don't interfere with us at all, at all.

When her next son, Angus, married, he and his French wife Mary followed family tradition and spent the first few years with Angus's parents, and, as Mary remarked, she even began to understand Gaelic as the Morrisons continued to use it as their everyday language. Thus, neither intermarriage nor religion precipitated the change from Gaelic to English.

Availability of work was, and is, a huge factor in dictating movement of population; thus, in the late 1870s and 80s, when the Canadian Pacific Railway was being built, it was inevitable that more 'outsiders' came in. Some were English-speakers from 'across the line', others were Québecois who worked alongside the Gaels. Naturally, some made their homes in railway towns such as Milan, which is the highest point on the railway east of the Rockies. By the time John MacKenzie moved there, at the age of twenty-three, 'there were exactly four French-speaking families in Milan' in 1915.

During those years there was also a steady movement of young people, mostly men, who 'went out west'. To begin with it was often for a sense of adventure, to make a 'quick dollar', that they went. Some went to look for better land, for, even when John Ramsay of Kildalton visited the area in 1870, he sensed discontent among some of the Lewismen who seemed to have forgotten just how bad their situation on the Isle of Lewis had been. He observed that they were already focusing on the disadvantages of the land granted to them by the British North American Land Company.[20] Predictably, some decided not to return, as there were usually brothers and sisters to carry on the family farm, and, in any case, many of the farms were not big enough or fertile enough to be sub-divided among several sons, so there was less reason to return to the Eastern Townships. Sometimes a sister would join her brother out west, or she would go 'to the Boston States' to work in domestic service. Even by the 1920s, the 'migrant labour' pattern common during the years of 'haying in Vermont' (Chapter 3), had evolved into one that was much more permanent, as former school-teacher and local historian Annie I. Sherman records:

> When Henry Ford started to make his Ford motor car, he attracted many young men from Lingwick to work in his plant in Detroit. His $5.00-a-day wage was good news and big news at that time. Many left home to seek employment with him. Large numbers of Scottish families settled in Detroit and the Lewis Society was formed where they met together regularly. Many of these families did well for themselves.[21]

Wherever they went to earn a wage, the hard workers and adventurers could always go back home for a holiday, and could usually help to support the family by sending money or the occasional parcel of clothing or other goods. The pattern was also very common among the older French families, who, like the Gaels, enjoyed the occasional boost to household expenses, as Oscar Dhu wrote in his poem 'Christmas in Quebec':

> Ma Joe sen' me twenty dollar,
> Jus' las' week from Lowhell, Mass.[22]

Mary Morrison, whose family, *les Martins*, moved into the area before she was born, estimated that this ebb and flow of population began before the turn of the century:

> In Stornoway where I was born we were across from some Morrisons — when we [my family] went to Stornoway it was all Scotch development...And the people in Stornoway they start[ed] to move away. When the kids would get older they would move to the States to work, or go out west where there was work and an easier life.

As long as it was only·'the odd one', most families were big enough to sustain a comfortable balance between those at home and those away, and could maintain the continuity necessary to the upkeep of home and farm.

During the 1914–18 War, however, all this was to change. So many young 'Scotchmen' enlisted that it was not just individual families but entire communities that suffered the drastic consequences.[23] To begin with, nobody could possibly have seen the far-reaching effects; the call-up of men to fight for the Old Country was strongly influenced by the fact that most of the immigrants felt loyal to the homeland. Optimistically they signed up, thinking it would be short-term, and that life would be back to normal as soon as it was over. Even the bitter experience of the First World War did not dampen the spirits of those who enlisted for the Second, as veteran Bill Young explained:

> Another big thing was the two World Wars...And Scotstown suffered heavily in the First War. At Ypres...and places like that, they lost a tremendous amount of men. And then in the last war, you had the same thing — you had a heavy enlistment all through there, 'English-speaking' again, you see. And then one entire regiment was wiped out at Hong Kong, eh? Well, that was fellows I went to school with. Well, the whole class I went to school with were in that thing — my brother-in-law...I don't know how many. Then of course, I, being raised in a Scottish district, thought I would go to Montreal and join the Black Watch; but fortunately, or unfortunately, I got side-tracked and joined an artillery unit. My brother joined the Black Watch and he was taken prisoner at Dieppe, (he's living up in St. Catherine's, now). So, there you had it again! Our whole high school classes that I went to school with disappeared out of the picture — they were killed or taken prisoner. Disappeared. There were no younger people left to take over.

As was the case in crofting and farming communities in Britain, not everyone over the age of conscription was called up, but large families were suddenly reduced to having one son at home, who would find himself with ageing parents and the full responsibility of running the farm. For example, in the case of Maryann and 'R.E.' Morrison, by then in their late sixties, their busy household, which also included a very elderly, bed-ridden grandparent, had to be run with the help of only one son, Angus, and a daughter, Eva. When Angus got married and brought his new bride to his parents' homestead the young couple took over more and more of the heavy work. Nevertheless, when Angus and Mary began to have their own family, Mary's rôle had to adjust according to their needs. With no brothers left to help with the ploughing, wood-cutting or 'men's work', and no sisters to help care for animals or lend a hand with planting and harvesting as they once did — to say nothing of the cooking, baking, housework, wool and needlework — when R.E.'s health began to decline it was decided it would be too much for the younger couple to manage all the farming chores and the care of their ageing parents besides. In 1943 they made their decision to sell the farm, little knowing that the buyer had no intention of farming, but would, instead, run a lumber business, which, even fifty years later, and under new ownership, is still profitable. Ironically, much of the new timber is cut from the area which once was fields and meadows, cleared by labour and toil by the first settlers, which, after years of being abandoned and neglected, is now 'all growed over'.[24]

At the same time as Scotch farms were being sold, there was an increasing demand for land by French from north of the area, mainly Comté Beauce, usually from large farming families without enough land to sub-divide between sons. Caught in a 'land-squeeze', they began to buy up the land as fast as it became available — 'you wouldn't blame them, and land was cheap.' At first it appeared to be 'just the occasional farm' that went up for sale, because the 'old folks could no longer manage it and the young ones had moved away.'[25]

Among the Gaels there was also another scenario, which began with the departure of the younger generation to get a university or college education. Until the First World War only young men who were training for the ministry had the privilege of a tertiary education, but, in the years that followed, many more young people, 'even the girls', were given the opportunity, as former school-teachers Muriel Mayhew, Ruth Nicolson and Bernice Laurila could attest. Not only were there teachers, but also nurses, doctors, lawyers and engineers whose professions took them outwith the area. When it came time for the old folk to hand over the working of the land to the young, they found that they had no willing candidates for the job. Some of 'the girls' *did* come back to teach or nurse, but generally they married into families whose sons were needed in similar circumstances. One by one, almost inevitably, 'Scotch farms' went up for sale, till, by the 1950s, the pattern had escalated so rapidly that there was no going back.

Meanwhile, the older, already established French families, such as the Legendres in Stornoway and the Poulins who kept the Post Office in Milan, were also educated in English-speaking schools. In discussing this subject, Ellen Legendre and her brother Alphonse ['Pit'] gave the French perspective of 'what happened'. They began with education, never doubting the fact that their parents believed the schooling offered by the Scotch to be better than that available in the French schools:

> [There was] a big difference in education...there certainly was. And our Bishop there in Sherbrooke — he came here when my sister died — he himself said that he thought that the good part of us, or the good spirit, came from the Scotch people.

After their elementary schooling in Stornoway, Ellen and her sisters were sent as boarders to the convent school in Coaticook.[26] Ellen later trained as a nurse while her brothers were trained at home to take over the family business. Pit added that in those days their Gaelic neighbours 'were much better set up than the French,' and could afford to send their children to 'places like MacDonald College in Montreal.' He confirmed that this eventually led to the fact that 'they sold out — The French people from Beauce started to come and buy their farms. The first thing we knew we had lost our good Scotch people...'[27]

Steadily and relentlessly, changes began to affect the society and the landscape, a process that continued till the 1970s, and when I interviewed the Legendres there was only one Gaelic-speaker left in Stornoway. (There are none today.) When I asked Ellen Legendre if she sensed any resentment between the French and the Gaels, she said that there was absolutely none in the early days when her family built the mills, she felt none her own youth, and (making no comment on the intervening years) she concluded that there is 'none today because there are no Gaels left to feel resentful.' Then, emphasising the accord between the French and the Scotch, she told of the time her father, then Mayor of Stornoway, insisted that 'as long as there is a Legendre in the town it will remain STORNOWAY out of respect for their good Scotch neighbours.' (Chapter 2)

After the Second World War, 'when the boys came home', the Canadian Government introduced a policy that also affected settlement of land. By way of reward or compensation for 'fighting for king and country', returning servicemen were offered sizable plots of land on which they could build homes 'and a better future'. For the Eastern Townships the location was Lennoxville and, though it was fifty miles from the core of the Scotch settlement, undoubtedly there were many factors in favour of this scheme. After six years of war and absence from civilian life, morale was low and there was a need for people start anew. Looking at parts of Lennoxville today, where war veterans and their young wives settled, no-one could doubt the energy that must have driven couples such as Bill and Kay Young, Herbert and Muriel Mayhew, Gordon and Lois Matheson (all of whom built homes in Atto Street). With due credit to the government, the project succeeded in its aims, and, content with their new surroundings, these families could still keep a link with their origins by returning to Milan, Scotstown, and the Megantic area whenever family or community attracted them.

From his home in Lennoxville, still surrounded by most of the friends who had created the 'new' neighbourhood, Bill Young looked back over the years that had changed the face of the area he had known as a youth in Scotstown. Though several of the points he raised were also made by the Legendres, Bill's perspective summarises the views held by many of the 'older families':

> And then, if you stop and figure, or you could look at the records of the younger folks born and brought up there, of Scottish descent, from both periods, like after the First War and after the Second War. Before the Second War, there was a tremendous amount of talent went out of this area. There were schoolteachers, doctors — all kinds of them graduating in that particular period. Nurses — and they just spread and no matter where you go in Canada today, and parts of the United States, you run across people and their origin is Megantic. It's tremendous, you know.
>
> Well, after the First World War, everyone [who wanted to leave] went to the States — practically all of them. I had an uncle that was in the army and he came back — he was taken prisoner at Ypres [laughs] and after the war he came back and he stayed here a year, right, in Canada, and then he went right to the States…He went to Detroit. Detroit was the big industrial centre then. It was springing up, eh? And then, he drifted from there to California. Now you'll find a lot of people in California from around these parts. And he died there, eh, five or six years ago. So wherever you go — my brother's in Ontario; my wife's sister is in Ontario; uh, people from all through here are all through Ontario.
>
> MB: Do the Scots who are left resent the French take-over of their area in any way?
>
> BY: Well, no, because the older Scottish people, they get along very well with the French, in the beginning. You see, there was no such thing [as resentment]. The Scottish have always seemed to be able to get along, no matter where they went, which is perhaps one of their strong points, eh? They could settle anywhere, and — No, they didn't [resent the French]! When I was a child there were French and there were Scotch. Oh, let us put it in a bigoted way — we thought we were the better race and we kept it that way! [laughs] But there was

no, there was no down to, you know, any of this hatred, or anything [that we are beginning to detect in the society of the 1970s]. We associated with French kids; we played with them; we chatted. And there were French families that learned to speak the Gaelic!

MB:…is it possible for you to look back objectively and consider whether or not you were economically better off than the French?

BY: No, no [he implies there was no question but that they were.] We were economically better off in the sense that we received an [advanced] education and they didn't. Now there's the root of the whole evil…The fact that their school system was separate from ours and they were under the domination of the church — completely!

MB: But did the Scots not have to memorise the Bible and the Catechism — ?

BY: Yeah, we had to have that thoroughly ingrained in us…but the teacher was boss [as opposed to the priest or the church]. She held the sway, and if we came home with stories about being picked on, we were picked on when we got home. they'd say, 'Go back to school; it's a place for you to learn…while you're there you will learn, or else! 'You've got to have discipline. I don't care who you are. This permissive society is for the birds! You've got to have discipline. You've got to have it. Well there again, we've fallen far down the ladder…

One by one the small schools originally set up by the Scotch settlers closed down and the old churches began to change hands. The Presbyterian Church in Marsboro, for example, was sold to the Catholic community who added a tall spire and several holy statues to the grounds; the one in Megantic was also sold, and eventually became a restaurant-cum-gallery in the 1970s, though by 1993 it was up for sale again, empty, with *'Maison à vendre'* on the door. How could the present-day visitor possibly know that this little brick building was once the place of worship of Gaelic-speaking inhabitants of the town? Only the most elderly Gaels know that it stands as a monument to the overbalancing of their very fragile culture.

The shift in population from Gaels to French had gained momentum so rapidly that nobody of either group seems to remember a stage when there was half-and-half. Suddenly the Gaels were by far in the minority, and the French had taken over so successfully that most did not seem to have any idea that the community they regarded as home had originally been carved out in the mid-19th century by a group of Presbyterians from Scotland. By the 1970s, many families were second and third generation descendants of the incomers from Comté Beauce, who had never even heard of Scotland, far less considered its significance to the land they farmed.

The emerging demographic pattern was further complicated in the late 1960s and early 1970s when a new wave of immigrants appeared, who were regarded by the resident population as 'hippies' or 'back-to-the-landies'. Most were young Canadians from the Montreal area and Americans from 'across the line', children of the 'flower-power' years, discontented with the social climate that contradicted their ideals of peace and goodwill. Many had been students during the years when the Vietnam war prompted thousands of America's conscientious objectors, colloquially known as 'draft-dodgers', to move to Canada. While each had a different story to tell, collective experience suggested that their optimism and hope of creating a new society with greater equality and freedom had evaporated; the 'good life' had gone bad, and many felt a need to get out and start anew. Most were from professional families, and, having chosen not to go down the same road as their parents, had either rejected or abandoned the option of a university education and used the allocated capital to bail out of the social mess.

The local people formed first impressions that fitted the newcomers into the stereotype of the hippy: personal appearance was unconventional (a tendency to 'dress down' rather than 'dress up'); males were bearded and both sexes had long hair; most tended to reject modern inventions (even electricity and the advantages of plumbing); they favoured the horse over the tractor; outside their farms they preferred to travel in vintage vehicles; and they turned up at every auction, community cider-pressing, or bean supper. On their side they had youth, health, strength, determination, a modest amount of capital and a great deal of enthusiasm. Only time would tell if they would 'stay the course', make anything of the recently acquired land, or alter the first impressions of the old-timers.

Since they were my contemporaries — most of us were in our twenties at the time — I got to know several of them while living in Milan. I valued their friendship, not only for the social aspect, but also because they gave me an important insight into their perception of the society into which they had moved. From many discussions, I sensed a keen interest in the history of the area and of individual farms — for example, there was a satisfaction for one newcomer in finding out that his farm at the top of Milan, which has one of the finest views in the Eastern Townships, was originally settled by pioneers from Scotland, a family from the Outer Hebrides, Gaelic-speakers, MacDonalds, whom he came to know as 'Ruth Nicolson's people'. Questions would arise in the course of conversation, so that individuals gradually pieced together a picture of the way of life of the first settlers — where exactly did they come from and why? What was it like for someone of my generation to live on the Isle of Lewis, to go to school there? Did folk learn this skill or that in Quebec or did they bring it with them? The sort of questions this book seeks to answer were woven in and out of my encounters with them, leaving no doubt as to their interest in the culture of their predecessors.

Of those who stayed on, almost all have learned French and many now use French as their everyday language. Their children automatically go to French schools (some would go by choice but, in any case, there are no English schools left in the area), so that they all associate with monoglot French-speaking children, thus reinforcing the place of French in the lives of the second generation. They have integrated well with the local population and, in so doing, individuals have gained more of the insider's view of issues that do, or do not, concern the area. Within their twenty-five years they too have seen many changes — they have watched 'Scotch farms' change hands, sometimes several times over, and point to this quick turn-over as one of the factors that intensifies cultural confusion among the young. 'If you buy a farm from a French family who bought it from a French family, you're not going to know that it was originally owned by a Scotch family. In any case, all of the Scotch families are English-speaking and the average person here is going to think they're *Anglais*' — so runs a typical explanation. While they appreciate the fact that the oldest Scotch and French families have a strong sense of their shared past, they compare the present-day schooling to that of the Legendres and the Poulins, pointing out that their children 'don't really learn anything about Quebec history except that the French were here first.' And so emerges Quebec's biggest political and social issue — separatism. Their teenage children join in and confirm they hear 'a lot about that at school.'

In a paper entitled 'Whose Periodisation? Francophone Historians and the Canadian Past', Peter D. Marshall surveyed school text-books dealing with Canada's history, and, in making a plea for a comprehensive book covering all aspects of the nation's history, he emphatically repeated that there is 'no such book' available for schools. Having studied the material available, he drew attention to particular omissions in Quebec's portrayal of Canadian history, implying that historians of the province have preferred to highlight whatever aspects suit the cause they wish to promote — in this case nationalism. Moulding texts to fit an intended propaganda is, of course, not specific to Quebec, nor is it a recent phenomenon; it is as old as written history — Julius Cæsar gave a biased account of the Gauls; school text-books in Canada portrayed the horrendous slaughter of Newfoundland's Beothick Indians as 'disappearance'; certain European texts are reported to have been re-written to omit contributions made by Jews, and so on. Marshall appeals to historians and academics to come up with a more balanced view for Quebec's school children. Meanwhile, during the past three decades, not a man, woman, or child, Francophone or Anglophone, could fail to have been impressed by the repetition of information centred on Quebec Nationalism and the issues of language and separatism.[28]

Observing recent changes in the light of the social, cultural, and political environment that makes up this part of Quebec today, it is not surprising that the majority of the youngest generation of incomers are nationalists who have no reason to seek out the history of the area. Intensely proud of their French language and culture, and rightly so, to them 'les Anglais' represent an authoritarian, arrogant, superior attitude which has threatened them throughout history. Few have any understanding that Scottish is not English, just as Canadian is not American, and, regarding language and culture as synonymous, have no need to consider that there are worlds of difference between the cultures of England, Scotland, Ireland, Wales, America, Canada, Australia, South Africa, New Zealand, all of which share the common language of English. Of course the French themselves share a language with Switzerland, Belgium, Luxembourg, Morocco, Algeria, Louisiana, St. Pierre etc. But only a small minority who have visited France begin to consider the concept, when they are shocked by the discovery that most French people claim to have little in common with the Québecois, have no interest in their politics, and may even ridicule the way they speak French. Furthermore, even when the tension generated by Quebec nationalism and separatism was at its height in Canada, an examination of the coverage of it in France's popular journal *l'Esprit* concluded that, 'Quebec nationalism is a phenomenon for explanation rather than support'.[29] It is at this point that the Québecois might consider that the Scots have a certain empathy for a culture so entirely misunderstood by a nation speaking the same language.

Even in the early 1970s, before the establishment of Quebec's uni-language policy, children from 'Scotch families' felt pressured by issues of language and politics. In 1976, Bill Young, whose children were among that group, observed:

> Now that they've started this, eh, separatism, which of course, you know about
> — anybody knows what that is…Our young people are leaving, like my son,
> and daughter, Laurie, there. Uh, chances are they may not be able to find what
> they want, a living, compared to the United States system, around here —
> they'll leave. They'll leave this area.

And leave they did, along with countless others of their generation who, by the following decade, had simply had enough. When they return on holiday each year, they renew ties with kinsfolk, catch up on all the changes, visit, relax, before returning to new challenges and adopted surroundings. As with many Gaels from past generations, their cultural defeat has dispersed them, forcing them to seek personal achievement in new challenges. And, since they feel it is now too late for the Quebec Gaels to rescue their language from extinction, it seems better for the young not to watch the death at close quarters. Meanwhile, those who are left hold on to the hope that their French neighbours may at least acknowledge the part played by their Gaelic forebears in this part of Quebec.

For long enough it seemed like a faint hope, then, in the early 1990s there was a most unexpected turn of events. The town of Megantic, now entirely

French-speaking, formed a committee,'Rues principales', under the auspices of 'Héritage Canada' to commemorate the centenary of the death of town's most famous son, a Lewisman, Donald Morrison, the so-called Megantic Outlaw. The event was to be the highlight of a weekend festival, *'Hômmage aux premiers arrivants Ecossais:* A tribute to the first Scottish Settlers'.

The idea originally grew out of the popularisation of the best known story from the Eastern Townships, first written in the poem by Oscar Dhu, then over the years in several books, radio programmes and television documentaries, and finally, in a French novel that caught everybody's attention. *L'héros,* Donald Morrison, was already a household name among the older French people — many had parents and grandparents who knew him personally. His story was retold with all the colour, romance, adventure and popular appeal of a 'Mills and Boone' or a 'Harlequin Romance', with Donald gazing into the eyes of his sweetheart on the front cover. In no time at all, the popularity of the novel, with its genuine connection to Megantic, had the whole town declaring him *'notre héros'*. So central is Morrison's life to the re-awakening of a new understanding of local history, that I will summarise the story that is so well known to every inhabitant of the area.

Donald Morrison, the youngest son of Lewis immigrants, was born in Lingwick in 1858. His father, struggling to 'make a go of things', mortgaged their farm in Megantic to a money lender, Col. Malclolm MacAulay (from Ross-shire). In 1880, Donald went out west to earn money as a cowboy to pay off the $900 debt. For seven years he sent money home to Megantic before returning to enjoy the fruits of his labours. MacAulay denied receiving a penny and had just sold the farm to a French family, *les Duquettes.* Outraged, Donald put the case into the hands of lawyers, but after three months and a fortune in fees, nothing happened. One winter night the barn burned down; Donald, the prime suspect, was charged with arson which he denied. Not long afterwards, he was standing near the house and, in the lamp-lit room, could see Mme Duquette winding the clock. Resenting the newcomers' comfort, Donald took aim at the hand of the clock, fired a perfect shot through the window which sheared the hand, but also terrified the poor woman out of her wits. Already accused of arson, Donald was charged with attempted murder. A warrant was issued for his arrest, Donald went on the run, and by the end of 1888, was famous from coast to coast as a 'Canadian Rob Roy'. Letters of protest to newspapers earned him the sympathy of a Sherbrooke judge who agreed to negotiate. Morrison came out of hiding, but infuriated the judge by insisting he would proceed only if his parents were re-instated in the house. Furious, the judge returned to Montreal and a big-scale manhunt began offering a reward out for his capture. Posters were everywhere, **WANTED! Donald Morrison,** but both Gaels and French protected him — for example, the Legendres hid him in their grist mill, Maryann Morrison brought him food, and so on.

Next on the scene comes American bootlegger, Lucien Warren, determined to claim the bounty — he'll get Donald, dead or alive, so he installs himself in the

American Hotel in Megantic, waiting. On June 22, 1888, when Warren least expects it, Morrison saunters up the main street unrecognised. Tipped off by a bar-room companion, Warren leaps to his feet, and, with hand on hip, challenges Morrison to surrender or he'll shoot him dead. Morrison tells him to keep his distance and put his gun away, but Warren is determined. Seconds later Warren lies dead with Morrison's bullet through his neck.

Now the manhunt is serious; there's a price of $3,000 on the Outlaw's head and for nine months the fugitive is protected loyally by Scots and French sympathisers, eight of whom are arrested and imprisoned without bail. In April 1889 a local judge meets with Donald then declares a truce, but, despite this, Donald was shot visiting his parents' cabin in Milan on Easter Sunday. Loaded onto a buck wagon he was taken to jail in Sherbrooke, tried on October 9th, and, after listening to the jury of twelve English-speaking settlers (not a Gael among them), the judge sentenced Donald to eighteen years in prison. Letters of protest and outrage eventually resulted in the St. Andrews Society of Montreal taking up his case. On June 19, 1894, still suffering from neglected gunshot wounds and tuberculosis contacted in jail, he was released and taken to hospital in Sherbrooke where, a few hours later, he died. To this day, people say he died 'a free man'.

The tragedy of Morrison's death weighed so heavily on the Gaels that even on occasions when it was discussed in the *taighean cèilidh* nobody would ever retell the complete story. Parts of it would be analysed, moral issues raised, and some people even claimed that his death marked the beginning of the end of the Gaelic community which never recovered from the bitter blows of injustice. [30] Like the Jacobites, they saw local loyalty mirrored in the fact that neither Gael nor Frenchman claimed the price on Morrison's head. Now finally, reflecting a messianic theme, through death comes salvation when Morrison's people, the Gaels, are given an honoured place in Quebec's history.

In 1994, the centenary of his death, a French dramatisation of the story was performed on the main street of Megantic on the opening Friday of the weekend festival. The 'set' was the American House Hotel, like the scene from an old movie, with front-porch bar-room and sawdust floor. The audience, lining the street below, recognise Lucien Warren. As he sits boasting, Morrison appears; the atmosphere is tense, the audience hushed, as they watch the meeting; then comes the shooting and a huge cheer goes up from the crowd when Warren falls dead. Morrison is everybody's hero. Slowly the street empties as spectators plan to meet the next day at the fête.

The rest of the celebration was held at the Veterans' Park by Lac Mégantic. The bandstand in the centre featured Scottish music, while the perimeter of the park was lined with tented stalls of local craftspeople displaying and selling quilts, woven articles, tartan (imported), needlework, wood-carving, and so on. Under a banner of 'Ceud Mìle Failte', people crowded in to taste scones with butter and jam — Ruth had baked 750 of them, 500 oatmeal scones and 250 white. For many it was their first taste of 'Scotch food — the kind that Donald Morrison ate'; they lingered, chatted, asked questions and responded enthusiastically to the warm hospitality. Meanwhile, a pipe band from Montreal played, Highland dancers danced and there was an 'interpretative display' in a nearby church. Director of Rues Principales, Danielle Tremblay, was quoted in *The Record* (Sherbrooke, July 11) as saying 'It's important to honour the founders of the city and help people learn more about their history,' and her assistant, Steven Stearns added 'I think it's important for the French Canadians in Megantic to learn what happened here many years ago. The Morrison story is a historic event, it's important for the town.' The event, attended by more than 2,000 people, was a great success, but that was only the beginning.

In 1995 the committed planned a much wider outreach, with publicity all over Quebec and every aspect as authentic as possible. Again the theme was *'Hômmage aux premiers arrivants Ecossais:* A tribute to the first Scottish Settlers', and, while the Morrison drama would be performed by the same French actors, this time it was to be part of the entertainment in the park. A special building, the old railway station, was converted into a museum to interpret the story of *les Ecossais,* and there was to be a Grand Opening with the Mayor, the Minister of Culture and other dignitaries. The committee asked me to prepare photos, locate objects and write a documentary text which they would translate; they would also mount the photos, collect the items on loan, and display the bi-lingual exhibition to its best advantage. The plan was to serve tea and scones, have short concert sets of Gaelic songs, music on the bagpipes and fiddle (like Donald Morrison would have heard) with brief explanations for the visitors. Could I arrange that too?

The Opening was a splendid occasion — red carpet, welcome speeches, standing room only. As invited guests finished their tea, throngs of people were ready to take the first table available. Meanwhile, they edged in to examine the displays, chatting, pointing, questioning, explaining and eventually sitting down to tea, scones and oatcakes. The warmth and hospitality was such as had not been seen for several decades, reminding the oldest families, Scotch and French alike, of times such as Russell MacIver liked to tell — 'remember, when the French fellow came and asked Big Neil you-help-raise-big-barn?…and those Stornoway Legendres could talk Gaelic with the best of them.' By the end of the weekend, the festival had given thousands of Québecois a chance to hear the story of Megantic's first settlers, to enjoy Gaelic songs and music on bagpipe and fiddle, to taste their Scotch whisky, tea and scones, and to share hospitality together. The numerous events that filled the weekend, too many to list, left us in no doubt that the committee of Rues Principales had achieved their aims. As their guests, my son Martyn (the main musician) and I were deeply moved to watch the appreciation of our music and songs, especially of the old-time French fiddlers (one in his eighties) almost in tears as they jigged their feet to the tunes of *le jeune Ecossais*. One old-timer shouted loudly for 'Beeg John MacNeil' and when he instantly got the tune he wanted he was ecstatic, for the only language he and Martyn had in common was *le musique du violon*.

When I began this study of the Hebridean traditions of the Eastern Townships, one of my greatest hopes was that Quebec would still be capable of identifying the contribution of a minority group and might value its place in the wider context of the culture of the province. I see this fresh venture, initiated by the local French people, as an opportunity for the Québecois to take pride in the close association between the French and the Gaels. And, when they look backwards to cite the history of Champlain and Cartier, they might even consider that there is an older alliance that dates back over seven hundred years to a bond between Scotland and France, the Auld Alliance.

While this book has been almost entirely about the Eastern Townshippers of Hebridean descent, it has been written not only for them and for people in Lewis and Harris to whom they are distantly related, but also for all Quebecers and Québecois, whatever language they speak, whatever town or village they inhabit, whatever farm they farm, whatever woodlot they cut, whatever sugar bush they tap — may they appreciate the events that led to its creation and the people who carved it out of a wilderness.

Notes

1. See p. i of the Introduction where I quote the article from *The Clansman News* of 1970, 'The Scottish Highlands of Quebec: Gaidhealatachd Chuibeic'.

2. Angus Calder, *Revolving Culture: Notes from the Scottish Republic,* pp. 1 and 4.

3. *Op cit,* pp. 3-4 and 15-16.

4. *Op cit,* p. 16.

5. *Op cit,* p. 3.

6. Oscar Dhu himself 'crossed the line' when he moved to the United States in 1899. He made his home in Seattle where he died in 1923.

7. 'Tony' means fashionable, suggesting people who had been to the city.

8. Buchanan had the store in Gould

9. i.e. Crown Land, or land that was not owned by anyone.

10. Family (either Irish or English) in Gould; he was the post-master. Since a lot of people there couldn't speak anything but Gaelic in the early days, he would have had the basic phrases for everyday communication.

11. This is what Donald sings; Oscar Dhu has *'Ca mar u ha u fean a diubh'* [sic] in his printed text. In this, and the next verse, the rhythm of the third line is repeated for the fourth line, then the final line returns to the rhythm of the other stanzas.

12. Nowadays local people now pronounce 'plaid' like *plad* as they do in the U.S.A. Apparently in Oscar Dhu's day it was as in Scotland.

13. Oscar Dhu's version has 'buirdly'.

14. Oscar Dhu has "Beinn Oran' and 'Chaibar Faidth' in his published version.

15. See also *By Trench and Trail* pp. 116–119.

16. Johnnie 'Bard' MacLeod, op cit, p. 55, my italics.

17. Though there were several others not named here, these families were still very much in the minority.

18. *Op cit,* p. 10.

19. John L. Campbell *Songs Remembered in Exile,* footnote to p. 27.

20. John Ramsay, *Diary of his Trip to Canada in 1870,* p. 62 ff.

21. Annie Isabel Sherman, *History: The Families of Sherman-MacIver with Stories of People and Places on the Eastern Townships,* p. 57.

22. Oscar Dhu, 'Christmas in Quebec'. The 'parcel from America' is also well-known to many Scottish families who, especially between the wars, and even into the 1950s, looked forward to this boost to family goods.

23. To this day, Canada's involvement in the two world wars is a very emotive subject, giving rise to heated discussion, varying opinions, and criticism of both the Canadian and the British Governments. It is also the subject of several books and articles. *From Romance to Reality,* edited by Peggy O'Hara, deals with the subject of war brides.

24. It is always a source of wonder to visitors from Scotland, especially those from the Outer Hebrides where trees are not only difficult, but impossible, to cultivate, that windfall seedlings grow like weeds, and in the space of one generation land that was once farmed becomes 'all growed over' [with trees], as the local people say.

25. Quotations are from several tapes, many repeated as if part of an oft-repeated discussion.

26. J.I. Little notes that when Ferdinand Legendre sent his children to the Protestant School he was told by the curé *[incorrectly]* that this was against the law. Op cit, p. 233 and endnote 61; my square brackets.

27. Despite widespread evidence, J. I. Little suggests that the idea that the Scots 'became overqualified for farm life is actually a myth'. *Crofters and Habitants,* p. 242. He concedes that, in general, the Scots opened schools earlier in the year and hired better quality teachers, (p. 242), and suggests that *'if* the Scots placed more emphasis on educating their children than did the French Canadians, that impulse appears to have originated with their Bible-centred evangelicalism.' p. 256. (My italics, for there can be no *if* in such a strongly supported fact.)

28. The theme of the conference sponsored by the Centre of Canadian Studies at the University of Edinburgh in May 1994 was 'Canada's Centuries: Periodisation As a Strategy for Understanding the Canadian Past'.

29. Lee S. Rotherham, 'Québec's Loudhailers: A Conflict of Nationality in the Journal Esprit', *British Journal of Canadian Studies*, Vol. 8, pp. 191–210.

30. Patrick Cavanagh suggests that Morrison's death was the beginning of the demise of the Scots in the E Townships. The death was symbolic of a dying community

See also, James Shaw Grant, 'Quiet Clearance in Quebec', *Stornoway Gazette*, Sept. 10, 1983 — his series 'In Search of Lewis — 127' Grant gives a good summary of the story, with a final note:

> Somehow the story is symbolic of the dying community, imprisoned in circumstances from which it cannot break free. An unhappy tailpiece to the history of the clearances which shows us that the same basic pressures are still quietly and subtly at work in a manner which does not even leave us with a grievance to cherish against an evicting landlord.
>
> But at least it helps us to identify the real problem.

Bibliography

Abbreviations

CCFS	Canadian Centre for Folk Culture Studies, NMM
JAF	Journal of American Folklore
JFSAC	Journal of the Folklore Studies Association of Canada
MS	Mercury Series
MUN	Memorial University of Newfoundland
NMM	National Museum of Man/ Museum of Civilization, Ottawa
SHR	*Scottish Historical Review*
TGSI	Transactions of the Gaelic Society of Inverness
TCI	*Tradition and Cultural Identity*
NIF	Nordic Institute of Folklore

Adam, Margaret I. 'Eighteenth Century Landlords and the Poverty Problem', *SHR*, Vol. XIX, No. 73, (Oct. 1921), pp. 1–20 and No. 75, (Apr. 1922), pp. 161–179.

Adam, Margaret I. 'The Causes of the Highland Emigrations of 1783 and 1803', *SHR*, Vol. XVII, No. 66, (Jan. 1920), pp. 73–89.

Adam, Margaret I. 'The Highland Emigration of 1770', *SHR*, Vol. XVI, No. 64, (July, 1919), pp. 281–293.

Adams, G.B. 'The Work and Words of Haymaking', *Ulster Folklife,* 12 (1966) pp. 66–91; 13 (1967) pp. 29–53.

Adams, Ian & Meredyth Somerville. *Cargoes of Despair and Hope: Scottish Emigration to North America 1603–1803*, Edinburgh, 1993.

Adams, Margaret I. 'The Causes of the Highland Emigrations of 1783–1803', *SHR*, 17, 1920, pp.73–89.

Alexandrin, Barbara and Robert Bothwell. *Bibliography of the Material Culture of New France*, NMM, Ottawa, 1970.

Anderson, P. *Guide to the Highlands and Islands of Scotland*, Edinburgh, 1850.

Apte, Mahadev L. and Judit Katona-Apte. 'Diet and Social Movements in American Society: The Last Two Decades' in Fenton & Kisbán (eds) *Food in Change,* Edinburgh, 1986, pp. 26–33.

Argyll, John George. *Canadian Life and Scenery with Hints to Intending Emigrants and Settlers,* Piccadilly: The Religious Tract Society, 1886.

Armstrong, George H. *The Origin and Meaning of Place Names in Canada,* Toronto, 1930, 1972.

Arthur, Eric and Dudley Witney. *The Barn: A Vanishing Landmark in North America,* Toronto, 1972.

Avis, Walters S. (ed). *A Dictionary of Canadianisms on Historical Principles,* Toronto, 1967.

Bagnell, Kenneth. *The Little Immigrants: the Orphans Who Came to Canada,* Toronto, 1980.

Baines, Patricia. *Spinning Wheels: Spinners and Spinning,* London, 1977 & 1979.

Barbeau, Marius. 'Boily le ramancheur', *Liaison,* No. 13, Montreal, 1948, pp. 145–153.

Barbeau, Marius. 'Maple Sugar', *Canadian Geographical Journal*, 38, Apr. 1949, pp. 176–189.

Barbeau, Marius. 'The Origin of the Hooked Rug', *Antiques*, LII:2 (Aug. 1947), pp. 110–113.

Barbeau, Marius. *I Have Seen Quebec*, Toronto, 1957.

Barber, Mary and Flora MacPherson. *Christmas in Canada*, Toronto, 1959.

Barker, T.C., J.C. MacKenzie, and J.Yudkin (eds). *Our Changing Fare: Two Hundred Years of British Food Habits,* London, 1966.

Barnett, H.G. *Innovation: The Basis of Cultural Change*, New York, Toronto, London, 1953.

Bauman, Richard. 'Quaker Folk-Linguistics and Folklore' in Ben-Amos &. Goldstein (eds) *Folklore Performance and Communication*, The Hague, 1975.

Beattie, Jessie Louise. *Black Sheep Folklore of Canada*, Hamilton, Ont., 1981.

Beattie, Susan. *A New Life in Canada: the Letters of Sophia Eastwood, 1843–1870*, Toronto, 1989.

Beck, Horace (ed). *Folklore in Action: Essays for Discussion in Honour of MacEdward Leach,* American Folklore Society, 1962.

Beechan, H.A. and John Higgs. *The Story of Farm Tools,* Young Farmers' Club Booklet No. 24, 2nd ed., London, 1961.

Beith, Mary. *Healing Threads: Traditional Medicines of the Highlands and Islands*, Edinburgh, 1995.

Belden, H. & Co. *Illustrated Atlas of the Eastern Townships and South Western Quebec, 1881,* repr. Port Elgin, Ont., 1972.

Ben-Amos, Dan and Kenneth S. Goldstein (eds). *Folklore Performance and Communcation*, The Hague, Netherlands, 1975.

Bennett, Margaret. 'The Pot of Gold', in *Legends Told in Canada,* compiled by Edith Fowke, Toronto, 1994.

Bennett, Margaret. 'A Codroy Valley Milling Frolic' in *Folklore Studies in Honour of Herbert Halpert: A Festschrift,* ed. K.S. Goldstein and N.V. Rosenberg, MUN Folklore and Language Publication Series, St. John's, Newfoundland, 1980. pp. 99–110.

Bennett, Margaret. 'Gaelic Song in Eastern Canada: Twentieth Century Reflections', in *Canadian Folklore canadien*, Ottawa, 1992, pp. 21–34.

Bennett, Margaret. 'Gaelic Songs in Quebec', Proceedings of the Conference of the Association of Scottish Literary Studies at Aberdeen, Aug. 26–29, 1993, forthcoming Aberdeen, 1994.

Bennett, Margaret. 'Parlez Moi de Bretagne, d'Irelande, d'Ecosse' in *C.B.C. Journal,* Montreal, 1991, pp. 58–59.

Bennett, Margaret. 'Plant Lore in Gaelic Scotland', in *Flora of the Outer Hebrides,* ed. R. Pankhurst, British Museum of Natural History, London, May 1991, pp 56–60.

Bennett, Margaret. 'Scottish Gaelic, English, and French: Some Aspects of the Macaronic Traditions of the Codroy Valley, Newfoundland' *Regional Languages Studies...Newfoundland,* St. John's, May 1972. pp. 25–30.

Bennett, Margaret. 'Scottish Hebridean Traditions in Quebec: Yesterday and Today', Proceedings from the Conference on Quebec, British Association of Canadian Studies at Birkbeck, March 1994, *The London Journal of Canadian Studies*, London, 1995.

Bennett, Margaret. 'The Folklore of Plants in Scotland', in J.H. Dickson & R.R. Mill (eds) *Plants and People: Economic Botany in Northern Europe, 800–1800*, Edinburgh, 1994.

Bennett, Margaret. 'Weather Sayings from Banffshire', *Tocher* 47, pp. 310–12.

Bennett, Margaret. *Scottish Customs from the Cradle to the Grave*, Edinburgh, 1992.

Bennett, Margaret. *The Last Stronghold: Scottish Gaelic Traditions of Newfoundland,* St. John's & Edinburgh, 1989.

Bennett-Knight, Margaret. 'First Impressions of a New World'; 'Learning the Language'; 'Novel Situations'; 'Life Among Strangers'; 'Tales of Lying'; and several other contributions in Magnus Einarson (ed), *Nothing But Stars: Leaves from the Immigrant Saga,* NMM, MS, no. 51, Ottawa, 1984. pp. 19, 38, 47, 56, 59, 81, 93, 113.

Bennett-Knight, Margaret. 'Folkways and Religion of the Hebridean Scots in the Eastern Townships' in *Cultural Retention and Demographic change: Studies of the Hebridean Scots in the Eastern Townships of Quebec*, edited by Laurel Doucette, NMM MS, No. 34, Ottawa, 1980, pp. 45–144.

Berg, Gösta. *Sledges and Wheeled Vehicles: Ethnological Studies from the View-Point of Sweden*, Nordiska Museets Handlingar, 4, Stockholm, 1935.

Berthoff, Rowland T. *British Immigrants in Industrial America: 1790–1950*, Harvard Univ. Press, Cambridge, l953.

Best, Henry B.M. 'The Auld Alliance' in S.W. Reid (ed), *The Scottish Tradition in Canada*, Toronto, 1976, pp. 15–26.

Bibliothèque Nationale du Québec. *Regard sur les Collections de la Bibliothèque Nationale du Québec*, Montreal, 1987.

Bird, Michael. *Canadian Folk Art, Old Ways in a New Land*, Toronto, 1983.

Blake, Annie (interview by Elizabeth Goudie and Doris Saunders). 'No Pants in My Day' in *Them Days*, 3, 1, (1977), p. 13.

Blake, J.L. 'Distribution of Surnames in the Isle of Lewis' in *Scottish Studies*, 10, 1966, pp. 154–61.

Blanchette, Jean-François (ed). *People and Things*, special issue of *Canadian Folklore canadien*, & 'A Bibliography of Folk Material Culture in Canada 1965–1982', No. 4, 1982.

Bloomfield, Morton W. and Charles W. Dunn. *The Role of the Poet in Early Societies*, Cambridge, 1989.

Bø, Olav. 'The Rôle Played by Tradition in a Local Community Today and Earlier' in *TCI*, Turku, 1988, pp. 143–157.

Boily, Lisé and Jean-François Blanchette. *The Bread Ovens of Quebec*, NMM, Ottawa, 1979.

Bonavia, George. *Focus on Canadian Immigration*, Ottawa, 1977.

Born, W. 'Types of the Spinning Wheel', *Ciba Review*, 28, (Dec. 1939), pp. 998–1002.

Bowles, Ella Shannon. *Handmade Rugs*, Boston, 1927.

Brander, Michael. *The Emigrant Scots*, London, 1982.

Bridenbaugh, Carl. *The Colonial Craftsman*, New York & London, 1950.

Brightbill, Dorothy. *Quilting as a Hobby*, New York, 1963.

British American Land Company. *Information Respecting the Eastern Townships of Lower Canada, in which the British American Land Company Intend to Commence Operations for the Sale and Settlement of Lands in the Ensuing Spring*, London, 1833.

British Canadian Symposium on Historical Geography , Brian S. Osborne (ed). *The Settlement of Canada: Origins and Transfer: Proceedings of the 1975 British Canadian Symposium on Historical Geography*, Queen's Univ., Kingston, 1975.

British Wool Marketing Board. *British Sheep Breeds: Their Wool and Its Uses*, Isleworth, n.d.

Broadfoot, Barry. *The Pioneer Years 1895–1914*, Toronto, 1976.

Brown, L. K. and K. Mussell (eds). *Ethnic and Regional Foodways in the United States*, Knoxville, 1984.

Brown, Nelson Courtlandt. *Logging*. New York and London, 1949.

Bruce, Jean. *After the War*, Don Mills, Ont., 1982.

Brück, Ulla. 'Identity, Local Community and Local Identity' in *TCI*, Turku, 1988, pp. 77–92.

Brunvand, Jan Harold. *The Study of American Folklore*, New York, 1968.

Bryant, C.A., A. Courtney, B.A. Maukesberry, and K.M. DeWalt. *The Cultural Feast: An Introduction to Food and Society*, New York, 1985.

Bryant, Ralph Clement. *Logging*, New York & London, 1913.

Brye, David L. (ed). *European Immigration and Ethnicity in the United States and Canada: a Historical Bibliography*, Santa Barbara, CA, 1983.

Buchanan, John Lane. *Travels in the Western Hebrides: from 1782–1790*, London, 1793.

Buchanan, Roberta. "Country Ways and Fashions': Lydia Campbell's *Sketches of Labrador Life* — A Study in Folklore and Literature' in Gerald Thomas and J.D.A. Widdowson (eds). *Studies in Newfoundland Folklore: Community and Process,* St. John's, 1991, pp. 289–308.

Buchanan, Ronald H. 'A Decade of Folklife Study', *Ulster Folklife,* 11 (1965) pp. 63–75.

Bucher, Robert C. 'The Continental Log House', *Pennsylvania Folklife,* 12:4 (Summer, 1962), pp. 14–19.

Buie, T.S. 'Rail Fences', *American Forests,* 70:10 (Oct., 1964), pp. 44–46.

Bulletin of the Folklore Studies Association of Canada, Quarterly, 1976–.

Bumsted, J.M. *Interpreting Canada's Past,* Toronto, 1986.

Bumsted, J.M. *The People's Clearance: Highland Emigration to British North America 1770– 1815,* Edinburgh, 1982.

Bumsted, J.M. *The Scots in Canada,* Ottawa, 1982.

Burne, Charlotte S. *The Handbook of Folklore,* rev. London, 1914.

Burnet, Jean R. *Coming Canadians: an Introduction to a History of Canada's Peoples,* Toronto, 1988.

Burnham, Dorothy K. *The Comfortable Arts: Traditional spinning and Weaving in Canada,* Ottawa, 1981.

Burnham, Harold B. and Dorothy K. Burnham. *'Keep Me Warm One Night': Early Handweaving in Eastern Canada,* Toronto, 1972.

Burt, A.L. *The Old Province of Quebec,* Minneapolis, 1933.

Burt, Capt. Edward. *Letters from a Gentleman in the North of Scotland to his Friend in London... begun in 1726,* 2 vols., London, 1754 & 1815.

Burton, John G. *The Scots Abroad,* 2 Vols., Edinburgh, 1864.

Butler, Gary. 'Participant Interaction, Truth, and Belief in the Legend Process', *Culture & Tradition,* 5, 1980, pp. 67–78.

Cage, R.A. *The Scots Abroad: Labour, Capital, and Enterprise, 1750–1914,* London, 1985.

Calder, Angus, *Revolving Culture: Notes from the Scottish Republic,* London & New York, 1994.

Cameron, Rev. J. 'The Parish of Stornoway' in *New Statistical Account,* 14, 1845, pp. 115–140.

Camp, Charles (ed). *Time and Temperature,* A Centennial Publication of the American Folklore Society, Washington, 1989.

Campbell, D. and R.A. MacLean. *Beyond the Atlantic Roar: A Study of the Nova Scotia Scots,* Ottawa, 1974.

Campbell, John C. *The Southern Highlander and His Homeland,* The University of Kentucky Press, 1921 (reprint).

Campbell, John Francis (of Islay). *Popular Tales of the West Highlands,* 4 vols., Edinburgh, 1860–62.

Campbell, John G. *Superstitions of the Highlands and Islands of Scotland,* Glasgow, 1900.

Campbell, John G. *Witchcraft and Second Sight in the Highlands and Islands of Scotland,* Glasgow, 1902, repr. East Ardsley, 1974.

Campbell, John L. *Songs Remembered in Exile,* Aberdeen, 1990.

Campbell, John L. and Francis Collinson. *Hebridean Folksongs,* Oxford, Vol. I, 1969; Vol II, 1977; Vol. III, 1981.

Campbell, John L. and Trevor H. Hall, *Strange Things: The Enquiry by the Society for Psychical Research into Second Sight...* London, 1968.

Campbell, R. H. *Scotland Since 1707,* Oxford, 1956.

Canada, Government of. *Census Report of the Canadas, 1860–61,* Ottawa, 1861.

Canada, Government of. *Notice Issued by His Majesty's Chief Agent for the Superintendence of Emigrants in Upper and Lower Canada,* Quebec, 1833.

Canada, Government of. *The Settler's Guide: or, the Homesteader's Handy Helper,* Montreal, 1896.

Canada, Government of. *Census of Canada, 1871–91,* Ottawa, 1891.

Canada, Government of. *Census Report of the Canadas, 1851–52*, Ottawa, 1852.

Canada, Government of. *Minutes of Evidence, Crown Lands and Emigration*, n.p., 1839.

Canada, Government of. *The Eastern Townships: Information for Intending Settlers*, 3rd edn., Ottawa,1881.

Canadian Consultative Council on Multiculturalism. *First Annual Report of the Canadian Consultative Council on Multiculturalism*, presented to the Hon. John Munro, Minister Responsible for Multiculturalism, 1974,. Ottawa, 1975.

Canadian Consultative Council on Multiculturalism. *Multiculturalism as State Policy*, Conference Report, Second Canadian Conference on Multiculturalism, Ottawa, 1976.

Canadian Encyclopedia, The, 3 vols., Edmonton, 1985.

Canadian Ethnic Studies, Special Issue 'Ethnic Folklore in Canada',JFSAC,Vol. 7, No. 2, 1975.

Canadian Folklore canadien, Special issue,'Foodways/ L'alimentation',JFSAC,Vol. 12, No. 1, 1990.

Canadian Folklore canadien. Special issue,'Folktales in Canada', JFSAC,Vol. 1, 1979.

Canadian Industries Limited. *Blasters' Handbook*, Montreal, 1964.

Careless,J.M.S. *The Pioneers.An Illustrated History of Early Settlement in Canada*,Toronto, 1973.

Carlisle, Lilian Baker. *Pieced Work and Appliqué Quilts at Shelbourne Museum*, Museum Pamphlet Series, number 2, Shelburne, 1957.

Carmichael,Alexander. *Carmina Gadelica.* 6 vols., Edinburgh, 1928–71.

Carpenter, Carole H. *Many Voices:A Study of Folklore Activities in Canada and their Rôle in Canadian Culture*, CCFCS, MS 26, Ottawa, 1979.

Carruthers,William A. *Emigration from The British Isles*, London, 1929.

Cattermole,William. *Emigration:The Advantages of Emigration to Canada*, London, 1831.

Chambers,Robert. *Popular Rhymes of Scotland,* new ed., London & Edinburgh, 1870, repr. Detroit, 1969.

Chambers,Robert. *Book of Days,* 2 vols., London & Edinburgh, 1862-64.

Channell,Leonard S. *History of Compton County and Sketches of the Eastern Townships, District of St. Francis and Sherbrooke County*, Cookshire, Quebec, 1896, repr. Belleville, Ont., 1975.

Charon, Milly (ed). *Between Two Worlds: the Canadian Immigration Experience*, Dunvegan, Ont., 1983.

Cheape, Hugh. 'Pottery and Food Preparation, Storage and Transport in the Scottish Hebrides' in Fenton & Kisbán (eds) *Food in Change,* Edinburgh, 1986, pp.111–121.

Christensen, Erwin O. *Early American Wood Carving*, Cleveland & New York, 1952.

Clark, S.D. *Church and Sect in Canada*,Toronto, 1948.

Clayton C. Purdy. *MacAulay: Isle of Lewis to Quebec*, Oracle Press, Baton Rouge, LA, 1986.

Cochran, Robert. "WHAT COURAGE!' Romanian 'Our Leader' Jokes',JAF,Vol. 102, No. 405, pp. 259–274.

Cohen,Anthony P. (ed). *Belonging: Identity and Social Organisation in British Rural Cultures*, Manchester, 1982.

Colby,Averil. *Patchwork Quilts*, Copenhagen, 1965.

Coleman,Terry. *Passage to America*, London, 1972.

Comeau, Fr. Léger. 'Multiculturalism — the Francophone Viewpoint', *Multiculturalism as State Policy*, Conference Report, Second Canadian Conference on Multiculturalism, Ottawa, Feb. 13–15, 1976, pp. 27–28.

Connor,Jennifer C. 'Folklore in Anglo-Canadian Medical Journals 1845–1897', *Canadian Folklore canadien*, 7, 1985, pp.35–53.

Conroy, Mary. *300 Years of Canada's Quilts*,Toronto, 1976.

Copeland,Jennie F. *Every Day But Sunday*, Brattleboro,Vermont, 1936.

Copland, Samuel. *Agriculture Ancient and Modern:A Historical Account of its Principles and Practice, Exemplified in Their Rise, Progress, and Development,* 2 vols., London, 1866.

Copp,James H. (ed). *Our Changing Rural Society: Perspectives and Trends*, Ames, Iowa, 1964.

Cormack, William Epps. *Narrative of a Journey Across the Island of Newfoundland in 1822,* London, New York, Toronto, 2nd ed. 1928.

Cowan, Helen I. *British Emigration to British North America,* Toronto, 1961.

Creighton, Helen, Graham George, et al. 'Marius Barbeau (1883–1969)'. CFMJ 12, 1984, pp. 42–59.

Creighton, Helen. *A Life in Folklore,* Toronto, 1975.

Creighton, Helen. *Bluenose Ghosts,* Toronto, 1957, repr. 1976.

Crepeau, Pierre (ed). *Médicine et Réligion Populaires: Folk Medicine and Religion,* NMM, MS, no. 53, Ottawa, l985.

Crofters Commission Report, Edinburgh, 1884.

Crowell, Ivan C. 'Little Old Mills of New Brunswick', *Collections of the New Brunswick Historical Society,* 19 (1966), pp. 79–87.

Culpepper, Nicholas. *Culpepper's Complete Herbal,* London, 1653 (rept. 1985, 1992).

Daiches, David (ed). *A Companion to Scottish Culture,* London, 1981 & Edinburgh, 1993.

Day, Catherine Matilda. *History of the Eastern Townships,* Montreal,1869.

Day, Catherine Matilda. *Pioneers of the Eastern Townships...,* Montreal, 1863, repr. 1973.

De Gaspé, Philippe-Aubert, père. *Canadians of Old,* Toronto, 1974.

De vos, George. 'Ethnic Identity and Minority status: Some Psychocultural Considerations' in Anita Jacobsson-Widding (ed), *Identity: Personal and Socio-Cultural,* Uppsala, 1983.

Dean, I. F. M. *Scottish Spinning Schools,* London, 1930.

Dégh, Linda, and Andrew Vázsonyi. 'The Hypothesis of Multi-Conduit Transmission in Folklore' in Ben-Amos &. Goldstein (eds) *Folklore Performance and Communication,* The Hague, 1975.

Dégh, Linda. *Folktales of Hungary,* Chicago, 1965.

Delargy, James. 'The Gaelic Story-teller, with some notes on Gaelic Folk-tales' in *Proceedings of the British Academy,* Vol. 31, 1945, pp. 177–221.

Devine, T.M. 'Landlordism and Highland Emigration' in *Scottish Emigration and Scottish Society,* Edinburgh, 1992, pp. 84–103.

Devine, T.M. *The Great Highland Famine: Hunger, Emigration and the Scottish Highlands in the Nineteenth Century,* Edinburgh, 1988.

Devine, T.M. (ed). *Scottish Emigration and Scottish Society,* Proceedings of the Scottish History Studies Seminar, University of Strathclyde, 1990–91, Edinburgh, 1992.

Dhu, Oscar. *see* MacKay, Angus.

Dickerman, Charles W. *How to Make the Farm Pay; Or, The Farmer's Book of Practical Information on Agriculture, Stock Raising, Fruit Culture, Special Crops, Domestic Economy and Family Medicine,* Philadelphia, 1871.

Dobson, Henry and Barbara Dobson. *The Early Furniture of Ontario and the Atlantic Provinces,* Toronto, 1974.

Dominion of Canada, Bureau of Statistics. *Census of Canada 1951,* 1961.

Donald Morrison, The Canadian Rob Roy, or *The Hunted Outlaw,* no author given. Montreal, 1899. [Bibliotheque Nationale du Quebec (HV6248 M6H85 1889)].

Dorson, Richard M. 'The Debate of the Trustworthiness of Oral Traditional History', in F. Harkort (ed.), *Volksüberriefung: Festschrift für Kurt Ranke,* Göttingen, 1968.

Dorson, Richard M. *Bloodstoppers and Bearwalkers,* Cambridge, 1959.

Dorson, Richard M. *The British Folklorists: A History,* Chicago, 1968.

Dorson, Richard M. (ed). *Folklore and Traditional History,* The Hague, 1973.

Dorson, Richard M. (ed). *Folklore Research around the World: A North American Point of View,* Bloomington, 1961. Also in *JAF,* LXXIV:294 (Oct.–Dec., 1961).

Dorson, Richard M. (ed). *The Handbook of American Folklore,* Bloomington, 1986.

Dorson, Richard M. *Buying the Wind*, Chicago & London, 1969.

Dorson, Richard M. *Folklore and Folklife: An Introduction*, Chicago & London, 1972.

Doucette, Laurel (ed). *Cultural Retention and Demographic change: Studies of the Hebridean Scots in the Eastern Townships of Quebec*, NMM MS, No. 34, Ottawa, 1980.

Drapeau, M. Stanislas. *Études sur les développements de la Colonisation du Bas Canada*, 1863.

Dresser, John A. 'The Eastern Townships of Quebec: A Study in Human Geography', *Royal Society of Canada (Transactions)*, 29, 1935, pp. 89–100.

Driedger, Leo (ed). *The Canadian Ethnic Mosaic: a Quest for Identity*, Toronto, 1978.

Drolet, Lisé et Claude Martineau. 'Marius Barbeau'. *Culture & Tradition*, 8, 1984, pp. 7–19.

Dunae, Patrick A. *Gentlemen Emigrants: from the British Public Schools to the Canadian Frontier*, Vancouver, 1981.

Dunbar, James. *Smegmatalogia; or the Art of Making Potashes and Soap, and Bleaching Linen*, Edinburgh, 1736.

Dundes, Alan. 'Defining Identity Through Folklore' in *Identity: Personal and Socio-Cultural*, in Anita Jacobsson-Widding (ed), Uppsala, 1983.

Dundes, Alan. 'Defining Identity Through Folklore', *Symposium on Identity, Personal and Socio-cultural*, Upsala, NIF No 12, 1982.

Dundes, Alan. 'Texture, Text, and Context', *Southern Folklore Quarterly*, 28 (1964), pp. 251–265.

Dundes, Alan. *Essays in Folkloristics*, Folklore Institute, Meerut, 1978.

Dundes, Alan. *Interpreting Folklore*, Bloomington, 1980.

Dundes, Alan. *The Study of Folklore*, Englewood Cliffs, NJ, 1965.

Dunkley, Nancy Rose. 'Studies in the Scottish Gaelic Folk-song Tradition in Canada', unpublished Ph.D thesis, Harvard University, Cambridge, 1984.

Dunn, Charles W. 'Gaelic Proverbs in Nova Scotia', *JAF*, 72, 1959, pp. 30–35.

Dunn, Charles W. *Highland Settler: A Portrait of the Scottish Gael in Nova Scotia*, Toronto, 1953, 1968, 1992.

Dunton, William Rush, Jr. *Old Quilts*, Catonsville, Maryland, 1946.

Dwelly, Edward, comp. *The Illustrated Gaelic-English Dictionary*, Glasgow, repr. 1971.

Dyck, Ruth. 'Ethnic Folklore in Canada: A Preliminary Survey', *Canadian Ethnic Studies*, 7, 1975, pp. 90–101.

Eastern Township Gazetteer and General Business Directory, St. John's, Lower Canada, 1867.

Einarsson, Magnus (ed). *Nothing But Stars: Leaves from the Immigrant Saga*, NMM MS, No. 51, Ottawa, 1984.

Ek-Nilsson, Katarina. 'The Social Functions of Festival Food' in Fenton & Owen (eds), *Food in Perspective*, Edinburgh, 1981, pp. 77–81.

Ekblaw, K.J.T. *Farm Structures*, New York, 1920.

Elliot, Bruce. *Irish Immigrants in the Canadas: A New Approach*, Kingston & Montreal, 1988.

Emmerson, George S. 'The Gaelic Tradition in Canadian Culture' in W. S. Reid (ed) *The Scottish Tradition in Canada*, Toronto, 1976, pp. 232–247.

Epps, Bernard. 'Immigrant File: When the First Scots Came from Lewis' in *The Record*, Sherbrooke, Oct. 21, 1988.

Epps, Bernard. *The Outlaw of Megantic*, Toronto, 1973.

Erixon, Sigurd. 'European Ethnology in our Time', *Ethnologia Europaea*, 1:1 (1967), pp. 3–11.

Erixon, Sigurd. 'Folklife Research in Our Time', *Gwerin*, 3 (1962), pp. 271–291.

Erixon, Sigurd. 'Regional European Ethnology', *Folkliv*, 1937:2/3, pp. 89–108; 1938, pp. 263–294.

Erixon, Sigurd. 'The North-European Technique of Corner Timbering', *Folkliv*, 1937:1, pp. 13–60.

Erixon, Sigurd. 'West European Connections and Culture Relations', *Folk-Liv*, 1938:2, pp. 137–172.

Evans, George Ewart. *Ask the Fellow Who Cuts the Hay*, London, 1956 & 1962.

Evans, George Ewart. *Spoken History*, London and Boston, 1987.

Fanning, Wayne W. 'Storytelling at a Nova Scotia General Store', *Culture & Tradition, 3*, 1978, pp. 57–67.

Farb, P. & G. Armelagos. *Consuming Passions: The Anthropology of Eating*, Boston, 1980.

Farm Buildings: A Compilation of Plans for General Farm Barns, Cattle Barns, Dairy Barns, Horse Barns, Sheep Folds, Swine Pens, Poultry Houses, Silos, Feeding Racks, Sheds, Farm Gates, Portable Fences, Etc., Chicago, 1907.

Farrow, Moira. *Nobody Here But Us: Pioneers of the North*, Vancouver, 1972.

Fenton, Alexander & Eszter Kisbán, *Food in Change: Eating Habits from the Middle Ages to the Present Day*, Edinburgh, 1986.

Fenton, Alexander & Trefor M. Owen. *Food in Perspective*, Proceedings of the Third International Conference on Ethnological Food Research, 1977, Edinburgh, 1981.

Fenton, Alexander, *Country Life in Scotland: Our Rural Past*, Edinburgh, 1987.

Fenton, Alexander, *The Island Blackhouse*, HMSO, Edinburgh, 1978.

Fenton, Alexander. 'Material Culture as an Aid to Local History Studies in Scotland', *Journal of the Folklore Institute*, II:3 (Dec. 1965), pp. 326–339.

Fenton, Alexander. *The Shape of the Past: Essays in Scottish Ethnology*, 2 vols., Edinburgh, 1986.

Ferguson, W. *Scotland 1689 to the Present*, Edinburgh, 1968.

Fergusson, Donald A. (ed). *Fad air Falbh as Innse Gall: Beyond the Hebrides*, Halifax, 1977.

Ferris, William R. 'Folksong and Culture: Charles Seeger & Alan Lomax', *New York Folklore Quarterly*, 24, 1973, pp. 206–218.

Filby, P. William (ed) with Mary K. Meyer. *Passenger and Immigration Lists Bibliography, 1538–1900: being a Guide to Published Lists of Arrivals in the United States and Canada.* Detroit, 1984.

Fine, Elizabeth C. *The Folklore Text: From Performance to Print*, Bloomington, 1984.

Finley, Ruth E. *Old Patchwork Quilts and the Women Who Made Them*, Philadelphia & London, 1929.

Finnegan, Ruth. *Oral Traditions and Verbal Arts: a Guide to Research Practices*, London, 1992.

Flinn, M.W., Smout, et al. *Scottish Population History from the Seventeenth Century to the 1930s*, Cambridge, 1977.

Foster, Annie H. & Anne Grierson. *High Days and Holidays in Canada*, Toronto, 1938.

Foster, George M. 'What Is Folk Culture?', *American Anthropologist*, 55:2, 1 (April–June, 1953), pp. 159–173.

Foster, Gilbert. *Language and Poverty: the Persistence of Scottish Gaelic in Eastern Canada*, St. John's, Nfld., 1988.

Foster, W.A. & Deane G. Carter. *Farm Buildings*, New York, 1922.

Fowke, Edith & Carole H. Carpenter (comps). *A Bibliography of Canadian Folklore in English*, Toronto, 1981.

Fowke, Edith. 'Canadian Folklore in English', *The Oxford Companion to Canadian Literature*, ed. Wm. Toye, Toronto, 1983, pp. 261–264.

Fowke, Edith. *Canadian Folklore*, O.U.P., Toronto, 1988.

Fowke, Edith. 'Labour and Industrial Protest Songs in Canada', JAF, 82, 1969, pp. 34–50.

Fowke, Edith. *A Reference List on Canadian Folk Music*, CFMJ 6, 1983, pp. 43–60, rpt. Calgary, 1984.

Fowke, Edith. *Folklore of Canada*, Toronto, 1976.

Fowke, Edith. *Lumbering Songs from the Northern Woods*, Memoir 55, AFS, 1970, rpt. Toronto, 1985.

Fowke, Edith. *Tales Told in Canada*, Toronto, 1986.

Fowke, Edith. *The Penguin Book of Canadian Folk Songs*, Harmondsworth, 1973 & Markham, Ont., 1986.

Fox, Cyril. 'Sleds, Carts and Waggons', *Antiquity,* V:18 (June, 1931), pp. 185–199.

Fraser, Alexander, L.L.D. 'The Gael in Canada'. *TGSI,* Vol. XXIII, 1902, p. 209.

Fraser, Jean. *Traditional Scottish Dyes and How to Make Them*, Edinburgh, 1983.

Freese, Stanley. *Windmills and Millwrighting*, Cambridge, 1957.

Furry, Margaret S. and Bess M. Viemont. *Home Dyeing with Natural Dyes*, United States Dept. of Agriculture publication, 1935, repr. Santa Rosa, California, 1973.

Fussell, G. E. *The Farmer's Tools: A.D. 1500–1900*, London, 1952.

Gagnon, Serge. *Quebec and its Historians in the Twentieth Century*, Montreal, 1985.

Galbraith, John Kenneth. *The Scotch*, Toronto, 1964.

Garigne, Philippe. *A Bibliographical Introduction to the Study of French Canada*, Westport, Conn., 1977.

Gates, Paul W. 'Official Encouragement to Immigration by the Province of Canada', *Canadian Historical Review*, 15, 1934, pp. 24–38.

Geikie, John C. *George Stanley; or, Life in the Woods*, London, 1864.

Georges, Robert A. 'Towards a Resolution of the Text/Context Controversy', *Western Folklore*, 39, 1980, pp. 34–40.

Georges, Robert A. & Michael Owen Jones. *People Studying People: The Human Element in Fieldwork*, Berkley, Los Angeles, London, 1980.

Gibbon, J. M. *The Scots in Canada*, London, 1911.

Gifford, Ann (ed). *Towards Quebec: Two mid-19th Century Emigrants' Journals*, London, 1981.

Giglioli, Pier Paolo. *Language and Social Context*, Harmondsworth, 1972.

Gilbert, John & Duncan P. Read. *Pioneer Life in Upper Canada,* Don Mills, Ont., 1972.

Gillies, William (ed). *Gaelic and Scotland: Alba agus a' Ghàidhlig,* Edinburgh, 1989.

Gillis, Heather M. & J. Estelle Reddin. 'Tapioca Pudding — Food's Interconnections', *Canadian Folklore canadien,* Special issue, 'Foodways/ L'alimentation', JFSAC, Vol. 12, No. 1, 1990, pp. 39–53.

Glassie, Henry, Edward D. Ives & John F. Szwed (eds). *Folksongs and Their Makers*, Bowling Green, 1970.

Glassie, Henry. *Pattern in the Material Folk Culture of the Eastern United States*, Philadelphia, 1968.

Glassie, Henry. The Types of Southern Mountain Cabin', in Jan H. Brunvand, *The Study of American Folklore*, New York, 1968, pp. 338–370.

Goldring, P. 'Lewis and the Hudson's Bay Company in the Nineteenth Century' in *Scottish Studies*, 24, 1980, pp. 23–42.

Goldstein, Kenneth S. 'The Collecting of Superstitious Beliefs', *Keystone Folklore Quarterly,* Spring, 1964, pp. 13–22.

Goldstein, Kenneth S. *A Guide for Field Workers in Folklore,* Hatboro, Pennsylvania, 1964.

Goldstein, Kenneth S. & Neil V. Rosenberg (eds). *Folklore Studies in Honour of Herbert Halpert: A Festschrift.* St. John's, 1980.

Gomme, Sir George Laurence. *The Handbook of Folklore*, London, 1890.

Gomme, Sir George Laurence. *Folklore as an Historical Science*, London, 1908.

Goodman, W. L. *The History of Woodworking Tools,* London, 1964.

Gould, Mary Earle. *Early American Wooden Ware and Other Kitchen Utensils*, Springfield, Mass., 1942 & Rutland Vt., 1962.

Gowans, Alan. *Building Canada: An Architectural History of Canadian Life*, Toronto, Oxford, 1966.

Graham, Ian C. C. *Colonists from Scotland*, New York, 1956.

Grant, I. F. 'An Old Scottish Handicraft Industry', *SHR*, Vol. 18, (1921), pp. 277–289.

Grant, I. F. *Highland Folkways*, London, 1980.

Grant, James Shaw. 'Quiet Clearance in Quebec', part of the series 'In Search of Lewis-127', *Stornoway Gazette,* Sept. 10, 1983.

Grant, Ted & Andy Russell. *Men of the Saddle: Working Cowboys of Canada,* Scarborough, 1978.

Gravel, Albert. *La Pousse Gaelique Ecossaise dans Les Cantons de L'est,* Pages d'histoire régionale, cahier no. 23, Sherbrooke, 1967.

Gravel, His Lordship Albert. *Donald Morrison: From Cowboy to Outlaw,* unpubl. ms (French) in Bishop's University Library, 1968, transl. by Ida MacDonald (Mrs Ross), Scotstown, Que., 1973.

Gray, Malcolm. *The Highland Economy,* Edinburgh, 1957.

Great Britain, Parliament of. *Report of the Agent General for Emigration on the Applicability of Emigration to Relieve Distress in the Highlands,* 1837.

Great Britain, Parliament of. *Papers Relative to Emigration to Canada,* 1842.

Great Britain, Parliament of. *Report from Her Majesty's Commissioners for Inquiry into the Administration and Practical Operation of the Poor Laws in Scotland,* Vols. 21–24, 1844.

Great Britain, Parliament of. *Report of the Select Committee on Emigration, Scotland,* Parliamentary Papers, Vol. 27, Np. 6, 1841.

Greenhill, Basil. *The Great Migration: Crossing the Atlantic under Sail,* National Maritime Museum, London, 1968, 1976.

Gregor, Rev. Walter. *Notes on the Folk-Lore of the North-East,* PFLS 7, London, 1881.

Grierson, Su. *The Colour Cauldron: the History and Uses of Natural Dyes in Scotland,* Perth, 1986.

Grigor, Iain F. *Mightier Than a Lord: The Highland Crofters' Struggle for Land,* Stornoway, 1979.

Guillet, Edwin C. *Early Life in Upper Canada,* Toronto, 1933, 1964.

Guillet, Edwin C. *Pioneer Arts and Crafts,* Toronto, 1940, 1968.

Guillet, Edwin C. *The Great Migration: The Atlantic Crossing by Sailing Ships Since 1770,* Toronto & New York, 1937.

Gullick, Mary I. 'The Historical and Social Context of Quilt Make-up in Weardale', unpublished M.Litt., University of Sheffield, 1991.

Hale, Richard W., Jr. 'The French Side of the Log Cabin Myth', *Proceedings of the Massachusetts Historical Society,* LXXII (Oct. 1957–Dec.1960), pp. 118–125.

Hall, Eliza Calvert. *A Book of Hand-Woven Coverlets,* Boston, 1931 & Rutland, Vt., 1966.

Halpert, Herbert & John D.A. Widdowson. 'Folk-Narrative Performance and Tape Transcription, Theory versus Practice', *Lore and Language,* 5:1, 1986, pp. 39–50.

Halpert, Herbert. 'Coming into Folklore More Than Fifty Years Ago', JAF, 105/418, 1992, pp. 442–457.

Halpert, Herbert. 'Vitality of Tradition and Local Songs', *Journal of International Folk Music Council,* 3, 1951, pp. 35–40.

Halpert, Herbert. *A Folklore Sampler from the Maritimes,* St. John's, 1982.

Hand, Wayland D. 'American Folklore After Seventy Years: Survey and Prospect', *JAF,* 73:287 (Jan.–March, 1960), pp. 1–11.

Hand, Wayland D. (ed) 'Popular Beliefs and Superstitions from North Carolina', *The Frank C. Brown Collection of North Carolina Folklore,* Vol. VI, Durham, N.C., 1961.

Hansen, M.L. *The Atlantic Migration, 1607–1860,* New York, 1940, repr. 1961.

Haring, Lee. 'Performing for the Interviewers A Study of the Structure of Context', *Southern Folklore Quarterly,* 36, 1972, pp. 383–398.

Harney, George E. *Barns, Outbuildings and Fences,* New York, 1870.

Harper, Marjory. 'The Juvenile Immigrant: Halfway to Heaven, or Hell on Earth?' in *The Immigrant Experience,* Guelph, 1992, pp. 165–183.

Harper, Marjory. *Emigration from North-East Scotland,* 2 vols. *Willing Exiles* (Vol. I) & *Beyond the Broad Atlantic* (Vol. II), Aberdeen, 1988.

Harrington, Lyn & Richard Harrington. *Covered Bridges of Central and Eastern Canada*, Toronto, 1977.

Harris, Leslie. 'Without Strap Nor String' in *Folklore and Oral History*, Canadian Aural/Oral History Association, St. John's, Nfld., 1975, pp. 5–14.

Harrison, Phyllis (ed). *The Home Children: their Personal Stories*, Winnipeg, 1979.

Henning, Darrel D. 'Maple Sugaring: History of a Folk Technology', *Keystone Folklore Quarterly*, XI:4 (Winter, 1966), pp. 239–274.

Henry, Lorne J. & Gilbert Paterson. *Pioneer Days in Ontario*, Toronto, 1938.

Herzog, George. 'The Study of Folksong in America', *Southern Folklore Quarterly*, 2, 1938, pp. 59–64.

Hibbert, Joyce. *The War Brides*, Toronto, 1978.

Higgs, J.W.Y. *Folk Life Collection and Classification*, Handbook for Museum Curators, Part C, Section 6, London, 1963.

Gladstone, Mary, *The Big Cloth: The History and Making of Harris Tweed*, Beauly, 1981.

Hill, Douglas. *Great Emigrations: The Scots to Canada*, Gentry Books, London, 1973.

Hill, Douglas. *The Scots to Canada*, London, 1972.

Holbrook, Stewart H. *The American Lumberjack,* New York, 1962, first publ. as *Holy Old Mackinaw*, 1938.

Honko, Lauri (ed). *Tradition and Cultural Identity*, NIF, No.20, Turku, 1988.

Honko, Lauri & Vilmos Voigt (eds). *Genre, Structure and Reproduction in Oral Literature,* Budapest, 1980.

Honko, Lauri. 'Empty Texts, Full Meanings: On Transformal Meaning in Folklore', *Journal of Folklore Research*, 22, 1985, pp. 37–44.

Honko, Lauri. 'Studies on Tradition and Cultural Identity: An Introduction' in *TCI*, Turku, 1988, pp. 7–26.

Honko, Lauri. 'The Unesco Perspective on Folklore', *Folk Fellows Network*, No 3, Helsinki, 1992.

Hooper, Edward James. *The Practical Farmer, Gardener and Housewife; or, Dictionary of Agriculture, Horticulture and Domestic Economy*, Cincinnati, 1842.

Hopkins, Alfred. *Modern Farm Buildings*, New York, 1913.

Hoppál, Mihály. 'Genre and Context in Narrative Event: Approach to Verbal Semiotics' in *Genre, Structure and Reproduction in Oral Literature*, L. Honko & V. Voigt (eds), Budapest, 1980, pp. 107–128.

Hörandner, Edith. 'Storing and Preserving Meat in Europe: Historical Survey' in Fenton & Kisbán (eds) *Food in Change,* Edinburgh, 1986, pp. 53–58.

Hörandner, Edith. 'The Recipe Book as a Cultural and Socio-Historical Document' in Fenton & Owen (eds), *Food in Perspective*, Edinburgh, 1981, pp. 119–144.

Hultkrantz, Ake (ed). *International Dictionary of Regional European Ethnology and Folklore: General Ethnological Concepts*, Copenhagen, 1960.

Hunter, James. *A Dance Called America,* Edinburgh, 1994.

Hunter, James. *The Making of a Crofting Community*, Edinburgh, 1976.

Hymes, Dell. 'Breakthrough into Performance' in Ben-Amos &. Goldstein (eds) *Folklore Performance and Communication*, The Hague, 1975.

Ickis, Marguerite. *The Standard Book of Quilt Making and Collecting*, New York, 1949, repr. Dover, N.Y., 1959.

Ives, Edward D. *Joe Scott, the Woodsman Songmaker*, Urbana, 1979.

Ives, Edward D. *Larry Gorman, The Man Who Made the Songs*, Bloomington, 1964.

Ives, Edward D. *Lawrence Doyle, the Farmer-Poet of Prince Edward Island*, Orono, 1971.

Ives, Edward D. *The Tape-Recorded Interview: A Manual for Field Workers in Folklore and Oral History*, Knoxville, 1974.

Ives, Edward D. 'The Study of Regional Songs and Ballads', *The Handbook of American Folklore*, ed. Richard M. Dorson, Bloomington, 1986.

Jackel, Susan (ed). *A Flannel Shirt and Liberty: British Emigrant Gentlewomen in the Canadian West, 1880–1914*, Vancouver, 1982.

Jackson, Kenneth. 'Folktale in Gaelic Scotland', *The Proceedings of the Scottish Anthropological and Folklore Society*, Vol. IV, No. 3, 1952, pp. 132–139.

Jansen, Wm Hugh. 'Ethics and the Folklorist' in *The Handbook of American Folklore*, R. M. Dorson (ed), Bloomington, 1986.

Jenkins, J. Geriant. 'Folk Life Studies and the Museum', *Museums Journal*, 61:3 (Dec., 1961), pp. 3–7.

Jenkins, J. Geriant. *Traditional County Craftsmen*, London, 1965.

John Hare, Marc Lafrance, David T. Ruddel, *Histoire de la ville de Québec 1608–1871*, NMM, Ottawa, 1983,

Johnson, Cuthbert W. *The Farmer's Encyclopaedia, and Dictionary of Rural Affairs*, Philadelphia, 1844.

Johnson, J.B. & B. Fowles. *Our Heritage of Our Maine Wildflowers*, Rockland, 1978.

Johnson, Stanley C. *A History of Emigration from the United Kingdom to North America 1763–1912*, London, 1913.

Johnston, H.J.M. *British Emigration Policy 1815–1830*, London, 1972.

Jones, J.P. *History of Lake Megantic: 1760–1921*, Unpubl. ms at National Archives, (MG 30, H17).

Jones, Michael Owen. 'The Study of Traditional Furniture: Review and Preview'. *Keystone Folklore Quarterly*, XII:4 (Winter, 1967), pp. 233–245.

Jordan, Philip D. 'The Folklorist as a Social Historian', *Western Folklore*, XII:3 (July, 1953), pp. 194–201.

JAF Canadian issues. 'Contes populaires canadiens', *JAF* 29:1, 1916; 30:1, 1917; 32;1, 1919; 36:3, 1923; 39:4, 1926; 44:3, 1931; 53:3, 1940.

Karp, Ellen (comp). *Many Are Strong Among the Strangers: Canadian Songs of Immigration*, CCFCS MS 50, NMM, Ottawa, 1984.

Kauffman, Henry J. *Early American Ironware: Cast and Wrought*, Rutland, Vt., 1966.

Kennedy, David Sr. *Incidents of Pioneer Days at Guelph and the County of Bruce*, Toronto, 1903, repr. 1973.

Kerrigan, Catherine (ed). *The Immigrant Experience*, Proceedings of a Conference at the University of Guelph, 1989, Guelph, 1992.

Kesteman, Jean-Pierre. *Histoire du Lac Mégantic,* Lac Megantic, 1985.

Keyfitz, Nathan. 'How the Descendants of English Speakers See the Speakers of Other Languages and Their Descendants', *Multiculturalism as State Policy*, Report, Second Canadian Conference on Multiculturalism, Ottawa, 1976, Proceedings, pp. 65–79.

Kidd, Henry G. *The Megantic Outlaw*, Toronto, 1948.

King, Arden R. 'A Note on Emergent Folk Cultures and World Culture Change', *Social Forces*, 31:3 (March, 1953), pp. 234–237.

Kittredge, L. *Witchcraft in Old and New England*, Cambridge, Mass., 1929.

Kluckhohn, Clyde. 'Bronislaw Malinowski, 1884–1942', *JAF*, Vol 56, Jul.–Sept., 1943, No. 221, p. 214.

Klymasz, Robert B. 'The Ethnic Joke in Canada Today', *Keystone Folklore Quarterly*, 15, 1970, pp. 167–73.

Kniffen, Fred, & Henry Glassie. 'Building in Wood in the Eastern United States: A Time-Place Perspective', *The Geographical Review*, LVI:1 (Jan. 1966), pp. 40–66.

Kopsa-Schön, Tuula. 'The Gypsy Identity and Tradition in Cultural Interaction' in *TCI*, Turku, 1988, pp. 175–194.

Koroleff, Alexander Michael, & Ralph C. Bryant. *The Transportation of Logs on Sleds*, Yale University School of Forestry Bulletin, 13, New Haven, 1925.

Krappe, Alexander Haggerty. *The Science of Folk-Lore*, London, 1930.

Kundegraber, Maria. 'Plants and Herbs as a Food of the People: An Example from West Steiermark, Austria' in Fenton & Owen (eds), *Food in Perspective*, Edinburgh, 1981, pp. 171–177.

Labelle, Ronald. 'A Case Study of Folk Religion Among Quebec's Stone Cutters', *Laurentian Review*, No. 12, 1979, pp. 51–63.

Lacourcière Luc. 'A Survey of Folk Medicine in French Canada from Early Times to the Present', *American Folk Medicine*, W. D. Hand (ed), Berkely, 1976, pp. 203–214.

Lajoie, Paul G. *Agricultural Lands in Southern Quebec: Distribution, Extent, and Quality*, Ottawa, 1975.

Lalumière, Guy, et al. *Stornoway 1858–1983*, Les Albums Souvenirs Québecois, Sherbrooke, 1983.

Landry, René. 'Archival Sources: A List of Selected Manuscript collections at the Canadian Centre for Folk Culture Studies, NMM, Ottawa', *Canadian Ethnic Studies*, 7, 1975, pp. 73–89.

Laperrière, Guy. *Bibliographie d'Histoire des Cantons de L'Est — History of the Eastern Townships: A Bibliography*, Sherbrooke, Quebec, 1986.

Lawson, Bill. *A Register of Emigrant Families from the Western Isles of Scotland to the Eastern Townships of Quebec, Canada,* Compton County Historical Museum Society, Eaton Corner, Quebec, 1988.

Leach, Edmund. *Culture and Communication*, Cambridge, 1976.

Leach, MacEdward. 'Problems of Collecting Oral Literature', *Publications of the Modern Languages Association*, LXXVII, (1962), pp. 335–340.

Leach, MacEdward. 'Celtic Tales from Cape Breton' in *Studies in Folklore* ed. W.E. Richmond, Bloomington, 1957, pp. 40–54.

Leach, Maria (ed). *Funk & Wagnalls Standard Dictionary of Folklore, Mythology, and Legend*, 2 vols., New York, 1949 & 1950.

Leechman, Douglas. 'Good Fences Make Good Neighbours', *Canadian Geographical Journal*, LVI:4 (Oct., 1966), pp. 467–496.

Leeson, Alice M. 'Certain Canadian Superstitions', *JAF*, 10, 1897, pp. 76–78.

Lenman, Bruce. *An Economic History of Modern Scotland 1660–1976*, London, 1977.

'Lennoxville: Wool Shop latest victim of the Times' in *The Record*, Sherbrooke, May 19, 1993.

Leonard, John. 'Settlement of the Gaelic Part of the Province', *Sherbrooke Daily Record*, Feb. 22, 1930.

Lewin, Kurt. *Field Theory in Social Science*, London, 1952.

Lewis H. Harry. 'Population of Quebec Province: Its Distribution and National Origins', *Economic Geography*, 16, 1940, pp. 59–68.

Linklater, Clive (on behalf of the National Indian Brotherhood). 'Special Presentation', *Multiculturalism as State Policy*, Conference Report, Second Canadian Conference on Multiculturalism, Ottawa, 1976, Proceedings, pp. 173–177.

Little, J. I. *Crofters and Habitants: Settler Society, Economy, and Culture in a Quebec Township, 1848–1881*, Montreal & Kingston, 1991.

Little, J. I. *Nationalism, Capitalism, and Colonization in Nineteenth-Century Quebec: the Upper St Francis District*, Montreal, Kingston & London, 1989.

Little, J.I. 'From the Isle of Lewis to the Eastern Townships: The Origins of a Highland Settlement Community in Quebec, 1839–81' in *The Immigrant Experience*, Guelph, 1992

London, J.C. *An Encyclopaedia of Cottage, Farm, and Villa Architecture and Furniture*, London & New York, 1869.

Long, Amos, Jr. 'Outdoor Privies in the Dutch Country', *Pennsylvania Folklife*, 13:3 (July, 1963), pp. 33–38.

Long, Amos, Jr. 'Pennsylvania Summer-Houses and Summer-Kitchens', *Pennsylvania Folklife*, 15:1 (Autumn, 1965), pp. 10–19.

Long, Amos, Jr. 'The Woodshed', *Pennsylvania Folklife*, XVI:2 (Winter, 1966–1967), pp. 38–45.

Lowrie, Robert H. 'Oral Tradition and History' *JAF*, XXX (April–June, 1917, pp. 161–167.

Lumley, Frederick. *Means of Social Control*, New York, 1925.

Lynch, Michael. 'Scottish Culture in its Historical Perspective' in *Scotland: A Concise Cultural History*, edited by Paul H. Scott, Edinburgh & London, 1993, pp. 15–45.

Lynch, Michael. *Scotland: A New History*, London, 1991.

MacBain, A. *Place-names in the Highlands and Islands*, Stirling, 1922.

MacBain, Alexander. 'Old Gaelic System of Personal Names', *TGSI*, Vol. XX, 1897, p.279.

MacCallum, Urr. Gilleasbuig. *Laoidhean agus Dàin Spioradail [Spiritual Hymns and Poems.]* Glasgow, 1894.

MacDonald, Alexander. 'Social Customs of the Gaels', *TGSI*, 32, 1925, PP. 272–300 & 33, 1926, pp. 122–145.

MacDonald, Alphonse (comp). *Cape Breton Songster: A Book of Favourite English and Gaelic Songs*, Sydney, N.S., 1935.

MacDonald, Donald. *Lewis: A History of the Island*, Edinburgh, 1978 & 1983.

MacDonald, Donald. *The Tolsta Townships*, Tolsta, Isle of Lewis, 1984.

Macdonald, Dorothy K. *Fibres, spindles and Spinning Wheels*, n.p.: Royal Ontario Museum of Archaeology, 1950.

MacDonald, Dr. Donald of Gisla. *Tales and Traditions of the Lews*, Stornoway & Paisley, 1967.

MacDonald, George. *Peasant Life: Sketches of the Villagers and Field-Labourers in Glenaldie*, London, 1871.

MacDonald, Norman. *Canada: Immigration and Colonization, 1841–1903*, Toronto, 1966.

MacDonald, Rev. M.N. 'Letter to the Editor', *Sherbrooke Daily Record*, Aug. 7, 1949.

MacDonald, Rev. M.N. *Family Tree and Some Reminiscences of Early Days in Winslow and Whitton, Quebec*, Avonmore, n.p., n.d., repr. Sherbooke, 1973.

MacDonell, John A. *Early Settlement and History of Glengarry*, Montreal, 1893.

MacDonell, Sr Margaret. *The Emigrant Experience: Songs of Highland Emigrants in North America*, Toronto, 1982.

MacDougall, Alexander G. 'The Presbyterian Church in the Presbytery of Quebec, 1875–1925', M.A. thesis, McGill University, 1960.

MacEachern, Rev. Dugald. 'Highland Second Sight', *TGSI*, Vol. XXIX, 1922, p. 290.

MacEwan, J.W. Grant. *Blazing the Old Cattle Trail*, Saskatoon, 1962.

MacEwan, J.W. Grant. *Hoofprints and Hitching Posts*, Saskatoon, 1964.

MacEwan, J.W. Grant. *John Ware's Cow Country*, Edmonton, 1960.

MacEwan, J.W. Grant. *The Sodbusters*, Toronto, 1948.

MacFarland, Rev. A.M. 'Gaelic Names of Plants: Study of their Uses and Lore', *TGSI*, Vol. XXXII, 1929, p. 1.

MacInnes, John. 'Gaelic Poetry and Historical Traditon', *The Middle Ages in the Highlands*, ed. Lorraine MacLean, Inverness, 1981, pp. 142–163.

MacInnes, John. 'Gaelic Poetry in the Nineteeth Century', *The History of Scottish Literature*, Vol. 3, D. Gifford (ed), Aberdeen, 1988, pp. 377–396.

MacInnes, John. 'The Gaelic Perception of the Lowlands' in *Gaelic and Scotland: Alba agus a' Ghàidhlig*, W. Gillies (ed), Edinburgh, 1989, pp. 89–100.

MacInnes, John. 'The Oral Tradition in Scottish Gaelic Poetry', *Scottish Studies*, 12/1, pp. 29–44.

MacInnes, John. 'The Seer in Gaelic Tradition', pp. 10–24 in *The Seer in Celtic and Other Traditions*, H. E. Davidson (ed), Edinburgh, 1989.

MacInnes, Rev. Duncan. 'Notes on Gaelic Technical Terms, with Illustrations of a Highland Cottage', *TGSI*, Vol. XIX, 1895, p. 213.

MacInnes, Rev. John. *The Evangelical Movement in the Highlands of Scotland, 1688 to 1800,* Aberdeen, 1951.

MacKay, Angus (Oscar Dhu). *By Trench and Trail in Song and Story*, Seattle & Vancouver: MacKay, 1918.

MacKay, Angus (Oscar Dhu). *Donald Morrison, the Canadian Outlaw: A Tale of the Scottish Pioneers.* n.p., 1892, repr. Sherbrooke, 1965, 1975. 'Enhanced Centennial Edition' ed. & introduced by Thomas A McKay, Arlington, 1993.

MacKay, Donald. *Scotland Farewell: The People of the Hector*, Toronto, 1980.

MacKay, Donald. *The Lumberjacks*, Toronto, 1978.

MacKay, William. 'Life in the Highlands in the Olden Times as Ilustrated by Old Writings', *TGSI*, Vol. XXIX, 1914–19, pp. 1–18.

MacKenzie, Alexander. *The History of the Highland Clearances*, Glasgow, 1883, rev. 1946.

Mackenzie, George A. (ed). *From Aberdeen to Ottawa in Eighteen Forty-Five: The Diary of Alexander Muir*, Aberdeen, 1990.

MacKenzie, Osgood Hanbury. *A Hundred Years in the Highlands*, London, 1921 (many reprints), rev. 1965.

MacKenzie, William. *Old Skye Tales*, Glasgow, 1934.

MacKenzie, William. *Old Skye Tales: Further Traditions, Reflections and Memories of an Octogenarian Highlander*, Glasgow, 1934.

MacKinlay, D. *The Island of Lewis and its Fishermen Crofters,* London, 1878.

MacKley, Florence M. *Handweaving in Cape Breton*, Sydney, N.S., 1967.

MacLaren, Allan A. (ed). *Social Class in Scotland: Past and Present*, Edinburgh, 1976.

MacLean, Calum. 'Death Divination in Scottish Folk Tradition', in *TGSI*, 42(1953–9), pp. 56–67.

MacLeod, John Austin (Johnnie Bard), *Memoirs of Dell* , unpubl. ms. Kingston, 1971.

MacLeod, M.C. *Setttlement of the Lake Megantic District in the Province of Quebec, Canada*, n.p. [New York]. 1931.

MacLeod, Norman. *Reminiscences of a Highland Parish,* London, n.d. (late 1800s).

MacNeil, Joe Neil. *Sgeul gu Latha: Tales Until Dawn. The World of a Cape Breton Gaelic Story-Teller*, ed. John Shaw, Kingston & Edinburgh, 1986.

Macrae, Marion. *The Ancestral Roof, Domestic Architecture of Upper Canada*, Toronto, 1963.

Malchow, Howard L. *Population Pressures: Emigration and Government in Late Nineteenth-Century Britain*, Palo Alto, California, 1979.

Martin, Martin. *A Description of the Western Isles of Scotland circa 1695*, Edinburgh, 1716, Glasgow, 1884, & Stirling, 1934.

Mather, Eugene Cotton & John Fraser Hart. 'Fences and Farms', *The Geographical Review,* XLIV:2 (April 1954), pp. 201–223.

Mayhew, H. Carl. *The History of Canterbury County, Quebec*, Lennoxville, 1970.

McDonald, Neil T. *The Baldoon Mysteries: A Weird Tale of the Early Scotch Settlers of Baldoon,* Wallaceburg, Ont., 1871, 3rd edn., 1910.

McKechnie, Robert E. *Strong Medicine*, Vancouver, 1972.

McKendry, Ruth. *Quilts and Other Bed Coverings in the Canadian Tradition*, Scarborough, 1979.

McKillop, Dugald McKenzie. *Annals of Megantic County*, Lynn, Mass., 1902, repr. by Mrs Arthur Mimnaugh (Cora McKillop), Inverness, Que., 1962, 1966, 1981.

McLeod, Duncan. *The Milan Story*, Sherbrooke (privately published), 1977.

McMichael, R.N. 'The Potato Famine of the 1840s in the Western Highlands and Islands of Scotland', M.A. thesis, University of Edinburgh, 1973.

McNeil, Bill. *Voice of the Pioneer*, 2 vols., Toronto, 1978 & 1984.

McNeill, F. Marian. *Hallowe'en: Its Origin, Rites and Ceremonies in the Scottish Traditions.*, Edinburgh, 1970.

McNeill, F. Marian. *The Scots Kitchen: Its Traditions and Lore,* London & Glasgow, 1929, 17th reprt. 1961.

Meade, R. K. 'Mode of Cultivating Indian Corn. Harrows', *Memoirs of the Philadelphia Society for Promoting Agriculture*, IV (1818), pp. 184–187.

Memoirs of a Highland Lady: The Autobiography of Elizabeth Grant of Rothiemurchus... 1797–1830, Edinburgh, London, 1898. (edited by Lady Strachey), Several editions;1911 edition used here.

Mercer, Henry C. 'The Origins of Log Houses in the United States', *A Collection of Papers Read Before the Bucks County Historical Society*, V (1926), pp. 568–583. Also in *Old-time New England*, XVIII:1 (July, 1927); XVIII:2 (Oct. 1927).

Meredith, Mamie. 'The Nomenclature of American Pioneer Fences', *Southern Folklore Quarterly*, XV:2 (June, 1951), pp. 109–151.

Mewitt, Peter G. 'Associational Categories and the Social Location of Relationships in a Lewis Crofting Community' in Anthony P. Cohen (ed), *Belonging: Identity and Social Organisation in British Rural Cultures*, Manchester, 1982, pp. 101–130.

Meyer, Duane. *The Highland Scots of North Carolina, 1732–66*, Oxford, 1961.

Milner, Elizabeth Hearn. *Huntingville, 1815–1980: a Story of a Village in the Eastern Townships of Quebec*, Lennoxville, Quebec, 1981.

Minhinnick, Jeanne. *Early Furniture in Upper Canada Villages, 1800–1837*, Toronto, 1964.

Mitchell, Arthur. *The Past in the Present*, Edinburgh, 1880.

Moir, John S. *Enduring Witness: A History of the Presbyterian Church in Canada*, Toronto, 1974.

Montell, W. Lynwood. *From Memory to History*, Nashville, 1981.

Montell, W. Lynwood. *The Saga of Coe Ridge: A Study in Oral History*, Knoxville, 1970.

Moodie, Susanna. *Roughing it in the Bush; or, Life in Canada*, 2 vols., London, 1852. Carl Ballstadt (ed), Ottawa, 1988 & 1995.

Morrison, N. 'Vegetable Dyeing in Lewis', *Scottish Field*, June, 1929, p. 28.

Morrissey, Charles T. 'The Case for Oral History', *Vermont History*, XXXI:3 (July, 1963), pp. 145–155.

Mullowney, John J. *America Gives a Chance*, Florida, 1940.

Myres, John L. 'Folkmemory', *Folk-Lore*, Vol. XXXVII, 1926, pp. 12–34.

Greenhill, Basil., *The Great Migration: Crossing the Atlantic Under Sail,* National Maritime Museum, London, 1968.

NicLeòid, Babi. *Gaelic Proverbs*, Club Leabhar, Inbhirnis, 1973.

O Suilleabháin, Seán. *A Handbook of Irish Folklore*, Folklore Associates, Hatboro, 1942, repr., 1963.

O'Bryan, K.G., J.G. Reitz, & O.M. Kuplowska. *Non-Official Languages: A Study in Canadian Multiculturalism*, Ottawa, 1976.

O'Hara, Peggy (ed). *From Romance to Reality*, Cobalt, Ont., 1983.

Og, Alistair. 'The Highland Ceilidh', *Celtic*, Vol. I, 1876, p. 40.

Olson, Ian A. 'Scottish Contemporary Music and Song: An Introduction' in *Scotland: Literature, Culture, Politics*, Anglistik & Englischunterricht, Band 38/39, Peter Zenzinger (ed), Heidelberg, 1989, pp. 139–166.

Opie, Iona, & Moira Tatem (eds). *A Dictionary of Superstitions*, Oxford & New York, 1992.

Oring, Elliot (ed). *Folk Groups and Folklore Genres: A Reader*, Logan, 1989.

Oring, Elliot (ed). *Folk Groups and Folklore Genres: An Introduction,* Logan, 1986.

Ornstein, Lisa. 'Instrumental Folk Music of Quebec: an Introduction', *CFMJ*, 10, 1982, pp. 3–11

Oscar Dhu. *see* MacKay, Angus.

Overbeek, Johannes. *Population and Canadian Society*, Toronto, 1980.

Palardy, Jean. *Early Furniture of French Canada,* Toronto, 2nd edn., 1965.

Palmer, H. *Land of the Second Chance*, Lethbridge, 1972.

Palmer, Howard. 'Reluctant Hosts: Anglo-Canadian Views of Multiculturalism in the Twentieth Century', *Multiculturalism as State Policy*, Conference Report, Second Canadian Conference on Multiculturalism, Ottawa, 1976, Proceedings, pp. 81–118.

Palmer, Judi. *Dyeing with Natural Dyes*, Wellingborough, 1980.

Palmer, Roy. *Britain's Living Folklore*, London, 1991.

Parades, Americo & Richard Bauman (eds). *Towards a New Perspective in Folklore*, Austin & London, 1972.

Paradis, Michèle. 'Du jardin à votre assiette…le jardin potager en milieu rural', *Canadian Folklore canadien*, Special issue, 'Foodways/ L'alimentation', JFSAC, Vol. 12, No. 1, 1990, pp. 83–98.

Paradis, Roger. 'Henriette, la Capuche: The Portrait of a Frontier Midwife', *Canadian Folklore Canadien*, Vol. 3, No. 2, 1981, pp. 110–126.

Parry, Caroline. *Let's Celebrate! Canada's Special Days*, Toronto, 1987.

Peterson, Roger T. *A Field Guide to the Birds*, Boston, 2nd edn. 1975.

Peterson, Vicki. *The Natural Food Catalogue*, London, 1978.

Peto, Florence. *American Quilts and Coverlets*, New York, 1949.

Petrone, Penny. *Canadian Indian Literature*, 1980.

Petty, W. 'An Apparatus to the History of the Common Practices of Dyeing' in *The History of the Royal Society of London*, London, 1702.

Phillips, Yvonne. 'The Syrup Mill', *Louisiana Studies*, IV:4 (Winter, 1965), pp. 354–356.

Plant, Marjorie. *The Domestic Life of Scotland in the Eighteenth Century*, Edinburgh, 1952.

Pocius, Gerald L. 'Material Folk Culture Research in English Canada: Antiques, Aficionados and Beyond', *Canadian Folklore canadien*, No. 4, 1982, pp. 27–42.

Pratt, Rev. John B. *Buchan*, Aberdeen, Edinburgh & London, 1858, repr. Turriff, 1978.

Prebble, John. *The Highland Clearances*, London, 1963.

Pugh, Lamont. 'Hog-Killing Day', *Virginia Cavalcade*, VII:3 (Winter, 1957), pp. 41–46.

Purdy, Clayton C. *MacAulay: Isle of Lewis to Quebec*, Baton Rouge, LA, 1986.

Quebec, Government of (Lower Canada). *First and Second Reports of the Special Committee Appointed to Inquire into the Causes which Retard the Settlement of the Eastern Townships of Lower Canada*, Quebec, 1851.

Quebec, Government of (Lower Canada). *List of Lands Granted by the Crown in the Province of Quebec from 1763 to December 31, 1890*, Quebec, 1891.

Quebec, Government of (Lower Canada). *The Province of Quebec and European Emigration*, Quebec, 1870.

Quebec, Government of (Lower Canada). *The Settler's Guide*, Quebec, 1905.

Radford, E. & M.A. *Encyclopaedia of Superstitions*, London, 1948, rev. 1961.

Ramsay, Dean E.B. *Reminiscences of Scottish Life and Character*, New York, 1873. (Many editions).

Ramsay, Freda. *John Ramsay of Kildalton: Being an Account of his Life in Islay and including the Diary of his trip to Canada in 1870*. Toronto, 1969, repr. Aberfeldy, 1988.

Ramsay, John. *Scotland and Scotsmen in the Eighteenth Century*, 2 vols., London, 1888.

Randolph, Vance. *Ozark Magic and Folklore*, New York, Toronto, London, 1947; New York, 1964.

Rattray, W. J. *the Scot in British North America*, 4 Vols., Toronto, 1880–94.

Rawson, Marion Nicholl. *Little Old Mills*, New York, 1935.

Redmond, Gerald. *The Caledonian Games in Nineteenth-Century America*, Cranbury, N.J., 1971.

Reid, W. Stanford (ed). *The Scottish Tradition in Canada*, Toronto, 1976.

Reid, W. Stanford. 'The Scottish Protestant Tradition' in W. S. Reid (ed) *The Scottish Tradition in Canada*, Toronto, 1976, pp. 118–136.

Richards, Eric. *The Highland Clearances*, London, 1982.

Riedl, Norbert F. 'Folklore and the Study of Material Aspects of Folk Culture', *JAF*, 79:314 (Oct.–Dec., 1966), pp. 557–563.

Roberts, Isaac Phillips. *Autobiography of a Farm Boy*, Ithica, 1916, repr. 1946.

Robertson, Elizabeth Wells. *American Quilts*, New York, 1948.

Rolph, Thomas. *Emigration and Colonization: Embodying the Results of a Mission to Great Britain and Ireland, during the Years 1839, 1840, 1841, and 1842; Including Correspondence… Descriptive Accounts of Various Parts of the British American Provinces*, London, 1844.

Rosander, Göran. 'The 'Nationalisation' of Dalecarlia' in *TCI*, 1988, pp. 93–142.

Rosenberg, Neil V. *Folklore and Oral History*, Papers from the Second Annual Meeting of the Canadian Aural/Oral History Association at St. John's, 1975, St. John's, 1978.

Ross, Aileen D. 'The Cultural Effects of Population Changes in the Eastern Townships', *Canadian Journal of Economics and Political Science*, 9, 1943, pp. 447–462.

Ross, Aileen D. 'Population Changes in the Eastern Townships', *Canadian Forum*,, 33, 1953, pp. 128–130.

Ross, Mabel. *Encyclopaedia of Handspinning*, London, 1988.

Ross, W.C.A. 'Highland Emigration', *Scottish Geographical Magazine*, May 1934, p. 155–166.

Rotherham, Lee S. 'Québec's Loudhailers: A Conflict of Nationality in the Journal <u>Esprit</u>', *British Journal of Canadian Studies*, Vol. 8, No. 2, 1993, pp. 191–210.

Rowles, Edith. 'Bannocks, Beans, and Bacon: an Investigation of Pioneer Diet', *Saskatchewan History*, No. 5, Winter, 1952, pp. 1–15.

Roy, Carmen. *An Introduction to the Canadian Centre for Folk Culture Studies*, MS 7, NMM, Ottawa, 1973.

Ruddel, David T. *Quebec City 1765–1832: The Evolution of a Colonial Town*, MS, NMM, Ottawa, 1987.

Rudin, R. 'The Megantic Outlaw and His Times: Ethnic Tensions in Quebec in the 1880s' in *Canadian Ethnic Studies*, 18, 1, 1986, pp. 16–31.

Russell, Carl P. *Guns on the Early Frontiers*, Berkeley & Los Angeles, 1957, repr. 1962.

Salaman, R.N. *The History and Social Influence of the Potato*, Cambridge, 1949.

Sandsdalem, Unni. 'Identity and Local Society: Setesdal Today' in *TCI*, NIF, No.20, Turku, 1988, pp. 159–174.

Scholes, Alexander G. *Education for Empire Settlement: a Study of Juvenile Migration*, London, 1932.

Schwartz, Herbert T. *Tales from the Smokehouse*, Edmonton, 1974.

Scott, Paul H. *Cultural Independence,* Edinburgh, 1989.

Scott, Paul H. *In Bed With an Elephant*, Edinburgh, 1983.

Scott, Paul H. *Scotland: A Concise Cultural History*, Edinburgh & London, 1993.

Scott, Sir Walter. *Tales of a Grandfather: Being the History of Scotland from the Earliest Times*, Edinburgh, 1869 (several eds).

Séguin, Robert-Lionel. *Les Granges du Québec du XVIIe au XIXe siècle*. Musée National du Canada Bulletin No. 192 No. 2, Ottawa, 1963.

Sellar, Robert. *The Tragedy of Quebec: The Expulsion of its Protestant Farmers*, Toronto, 1907, repr. 1974.

Selmer, Jørgen. 'Cultural Groups and the Study of Life-Styles and Cultural Identity' in *TCI*, Turku, 1988, pp. 47–75.

Senécal, André & Nancy Crane. *Quebec Studies: A Selected Annotated Bibliography*, Burlington, Vt., 1982.

Shaw, Margaret Fay. 'Gaelic Folksong from South Uist', *Studia Memoriae Bela Bartok Sacra*, Budapest, 1957.

Shaw, Margaret Fay. *Folksongs and Folklore of South Uist*, London, 1955.

Sheppard, Muriel Earley. *Cabins in the Laurel,* Chapel Hill, 1935, repr. 1946 & 1991.

Shepperson, Wilbur S. *British Emigration to North America*, Oxford, 1957.

Sherbrooke Daily Record, 'Old Home Week Marked by Cemetery Visit', Sherbrooke, Aug. 8, 1949.

Sherman, Annie Isabel. *History: The Families of Sherman-MacIver with Stories of People and Places on the Eastern Townships*, Sherbrooke, 1971.

Shorter Catechism, The. Agreed upon by the Assembly of Divines at Westminster, London & Glasgow, many editions.

Shurtleff, Harold R. *The Log Cabin Myth*, Cambridge, Mass., 1939.

Siirtolisuus: Migration, Journal of the Institute of Migration, Turku, vol. 4, 1996.

Sime, J. G. *In a Canadian Shack*, London, 1937.

Simons, Elizabeth Radin. 'The NASA Joke Cycle: The Astronauts and the Teacher', *Western Folklore* Vol. XLV, No. 4, 1986, pp. 261–277.

Singer, Charles, E.J. Holmyard, A.R. Hall, & Trevor I. Williams. *A History of Technology*, 5 vols., London, 1954–1958.

Skelton, Mrs Isobel (Murphy). *The Backwoods Woman: A Chronicle of Pioneer Life in Upper and Lower Canada*, Toronto, c. 1924.

Skelton, O.D. *The Life and Times of Sir Alexander Galt*, Toronto, 1920.

Sloane, Eric. *A Museum of Early American Tools*, New York, 1964.

Smith, H.R. Bradley. *Blacksmiths' and Farriers' Tools at Shelburne Museum — A History of Their Development from Forge to Factory*, Shelburne, Vt, 1966.

Smith, P.A.L. *Boyhood Memories of Fauquier*, Richmond, 1926.

Smout, T.C. *A Century of the Scottish People 1830–1950*, London, 1987.

Smout, T.C. *A History of the Scottish People 1530–1830*, London, 1969.

Smyth, Willie. 'Challenger Jokes and the Humour of Disaster', *Western Folklore* Vol. XLV, No. 4, 1986, pp. 243–260.

Somers, Robert. *Letters from the Highlands on the Famine of 1846,* Glasgow, 1848, repr. Inverness, 1985.

Steensberg, Axel. *Fire-Clearance Husbandry: Traditional Techniques Throughout the World*, Copenhagen, 1993.

Stein, Mary Beth. 'The Politics of Humour: The Berlin Wall in Jokes and Graffiti', *Western Folklore*, vol. XLVIII, 1989, pp. 85–108.

Stephens, Henry. *The Book of the Farm Detailing the Labours of the Farmer, Farm-Steward, Ploughman, Shepherd, Hedger, Farm-Labourer, Field-Worker, and Cattle-Man.* Fourth edn, Edinburgh & London, 1889.

Stewardson, John E. 'Regina's Day of Wrath: Killer Cyclone of 1912' in *The Beaver*, June/July 1993, pp. 12–16.

Stewart, Charles H. *The Eastern Townships of the Province of Quebec: A Bibliography...*, Montreal, 1930.

Struthers, Edward James. *The Early Settlement of the Eastern Townships*, Lennoxville, 1972.

Swayze, Nansi. *Canadian Portraits: The Man Hunters*, Toronto, 1960.

Sydow, Carl Wilhelm von. *Selected Papers on Folklore*, Laurits Bødker (ed), Copenhagen, 1948.

Symons, Harry. *Fences*, Toronto, 1958.

Szromba-Rysowa, Zofia. 'The Social Aspect of the Popular Diet in Poland with Special Consideration of Eating Customs...' in Fenton & Owen (eds), *Food in Perspective*, Edinburgh, 1981, pp. 267–275.

Szwed, John. *Private Cultures and Public Imagery: Interpersonal Relations in a Newfoundland Peasant Society*, Newfoundland Social and Economic Studies No. 2, MUN, St. John's, 1966.

Tallman, Marjorie. *Dictionary of American Folklore*, New York, 1959.

Tannahill, Reay. *Food in History*, New York, 1973.

Tarasoff, Koomza J. *Traditional Doukhobor Folkways: An Ethnographic and Biographic Record of Prescribed Behaviour*, MS, No. 20, NMM, Ottawa, 1978.

Taylor, Helen V. *A Time to Recall: The Delights of a Maine Childhood*, New York, 1963.

The Harmsworth Encyclopaedia. London, 10 vols., 1906.

The Record, Sherbrooke, July 11, 1994.

Thomas, C. *Contributions to the History of the Eastern Townships*, Montreal, 1866.

Thomas, Gerald & J.D.A. Widdowson (eds). *Studies in Newfoundland Folklore: Community and Process,* John's, 1991.

Thompson, Francis. *Harris Tweed: The Story of a Hebridean Industry*, Newton Abbot, 1969.

Thompson, G.B. *Primitive Land Transport of Ulster,* Transport Handbook No. 2, Belfast, 1958.

Thompson, G.B. *Spinning Wheels (The John Horner Collection),* Belfast Museum & Art Gallery Publcation No 168, Belfast, 1964.

Thompson, Georges. *Up to Date; or, The Life of a Lumberman*, Petrborough, 1895.

Thompson, Stith. 'Advances in Folklore Studies' in A.L. Kroeber (ed), *Anthropology Today: An Encyclopaedic Inventory*, Chicago, 1955, pp. 587–596.

Thomson, Derick S. 'The Gaelic Oral Tradition', *The Proceedings of the Scottish Anthropological and Folklore Society,* Vol. V, No. 1, 1954, pp. 1–18.

Thomson, Frank. *Harris and Lewis: The Outer Hebrides*, Newton Abbot, 1968.

Thomson, James. *For Friends at Home: a Scottish Emigrant's Letters from Canada, California... 1844–1864*, Montreal, 1974.

Thresh, Christine. *Spinning with a Drop Spindle*, Santa Rosa, CA, 1972.

Thurstan, Violetta. *The Use of Vegetable Dyes,* Northgates, Leicester, 1977.

Tocher: Tales, Songs and Tradition Selected from the archives of the School of Scottish Studies, Edinburgh, No. 42 (Scots Overseas), 1989 & No 47 (1993–94).

Traill, Catherine Parr. *Canadian Wild Flowers,* Toronto, 1868.

Traill, Catherine Parr. *Studies of Plant Life in Canada; or, Gleanings from Forest, Lake and Plain,* Toronto, 1885.

Traill, Catherine Parr. *The Backwoods of Canada, being letters from the Wife of an Emigrant Officer, illustrative of the Domestic Economy of British America*, London, 1836, repr. Toronto, 1989.

Traill, Catherine Parr. *The Canadian Settler's Guide.* Toronto & Montreal, Repr. 1969.

Traill, Catherine Parr. *The Female Emigrant's Guide, and Hints of Canadian Housekeeping*, n.p., 1854.

Traill, Catherine Parr. *The Young Emigrants; or, Pictures of Life in Canada , Calculated to Amuse and Instruct the Minds of Youth,* Toronto, 1826.

Traquair, Ramsay. 'Hooked Rugs in Canada', *Canadian Geographical Journal*, XXVI:5 (May, 1943), pp. 240–254.

Tyrwhitt, Janice. *The Mill,* Toronto, 1976.

Usher, Bill & Linda Page-Harpa (eds). *For What Time I Am in the World: Stories from Mariposa,* Toronto, 1977.

Utley, Lee Francis. 'The Bible of the Folk', *California Folklore Quarterly,* Vol. 4, Jan. 1945.

Van Lent, Peter. 'La Vie de l'Habitant: Quebec's Folk Culture of Survival', *New York Folklore,* 7, winter 1981, pp. 57–65.

van Wagenen, Jared. *The Golden Age of Homespun*, New York, 1963.

Vaudry, Richard W. 'The Free Church in Canada, 1844–1861' Ph.D. thesis, McGill University, Montreal, 1984.

Via, Vera V. 'The Old Rail Fence', *Virginia Cavalcade*, XII:1 (Summer, 1962), pp. 33–40.

Vince, John. *Mills and Millwrighting*, Shire Album 33, Aylesbury, 1978.

Wagner, Gillian. *Barnardo*, London, 1979.

Wagner, Gillian. *Children of the Empire*, London, 1982.

Walker, Bruce. 'The Flesher's Trade in Eighteenth and Nineteenth-Century Scotland...' in Fenton & Kisbán (eds) *Food in Change,* Edinburgh, 1986, pp.127–137.

Wallace, Clarke. *Wanted — Donald Morrison: the True Story of the Megantic Outlaw,* Toronto, 1977.

Weaver, Emily P. *A Canadian History,* Toronto, rev. edn., 1919.

Weaver, Jack W. & DeeGee Lester (eds). *Immigrants from Great Britain and Ireland: a guide to Archival and Manuscript Sources in North America,* Westport, Conn., 1986.

Webb, J.R. 'Syrup Making', *North Carolina Folklore*, I:1 (June, 1948), p. 17.

Webster, Marie D. *Quilts: Their Story and How to Make Them,* Garden City, 1928.

Wells, David A. *The Year-Book of Agriculture: or, The Annual of Agricultural Progress and Discovery, for 1855 and 1856,* Philadelphia, 1856.

Welsh, Peter C. 'Woodworking Tools, 1600–1900' *Contributions from the Museum of History and Technology,* U.S. National Museum Bulletin 241, Paper 51, Washington, 1966, pp. 178–228.

Welsh, Peter C. *Tanning in the United States to 1850,* U.S. National Museum Bulletin 242, Washington, 1964.

Whitaker, Ian. 'The Harrow In Scotland', *Scottish Studies*, 2:2 (1958), pp. 149–165.

Whyte, Donald. *A Dictionary of Scottish Emigrants to Canada before Confederation,* Toronto, 1986.

Wickens, Hetty. *Natural Dyes for Spinners and Weavers,* London, 1983.

Wildhaber, Robert. 'A Bibliographical Introduction to American Folklife', *New York Folklore Quarterly*, XXI:4 (Dec., 1965), pp. 259–302.

Wiley, H.W. 'Table Syrups', *Yearbook of the United States Department of Agriculture: 1905,* Washington, 1906, pp, 241–248.

Williams, Henry Lionel. *Country Furniture of Early America,* New York & London, 1963.

Wilson, William A. 'The Deeper Necessity: Folklore and the Humanities', JAF 101, 1988, pp. 156–67.

Wolcott, Stephen C. 'The Frow — A Useful Tool', *The Chronicle of the Early American Industries Association*, I:6 (July, 1934), pp. 1–3.

Woodsworth, J.S. *Strangers Within Our Gates,* Winnipeg, 1909.

Yoder, Don. 'Folk Cookery' in R. Dorson (ed) *Folklore and Folklife: An Introduction,* Chicago, 1972.

Yoder, Don. 'Historical Sources for American Traditional Cookery: Examples from the Pennsylvania German Culture', *Pennsylvania Folklife*, 20 (1971), pp. 16–29.

Yoder, Don. 'Sauerkraut in the Pennsylvania Folk Culture', *Pennsylvania Folklife*, 12:2 (Summer, 1961), pp. 56–69.

Yoder, Don. 'The Folklife Studies Movement', *Pennsylvania Folklife*, 13:3 (July, 1963), pp. 43–56.

Youngson, A. J. *After the Forty-Five: The Economic Impact on the Scottish Highlands,* Edinburgh, 1973.

Zelinsky, Wilbur. 'Walls and Fences', *Landscape*, 8:3 (1959), pp. 14–20.

Zimmerly, David (ed). *Contextual Studies of Material Culture,* NMM, Ottawa, 1978.

Zumwalt, Rosemary L. *American Folklore Scholarship: A Dialogue of Dissent,* Bloomington & Indianapolis, 1988.

Index